CHRÉTIEN CONTINUED

Chrétien Continued

A Study of the Conte du Graal *and its Verse Continuations*

MATILDA TOMARYN BRUCKNER

OXFORD
UNIVERSITY PRESS

OXFORD

UNIVERSITY PRESS

Great Clarendon Street, Oxford OX2 6DP

Oxford University Press is a department of the University of Oxford.
It furthers the University's objective of excellence in research, scholarship,
and education by publishing worldwide in

Oxford New York

Auckland Cape Town Dar es Salaam Hong Kong Karachi
Kuala Lumpur Madrid Melbourne Mexico City Nairobi
New Delhi Shanghai Taipei Toronto

With offices in

Argentina Austria Brazil Chile Czech Republic France Greece
Guatemala Hungary Italy Japan Poland Portugal Singapore
South Korea Switzerland Thailand Turkey Ukraine Vietnam

Oxford is a registered trade mark of Oxford University Press
in the UK and in certain other countries

Published in the United States
by Oxford University Press Inc., New York

British Library Cataloguing in Publication Data
Data available

Library of Congress Cataloging in Publication Data
Data available

Typeset by SPI Publisher Services, Pondicherry, India
Printed on acid-free paper by the
MPG Books Group
in the UK

ISBN 978–0–19–955721–9 (Pbk.)

1 3 5 7 9 10 8 6 4 2

à mes plus que pères et mère

John J. McCann, Peter Haidu, and Nancy Freeman Regalado
mentors par excellence

Preface

This book grows out of a certain sense of dissatisfaction, that other side of desire. Having avoided writing on the *Conte du Graal* for a good part of my career, given its unfinished state and the thorny question of religion's role, which frequently leads to readings that place the complex ambiguity of Chrétien's romance on a reductive rack of allegorical explication, I preferred to avoid *Perceval* in favor of Chrétien's other romances. But the *Conte* eventually proved irresistible: once Keith Busby, Douglas Kelly, and Norris Lacy asked me to write a chapter on intertextuality for *The Legacy of Chrétien de Troyes*, I could no longer avoid its claims as I tackled its relationship to the *Perceval* Continuations.

Dissatisfaction and desire combined to make me, like so many others, a prisoner of what continues to seem like the unattainable achievement of the Grail, no matter how many endings accumulate for Chrétien's initial romance. But I determined to find a better way—better at least from my critical viewpoint—to deal with the issues of religion atypically inserted into the Arthurian world, a more satisfying way to understand how they relate to the other parts of Chrétien's romance. Through analysis of narrative and structure, I followed the religious strands in conjunction with other major threads of the romance, courtly and chivalric issues that caught my puzzled attention, especially points of contradiction that marked the paths of my (re)reading and, it seemed to me, that of successive continuators who were also reading Chrétien. Eventually I discovered that the apparently random accumulation of articles and papers such analyses generated, at first independent of each other, later brought together, in fact retraced the three-part sets of advice Perceval received three times—as if even we dull readers, like the simpleton Perceval, must eventually get the message, unconsciously and then, if we are persistent, more consciously and perhaps more constructively.

Hence this book and my argument, pursued from chapter to chapter, that Chrétien's authorship appears (however surprisingly for modern readers) not only in the 9,000 verses of his unfinished romance but across four continuations whose successive authors follow the guiding hand inscribed in 'the old Perceval'. I do not spend much time at the Grail Castle: it has already received so much attention. I have preferred to look elsewhere to pursue less obvious points of dialogue between Chrétien and the continuators. But there again you will see that I have eventually been lured back to the Fisher King's castle and the Grail, as I move toward the end of this quest. And so, this is not a book about the Grail... though it is a book about the Story of the Grail.

In pursuit of that story, I have benefited from the help and support of many people and institutions. I would first like to thank the presses who granted me permission to reproduce material from already published articles: Editions Rodopi, Rowman & Littlefield, Librairie Droz, Kümmerle Verlag, and Palgrave Macmillan. Parts of Chapter 1 are based on Bruckner (2006a); Bruckner (1996) forms the basis of Chapter 3. Earlier stages of the fourth chapter appear in Bruckner (1999), (2003a), and (2003b). Finally, Bruckner (2000a) provides the starting point for Chapter 5.

I would also like to express my gratitude to the Bibliothèque nationale de France for permission to reproduce the manuscript images that appear on the dust jacket and throughout the book. In particular, I would like to thank Philippe Aveline who steered me to the wonderful transferability of digital images and saved me from the problems of mistaken orders and the perils of international delivery.

Among colleagues and friends, my personal and professional thanks go first to Douglas, Keith, and Norris, who started me on this path and supported me in multiple ways along the byways that led finally to ending it. I am also grateful to a number of colleagues who read parts of the manuscript in the form of earlier papers and articles, or as chapters in the process of revision for the book: I have benefited greatly from the feedback of Virginie Greene and Sophie Marnette on Chapter 1, Zrinka Stahuljak on Chapters 2 and 3, Peggy McCracken who encountered an early form of the conclusion when she invited me to speak in a session at Kalamazoo on 'Gender and the Grail' and a version of Chapter 3 presented to the Medieval Seminar at the University of Michigan in October 2005. My thanks to all the participants in that seminar for their receptive eyes and ears: Elizabeth Allen, Theresa Coletti, Kathy Lavezzo, Paula Leverage, and Andrea Tarnowski. In particular, I would like to thank Kathy for her suggestion that the image of the lady and the tent might serve as an emblem for my entire book.

Several friends and colleagues were instrumental in introducing me to different fields of study connected to this project. Frans van Liere was most generous in sharing with me his expertise in the areas of biblical reception and exegesis in the Middle Ages. Dr Joseph Youngerman gave me advice and his own collection of books and articles for my introduction to the works and theories of Melanie Klein. An anonymous reader for OUP encouraged me to situate the *Perceval* Continuations in the wider context of Grail stories (particularly but not only in the English tradition), in order to show their common concerns and open my book to a wider group of readers who could benefit from an overview of how the verse continuations contribute to later rewritings of the Grail story. To all of them I offer my gratitude and thanks.

Simon Gaunt, who served as one of the readers for OUP, was equally generous in his support for my book, not least in recognizing the importance of rediscovering the first Grail romance in its medieval context as part of an ensemble of romance continuations brought into alignment in a variety of medieval compilations. I offer him heartfelt thanks both for specific suggestions for the revision process (including integration of manuscript illustrations), as well as his general concern that the book be accessible to readers beyond the usual suspects of Chrétien devotees. I thank Oxford University Press for accepting his and the other reader's recommendations. As I have passed successively through the expert hands of Valerie Shelley, Andrew McNeillie, and Jacqueline Baker, each of my editors at OUP has served as a valuable guide. My thanks to all of them for their support, patience, and precision. I would also like to thank Jennifer Dunn, a doctoral student at Boston College whose work on organizing the index was indispensable. Thanks and gratitude for technical support go as well to Robyn Ochs in the Department of Romance Languages and Literatures at Harvard University, where I was a Visiting Professor of French through the final stages of preparing all the materials for publication. As I think back to the beginning of this process, I cannot forget Sarah Kay who suggested that I consider publishing with Oxford: a special thank you for her confidence and encouragement.

Support received in the form of grants, not to mention letters of recommendation for grant proposals, played an important role in helping me secure the extended time needed to bring such a large-scale project to its conclusion. Warm thanks for the thankless task of writing those letters goes to E. Jane Burns, Kevin Brownlee, Peter Haidu, David Hult, Douglas Kelly, Peggy McCracken, and Nancy Freeman Regalado. I am grateful to Boston College for awarding me a number of research fellowships, grants, and sabbaticals, as well as to the National Endowment for the Humanities for naming me a Fellow for the calendar year 2006. Please note that any views, findings, conclusions, or recommendations expressed in this book do not necessarily reflect those of the National Endowment for the Humanities.

Words will not be sufficient but must nevertheless be pressed into service to thank most particularly Peter Haidu and Nancy Regalado, two friends and colleagues who have been my constant teachers and mentors over many years. Both of them read the complete manuscript in its earliest state and helped me discover what I had left unsaid, unexplained, unarticulated, unjustified. My revisions may not have answered all their questions nor reached their highest standards, but the final shape of this book owes them both a debt of gratitude that cannot finally be repaid. To Peter, my thanks for the intellectual nourishment he has unfailingly offered and my gratitude for his ever sharp critique combined with unshakable enthusiasm for my work. To Nancy, my thanks for her ever-renewed gift of self expressed in an uncanny ability to put herself in the service of another person's point of view, to search out every nook and cranny, from titles to stylistic tics, from the general argument to specific details, as she forced me to figure out what I was trying to say. This book is dedicated to them and to John J. McCann, friend of many years, my earliest mentor and first French teacher who back in high school inspired me and put me on the 'droit chemin' whose curious twists and turns I continue to follow. My deepest thanks to all three.

Finally, I would like to thank my family: Raphael and Daniel, two sons who listened appreciatively to their mother's stories about Perceval and taught me about boys growing up; my husband Edward, whose patience and love accept so generously the quirks of a medievalist wife.

Newton   MATB

Contents

List of Illustrations   xiii

Introduction   1
Overview of the Corpus   4
Perceval Continuations and Grail Rewritings   11
Verse and Prose/Centripetal and Centrifugal Textuality   15
Key Traits of the *Conte du Graal*   17
On Ending and Endlessness   22
Reading (Through) Collective Authorship   25

1. Authorial Relays   32
Authors' Names   33
Anonymous Chrétien   42
Interlacing Wauchier de Denain   44
Manessier's Closing Signature   54
Collective Authorship and Gerbert   59
Back to the Story and Chrétien   72

2. Telling Tales, Of Maidens in Tents   86
Textual Intercourse and Human Development   87
Chrétien's Criss-crossing Itineraries   91
Perceval and the Tent Maiden: Simulating Rape   95
Too Little and Too Much for the Ladies' Man   98
Gauvain and the Male Pucele: Thinking About Rape   100
The First Continuation's Gauvain: Confessing Rape   105
Gerbert's Gauvain: Acting out Rape   109
Retelling Love Stories: Writing Forward and Back   112

3. Sons and Mothers, Mothers and Lovers   116
Protecting Mothers: Connections and Contradictions   119
The Sin of the Mother   124
Nature and Nurture   127
The Marginalization and Restoration of Mothers   132
Mothers and Siblings: From the *Conte* to the First Continuation   135
The Sexuality of Mothers   137
The Good Mother and the Beloved   143

4. Violent Swords and Utopian Plowshares   149
Violence at the Heart of Romance   149

What is a Lance?   153
Collapsing Oppositions   157
Isaiah's Utopian Vision in Arthurian Garb   163
Re-reading Oppositions   165
Unending Questions   168
Grail Quests and the Ends of Violence   173
Manessier's Resolution   179

5. Middles, Beginnings, and Ends   187

A Beginning for Middles and Endings   187
Verbatim Repetition: A Biblical Example   192
Gerbert's Grail-like Barrels   198
Grail Castle Visits Multiplied   204

Conclusion   213

Appendix 1   229
Appendix 2   235
Bibliography   237
Index   255

List of Illustrations

Fig. 1. BN, fr. 12576, f. 1. Perceval kneels before a knight he mistakes for God, as the knight's companions look on (top register). On the bottom left, Perceval asks Yvonet to show him King Arthur (seated at the table); on the right, Perceval kills the Red Knight with a javelin. By permission of the Bibliothèque nationale de France.   8

Fig. 2. BN, fr. 12577, f. 149v. Perceval plays with the Magic Chessboard in the Second Continuation. By permission of the Bibliothèque nationale de France.   49

Fig. 3. BN, fr. 12576, f. 201v. Gauvain and the lady of the tent in Gerbert's Fourth Continuation. By permission of the Bibliothèque nationale de France.   89

Fig. 4. BN, fr. 12577, f. 1. Perceval says goodbye to his mother, who then falls down and dies (left top and bottom). On the top right, Perceval kneels before the first knights he has ever encountered; on the bottom register, he kills the Red Knight. By permission of the Bibliothèque nationale de France.   122

Fig. 5. BN, fr. 1453, f. 85. The rubric announces that Caradoc bathes in a tub, as does his beloved, and the snake entwines around the knight's arm. By permission of the Bibliothèque nationale de France.   144

Fig. 6. BN, fr. 12577, f. 74v. At the Grail Castle, while seated at a table with the Fisher King, Gauvain witnesses the Grail procession. By permission of the Bibliothèque nationale de France.   205

Fig. 7. BN, fr. 12576, f. 261. Perceval kneels before a maiden who holds the partially covered Grail, while an angel reaches toward it from heaven. By permission of the Bibliothèque nationale de France.   224

Introduction

il faut encore une fois partir de l'image du puzzle ou, si l'on préfère, l'image
d'un livre inachevé, d'une 'œuvre' inachevée à l'intérieur d'une littérature
jamais achevée. Chacun de mes livres est pour moi l'élément d'un ensemble.

Georges Perec, 'Entretien: Perec/Jean-Marie Le Sidaner'

From the building of cathedrals to the formation of epic and romance cycles,
continuation assumes many different guises in the Middle Ages. The slow
accretion of large scale projects may reflect contemporary means and technology,
but it represents an aesthetic choice as well: medieval taste delights in continuation. Within the literary domain, this predilection appears in the grouping of
chansons de geste around the central figures of Charlemagne or Guillaume
d'Orange, in the multiple romance cycles of Alexander or the Grail, in the two
parts of the *Roman de la Rose*, as in the proliferating branches of the *Roman de
Renart*. Cycles, sequels, retellings, and rewritings invariably raise questions about
how stories are joined, when and how stories end, what makes a whole, what
changes in meaning emerge across their continuities and discontinuities, what is
the nature of authorship in the context of medieval invention and manuscript
culture. The central argument of this book addresses these questions to demonstrate how Chrétien de Troyes's unfinished Grail story, a potent site for generating romance continuations from the late twelfth through the fifteenth centuries,
continues to guide his successors through the patterns and puzzles inscribed in
his enigmatic romance. It might be argued that, even before the modern
rediscovery of his romances in the nineteenth and early twentieth centuries,
Chrétien's influence, exerted directly through his own works or indirectly
through prose rewritings, extends beyond the medieval period across the gulf
typically seen as dividing the Middle Ages from the Renaissance. The work of a
writer like Pierre Sala or the successive editions of medieval romances by early
printers and booksellers suggest that our notions of periodization need a thor-
ough rethinking in light of textual production and reproduction in the fifteenth
and sixteenth centuries.[1]

Chrétien Continued: A Study of the Conte du Graal *and its Verse Continuations*
offers the first book-length examination of all four verse continuations that line

---

[1] See *Legacy* (1987–8) and *Manuscripts* (1993) for a large variety of articles that explore
Chrétien's influence and afterlife.

up in the wake of Chrétien's romance, which medieval scribes as well as modern editors and readers commonly designate as *Perceval*, a title conveniently furnished by the first hero's name. As my own title indicates, this book is as much about the *Conte du Graal* as it is about the continuations. In order to explore their ongoing dialogue, I analyze key features of the originating text to establish how and where the patterns set up by Chrétien resurface in the verse continuations, whose additions and rewritings, in turn, throw new light back on the *Conte* to reveal the kinds of problems Chrétien's medieval readers and writers respond to in his text. On the level of content, these questions focus on society and the individual; love, gender relations, and family ties; chivalry, violence, and religion; on the formal level, they highlight issues of collective invention and intertwined heroes, interpretation, rewriting, and canon formation.

Just as the particular and the general constantly entertain the potential for interactive dialogue, so my study of Chrétien's strangely decentered romance joined to successive continuations operates on a more abstract dimension as well: its very specificity outlines a theoretical reflection on the poetics of continuation that function in this cycle and widely throughout medieval literature. The overview that emerges from detailed textual analyses, whether particular to the *Perceval* Continuations or shared with other literary cycles in verse and prose, should thus serve scholars, students, and general readers interested in broader notions of continuation, contradiction, and collective authorship, as well as specialists of medieval French literature. While my attention stays squarely focused on the medieval examples before me (which constitute an enormous textual edifice through their accumulated length), literary practice and popular culture in a postmodern world show great interest in similar kinds of experiments with serial works.

Our understanding of contemporary performance is deepened by expanding our historical grasp of literary precedents, both as they differ from and anticipate current productions. If from a modern perspective, we limit Chrétien's authorship to the 9,000-plus verses of his unfinished romance, I demonstrate here that, within the terms of medieval practice, Chrétien continues to exert authorship throughout the cycle, as continuators write freely but remain faithful to his tutelage through the continuing presence of the *Conte du Graal* inscribed at the head of each manuscript compilation.[2]

For those already familiar with the continuations and the relatively few studies they have attracted, this claim may appear surprising. As indicated by multiple editions, translations, and a rich bounty of critical writings, modern scholarship has given ample attention to the powerful synthesis offered by the *Lancelot-Grail*, the anonymous prose romances (also known as the Vulgate Cycle) that absorbed

---

[2] Genette's theoretical discussion of *continuation* and *suite* includes the same notion of a guiding spirit extending from the original work, finished or unfinished, on through the (new) ending or prolongation (1982: 181–3).

and rewrote Chrétien's Grail romance into the chronicle of Arthurian history composed in the early part of the thirteenth century and the source of most modern rewritings since Thomas Malory's *Morte d'Arthur* brought it into the English literary tradition in the late fifteenth century. By contrast, the four verse continuations have yet to garner much critical attention, even though they have been available as a group and in multiple versions since the publication of William Roach's monumental, multi-volumed edition, completed in 1983 (an edition of the Fourth Continuation appeared separately in three volumes, started by Mary Williams in 1922 and completed by Marguerite Oswald in 1975). The verse continuations remain undeservedly marginalized in modern critical discourse in large measure because, for modern readers, their apparently miscellaneous and inconsistent accumulation of materials makes it difficult to see them as acceptable continuations. We are disappointed that the continuators appear to know no better than we do how Chrétien planned to solve the puzzles of a work that in so many respects seems to challenge the model of Arthurian romance that Chrétien generated in his previous romances.[3] To what end did he introduce religious issues into the matter of Britain? How would he explain the relationship between the two heroes—and their mothers, usually unnoticed in romance? Would Perceval return to the Grail Castle and, with the Grail quest completed, to his beloved Blancheflor? The continuations fail to answer our questions according to expectation, if at all; they do not form a recognizable or satisfactory whole in relation to Chrétien's romance.

Yet the manuscript tradition requires us to accept the implicit claim of oneness extending across the obvious multiplicity of sometimes discordant voices variously combined in a dozen manuscript compilations. Indeed, most medieval readers would have encountered the *Conte du Graal* not by itself but as part of an ensemble, diversely combined with one, two, three or four continuations. It might be argued that *Perceval* survives in many more copies than other romances by Chrétien (eighteen versus an average of twelve to fourteen for *Erec*, *Cligès*, and *Yvain*; seven for *Lancelot* within the extant corpus of forty-five manuscripts and fragments) precisely because of the interest generated by the continuations. Seen in that light, the verse continuations reward our attention not only by revealing their own underestimated merits but also by helping us discover, as they pursue their dialogue with Chrétien on a variety of levels (narrative and structural, as well as thematic), the crucial issues embedded in the Grail story under his authorizing signature.

---

[3] Chrétien's four earlier romances are usually ordered and approximately dated as follows: *Erec et Enide* (c.1165–70) and *Cligès* (c.1170–7), followed by *Le Chevalier de la Charrette* (*Lancelot*), and *Le Chevalier au lion* (*Yvain*), the last two composed between 1177 and 1181, either simultaneously or alternately, judging by their intertwined plots and the three references to *Lancelot* included in *Yvain*.

OVERVIEW OF THE CORPUS

A short introduction to the whole corpus analyzed here will help explain a number
of significant choices that underpin this study. At the behest of Philip of Flanders,
Chrétien composes *Le Conte du Graal* (*c*.1181–91, the date *ante quem* furnished by
Philip's death on crusade in Acre). When his narrative ends in the midst of the
Guiromelant episode as Gauvain's messenger arrives at Arthur's court, the anonymous First Continuation (late twelfth century) picks up the thread of Gauvain's tale
and carries his story forward (including one or two Grail Castle visits, depending on
the version), while adding its own displacements by inserting into the narrative
sequence the story of two more heroes, Caradoc and Gauvain's brother Guerrehés.
The Second Continuation by Wauchier de Denain (late twelfth century) returns to
Perceval and brings him back to the Grail Castle after a long series of adventures
have taken him on parallel quests for the Chessboard Lady (and a brief return to
Blancheflor). A Third Continuation by Manessier (*c*.1214–27), which begins
during Perceval's visit with the Fisher King (interrupted by the untimely end of
the Second Continuation), affirms his achievement of the Grail quest but sends him
off on a quest for family vengeance before completing Perceval's life story with an
account of his edifying end as king, then hermit and priest. In two manuscripts, a
Fourth Continuation by Gerbert de Montreuil (*c*.1226–30) has been inserted
between the Second and Third.[4] Gerbert begins at the same place as Manessier
(and probably wrote without knowledge of his continuation), but he interprets
Perceval's performance at the Grail Castle as still in need of improvement: a new
series of adventures take him back to many of the highpoints of his wanderings in
the *Conte* and include a chaste marriage with Blancheflor before his now successful
return to the Grail Castle (at which point the narrative of the Third Continuation
resumes). Coming after the popular recasting of Chrétien's romances in the prose
romance cycle, the last two continuators demonstrate the influence of the *Queste del
Saint Graal* by reinserting religious issues after the more courtly adventures of the
First and Second Continuations. Both Gerbert and Manessier present a Grail hero
who must remain virginal; and both move Gauvain into a marginal role in relation
to Perceval.[5]

The ensemble of four continuations creates an enormous cycle of romances,
some 75,000 verses long, whose pattern of accumulation can be summarized as
follows:

---

[4] Only the name Gerbert appears in the text of the Fourth Continuation but he has been
identified with Gerbert de Montreuil who also wrote the *Roman de la Violette* (*c*.1227–9).

[5] Cf. Busby's overview of the different spirit that characterizes each segment of the cycle:
'Chrétien, spiritual and mystical; the First Continuation, wildly supernatural, exuberant and
archaic; the Second Continuation, secular and conventional; Manessier, rational and reassuring;
Gerbert de Montreuil, solemn and sermonizing' (2006: 229).

(P) *Le Conte du Graal* (*Perceval*) by Chrétien de Troyes, *c.*1181–91
(1) The First, or Gauvain Continuation, end of twelfth century
(2) The Second, or Perceval Continuation by Wauchier de Denain, end of twelfth century.[6]
(3) The Third Continuation by Manessier, *c.*1214–27
(4) The Fourth Continuation by Gerbert de Montreuil, written c.1226–30, inserted between the Second and Third Continuations in mss TV, *c.*1250 (or later)

The anonymous First Continuation shows a particularly complex development. Roach's edition offers a selection of manuscripts from three different groups, published in separate volumes, in order to make available the Mixed, Long, and Short Redactions (vols. I, II, and III, part 1, respectively). Although the editor can draw no conclusions about 'the manner in which the individual redactions developed into the state in which they now exist' (I, xxxix), the short version (found in five manuscripts), with its single, very disparate Grail Castle visit for Gauvain, appears to have preceded the others. Both the Long Redaction (four manuscripts) and Mixed Redaction (two manuscripts) add another Grail Castle visit to bring it more in line with Chrétien's episode, as we shall see in Chapter 5.[7]

A detailed list of manuscripts and their combinations reveals the variety of states found in the tradition and the great diversity of reception enjoyed by *Perceval* (Busby, ed. 1993: xxxix). It also highlights the dominant role played by the combination P 1 2 3 within the overall distribution, even though different redactions of the First Continuation add further variations within that 'canonical' form. The table orders the manuscripts by sigla; it indicates date and provenance, identifies which other romances by Chrétien are included in the manuscript (if any) and which continuations (if any) follow the *Conte du Graal.*[8] Like the *enfances* added to epic cycles, 'prequels' appear in two manuscripts: the *Elucidation* (E) precedes Chrétien's prologue; *Bliocadran* (B) follows it.[9] The former includes both exordium and narrative, which furnishes explanations (the origins of disaster for the kingdom of Logres, for example) and anticipates events to

---

[6] Busby dates the earliest form of the First Continuation before 1200 (2006: 222) with the Second Continuation composed immediately after *c.*1200 (229); all four continuations were 'in existence by c. 1225, or shortly thereafter' (228).

[7] Roach's outline of the plot and division into five sections, each with a varying number of episodes gives a clear overview of what the different versions and manuscripts have in common and where they differ (I, xlvi–lxii). See App. 1, where I have reproduced Roach's division into segments and episodes for the first three continuations and added a similar brief analysis of Gerbert's continuation, in order to help orient readers who may be more or less familiar with the *Perceval* Continuations.

[8] Detailed information on the manuscripts is given in Roach's edn. of the continuations (1965–83: I, xvi–xxxii), Busby's edn. of *Perceval* (1993: ix–xxxix), and numerous essays in *Manuscripts* (2003).

[9] Both prequels appear in the 16th-cent. French prose version printed in 1530 and in the German tradition as well (see Pickens 2006a: 215–16). I have not included the prequels in this study nor the later prose translation, although the persistence of interest in the cycle is noteworthy.

follow in an extended Grail romance (for example, Grail visits for Perceval and Gauvain). *Bliocadran* picks up the *Elucidation*'s chronology and leads into *Perceval*'s opening scene; most particularly it fills in the missing paternal genealogy for Chrétien's mother-centered hero (Pickens 2006a: 215–21).

A   Paris, Bibliothèque nationale, fonds fr. 794, includes all of Chrétien's romances copied by Guiot, first half of the thirteenth century, Champagne (P 1 short 2)

B   Berne, Bibliothèque de la bourgeoisie (Burgerbibliothek) 354, early fourteenth century, Eastern (?) (P)

C   Clermont-Ferrand, Bibliothèque municipale et interuniversitaire 248, second half of thirteenth century, Northern (P)

E   Edinburgh, National Library of Scotland, 19.1.5, first half of thirteenth century, Eastern (P 1 long 2 3)

F   Florence, Biblioteca Riccardiana 2943, mid-thirteenth century, Eastern (P)

H   London, College of Arms (Heralds' College), Arundel XIV, mid-fourteenth century, England (P)

K   Berne, Stadtbibliothek 113, late thirteenth century (2 + conclusion)

L   London, British Library, Additional 36614, second half of thirteenth century, Eastern (B P 1 short 2)

M   Montpellier, Bibliothèque interuniversitaire, Section Médecine H 249, late thirteenth century, Northern (P 1 long 2 3)

P   Mons, Bibliothèque universitaire et publique 331/206, mid-thirteenth century, Northeastern (E B P 1 short 2 3)

Q   Paris, Bibliothèque nationale, fonds fr. 1429, second half of thirteenth century, Champagne (P 1 long 2 3)

R   Paris, Bibliothèque nationale, fonds fr. 1450, inserts all of Chrétien's romances into Wace's *Brut*, second quarter thirteenth century, Northeastern (P 1 short)

S   Paris, Bibliothèque nationale, fonds fr. 1453, early fourteenth century, Paris (P 1 short 2 3)

T   Paris, Bibliothèque nationale, fonds fr. 12576, second half of thirteenth century, Northeastern (P 1 mixed 2 4 3)

U   Paris, Bibliothèque nationale, fonds fr. 12577, first half of fourteenth century, Paris (P 1 long 2 3)

V   Paris, Bibliothèque nationale, nouvelles acquisitions françaises 6614, second half of thirteenth century, Northeastern (incomplete, especially Manessier) (P 1 mixed 2 4 3)

a   Annonay fragments, late twelfth or early thirteenth century, includes parts of all Chrétien's romances except *Lancelot*, Champagne (P fragments)

l   Two fragments of *Perceval*, first half of thirteenth century, Northeastern (P fragments)

p   Prague, Bibliothèque de l'Université (Clementium) 220, end twelfth or early thirteenth century, Northeastern (P fragments)

q   Paris, Bibliothèque nationale, fonds fr. 1429, a fragment of *Perceval* added to the beginning of manuscript Q, first half of thirteenth century, Champagne (P fragments)

A brief analysis of the data included here can give some sense of the dissemination and readership that characterize *Perceval* and the continuations. Among Chrétien's romances, the *Conte du Graal* appears in the most varied contexts, from author collections and romance or genre collections to the cycle of verse continuations (Busby 2005: 69–72). The geographical distribution of manuscripts indicated by place of origin and dialect particularly associates *Perceval* and the continuations with northeastern France, perhaps not surprisingly since the two patrons named by Chrétien and Manessier were both counts of Flanders.[10] While the Annonay fragments suggest the manuscript originally included a complete collection of Chrétien's romances and thus offer the closest witness to Chrétien's activity as writer (perhaps as early as the late twelfth century), the majority of the manuscripts date from the thirteenth century; four are produced in the fourteenth. But Chrétien and the continuations continue to circulate among readers at least through the sixteenth century, as evidenced by a printed version in French prose, published in 1530, which contains the *Elucidation* and a shortened version of *Bliocadran*, *Perceval* and the three standard continuations. Printing and prosification thus considerably extend the textual life of the entire cycle, thanks to their modernized forms.[11] But there is evidence as well that even earlier manuscripts continue to circulate in the sixteenth century: in the bottom margin of ms. T's first folio (see Fig. 1), a handwritten note extends across two columns and reads, 'Ce livre appartient a Mons de la Hargerie qui l'a preste a madame de Contay qui a promis lui rendre' (This book belongs to Monseigneur de la Hargerie who has lent it to Madame de Contay who has promised to return it to him). These are most likely Françoise de Contay (born *c*.1490) and her contemporary François de Raisse (whose signature appears on f. 284v).[12]

The entire page gives evidence of the wear and tear of repeated handling, with its blotches, stains, and rubbings. The historiated letter in the third column, which shows Perceval standing and looking down (saddling his horse?), is barely legible, though the miniature on the top left still colorfully represents key episodes at the beginning of the romance and clearly marks the opening page

---

[10] For an overview of all Chrétien manuscripts, see the catalogues presented by Terry Nixon, particularly those arranged by place of origin (2: 15–16), by scribes and production (17), as well as the 'Index of Former Owners' by Roger Middleton (2: 87–176) in *Manuscripts* (1993). Of the eighteen manuscripts and fragments, twelve come from the northeastern or eastern regions of France, three from Champagne, two from Paris, and one from England.

[11] Roach identifies this 16th-cent. printed version as G (I, xxxii).

[12] *Manuscripts* (1993: 2, 117–18, 216–31); see esp. 227–8 (where Middleton cautions us against assuming that Madame de Contay intended to read the borrowed manuscript) and 275.

Fig. 1. BN, fr. 12576, f. 1. Perceval kneels before a knight he mistakes for God, as the knight's companions look on (top register). On the bottom left, Perceval asks Yvonet to show him King Arthur (seated at the table); on the right, Perceval kills the Red Knight with a javelin.

of Chrétien's romance and the entire cycle. As Alison Stones has observed, first miniatures tend to be different from others (1993: 1, 232) and such is the case here, since it is the only illustration in the series to represent several scenes together in an elaborate four-part structure.

The specific images included deserve further commentary, and I shall return to them in later chapters, but for the moment they may best serve to call attention to the general pattern of illustration, as well as the individual fit of image and text, as is typical of all romances, Arthurian or not.[13] In general, given the size of the cycle, a paucity of decoration and illustration characterizes these manuscripts, but among Chrétien's romances the *Conte du Graal* is nevertheless the most frequently illustrated, and their iconographic program gives us some insight into the ongoing medieval reception of *Perceval* and the continuations. As Keith Busby suggests, the apparently random choice of subjects chosen for representation in miniatures and historiated letters is best understood in the context of Chrétien's reception as a whole: certain scenes, episodes, and themes become favorites for later authors and no doubt the public as well (1993a: 1, 359). Among the scenes chosen from the continuations, the *Livre de Caradoc* is particularly well represented (Busby 1993c: 1, 370), while perhaps surprisingly for the modern public, representations of the Grail remain scarce across the illustrated manuscripts: only twelve miniatures in the five illustrated manuscripts, all of which date from the period in the thirteenth and fourteenth centuries when prose romances like the *Lancelot-Grail* and the *Prose Tristan* were at the height of their popularity. Laurence Harf-Lancner's analysis of the fantastic in these illustrations shows that the Christian marvelous (including the Grail as well as the diabolical) appears on average about as much as the Breton marvelous (1993: 1, 464). In the Chrétien section, only ms. U shows the Grail with the lance and sword and always shows it as a kind of ciborium, a vision projected back from the Christianization of the Grail in the later rewritings. Indeed, the iconography of the Grail, lance, and sword develops in the continuations and reflects the rival prose cycle (Baumgartner 1993: 1, 489–92). Despite the modern critical tendency to treat verse and prose romances as separate categories, illustrations, intertextual references, as well as medieval manuscript tradition in general suggest rather a dynamic of interaction between them, a continuity of practice and reception across their differences.[14]

Margot van Mulken points out that almost every *Perceval* manuscript is subject to partner shifts in the process of copying, making the choice of a critical edition especially problematic.[15] The few stable manuscripts, at the center of the manuscript configuration, T, L, and M, are the sought-after partners for the scribes of other manuscripts (1993: 2, 45). Manuscript T (BN, fr. 12576), written in a

---

[13] Baumgartner (1993: 1, 490). I shall have occasion to analyze a number of miniatures from S, T, and U, in order to follow the play between text and image in their ongoing reception.

[14] Busby (1993a: 1, 353–4), Bruckner (2000b: 15).

[15] For an overview of the state of scholarship on the entangled filiation of Chrétien manuscripts in general and those of *Perceval* in particular, see Busby's introd. to his *Perceval* edn. (1993: xl–xlviii).

Picard dialect and dated around 1250, is the most cyclical of the *Perceval*
manuscripts with all four continuations included.[16] In this study, it serves as
the primary object of analysis; it encapsulates one reading of the cycle, even as it
plays off multiple states of the set as a whole. For this reason, I have taken all
quotations of Chrétien's *Conte du Graal* from Roach's edition of T, while also
consulting Keith Busby's more recent critical edition of the romance, for which
T serves as the base manuscript.[17] Félix Lecoy, who based his Classiques Français
du Moyen Âge edition of *Perceval* on Guiot's copy (ms. A), offered this general
assessment of T: 'un bon manuscrit, mais dont la régularité est en grande partie
due à une révision ancienne du texte ... qui a l'inconvénient, me semble-t-il, de
donner du poème une version quelque peu affadie dans le détail de l'expression'.[18] I shall have more than one occasion to refer to T's efforts to coordinate all
the parts brought together in this rendition of the cycle.

An overview of the manuscript tradition necessitates some reflection on the
choice of title used here and elsewhere to identify Chrétien's work, since in certain
respects the two titles—*Le Conte du Graal* and *Perceval*—tell us rather different
things about this romance and how it is viewed. The first is the name as given by
the author in his prologue and, as we shall see in Chapter 1, it is unusual within
Chrétien's corpus, the only title that does not designate the hero either directly by
name or indirectly by pseudonym. To use Chrétien's title is to remind ourselves of
the first author's point of view on his composition and the air of mystery he has
willingly wrapped around a romance that purports to be about a large serving
dish.[19] The anonymous writer who composed the *Elucidation* similarly refers to 'li
Contes del Greal' (482), when he reframes Chrétien's romance.

The other title naming the first hero does not wait for the shorthand of
modern scholarship to come into currency. Already in the manuscript tradition
the explicits added by scribes to demarcate Chrétien's work, or the series of
romances that end with Manessier's continuation, privilege Perceval's name as
synecdoche.[20] When Guiot copies all of Chrétien's romances in BN, fr. 794, he

---

[16] The only other manuscript in which Gerbert's continuation appears is V, fragmentary but
clearly a twin of T: their decorative programs correspond closely; both are from the same exemplar,
and both were copied by the same scribe (Busby 1993b: 1, 52–3).

[17] Quotations from Chrétien's other works will be taken from *Romans* (1994b), unless otherwise
indicated.

[18] Quoted by Gouttebroze (1995: 167 n. 5).

[19] Pace Robert de Boron's and later rewriters' interpretation of the Grail as a cup or chalice,
Chrétien's descriptions make it clear that his Grail is a deep, wide serving dish in which we would
be surprised not to find a large fish (see Ch. 5).

[20] A number of medieval writers refer to Chrétien in general or allude specifically to his romances
by the hero's name (see the appendix in *Legacy* 1987–8: 1, 333–7). Of the thirteen references Van
Coolput lists, eight refer to Perceval or to Chrétien in the context of a Grail romance (including
three of the verse continuators). Of particular interest here is the reference in the *Roman de Hem*,
where Sarrasin seems to acknowledge both titles used to designate Chrétien's *Conte*: 'Oï avés ... du
romant que Crestiiens | Trova si bel de Perceval, | Des aventures du Graal' (475–8; qtd. 336–7: 'you
have heard about the romance that Chrétien composed so well about Perceval and the adventures of

writes 'Explycyt perceuax le uiel' ('here ends the old Perceval') to mark the passage from *Perceval* to the First Continuation (Roach I, xvii).[21] Ms. B (Berne, Bibliothèque de la Bourgeoisie 354), in which the *Conte du Graal* appears by itself, ends with 'Explicit li romanz de perceval' (Busby, ed. 394). Roach prints the three colophons found at the end of Manessier's Third Continuation (V, 344):

M   Explicit de perceval le galois
     (End of Perceval the Welshman)
T   Explicit li romans de percheval
     (End of the romance of Perceval)
U   Ci fenist li roumans De perceval le galois Le quel fu moult preus Et courtois Et plain de grant chevalerie Pour lamour dieu feni sa vie
     (Here ends the romance of Perceval the Welshman who was very worthy and courteous and full of great chivalry. For the love of God I finished his life story.)[22]

Each of these variations on Perceval's name as title reminds us that the first hero has in the long run been identified as dominant in the story of the Grail (at least where Galahad has not supplanted him and reduced his status to one among three). Most of these designations look back from a point of view embedded within the continuations and their dialogue with the master text, as it has been reinterpreted over and over again through the process of accumulation. The two different titles commonly used to designate Chrétien's last romance thus capture intersecting views, looking forward from his prologue and backward from a series of stopping points that mark the stages from the unfinished end of *Le Conte du Graal* through Manessier's epilogue.

PERCEVAL CONTINUATIONS AND GRAIL REWRITINGS

A quick review of *Perceval* and the continuations in relation to the many reinventions of the Grail story that proliferate across European literary traditions can give some idea of their weight and influence. If Chrétien has long been recognized as one of the most important medieval French writers, the focus here brings out not only how his literary capital generates multiple rewritings; it

the Grail'). Van Coolput does not include the famous passage in *Flamenca* where the narrator enumerates many tales told at the wedding celebration, including references to all five of Chrétien's romances (1960: 665–83). Among the excerpts named one concerns Perceval: 'L'autre comtet de Persaval | Co venc a la cort a caval' (671–2: another told of Perceval, how he came to court on horseback).

[21] Interestingly, in Guiot's famous manuscript, *Perceval* is separated from Chrétien's other romances and placed at the end of the compilation (Busby, ed. x), where it is followed by the First Continuation and a fragment of the Second Continuation (Roach I, xvii).

[22] Among manuscripts containing Manessier, the end is missing in EQS (Roach V, xv–xvii).

highlights as well how the *Perceval* Continuations extend his reach and conse-
quence. Within the French tradition, Robert de Boron links Grail history and
Perceval's genealogy to biblical and British history by composing (*c.*1200) his
Estoire dou Graal to explain the mysteries of the Grail and its relation to
Arthurian Britain. Robert transforms the *Conte*'s enigmatic object into the
Holy Grail by identifying it with the vessel from the Last Supper in which Joseph
of Arimathea collected Christ's blood. Robert's work marks the inception of a
'little Grail cycle', with versions in verse and prose: it includes the *Estoire* (or
Joseph d'Arimathie in the prose version), *Merlin*, and the *Didot-Perceval*.[23] The
last part of the trilogy picks up Perceval's extended story, eliminates Chrétien's
Gauvain section and the First Continuation, and concludes the story of the Grail
by way of the Second Continuation and the end of Arthur's kingdom as
recounted by the *Roman de Brut* (1155), Wace's translation and expansion of
Geoffrey of Monmouth's *Historia Regum Britanniae* (1138).

The anonymous prose romancers who elaborated Lancelot's story and combined it with the Grail quest to form the backbone of the Vulgate Cycle,
composed the *Lancelot* proper, the *Queste del Saint Graal* and the *Mort le Roi
Artu* between 1215 and 1230. The *Estoire du Saint Graal* and the *Estoire de
Merlin*, though composed after the 1230s, take their place at the beginning of the
cycle as the first two branches according to the story's chronology. These authors
mined Chrétien's romances as well as the Robert de Boron cycle: Perceval remains
an important knight in the *Queste* but his status as hero is reduced once the
Christological figure of Galahad takes center stage among multiple questers in
pursuit of the Holy Grail (as we shall see more fully in Chapter 4).

Scholars have not resolved the problem of deciding whether the *Perlesvaus*, another
Grail story written in prose, precedes or follows the *Queste*.[24] In this anonymous
romance from the first half of the thirteenth century, the author conceptualizes the
Grail quest as a violent struggle between the Old Law and the New. He picks up
Perceval's suspended story, framing it with a disquieting episode in which Arthur's
squire Cahus is killed, then elaborates three principal Grail quests: Gauvain's,
Lancelot's, and finally Perceval's. After his successful completion of the quest, Perceval
frees his mother (still alive in this version though she dies at the beginning of
Chrétien's), returns to the Grail Castle, then sails away to an unknown destination.
On the whole, *Perlesvaus* remains an enigmatic text, not least because of the way it

---

[23] There is some disagreement among scholars as to what exactly Robert wrote and whether the
verse or prose versions came first. Pickens presents an overview that generally credits Robert with the
verse *Estoire* and *Merlin*, and some form of the *Didot-Perceval* (2006b: 247–59). The *mises en prose*
by anonymous continuators remain identified with Robert in the manuscript tradition, whose
importance is attested by the large number of extant copies (some sixty manuscripts plus fragments).
Gowans argues for the precedence of the prose versions and credits Robert de Boron with only the
Joseph part of the cycle associated with his name. Her analysis has significant ramifications in
assessing the anti-Semitic character of Robert's writing, since the recurrent vilification of Jews that
appears in the verse *Estoire* is less prominent in the prose *Joseph* (2004: 21).

[24] For an overview of the romance and current scholarship, see Andrea M. L. Williams (2006).

mixes the Grail adventure with other marvels of Logres, contaminating orthodox Christian allegory with 'merveilleux païen'[25]—a trait that may echo Chrétien's own unexpected insertion of Christian material into the matter of Brittany.

Interestingly, the *Perlesvaus* romancer includes among Lancelot's adventures a beheading contest, a motif that figured prominently in the First Continuation's *Livre de Caradoc*. It will subsequently play an important role in the fourteenth-century *Sir Gawain and the Green Knight* and later middle English versions. The *Livre de Caradoc* also supplies a chastity test that finds echoes in the variants included in the *Lai du Cor* and the *Lai du Mantel* (end of the twelfth century), and these too have English language equivalents.[26] Other parts of the First Continuation inspire a number of works from the late fifteenth and early sixteenth centuries. Gauvain's encounter with the Tent Maiden (which will be analyzed in detail in Chapter 2) provides the storymatter for *The Jeaste of Sir Gawain*, which combines and reinvents the episode's two stages, widely separated in the Gauvain Continuation. The *Jeaste*, like *The Knightly Tale of Gologros and Gawane*, a Scottish romance that borrows materials from the adventure of the Chastel Orguelleus, is largely based on the 1530 printing of the First Continuation.[27]

With and without continuations, Chrétien's *Conte du Graal* can be followed into German, Welsh, and English versions. Widely disseminated in the German literary tradition, Wolfram von Eschenbach's *Parzival* (*c.*1200–10) completes and expands Chrétien's romance with introductory sections and a conclusion, redefining the Grail as an emerald stone and organizing his narrative around the theme of loyalty and faithfulness (Wynn 185, 192).[28] In the fourteenth century, Philipp Colin and Claus Wisse frame *Parzival* with the two prequels and three continuations from the French tradition to produce their 'new Perceval'.[29]

The Welsh romance, *Peredur*, dates from the thirteenth century and demonstrates a more problematic relationship with Chrétien's romance. Given the significant differences between them, scholars debate whether the author of *Peredur* knew Chrétien: might both authors have been working from similar materials? Nevertheless, close analysis of certain parallels between them suggests that the Welsh romancer, although clearly reworking Celtic traditions, was very likely influenced by Chrétien in parts of his tale.[30] Some episodes seem to echo Gauvain

[25] Anne Berthelot quoted by Williams (2006: 264): 'L'Autre Monde incarné: Chastel Mortel et Chastel des Armes dans le *Perlesvaus*', in Buschinger and Spielwok (eds.), *König Artus und der heilige Graal* (Griefswald, 1994), 31.

[26] See the discussion by Gillian Rogers in *Arthur of the English* (2001: 219–24).

[27] W. R. J. Baron presents both romances, as well as *Gawain and the Green Knight*, in *Arthur of the English* (2001: 155–83).

[28] His later romance *Triturel* (*c.*1217) has no previous source but assumes knowledge of *Parzival*, as Wolfram elaborates but leaves unfinished a Grail story that later romancers will continue (Wynn 204–5).

[29] In his overview of the textual tradition, Roach identifies this German version as D (I, xxxiii). See also Pickens (2006a: 215).

[30] See Ian Lovecy's discussion in *Arthur of the Welsh* (1991: 171–80), as well as Jeffrey Gantz's introduction to his translation (1981: 21–5, 217–18).

materials and Perceval's chessboard adventures in the Second Continuation (Peredur has a whole series of love affairs in sequence), but most strikingly there is no Grail: at his uncle's castle he sees a bleeding lance and a bloody head carried on a platter, representing a crime against his family which he will later avenge.

Likewise, the author of *Sir Percyvell of Galles* may or may not have known Chrétien. In the first half of the fourteenth century, he too gives us a Perceval story in which the Grail has been replaced by the bloody head on a platter.[31] In Ad Putter's view, the anonymous English romancer has indeed reworked Chrétien's romance to give a clear direction to his narrative from start to happy ending. Percyvell's comic energy propels him ever forward from one adventure to the next (including the crucial meeting with the maiden in the tent) but ultimately back to the place he started from, when he is able to reunite with his mother in the forest, having restored her to sanity by returning with the ring she gave him at the moment of parting.

This inventory of works orbiting around Chrétien's *Conte* and the verse continuations serves to highlight how similar problems arise throughout the different rewritings, from varied attempts to give closure to the Grail story to thematic questions, whether centered on the relationship between Grail heroes and love or the issues raised by family, religion, and violence. But we can see this dialogue in continuity and difference acted out most directly across the expanse of the *Perceval* Continuations whose verses line up immediately with Chrétien's last, incomplete sentence, an implicit invitation to continue his suspended narrative.

If individually the continuations do not address all the complexities of Chrétien's *Conte*, across the accumulation of all four, they show remarkable fidelity in integrating important elements distilled from a compellingly dense and mysterious romance that seems to promise and withhold so much in terms of plot and meaning. However far they appear to wander from the master text, the continuators considered as a group respond sympathetically to the dynamic incongruities and essentially paradoxical structure of their model. Even when they cannot resolve the oppositions and contradictions built into the Grail story, they neither efface nor eliminate the difficulties. Remaining faithful to the complementary and contradictory spirit of the decentered *Conte du Graal*, they do not simplify tensions but tend rather to follow, through the process of rewriting and continuation, the impetus of Chrétien's own characteristic techniques.

Properly understood, the same miscellaneous character that strikes modern readers as inconsistent with our definition of a good continuation is what allows the set of four verse continuations to function as an appropriate and necessary response to the impossible combinations that Chrétien has written into his romance, requiring his readers to grapple with without suppressing the apparent

---

[31] While building his comparison on the assumption that the *Percyvell* poet knew Chrétien, Putter gives a summary of scholars and views for and against (2004: 193 n. 3).

contradictions, the multiple strands so resistant to resolution. Even so, across the meanderings of the four continuations, we can observe a certain flattening or reduction of the *Conte*'s incongruities, whether in the role of mothers and lovers or the character of the Grail hero. Such shifts reflect the popular influence of the *Queste del Saint Graal*, written after the Second Continuation and significantly dividing the four verse continuations into before and after.

VERSE AND PROSE/CENTRIPETAL AND CENTRIFUGAL TEXTUALITY

Since the better-known prose romances serve as a point of comparison throughout this study and clearly operate within the same horizon of expectation for medieval (as well as modern) readers and writers, a brief comparison between the *Lancelot-Grail* and the verse continuations, based on their relationship to Chrétien, helps identify both the nature of their differences as well as the features they share in rewriting his romances. In a chapter on intertextuality for *The Legacy of Chrétien de Troyes*, I coined the terms centripetal and centrifugal intertextuality to contrast the prose romances' absorption of Chrétien's works into the Vulgate Cycle with the more linear configuration of *Perceval* and its continuations. The anonymous author who rewrites *Le Chevalier de la Charrette* and places its generative power at the center of the Prose *Lancelot* uses condensation, amplification, and displacement to explode the boundaries of Chrétien's Knight of the Cart episode and expand the hero's story in multiple directions. Through the technique of the interlace and a narrator who has eschewed Chrétien's wit and irony in favor of the objective voice of the story itself ('ce dist li contes'), the prose authors recount Lancelot's entire biography within the history of Arthur's reign; they recast the quest for a now Holy Grail with a new Grail hero, Lancelot's son, and use it as the pivot between Lancelot and Guenevere's love story and the fall of Arthur's kingdom. In the *Queste del Saint Graal*, allegory displaces narrative as a rival mode of continuation. And though Manessier and Gerbert, the third and fourth continuators, resist the kind of allegorical program that characterizes the *Queste*'s rewriting of the 'Story of the Grail', they must nevertheless reconcile the influence of the prose interpretation with their fidelity to the *Perceval*. As a result, we see a difference between the first two and last two continuations, a new vector set by the *Queste* affecting their treatment of the two heroes, the compatibility of love and the Grail, and the ambiguity sustained by Chrétien's unfinished narrative, which nevertheless continues to furnish the starting point, quite literally in each of its manuscript renditions, for the expanding cycle in verse.

On the contrary, except for an abbreviated *Charrette* episode, Chrétien's text is no longer present in the prose cycle, though it continues to function as an intertext: a reservoir of material for the anonymous writers, a point of reference for readers who know both versions and can compare them.[32] But an alternate point of view for intertextual reception is also built into the prose cycle once its scope is sufficiently developed. So all-encompassing are its narrative amplifications, the *Lancelot-Grail* provides its own universe of discourse, its own matrix out of which further reinventions flow through episodes, quests, and branches, first to the *Mort le roi Artu*, then back to the prequels, the *Estoire del Saint Graal* and the *Estoire de Merlin*. True to the centripetal movement that characterizes the prose rewriting of Chrétien's Arthurian romances, the whole Vulgate Cycle reconfigures Lancelot's story at its core, just as *Le Chevalier de la Charrette* was absorbed into the center of the Prose *Lancelot*. In the back and forward movement of their overarching structure, both romance cycles, in verse and in prose, play with the desire for, as well as resistance to ending.

Centrifugal intertextuality provides an obvious metaphor for a set of texts that continue to move out and away from their common starting point, as the *Conte du Graal* remains in place, the first romance of a gradually expanding sequence. The phrase represents at the same time an image of the tension between center and ever receding periphery. Centrifugal intertextuality thus figures the way Chrétien's model serves as a repeating center throughout the series by remaining off-center at the narrative beginning, the place where all continuators return for inspiration and reinvention in order to set out anew, even as they pick up the linear thread of narration wherever their immediate predecessor left it. In the *Perceval* Continuations, the intertextual play goes beyond their common participation in models shared by romances in general—types situated at the level of character (King Arthur, Yvain, dwarves, damsels in distress, etc.), scenes (for example combat, hospitality), and situations (for example the Fair Unknown arriving at court). Their intertextual dialogue is more pointed, based on rewriting specific scenes or patterns from their common center/starting point.[33]

In this respect, two references to 'Crestien' found in ms. T's version of the First Continuation appear emblematic as they represent points of maximum convergence and divergence in the to and fro dialogue between continuators (or scribal editors) and the master text. The first occurs when Gauvain arrives at the Grail Castle and the narrator refers back to Chrétien's praise of the fortress: 'Crestïen en ai a garant' (I, 1234: 'I have Chrétien as guarantor'[34]). The reference to an earlier textual moment and author (who is not the current narrating *je*) is unambiguous, and readers can verify the allusion, should they so desire, by turning back the folios of any manuscript copy (or pages of a printed edition) to the place where

---

[32] For bibliography on the *Charrette* and the Knight of the Cart episode in the Prose *Lancelot* and further analysis of their relationship, see Bruckner (1987–8: 225, 237–49; 2003c).

[33] Burns analyzes the way certain narrative patterns (imprisonment, liberation, etc.) are repeatedly exploited by the prose romancers (1985: 85–109). These 'allomorphs' function in the Vulgate Cycle on a level between the generic patterns of romance and the more specific textual echoes from Chrétien in the *Perceval* Continuations.

[34] Unless otherwise indicated, all translations here and throughout the book are mine.

Perceval arrives at the Fisher King's castle in the *Conte du Graal*. The second reference, however, is a fabrication. It occurs in the interpolated *Livre de Caradoc* and supports the description of a harper automaton which had a custom 'for which Chrétien prized it all the more' (I, 4118: 'Dont Crestïens mix le prisoit'). Such an automaton appears nowhere in Chrétien's works and certainly not in the *Conte du Graal*, though medieval readers are perhaps less concerned than we are with the falsity of the claim. The sense of continuing on a narrative path initially laid out by Chrétien, sustained by the allusion to his authority, may satisfy a public listening to a romance read out loud rather than reading it from a conveniently edited book.

This initial view of centrifugal intertextuality as a metaphor describing the links between *Perceval* and the continuations requires further nuance, inasmuch as the same movement is already built into the unfinished *Conte* before being exploited and expanded by successive continuators. The peculiar nature of Chrétien's last romance—its decentering through the unexpected doubling of heroes, the puzzles, parallels, and contradictions set up through contiguity and accumulation, the logic of and/both operating between its two parts, the distinct character of its endlessness, and the characteristic indirection and displacement of its narrative rhythm—will reappear in the continuations. Brief discussion of these traits will help readers understand more fully in the chapters to follow what is at stake in the centrifugal textuality that operates within Chrétien's Grail romance, just as between *Perceval* and the four verse continuations.

KEY TRAITS OF THE *CONTE DU GRAAL*

In the *Conte du Graal*, Chrétien introduces a series of enigmas, contradictions, and incongruities that confront the paradoxes of human experience without resolving them. Combined with its unfinished state, these puzzles propel successive continuators to reread and rewrite Chrétien's story, weaving their continuations according to its dialectical movement.[35] As subsequent writers pick up his story, they respond to an implicit invitation to interpret as they rewrite, filling in the gaps, reorienting, even contradicting what came before. By learning how to read them as they read Chrétien, we may grasp how their additions point to what remains silent but ready to speak in the interstices of his romance, uncovered by repetitions and recontextualizations of the master text's narrative elements.[36]

[35] Is it a coincidence that Georges Perec has named the protagonist of his great book of puzzles, *La Vie mode d'emploi*, Percival Bartlebooth, whose first and last names evoke a variety of possible literary allusions? In the epigraph cited at the beginning of the Introduction, Perec was speaking of his whole corpus of works, but his words could also stand as epigraph to *Perceval*, whether within the context of Chrétien's own corpus or that of the continuations and the larger ensembles Perec evokes.

[36] I have borrowed this notion from Aviva Zornberg who uses it to describe (in psychoanalytical terms) the intertextual relation between midrash and Torah: the rabbinic glosses reveal what remains silent, just underneath, on the side, attached to what is there but not already said, uncovered by

In exploring the varieties of contradictory knowledge and practice, Chrétien is not unique among twelfth-century thinkers. A number of recent scholars have analyzed the importance of contradiction as a key figure for his contemporaries across a wide spectrum of writers and disciplines. In *Courtly Contradictions: The Emergence of the Literary Object in the Twelfth Century*, Sarah Kay studies the play of contradictions common to medieval logic, courtly literature, and the modern psychoanalytic models of Jacques Lacan. *Courtly Contradictions* sets up with broad as well as detailed strokes a historical and theoretical framework for a field in which much remains to be done. In her review of Kay's book, the medieval historian Constance B. Bouchard also points to two other paradigm-changing studies, Catherine Brown's *Contrary Things: Exegesis, Dialectic and the Poetics of Didacticism* and her own book, *'Every Valley Shall Be Exalted': The Discourse of Opposites in Twelfth-Century Thought*. In Bouchard's words, all three seek to 'reconceptualize the nature of contradictions common in twelfth-century texts, arguing that they were not (as was once assumed) set up almost accidentally by pre-modern authors struggling with literary forms, but rather were put into those texts quite deliberately by their careful and sophisticated authors' (2002). Even before this recent attention to the larger currents of 'the discourse of opposites', Rupert Pickens gave his study of the *Perceval* a subtitle that underlines this characteristic feature of Chrétien's art: *The Welsh Knight: Paradoxicality in Chrétien's* Conte del Graal.[37] I have been working on issues connected with contradiction in lyric and romance for many years: the problem surfaces with particular emphasis in *Shaping Romance* through discussions of how oppositions operate in a selection of twelfth-century fictions that typify the romance genre across a wide spectrum of different forms: their opposed terms are generally intertwined, mutually implicated and inseparable, that is, non-disjunctive, in Julia Kristeva's terminology (1969: 55–62). The current study takes me further into an exploration of how 'and/both' is the characteristic mode in these great explorations of the human condition, persistent forms of the imagination that continue to enthrall us.

Indeed, as defined by Chrétien's model, romance continuation eschews the restrictions of either/or and claims the non-Aristotelian logic of and/both through

repeating and recontextualizing the narrative elements of the biblical text (see the introd. to *Particulars of Rapture*, esp. 2–7). The poem by Wallace Stevens from which Zornberg takes her title, 'Notes Toward a Supreme Fiction', is not without interest for a study concerned with the creative tension between opposites. As she quotes it (2001: 10):

> Two things of opposite natures seem to depend
> On one another, as a man depends
> On a woman, day on night, the imagined
> On the real. This is the origin of change.
> Winter and spring, cold copulars, embrace
> And forth the particulars of rapture come.

[37] Other medievalists working on issues connected to opposition, contradiction, and complementarity, and on the connections between 12th-cent. dialectic and courtly literature, esp. in the romances of Chrétien de Troyes, include Hunt (1979) and Vance (1973 and 1987).

the process of juxtaposition and accumulation. Contiguity forces interpretation and further narrative elaboration. Under the impetus of this logic, what first appears as a predicament of difference becomes complementary rather than merely contradictory. As I demonstrate later in Chapter 4, Chrétien typically constructs oppositions whose architecture requires us to retain both sides: opposing terms remain present, equally valid, as they interact in a potentially creative tension that neither dismisses nor suppresses either one but forces us to deal with the paradoxical combination of both. Chrétien challenges us to read and reflect in the same mode of and/both in which he composes. We might compare the technique to Jean de Meun's theory of 'contrary things' (Guillaume de Lorris and Jean de Meun 1970: 21543), the oppositions that necessarily work together to clarify meaning by providing a gloss of opposing terms: 'les unes sunt des autres gloses' (21544).[38] As suggested by the accumulation of continuations and different versions in manuscript compilations, nothing once added may be left out in the quest for narrative fulfillment. Amplification across the patterns of the syntagm continually increases the potential for discerning (or changing) possible meaning(s). In the *Perceval* cycle, continuation thus encompasses paradox, oppositions, and contradictions; it allows their dualities to stand in dynamic interaction across successive rewritings of the narrative. Continuation operates as a formal principle, but it is equally constitutive at the levels of content and meaning.

Most significantly, the logic of and/both is already inscribed in the two parts of Chrétien's *Conte du Graal*, which begins with Perceval's story and then without warning adds that of Gauvain, some 4,000 verses into the narratives. As promised, the narrator subsequently returns to Perceval, but only to insert a single episode, dropped into the middle of the ongoing series of Gauvain's adventures: Perceval's visit to his hermit uncle takes place five years into the future in relation to Gauvain's timeline, which nevertheless resumes after the interruption exactly where the narrator left him. The second hero is now engaged in a quest for the bleeding lance, thus auguring some convergence with Perceval's quest to return to the Fisher King and ask the two questions he failed to ask during his first calamitous visit: whom does the Grail serve? why does the lance bleed? When both plot lines are left suspended in midsentence (as confirmed by a number of manuscripts without continuations), each hero has occupied half of the narrative, a distribution that the first two verse continuators faithfully imitate along with a reprise of the lopsided interlace of their overlapping itineraries.[39]

---

[38] Jean de Meun is a connoisseur of contraries as the author of an enormous and encyclopedic continuation added to Guillaume de Lorris's *Roman de la Rose* (*c.*1230 and 1270–80 for the two parts). See Regalado on definitions in scholastic reasoning and Jean de Meun's use of the concept (1981). Cf. Dragonetti's discussion in *Le Mirage* where he links the 'contraires choses' to the relationship between the two authors of the *Roman de la Rose* (1987: 207–9). We might think of Chrétien's *Conte du Graal* as providing a gloss of itself, his previous romances, and romance as genre (see below).

[39] Even the last two continuations, remembering the pattern of their two-hero model, reserve some portion of the narrative for Gauvain within the overall dominance now accorded Perceval.

It is hard to underestimate the disorienting effect created by Chrétien's unexpected doubling and decentering of heroes in a romance that far exceeds his usual 6,000 to 7,000 verses with no end in sight. The confusion registered by earlier scholars can give some sense of how anomalous the combination appears in the context of twelfth-century romance in general and Chrétien's corpus in particular. In the 1950s and 1970s, medievalists debated if Chrétien had left one romance or two: one for Gauvain and another for Perceval, scrambled together by some scribe-editor. Frappier (1977a, 1977b) defended the unity of Chrétien's double-stranded romance against Martin de Riquer's hypothesis of two distinct romances (1957). When Stefan Hofer speculated that a *remanieur* might have written the Gauvain section and added it to Chrétien's romance of Perceval, the idea was hotly debated by colleagues who largely disagreed (1956: 15–30). No one argues nowadays for separating Chrétien's romance into two, but the on-going debates about the importance and meaning of Gauvain's adventures in relation to Perceval's quest offer testimony to the continuing difficulties many scholars have in admitting that the work may have two heroes of equal interest and value, even if (or as) they differ from each other. 'Oneness' produced by a 'molt bele conjointure' (*Erec* 14), however anomalous it may seem to us, still requires our critical attention as part of the production of meaning in this romance at both the narrative and semantic levels.

Of course, this is not the first time that Chrétien has composed a romance with more than one hero, but his previous examples look quite different: the establishment and testing of the couple in *Erec et Enide*, the two-generational stories of father and son consecutively told in *Cligès*. These multiples are more clearly defined in relation to each other, their hierarchical arrangement more obviously explained in the narrative design as well as the action of the plot. With his four earlier romances, Chrétien seemed to be systematically rewriting contemporary models.[40] Moving from his predecessors' romances of antiquity and the highly respected traditions of Greece and Rome—the *Roman de Thèbes* (1150–5), *Eneas* (1155–60), Benoît de Sainte-Maure's *Roman de Troie* (1160–5)—Chrétien claimed value for the matter of Britain. Complaining about the oral storytellers who corrupted and disrupted their matter by dismembering it, he touted the 'beautiful joining' of his own artful compositions, episodic narratives more concentrated than the epic scope of the *romans antiques* but longer and more complex than the compact, typically single-action plot of contemporary lays. Removing the tales of Arthur and his knights of the Round Table from the linear march of history encapsulated in Geoffrey's *Historia* and Wace's *Brut*, Chrétien opened a space for adventure, the marvelous, and the experiments of fiction. Across his corpus of five romances we can see both the movement away from and toward the expansions of antique romance, the tension between

---

[40] For more detailed discussion of how Chrétien rewrites his literary models, see Bruckner (2000b).

separating stories and reassembling them into larger groupings and potential cycles. There are implicit and explicit links connecting *Erec* and *Yvain*, *Le Chevalier de la Charrette*, and *Le Chevalier au Lion*, but the first four romances remain distinct within their textual boundaries, each centered around a single, primary hero: Erec, Cligès, Yvain, Lancelot.

Having created with this substantial series of works a new horizon of expectation for the entertainment and edification of his initiated courtly public, Chrétien once again rewrites romance and its connections with history in his final, unfinished composition. He reinvents quite specifically his own previous romances as well as more generally the generic model of what romance may be, as he continues to make it one of the most protean forms of medieval *inventio*. With this last work we can no longer take for granted any simple definition of Arthurian romance: 'a story of love and combat that (re)builds the hero's identity', or 'a hero propelled by love of his lady fights his way through adventures, achieves his quest and the reward for his love'. These formulations might work for Chrétien's four previous romances and those of his contemporaries who follow the model he distinguished from the romances of antiquity. Chrétien's reinventions have already resulted in a powerful release of energy for the imagination, but that process will be exponentially increased after his *Conte du Graal* revolutionizes romance yet again. By introducing new and unexpected matter, new configurations and new roles for his characters, new arrangements for his narrative and new questions for his readers, Chrétien designed a puzzle that continues to fascinate us today as much as it captivated his contemporaries, inspiring the multiple rewritings that propose radically different interpretations of his enigmas and contradictions.

Among the many disruptive questions posed for his readers and continuators is the problem of how to understand the relationship between two heroes who seem to start from radically opposed positions: the 'ex-centric' and foolish Perceval, an inexperienced adolescent raised in the Welsh forest far from Arthur's court and any knowledge of chivalry and courtliness; the suave Gauvain, the epitome of courtliness and prowess, central to the values and standards of Arthur's Round Table. These two heroes move surprisingly close to each other in the course of their adventures, strangely mirrored as we shall see in the chapters that follow. Contradiction and complementarity? The rapprochement between Perceval and Gauvain may startle us, though it is prepared to a certain extent by Chrétien's previous romances where each hero's trajectory moves him into parity with Arthur's nephew before surpassing him. In *Le Chevalier de la Charrette*, the narrator even gives us glimpses of Gauvain's quest to rescue Guenevere, which moves him into parallel with the hero and enhances Lancelot's success by contrast with his failure.[41]

---

[41] I would argue that the 'proto-quest' narrative of Gauvain's effort to rescue the queen in the *Charrette* anticipates his move into a more prominent role in the *Conte*, where his exploits as

These precedents have led numerous medievalists to continue assigning to Gauvain the secondary status he enjoys in the romances of Erec, Cligès, Yvain, and Lancelot. They treat him as a mere foil for Perceval, if they pay any attention to his part of the romance at all. Many scholars simply leave him out all together. I have nevertheless argued (1993a) that the *Conte du Graal*'s narrative requires us to read the two knights' sameness as well as their difference—the and/both logic just outlined—in order to recognize their double movement into heroic status. If we are to understand the kind of answers Chrétien may have anticipated for the questions embedded in his narrative puzzles, without collapsing the heroes' specificity we must nevertheless read across their interlaced itineraries, as if what happens to one happens to the other, at least on some level, from crisis and discovery to extraordinary adventure, from mothers to Grail mysteries (or the reverse). Dual centers of narrative interest, both heroes also demonstrate duality in their actions and reputations. They are both good and bad; their adventures result in success but also failure, which introduces a troubling new view of what the hero of romance is and does, how he relates to violence and to love relationships, how he coordinates chivalric practice and religious obligation, service in love and family ties.[42] In some yet to be explained way, Perceval and Gauvain need each other. The tasks set before them to build and rebuild the Arthurian ideal require multiple questers and multiple questions—a powerful model for subsequent romancers in verse as well as in prose. There are no longer simple solutions for a single hero in this last, unfinished romance, and the four verse continuators will variously pursue the diverse and intertwined paths outlined by the master text.

ON ENDING AND ENDLESSNESS

The unfinished state of Chrétien's romance is itself a major question that resists unambiguous answers. Was it left unfinished intentionally or unintentionally? How does the answer to that question affect the dialogue continuators maintain with the master text or the way we should read and interpret *Perceval* and its continuations? We can know nothing with certainty about Chretien's intentions, nor do we know if there is any biographical basis to Gerbert's claim in the Fourth

---

liberator and redeemer at the Roche de Champguin echo those of Lancelot in Gorre as much as they seem to anticipate Perceval's at the Fisher King's castle, both as present failure and potential success (see Chs. 2 and 3). The tendency to rank and compare heroes, already firmly established in Chrétien's romances, will continue to evolve into the kind of elimination contest that the Grail quest becomes in the *Queste del Saint Graal* or the repeated motif of comparing Tristan and Lancelot as both incomparably the best in the Prose *Tristan*.

[42] Cf. the role played by Gauvain in a series of Arthurian romances (including the *Perlesvaus*) collected together and played off against several branches of the *Roman de Renart* in Chantilly ms. 472, which Walters considers a Gauvain cycle (1998). As indicated above, Gawain frequently enjoys the starring role in middle English romance.

Continuation (written some thirty to forty years later) that Chrétien died before finishing the *Conte du Graal*. The historical Chrétien remains a cypher except for what we can glean from the works in his corpus (and that is subject to disputed attributions). Nevertheless, it seems to me highly unlikely that he would have set out to write a romance with no ending or without planning to end it. None of the continuators suggest that the task of continuation is superfluous: they take for granted that the story is obviously unfinished and calls for more (and more and more and more) on the way to an ending. Indeed, the pattern is reprised with the First, Second, and Fourth Continuations, all of which suspend ending but invite the closure finally offered by Manessier. With other fragmentary twelfth-century romances—Albéric de Pisançon's *Alexandre* (*c*.1110–30), Beroul's *Tristan* (*c*.1165–87)—it is equally difficult to determine if they were completed by their authors.[43] We can speculate that Chrétien found no way to solve the puzzles put into place or lost interest or died, but in the final analysis we simply have to admit that we do not know why the romance remained unfinished by its first author.

On the other hand, the argument advanced by a number of scholars for reading the *Conte* as in some sense complete in its unfinished state poses a different question, a question that may not have occurred to medieval readers (certainly not in the way we pose it). Given medieval textuality's different conceptions of textual unity and coherence, the importance of common sources, and what Zumthor has called the notion of the 'texte-fragment' whose beginning and ending may be located elsewhere in the literary tradition or in larger cultural patterns, such a question might be of little interest to medieval readers. But from a modern critical standpoint, it is clearly of great interest and resembles the sort of debate that attends the unfinished state of Guillaume de Lorris's *Roman de la Rose* in relation to Jean de Meun's continuation, though the argument based on the lyric character of the first part's suspended ending does not work for Chrétien's interrupted narrative sequence.[44] The tension implied in the notion that the *Conte* reaches closure in its unfinished state recalls the and/both logic of Chrétien's design and will thus be addressed here from different points of view in the chapters that follow. In particular, in analyzing how questions play a more important role than chivalric exploits (and even answers) when seeking solutions to the problems of violence, Chapter 4 argues that the *Conte* inscribes both the necessity of suspending closure and the impetus for continuations.

A pattern of problematic endings certainly appears in Chrétien's corpus. Even in those where the plot is firmly closed, the unresolved character of certain problems

---

[43] For a brief overview of fragmentation versus ending, see Kelly (1993: 6, 15). The hypothesis of two Berouls further complicates the question of how his version of *Tristan* may have ended. Berthelot discusses a later author, Baudoin Butor, who tried repeatedly to start a romance without advancing beyond the planning phase (2006).

[44] The same argument regarding lyric suspension has, however, been proposed for interpreting the way Chrétien 'ends' his part of the *Charrette* with Lancelot imprisoned in a tower, as opposed to Godefroi's narrative 'continuation' (see below and Ch. 1). For arguments on reading Guillaume's part as finished in its unfinished state, see e.g. Hult (1986) or Dragonetti (1987).

posed may put into the question the value of their narrative closure: in *Erec et Enide*, the question of deciding who in the couple and what are at fault; in *Cligès*, the incongruous relationship between the happy ending and the epilogue; in *Yvain*, the tension between the couple's reconciliation and Yvain's characteristic impetuosity. Although lack of closure operates similarly on the semantic rather than the narrative level in *Le Chevalier de la Charrette*, Godefroi de Leigni's role as a second author, finishing *Lancelot* with the first author's permission and following his guidance, introduces some notion of continuation into Chrétien's repertoire even before his last romance and, as such, has elicited extensive debate about possible motivation for the shift. Much of the speculation hinges on imagined difficulties in Chrétien's relationship to his patron, Marie de Champagne. Although the *Conte du Graal* also names a literary patron who has commissioned the task and supplied its source in a book, no one has suggested that some disagreement between Chrétien and Philip of Flanders interrupted the work—a reflection no doubt of the kind of gender politics that operate within romance as well as in the critical tradition.[45] In any case, what Chrétien's previous romances teach us is that the nature of ending (and endings) is complex; they contain multiple levels and layers of elements, some closed, some left open, often combined in perplexing ways.

If we focus more specifically on the *Conte* and its relation to the continuations, what stands out is the way Chrétien's Grail story both seeks and resists ending. The pattern instituted in Chrétien's romance is echoed in the accumulation of continuations, versions, and rewritings that pile up in the manuscript tradition. The tendency to end at a midpoint that calls for more narrative seems endemic to Grail romances of all sorts and characterizes Robert de Boron's trilogy as much as the verse continuations.[46] The peculiar kind of endlessness that characterizes the *Perceval* cycle, which appears fragmentary no matter how many continuations are added, reflects the decentered character of Chrétien's model: faithful to its logic of and/both, the verse continuations remain untotalizable across their accumulation and multiplication of possibilities, continuous and discontinuous, separate yet combined.[47] This book is in large measure an effort to understand, through the dialogue between the *Conte* and its continuations, the fundamental dichotomy between a desire for ending and the equally strong resistance to ending. It is a tension that has a strong stake in middleness, that is, the necessity to remain *in medias res* between a beginning and endpoint,

---

[45] See my effort to debunk and explain the persistence of this story of frustrated patronage (2005: 141–2, 151–2).

[46] Though his romances do not end mid-scene as Chrétien, the Second Continuation, and Gerbert do, Robert's trilogy also functioned, as suggested above, as a powerful generator of continuations in the 13th cent. The *Estoire* epilogue anticipates four narratives to follow, though these are not realized in subsequent writings.

[47] This feature accords with one of the definitions Michael Wood offers for 'the genre of the unfinishable work' (2007: 1394). Speaking of *The Arabian Nights*, whose textual tradition, like the *Perceval* Continuations', includes numerous additions, rewritings, translations, manuscripts, and interpretations, he sums up the view of Abdelfattah Kilito: 'there isn't an entirety' (1396). I shall return to other issues raised by his discussion in Ch. 4.

caught in the centrifugal dynamic that keeps the periphery moving out from yet still connected to the center. As we shall see, this middleness reflects the continual reconstruction of an ideal glimpsed by human imperfection, as well as the nature of the quest as it has been redefined in this romance.

READING (THROUGH) COLLECTIVE AUTHORSHIP

If, as I believe, the tutelary spirit of Chrétien guides the hands of successive continuators and shapes a kind of collective authorship, this should not imply that they have the authorization Godefroi claims in his epilogue. I do not imagine them sitting down with Chrétien's notes, as Maurice Wilmotte did in his effort to explain the accomplishments of the first (and anonymous) continuator, as we shall see in Chapter 1. They have surely not written what Chrétien himself might have written had he continued, but they have struggled with and engaged the problematics, at the levels of form and content, built into the initiating text. They continue to reread and rewrite 'Chrétien', that is to say the author as translated into the romance he has left them, with all the allure of its unfinished state. They share the same dynamic of displacement and indirection that propels Chrétien, as they follow in the byways of romance outlined for them and participate in the hermeneutics of patterning set up in the *Conte du Graal*. Commentary, signification, gloss emerge primarily from the designs woven through the narrative rather than any explicit comments and explanations offered by an authoritative voice belonging to the narrator or a privileged character. Hermits speak only occasionally here, more vociferously in the *Queste del Saint Graal* where the didactics of allegory and fixed meanings have replaced Chrétien's decentered, endlessly vital, and renewable quest for meaning.[48]

Following Chrétien's and the continuators' lead, I have traced in this book the sometimes haphazard process of reading an immense and non-totalizable cycle of romances with many different versions, multiple states reflected in a manuscript tradition that cannot be pinned down and placed, given the constancy of variation.[49] The textual vastness offers a lesson in humility, in fact multiple

---

[48] Cf. Krause's analysis of the hermits in Gerbert's continuation: however authoritative their statements appear, they fail to account for what the hero actually does (2003).

[49] Although the amount and kinds of variation differ significantly across genres and texts, van Mulken expresses what may have been many a scribe-editor's point of view (if not that of authors more concerned to safeguard the integrity of their text, as Chrétien demonstrates in the epilogue to *Yvain* and as the manuscript tradition of the *Conte* itself suggests): 'The literal, univocal transcription of a text was not considered to be extremely important. Of much greater importance was the "translatio studii", the accumulation of knowledge and the pursuit of completeness, and each time a copyist was entitled to adjust, modify, and change the text of successive versions with respect to the exemplar, the demands of his age, his dialect or his aesthetic sense' (1993: 48). Van Mulken's observation gives a salutary reminder about the materiality of textual transmission in the Middle Ages and its implications for understanding what concerns a medieval public desirous of finding the 'whole story', the kind of *summa* made available in vernacular romance cycles. Cf. Suzanne

lessons in getting lost, remembering (but perhaps inexactly), forgetting and rediscovering, trying to figure things out, find the right questions, as well as the right paths, heroes, and authors. Resembling the twists and turns of the *droit chemin*, this study is a product of chance and design, directed and undirected, unconscious and conscious efforts to see where certain inexhaustible patterns, most especially cruxes involving some kind of contradiction, whether formal or semantic, have led me (and the readers and writers before me). My path has followed the dialogue between Chrétien and the verse continuators to the places where I see a conjunction, incongruity, or contradiction that calls for further inquiry. Are there surprising omissions? No doubt. I have tended to avoid overworked places like the scene of the three blood drops against white snow or the mystery of the Grail and its procession, except insofar as they are inevitably at the heart of the matter, the decentered center of the *Conte du Graal* and therefore related to the conjunctions privileged for analysis here. This is not a book about the Grail, but it is an interrogation of the Story of the Grail launched by Chrétien and continued in verse by a series of writing entities from authorial to scribal, with many subcategories in between: romancers, continuators, *remanieurs*, editors, *compilatores*, redactors, and scribes.[50]

In the five chapters of this study, basing my argument on close readings of the texts, as well as detailed analyses of narrative structure and intertextual play, I follow the complex paths of continuity through contradiction designed by Chrétien and echoed by his continuators. They provide a guiding thread that leads to three major areas of tension: relations with the other sex, particularly, love and sexuality; violence and the role of chivalry; religious practice and values. These are the very topics that reappear in varied guise each time Perceval receives advice, first from his mother as he prepares to leave his forest home and find Arthur's court, then from his mentor, Gornemant de Goort, who officially makes him a knight and initiates him into the art of jousting along with the fine points of chivalric conduct, and finally from his hermit uncle during his Easter repentance and the renewal of his quest. However unusual Perceval's upbringing, disrupted by the upheavals of civil war and ongoing chivalric violence, his eventual passage from mother to father figure to maternal uncle mirrors the normal progress of a noble youth as he is initiated into family and society in the twelfth century.

Not surprisingly, the counsel so pointedly repeated connects to significant problems and obstacles encountered in the narrative, by Gauvain as well as Perceval. Rather more surprisingly, the subject matter privileged in this advice, like the unusual prologue that introduces Chrétien's *Conte*, offers new combinations. Religious elements no longer appear as part of the furniture of the Arthurian world

---

Fleishman's (1996) view of the tension between the 'monoglossia' of Old French grammars and the reality of variation in medieval usage.

[50] See the collection of articles included in *Auctor et Auctoritas* and especially the closing remarks of Jacques Dalarun (2001: 571–3).

but become visible as an issue to be addressed for the first time within the context of romance. Finding the right way to do so while remaining faithful to the incongruities of Chrétien's romance constitutes a major challenge for medieval continuators as well as modern commentators. I do not believe that Chrétien's romance offers itself to allegorical interpretation, for reasons that will become evident throughout this study, but I have taken authorization from his text to consider biblical reference where it seems relevant, whether on the level of content or form. In particular, I examine, as in biblical exegesis, the play of literal and figurative meanings invited by his elusive narrative. And biblical comparison will be of special interest on the level of narrative structure, inasmuch as the *Perceval* cycle viewed from the perspective of the manuscript tradition shares certain characteristics with the Bible as compilation. If the Bible functions as a book of books whose unity is accepted as a given yet requires elucidation in light of contradictions, mysteries, gaps, and repetitions, just so the successive segments of the verse continuations form an architectural whole whose continuities and discontinuities call for analysis and demonstration.

While I seek to integrate and account for the way religious issues and models enter into the complex dialogue of the Grail story, I do not automatically credit religious discourse as the final 'truth' of Chrétien's text, as do the hermits of the *Queste* or literary critics who seek a master key in allegory. The Christian practices and beliefs included in the *Conte du Graal* are no less problematized than the courtly and Arthurian values represented, as the verse continuations will confirm through their varied readings. The difficulties posed by trying to put both discourses into dialogue can be measured by readers' resistance (medieval and modern, my own as well as that of others), emblematized by the tendency of later romancers and some verse continuators to opt for focusing either on religious views (as in the *Queste*) or Arthurian adventure (as in the First and Second Continuations). If the logic of and/both that characterizes Chrétien's romance requires the strange mix of social and religious values, Arthurian and Christian traditions, then any single interpretive focus on one of the two strands comes at the expense (or neglect) of the other. Yet by the same logic, efforts to combine religious and secular elements through interpretation may seem equally illogical, as the forces of contradiction and complementarity continue to make one strand appear to jar with the other. Such is the predicament where Chrétien's romance places readers, rewriters, and critics, with no resolution in sight but plenty of advice to be followed across the complex itineraries represented.

Love, violence, and religion—three areas set an agenda not only for Perceval's education but for the writer's inscription and the readers' reception of his story; they continue to do so when readers subsequently take up the role of continuator or commentator. The set of crucial problems is thus reflected in the organization of this study's five chapters. Although each chapter inevitably involves the dynamic interaction and multiple connections among them, I generally follow the order of topics as they are introduced for the first time in the advice offered by Perceval's mother at the moment of his departure from her isolated manor. Each of the chapters explores the principle of continuation not only at the semantic level, as suggested by the repeated triad of topics, but also through the multiple forms of expression it assumes within Chrétien's originating romance, as in the reinventions of successive continuators. In Chapter 1, I focus on the collective nature of authorship linking Chrétien and the continuators by analyzing the rhetorical play of authors' names, whose placement in the text never coincides with the move from one segment to the next. Their appearance thus simultaneously masks and reveals the shifts between multiple authors across the entire cycle, as authorial naming, present or absent, plays throughout the continuations in counterpoint with the hidden moments of textual transition. If the first continuator's anonymity suggests a lack of authorization, Wauchier de Denain's name placed at the interlace leads to the discovery that, despite his apparent neglect of the Grail story in the Second Continuation, he remains paradoxically faithful to Chrétien's model by keeping open, through Perceval's adventures with the Chessboard Lady, the problematic conjunction of the Grail and love for Blancheflor. Manessier, on the contrary, uses his acts of naming in the epilogue as part of a strategy to put an end to Perceval's Grail quest, once and for all. His epilogue names not only himself as author but links his patroness, Jeanne of Flanders, to her ancestor Philip, thus establishing a genealogy that links the continuator with the (unnamed) first author and obscures the presence of any intermediary hands.

Gerbert's repeated self-naming furnishes a frame around his version of Perceval's return to Blancheflor. The fourth continuator thus places himself among multiple tellers of the tale even as he asserts his place as the one who hopes to finish it (though the manuscript tradition does not allow him to do so). Gerbert seeks to reconcile the pressures exerted by the prose cycle and its insistence on chastity for the Grail hero with his own desire to return to the wellsprings of Chrétien's romance (whose most significant episodes are reinvented through the fourth continuator's own imaginative twists, as Chapters 2 and 5 will show). Finally, Gerbert's references to his source lead back to the first author and his prologue, where Chrétien's own acts of naming are tied to problems of reading and interpretation, introduced by the fulsome praise of his literary patron, his acknowledged (and unacknowledged) biblical references, his model exegesis, as well as his incongruous combinations and clever ambiguities.

Love and sexuality set the agenda for the next two chapters. In Chapter 2, I examine the relationship within couples by following the interplay between sexuality, retelling, and rewriting. Perceval's comic caricature of rape, when he finds a beautiful maiden sleeping in a tent is reinvented as a more serious erotic encounter for Gauvain in the First Continuation. Although seduced by a maid eagerly awaiting his arrival at her tent, he later retells their story as rape. Gerbert gives Gauvain's adventure another turn in the Fourth Continuation, where it is replayed as a real rape, then transformed into love. These variations show how the relationship between love and the Grail remains unresolved across the cycle, even as competing ideologies (Christian and chivalric) reorient the tale.

Chapter 3 focuses on the alternately protective and destructive relationships between mothers and sons in *Perceval* and the First Continuation. Although the Veuve Dame dies when her son leaves the Welsh forest for the world of knights, she continues to play a significant role in Perceval's adventures (including erotic connections with Blancheflor and family connections to the Grail Castle). The issue of mothers and marriage unexpectedly returns when Gauvain's grandmother, mother, and sister appear at the Roche de Champguin, newly liberated from enchantment by Arthur's nephew in the last unfinished episode of Chrétien's romance. Problematic but essential connections continue to be traced between mothers, sexuality, sons, and lovers, as the first continuator extrapolates his anonymous elaboration of Gauvain's story and inserts the story of Caradoc, a son whose revelation of his mother's adultery leads to punishment and then cure with the help of his lady, configured as a kind of virginal mother.

Chapter 4 deals with the role of violence within the Arthurian ideal, made more acute as the heroes themselves are seen as aggressors against the innocent. Oppositions between courtly and noncourtly weapons, set up and subverted, suggest how Chrétien's romance explores human nature in relation to Isaiah's utopian vision of swords beaten into plowshares. The damage as well as the necessity of human aggression emerge through the sometimes conflicting registers of chivalric and Christian values. The questions Chrétien raises about the legitimacy of violence lead to different responses in the prose and verse rewritings: the Vulgate Cycle's collective Grail quest leads to the destruction of Arthur's kingdom, while the verse continuations as finished by Manessier retain Perceval's 'ex-centric', individual quest and tolerate the contradictions written into Chrétien. Prose rewritings of the Grail story offer rival versions that interact with the verse continuations, though each tradition develops and completes the Grail quest in radically different ways. Whereas Perceval's quest in the verse continuations remains an individual accomplishment celebrated by Arthur's court, the Vulgate's quest for the Holy Grail becomes a collective pursuit of salvation that heralds the catastrophic end of Arthur's reign. Contradictions and competing values are thus amplified to the breaking point in the prose cycle, while the verse continuations, echoing the dynamic of Chrétien's originating romance, maintain their tensions without forcing resolution.

Chapter 5 addresses the anomalies of narrative structure within Chrétien's romance and across the cycle by following the complex and shifting dance of beginnings, middles, and endings. A new perspective on the religious dimensions of Chrétien's text and its effects on later rewriting emerges from an odd verbatim repetition that frames the insertion of Gerbert's continuation between the Second and Third, thus creating a kind of loop in the narrative that keeps us in *medias res*. A similar pattern of exact repetition appears in the ordering of the history books within the biblical canon and leads to a comparison, based on compilational strategies and methods of reading, between the Bible as a set of books and the *Perceval* cycle, seen as a problematic whole with continuities and discontinuities. After this architectural macroview, analysis at the episodic level pinpoints first how Gerbert reinvents the Grail as two ivory barrels filled with a life-restoring balm, then follows the effects of repeated Grail visits in the First Continuation and in the transitions between the Second, Third, and Fourth (which echo the repeated retellings of the Grail episode in the *Conte*). These episodes emblematize the way the story is continually reborn through the narrative gloss offered by successive rewritings of Chrétien's Grail story.

As these summaries suggest, each chapter in this study includes analysis of the master text as well as its dialogue with the continuations, but not every chapter treats all four of the verse continuations. Chapter 1 does so in order to survey the question of collective authorship (through progressive discussion of authorial naming in the First, Second, Third, and Fourth Continuations, then back to Chrétien's *Conte*), while introducing the major issues and themes that will be examined on semantic and formal levels throughout the book. The comprehensive character of the discussion in Chapter 1 thus accounts for its unusual length in comparison with the chapters that follow. In Chapters 2 to 4, selected continuations are introduced, depending on the problems that first emerge in analysis of the *Conte du Graal* and then resurface intermittently across the cycle. In its focus on overall narrative structure, Chapter 5 once again looks over the entire cycle but also includes more detailed examination of Grail issues that connect Chrétien with Gerbert and the First Continuation.

As I said, this is not a book about the Grail, but rather a book about the 'Story of the Grail', which in its most immediate sense is simply the English translation of Chrétien's title for his romance, 'li Contes del Graal' (66), though it can no longer convey the sense of shock that Chrétien's 'story of the serving dish' must have given his earliest public. But the Story of the Grail also carries other meanings as well: the formulation implies that Chrétien's story matter is shared, traditional, not his alone, whether in the pre-history he claims in the book given by his patron (which may of course be a fiction) or in the post-Chrétien history created by those who take up his story to continue or make it their own. The Story of the Grail refers to Chrétien's romance, but it also tells the story of how the *Perceval* Continuations, the ever-enlarging narrative in verse, accumulate in the wake of the mother text under the banner of its prologue. This Story of the Grail rivals with other stories of the Grail, histories (*estoire*), and quests in prose.

In contrast to the volumes of articles and books that have repeatedly tried to answer the question, 'What is the Grail?', Chrétien's narrative does not ask nor does it seem to favor a search for definitions, since it formulates otherwise the questions that must be asked and routes elsewhere the answers to be received. In some sense, the reticence of the manuscript tradition in representing the Grail, as well as the iconographical ambiguities in the illustrations, corresponds to the *Conte du Graal*'s own elusive treatment of what is admittedly a powerfully fascinating object in the midst of a scene that we inevitably characterize as marvelous in both the strong and weak sense of the term.[51] In order to renew our understanding of Chrétien's unfinished romance through an approach that focuses on his dialogue with the continuations, I have tended to avoid the well-worn trail that leads to explaining the Grail, but like so many others, I finally found the pull irresistible despite my resistance. And so in the Conclusion, I broach the subject of the Grail more directly by picking up the threads linking Perceval's mother and the Grail, mothers and sons, sons and lovers and mothers, left dangling in the space between Chapters 2 and 3. In that itinerary of moving forward by returning back, I bring together analyses from all the previous chapters and see how they may take us farther, or rather, push us into the middle of mysteries that Chrétien has set before us, as before his medieval readers and continuators, by leaving unresolved so many contradictions and continuities in the human experience of paradox.

[51] See in vol. 1 of *Manuscripts* (1993), Rieger (398), Harf-Lancner (465), and Baumgartner (489–90, 497–8), who emphasizes that the iconography of the Grail as chalice reflects the influence of the prose romances and the Holy Grail.

1

Authorial Relays

Que por l'estoire consomer
Fait l'an lou conte durer tant.
Assez i avroit plus que tant,
Qui tot vorroit an rime metre;
Mais li miaudres est an la letre,
Et miaudres vient adés avant,
Que li contes vet amandant.

Second Continuation, IV 29202–8

(One makes the story last so long to bring it to an end. For one who wanted
to put all into rhyme, there would be much more; but the best part is written
[lit. in the letter], and better yet lies ahead as the story improves.)

Authorship in the context of medieval vernacular literature appears to be a concept
in search of a name, a practice taking shape before a definition, or even a series of
shifting definitions, can catch the freewheeling spirit of medieval literary production. If *l'écrivain*—the writer as metaphor of origin rather than the literally writing
scribe—does not yet exist in twelfth-century vocabulary and still poses methodo-
logical problems in thirteenth-century usage (Berthelot 1991: 19, 28–31), we have
to discover what and who occupies that conceptual ground in the context of the
notoriously unfinished and repeatedly continued romance of the Grail launched by
Chrétien de Troyes. The 'authorial relays' of my title conjure up an image of
successive figures—having some yet to be determined relation to the author—
who, like runners, pass along the baton of the text. The shared text is thereby
enabled to complete a trajectory from start to finish, beginning to end. A satisfying
metaphor for medieval authorship perhaps, but the image becomes richly problematic when that relay race connects Chrétien's *Conte du Graal* to the twists and
turns of four continuations, two prequels, and multiple combinations across twelve
manuscripts, the Middle High German translation and a sixteenth-century French
prose translation. Who authorizes this ever changing textual edifice? Who and what
is an author in such a context and how does authorship operate?

M.-D. Chenu's well-known article on the relation between *auctor, actor*, and
autor traces the links, switches, and slips in medieval Latin usage between notions
of general performance and specific acts of textual production.[1] In a kind of

---

[1] See Chenu (1927, and 1976: 353–60), Dragonetti (1987: 43–4), Minnis (1979: 385–98), and
essays included in *Auctor et auctoritas*. I would like to thank Michelle Bolduc for the last two
references, included in her discussion of *auctoritas* and the troubadours (2007).

chassé-croisé, the *actor* (from *ago*), one who does something, changes places with the *auctor* (from *augeo*), one who more specifically produces a book, while *auctor* in turn moves in the direction of *auctoritas* (the authority of origin, the one who initiates), and in the new form *autor* links up with authenticity as well. All these notions of production, authority, and authenticity will be useful here, if not immediately applicable, as they require some adjustment to the medieval vernacular context. However nominally challenged by their lack of a specific term, French writers of the twelfth and thirteenth centuries, and more specifically romancers, recognize and locate their role, with alternating pride and humility, within a set of multiple, authorizing functions: sources, storymatter, patrons, maxims, proverbs, parables, and, on occasion, their own proper names. Writing occurs along a continuum which includes authors, translators, continuators, redactors, interpolators, scribes, editors, and compilers, whose collective work, like the collection of authorizing elements claimed, are not always so easily disentangled for modern readers who name and care about the differences in ways that differ from their medieval counterparts.

The paradox of authorship that characterizes the entire structure formed by *Perceval* and its verse continuations suggests that Chrétien is and is not the author of those continuations; their authors are and are not individual continuators. In modern terms, we limit Chrétien's authorship to the originating and unfinished romance. But in terms of medieval practice, the complex set of connections author(iz)ed by Chrétien in the *Conte du Graal* initiate patterns through which his authority remains in play throughout the cycle, in the multiple ways to be examined across the chapters of this book. As a series of named and unnamed romancers write freely after Chrétien, they nevertheless compose 'sor Crestïen', as did Godefroi de Leigni in completing *Le Chevalier de la Charrette* (7105). Remaining under his tutelage, the continuators are tied individually and collectively to their common model, its narrative material, as well as its puzzles and problems. An inquiry into the specific role played by authors' names in the elaborate textual edifice built by Chrétien de Troyes and the four continuations offers a useful starting point to grasp how their dialogue develops. As the overall structure of this chapter will demonstrate, successive authors and continuations lead back repeatedly to the original author and his text: the fundamental movement of the cycle is as much backward as forward, as the linear acts of writing and reading give way to the roundabout acts of rereading and interpretation.

AUTHORS' NAMES

It is generally accepted that anonymous constitutes the degree zero of vernacular writers in the Middle Ages, though in certain generic contexts, this may be debatable: consider the hundreds of troubadours and trouvères named in lyric manuscripts.[2] But if we admit the general premise of anonymity, we must never-theless recognize in the case of romance a dynamic play operating between named and unnamed authors. Douglas Kelly's comprehensive list of medieval romances includes approximately 120 items for the twelfth and thirteenth centuries; 59 names account for 76 works (1993: xiii–xxi). No simple shift across the linear chronology appears; the play between named and unnamed romancers goes back and forth across the time span, depending on a variety of factors known and unknown, intentional, incidental, or accidental. While it is true that in many cases we have nothing more than a name with no *état civil* attached to it, the impetus to name authors is remarkable in its persistence.

Given this pattern, the use of their proper names by writers like Chrétien, Gautier d'Arras, Thomas d'Angleterre, Marie de France *et alia*, is precisely what fills the terminology gap for the 'author' writing in French in twelfth- and thirteenth-century usage, at least in the context of romance.[3] In this sense, when the vernacular author signs his or her proper name in the text, when that name is cited by another writer or recopied by scribe-editors and compilers, the act of naming makes a claim for authority that rivals that of the Latin *auctores*, the officially recognized authors in contemporary usage, in schools and in courts where clerical culture informs an aristocratic lay public.[4] As we shall see, across the *Perceval* cycle, Chrétien's author-ship gains in authority as it passes from production to authorization, from an act of self-naming that establishes his role as author to repeated invocations by continu-ators and scribes who name him as a way to authenticate their own acts of composition and writing. For his contemporaries at the courts of Champagne and Flanders, the name *Crestien* carries the weight of an historical person along with the function of vernacular author; for later readers and writers (including in all probability the continuators), Chrétien is what he wrote: the writing practices he inscribed under his proper name and the image of him that we formulate based on our knowledge, perception, and understanding of his works as they are embedded in the process of manuscript transmission.[5]

[2] On anonymity and the medieval author, see e.g. Dragonetti (1987: 9, 18), Baumgartner (1985a). In the context of troubadour poetry, *chansonniers* are frequently arranged by poets, and proper names abound in rubrics, as well as in the *tornadas* (envois) which name patrons, fellow poets, jongleurs, etc.

[3] Gautier d'Arras names himself in the epilogue to his romance, *Ille et Galeron* (1170–84), as does Thomas in the closing remarks to his *Tristan* (c.1170–75). Marie de France names herself in the prologue to the *Lais* (c.1170–80) and the epilogue to her *Fables* (c.1189–1208). As we shall see, these are the most likely, though not the only places to find author's names.

[4] On the links between proper names and signatures, the character of proper names, as well as use of the signature (often with riddles, anagrams, etc.) to confer authentification, see Fraenkel's study of the signature, based on documents from the 7th to the 16th cent. (1992). Her discussion of the philosophical problems surrounding the proper name and its referent, the ease with which a proper name can make fictional beings appear to be real (108–21), is particularly interesting in light of named medieval authors for whom we have no biographical information to verify their historical existence. I would like to thank Peter Haidu for bringing Fraenkel's book to my attention.

[5] See my discussion of medieval authorship in the context of Chrétien's unusually large, varied, and somewhat indeterminate corpus (2008).

The romance tendency to name authors thus sets up a continuum within the public's horizon of expectation, which ranges from anonymous to named authors whose proper names carry varying amounts of information. Without the para-textual apparatus of modern authorship—dust jackets, title pages, running heads, and so on—romancers who emerge from anonymity do so when their names penetrate textual boundaries by entering the space of writing. Named by others or by themselves in prologues and epilogues, less frequently *in medias res*, their proper names establish a kind of intermediary domain where the extra- and intradiegetic mix. In this meeting of inside and out, patrons' names like Philip of Flanders and his great niece Jeanne, the two literary patrons named at the beginning and end of the *Perceval* cycle, take on the same linguistic status as the named romancers and their literary characters. The presumption of a histor-ical referent built into the proper name (however unverifiable or fictional it may be) sets up a relationship between literary artifact and social setting—the courtly public of romance—and authorizes the particular arrangement and reinvention of the romance's source material (*estoire, conte, livre*), guaranteed by an authorial signature (and sometimes that of a scribe like Guiot added in a colophon). The author's proper name functions as a textual slot for accumulating literary 'capital' or as a magnet for attracting varieties of intertextual play. And in this respect, all names are definitely not equal, as the *Perceval* and its continuations amply demonstrate.

First let me emphasize that my study of authors' names will not follow the critical tradition of 'l'homme et l'œuvre'. My interest is directed rather toward the rhetorical effects set into motion by repeated acts of authorial naming in these romances. Although I may be unwilling to let fiction entirely subsume the play triggered by an author's proper name, I share Roger Dragonetti's interest in seeing how 'l'attribution des noms d'auteur relève pour une grande part des pratiques purement rhétoriques de l'écriture' (1987: 22). The proper names given in romance rarely resonate in relation to a biography of the author, and when the author/narrator does claim to speak from his personal experience, the persona he takes is typically the generic type of the lover whose story parallels or contrasts with that of his hero. Such romancers hide their names behind ano-nymity, as in *Partonopeu de Blois* (*c.*1182–5), *Le Bel Inconnu* (*c.*1185–95), or the first part of *Le Roman de la Rose*—whose poet/lover/dreamer is only exposed as the (unknown) author Guillaume de Lorris when named by the second author/continuator Jean de Meun speaking through the God of Love.[6]

In Chrétien and the Grail romances, that biographical pose is not deployed.[7] Author and storymatter remain distinct, even as they meet at the point of intersection signaled by the speaking voice of the narrator. The conjunction of author and narrator is frequently dramatized in prologues and epilogues where

---

[6] See Dragonetti's argument for reading the two authors' names as pseudonyms of a single author (1978a, 1978b, 1987).

[7] We might consider in that light the parallels set up by the *Estoire* author between his life and his story: see Baumgartner (1985a).

the romancer's name operates in third-person discourse. Indeed, it is the difference as well as the link between third-person author and first-person narrator (primarily singular, occasionally plural) that particularly distinguishes romance as a genre that depends on the resources of writing even when it is orally disseminated by reading out loud. As Sophie Marnette has demonstrated, the modern concept of implied author ill suits medieval romance where the narrating *I* assumes a whole range of functions (including that of author) but remains both more present than the modern implied author and, paradoxically, less responsible insofar as the medieval author makes no claim to being the unique source of the text (1998: 217–18). Anne Berthelot too signals the 'partial assimilation' of narrator and author (1991: 39). For medieval writers caught up in the role of creator, which problematically imitates that of the Creator, Berthelot emphasizes the way existence precedes essence, as it were: the author function emerges from inside the literary work as a '*persona* dont on raconte, ou qui raconte, les (ses) aventures, en faisant l'économie paradoxale d'une instance de narration' (38).[8]

What difference does a name make in this game of the author? Naming announces an identity, the identity of *je* and *il*, even as it opens the gap of their difference. The overlap simultaneously uncovers and covers over the space between inside and outside, keeps narrator and author in tandem throughout the text, although the third-person author designated by name appears only fleetingly in comparison with first-person interventions which repeatedly signal that the story as told reaches its public modulated through a particular narrating voice and point of view. When more than one author's name makes a claim on the same romance, the apparent constance of the narrating *I* disconcertingly wavers.[9] Chrétien's corpus anticipates such a shift in authorial identity, when Godefroi informs us retrospectively that he completed the *Charrette* with the first author's permission and in conformance with his design.

> Godefroiz de Leigni, li clers,
> A parfinee la charrete,
> Mes nus hom blasme ne l'an mete
> Se sor Crestïen a ovré,
> Car ç'a il fet par le boen gré
> Crestïen qui le comança. . . .
> Tant en a fet, n'i vialt plus metre
> Ne moins, por le conte malmetre.
>
> (7102–7, 7111–12)

---

[8] Cf. also the chapters on medieval authors in Dragonetti (1980) and Hult (1986).

[9] There has been considerable critical interest in studying the shift in the 'I' across the two parts of the *Roman de la Rose* and between Godefroi and Chrétien. The two named authors of the Prose *Tristan*, Luce de Gat in the prologue, Helie de Boron in the epilogue, present similar issues but the shift remains elusive, given the difficulty of identifying exactly which parts belong to which author in a work that, despite its enormous length, does not fit the model of text and continuation: there is no demarcation of parts belonging to a particular author, but rather a continuous narrative of interlaced heroes, in which parts of the Vulgate *Queste* are inserted into Tristan's story (Baumgartner 1990: 15–17, 46–7).

(The clerk Godefroi de Leigni has brought the *Charrette* to an end but no one should blame him if he has worked on Chrétien, for he did it with the good will of Chrétien who began it.)

Though the transition between Chrétien and Godefroi seems assured, many questions remain unanswered behind this unexpected doubling of authors.[10] And with the *Perceval* Continuations, the identity of authors becomes even more problematic.

For many modern readers it is not the appearance of continuity that has been disrupted by successive acts of authorial naming across the verse continuations. They have so often been dismissed for their very apparent discontinuities, their heterogeneous and contradictory accumulation of materials, it seems impossible to credit them as true continuations forming a coherent whole in relation to Chrétien's romance. And yet the manuscript tradition demands that we consider them as such to understand how medieval writers (authors and scribes) put them together and how medieval readers read them. As William Roach observes in the introduction to volume IV of his edition:

> it is clear that in all the manuscripts which have preserved both the First and the Second Continuations, the redactors and the copyists thought of the corpus as a single, continuous story. This fact is amply attested by the absence of breaks and transitions between the several Continuations, and also by the frequent allusions and references in the Second Continuation to incidents and episodes of Chrétien's *Perceval* and the First Continuation. (xvii)

Roach's observation, which applies equally to the Third and Fourth Continuations, reminds us that, between the romance framing of prologue and epilogue, where authors' names play their traditional role in authorizing proleptically and analeptically the text thus contained, none of the acts of authorial naming found in these manuscripts coincide with the textual moment of passing from one writer to another. The writing continues precisely in order to mask the shift in reference covered by the narrating *I*, whose changing identity will only be signaled after the fact. The repeated technique of delayed authorial naming that characterizes Chrétien's continuators seems, on the one hand, designed to fool the readers into missing the transitions and, on the other, insistently invites us to turn back and find the place (as in Jean de Meun's *Rose*).[11] The requirement to read forward and backward, the need to superimpose retroactively corresponding segments of narrative, the very techniques of writing and reading already inscribed in Chrétien's *Conte*, remain fundamental to the continuations. The succession and placement of authorial names play a key role in triggering and retriggering the system.

---

[10] Godefroi's epilogue has elicited numerous critical responses: see e.g. Frappier (1972b), Brownlee (1990), Hult (1989).

[11] Cf. Pickens on Robert de Boron and his *exordium a insinuatione* (1988: 25).

Reading the *Perceval* Continuations as a whole, however disparate the parts, also helps clarify an underlying logic that plays on fragmentation and continuation to realize *achèvement* (in both its French and English uses), a logic that is not without ramifications for other romances and other kinds of writing in the Middle Ages. Alexandre Leupin has identified the fundamental and contradictory impulses that build this immense textual edifice with what he calls 'la logique de la faille', a compelling image taken from the continuations themselves (1982). Anonymous as well as named romancers participated in this process. Close examination of their acts of authorial naming, present and absent in the manuscript tradition as it comes down to us, will lead us into the labyrinthine logic so characteristic of Chrétien's Grail romance, unfinished and continued through successive layers.

I refer to acts of naming present and absent because, although we have three continuators' names—Wauchier de Denain for the Second Continuation, Gerbert for the Fourth, and Manessier for the Third—we do not have a name for the first continuator who thus remains as anonymous as the other writing entities (interpolators, redactors, scribes, and compilers) who generally do not qualify for designation as authors. Within *Perceval* and its four continuations, as represented in the maximally cyclic manuscripts T and V, we thus encounter the whole gamut of authorial identity from anonymous to fully weighted proper name—but significantly they do not enter the scene of writing in that order.

The specificity of this narrative concatenation stands out more clearly against the larger context of other Grail romances that pick up and rewrite Chrétien's seminal story: Robert de Boron's trilogy, the *Perlesvaus*, the *Queste del Saint Graal*, and the Post-Vulgate Grail cycle. A number of anomalies involving the *Perceval* Continuations' form and authorship may explain, at least in part, why the verse continuations have received relatively little attention up to now—and why they deserve much more. Emmanuèle Baumgartner identifies a number of 'ruptures' that divide verse and prose romances from the beginning of the thirteenth century on. All romances (or new versions) of the Grail are composed in prose (except for the continuations), all other Arthurian romances in verse. There is no 'Gauvain en prose', although Arthur's nephew will star as hero in many verse romances. Emphasizing the underlying tendency of Grail romances to create an entire textual universe, Baumgartner signals an essential link connecting prose, cyclicization, and the Grail (1987–8: 168–9).

Marnette's statistical and qualitative analysis of data on author/narrators further confirms the tendency of Grail romances to opt for prose and anonymous authorship in order to be consistent with the type of truth claims associated with the Grail once Robert de Boron's version, which exercized enormous influence on subsequent writers, reinvents it as the Holy Grail (1998: 113–14, 203, 219). As Michel Zink points out (1987–8: 16, 18–20), verse romancers like Chrétien typically use their acts of self-naming to guarantee a notion of truth based on the romance's own internal logic and built by the narrating *I* through multiple perspectives. In Marnette's view, the *Estoire dou Graal* brings out a profound contradiction between named authors associated with verse romance and the subject of the Grail, whose truth is now connected to a monologic value system located outside romance in biblical history: Robert replaces Chrétien's mysterious serving platter by the 'holy vessel', the cup used for wine at the Last Supper and then, after the crucifixion, to collect Christ's blood.[12]

This descriptive logic is persuasive but repeatedly requires us to set aside the case of the verse continuations as exceptional. Yet these exceptions deserve further analysis precisely insofar as they accumulate anomalies in such an insistent fashion. Anomalous on three counts, the *Perceval* Continuations continue in verse; they continue to name authors; and they continue to associate Gauvain with the Grail quest (even if his role will be gradually reduced). We need to examine what these continuations tell us about Chrétien's romance and romance writing that may have been overlooked by other rewritings of the Grail story.

A quick overview of the specific acts of naming that both announce and efface the changes of gear from one author to another across the cycle will set the stage for exploring how each of the segments can be characterized by the name that stakes a claim to it and how those names function in relation to the larger textual architecture that emerges. If we consider the collection of authorial names given, their differences in status or role immediately mark out three subsets of texts.

(1) *Le Conte du Graal* remains in place as the initiating romance throughout the manuscript tradition.[13] In the prologue, 'Crestïens' twice identifies himself as author, his name forming a frame around the praise of his patron, as well as a kind of trumpet fanfare to announce the tale he is about to tell. 'Crestïens semme et fait semence | D'un romans que il encomence' (7–8: 'Chrétien sows and seeds a romance that he begins').

> Crestïens, qui entent et paine
> Par le comandement le conte
> A rimoier le meillor conte
> Qui soit contez a cort roial:...
> Oëz coment il s'en delivre.
>
> (62–5, 68)

(Chrétien, who takes pains at the count's command to rhyme the best story ever told in a royal court...Hear how he carries out the task.)

By the time Chrétien composes his last romance, his name has become a collection point, the point of intersection between two sets: four previous romances signed by the same name and the verse continuations that take off in direct descent from his

---

[12] Perhaps paradoxically, Robert de Boron himself wrote in verse, though his romance was quickly prosified and pseudonymously expanded, thus satisfying Baumgartner's and Marnette's analyses. If we accept Gowans's argument for crediting Robert with the prose version, the subsequent production of the versification may appear more problematic (2004).

[13] The only exception to this general rule is K, where the Second Continuation appears with neither *Perceval* nor the First Continuation. *Perceval* appears alone in three manuscripts and a number of fragments.

Grail story. Facing outside the text, Chrétien's name anchors his romances to particular places and time periods evoked by two patrons: here Philip of Flanders; in the *Charrette*, Marie de Champagne, the wife of Henry the Liberal, count of Champagne (together they place him, *c.*1160s–1191). Whatever transparence that name may have held for his contemporaries, it remains opaque as historical referent, an object of speculation for modern readers and critics. Within the text, 'Crestïens' has developed a lively presence, an identity synonymous with intra- and intertextual play. The public of connoisseurs Chrétien creates and expects as readers of romance recognizes in that proper name a certain kind of textuality, narrating voice, etc. 'Crestïens' has accumulated a thickness and weight incommensurate with that of his continuators who will show their deference through self-effacing anonymity as well as citation.[14]

(2) The First (or Gauvain) Continuation and the Second (or Perceval) Continuation, which both date from the end of the twelfth century, form a unit insofar as they continue largely under the aegis of Chrétien's authorship and together reprise the zigzagging pattern of interlace he set up between the two heroes.[15] One authorial name surfaces briefly in the Second Continuation, precisely at the moment when the interlace formula moves from Gauvain back to Perceval to introduce the final episodes toward the end of *Gauchier de Dondain*'s contribution. That is the name as it appears in E (Roach's base manuscript). Out of nine manuscripts, one omits it entirely and seven variations appear in the remaining eight. Arguments for and against identifying the author as Wauchier de Denain have recently been decided again in his favor.[16] What we do with that identification outside the text and how we read it inside in relation to both the First and Second, as well as the Third and Fourth Continuations, will require further commentary.

(3) The last two continuations, written in the first third of the thirteenth century, also form a subset, insofar as both Manessier and Gerbert are keen to situate their work in relation to the originating author. Both refer to the issue of interruption and continuation; both seek to clarify where they started 'in the middle'; and both look toward an ending. The third continuator announces his name twice, as did Chrétien, who remains unnamed but clearly designated in an epilogue that arches back to the distant prologue by way of a genealogy of patrons.

> . . . Jehanne la contesse
> Qu'est de Flandres dame et mestresse, . . .
> Dame, por vos s'en est pené
> Manessier tant qu'il l'a finé

[14] See the app. in *Legacy* vol. 1, which gives a list of quotations from other medieval writers who refer to Chrétien, thus indicating the extent of his renown and influence.

[15] They always appear together except in K (only the Second Continuation followed by a quick conclusion) and R (BN, fr. 1450), where *Perceval* and the First Continuation are integrated into a different cyclical structure in combination with Chrétien's other romances, all interpolated into the *pax arthuriana* of the *Roman de Brut*.

[16] Vial (1987), Roach, ed. V, xi–xii.

> Selonc l'estoire proprement,
> Qui conmença au soudement
> De l'espee sanz contredit.
>
> (V, 42643–4, 42657–61)

(Jeanne the countess who is lady and mistress of Flanders, . . . Lady, for you Manessier has worked so hard that he has finished it ['my book'] properly according to the story, he who began without contestation at the soldering of the sword.)

Jeanne could qualify as 'dame et mestresse' of Flanders between 1214 and 1227, during the imprisonment of her husband after the Battle of Bouvines (Roach, ed. V, xiii). Given the more or less contemporary dating of Gerbert's work (*c.*1226–30), most scholars accept the likelihood that Gerbert and Manessier worked independently of each other to pick up where the Second Continuation ended. Gerbert's desire to reach the end was apparently frustrated by a scribe editor who inserted his continuation between the Second and Third, which closes the series in the majority of manuscripts with continuations (eight out of twelve). Only the twin manuscripts T and V include Gerbert, whose authorial intervention frames Perceval's return to Blancheflor and includes multiple repetitions of his name, as well as an explicit acknowledgment that others before him have continued Chrétien: 'Gerbers, qui a reprise l'oevre |Quant chascuns trovere le laisse' (6998–9: 'Gerbert who has taken up the work again when each [other] poet leaves it').

This initial view of the Big Bang from Chrétien's densely-packed romance suggests a kind of lumpy collective authorship. The gradual spreading out of textual galaxies, attached to a series of author's names, guarantees the continuing authenticity of the Story of the Grail (at least for medieval readers of manuscripts). But the authorial identities present are decidedly irregular, unpredictably placed, and often as invisible as the universe's dark matter: three named continuators certainly do not account for all the writing gathered together. Before returning to Chrétien's signature located at the beginning of this literary explosion, we need to follow the series of continuations in order to examine in greater detail how authorial naming creates voids and fills in spaces, contributes to continuities and discontinuities across the whole textual edifice.

The rest of this chapter will thus examine each continuator from the first to the fourth, as a prelude to analyzing Chrétien's initial act of authorial naming in a prologue that, through scribal repetition, extends its reach to introduce the entire cycle. The varied rhetorical play associated with successive instances (or omissions) of naming the author will introduce a constellation of topics connected to the poetics of continuation explored in this chapter and further developed in those that follow. The anonymity of the first continuator inevitably raises the issue of textual boundaries, which reappears in the Second Continuation's naming at the interlace of heroes, as in the doubled acts of soldering that mark the joining of the Third and Fourth Continuations with Manessier's and Gerbert's retropective signatures. While Wauchier's middleness remains faithful to Chrétien's suspensions, his excursions into the amorous with Perceval's quest for the Chessboard Lady also anticipate a return in the Fourth Continuation to the problem of sexuality, Gerbert's own interlaced middleness (Manessier having definitively claimed the endpoint), and their collective construction of authorship. In the final segment of the chapter, Chrétien's repeated acts of authorial naming introduce the question of reading and interpretation, the hermeneutic problem so insistently staged in the *Conte du Graal*, so seductive for the readers and writers who follow.

ANONYMOUS CHRÉTIEN

The first continuator's anonymity suggests that he has no borrowed authority like Godefroi de Leigni to claim his status as writer—hence the effacement of his identity as difference, at least on the surface level of the narrating voice. What is at stake in this authorial silence? According to Godefroi, Chrétien was willing (for some unexplained reason) to allow another writer to continue his *Charrette*. On the other hand, Godefroi's defensiveness in explaining his role, his decision to delay mentioning it until after the fact, suggest that Chrétien's proper name in the prologue stakes a claim that should set his work apart in some way, even if the medieval writer situates himself in a different position from the modern, copyrighted author. Like other medieval writers, Chrétien defers to and cannibalizes the already written, acknowledges explicitly and implicitly multiple sources, materials, guarantors, and so on. But the authorial character he projects in his romances suggests someone who proudly lays claim to his own productions and productivity: the *Erec* prologue plays on his name and fame '[t]ant con durra crestientez' (26); the *Cligès* prologue begins with a long list of his works; the implicit rivalry with another romancer, Gautier d'Arras, appears in the praise of Marie de Champagne as a display of one-upmanship; the epilogue to *Yvain* declares that anyone who adds to his romance is adding lies, since Chrétien has already reported all that he heard; and the tone of the *Perceval* prologue is established by the opening figure of the sower, as well as the superlatives attached to 'le meillor conte | Qui soit contez a cort roial' (63–5).[17]

Gerbert alludes to his predecessor's death and thus establishes his right to continue.[18] By contrast, the First Continuation carries a sense of starting in close proximity to Chrétien, literally and figuratively, and then gradually moving farther away from him spatially and chronologically. This evolution appears in several guises in the verbal texture. In the first place, the Gauvain Continuation

---

[17] In Roach's edn., verses 64 and 63 are reversed. Zink reads that figure as making Chrétien the origin of all (1987–8: 18). Cf. motifs in troubadour lyric where poets like Jaufre Rudel assert control over their own production and seek to protect it from 'mouvance'.

[18] Guillaume de Lorris's death, as reported by the God of Love, works similarly to legitimate Jean de Meun's authorial intervention.

picks up immediately after the last unfinished sentence of Chrétien's *Conte* without in any way signaling a change of authorship. The eleven manuscripts that offer the First Continuation reflect successive stages of elaboration in which a kernel of episodes, established early in the process, remains constant, while variation and elaboration is such that the editor has published three separate volumes, required to adequately represent the Short, Long, and Mixed Redactions. The play of reinvention among these versions gives a picture of Chrétien's authorial presence and authority, still strongly felt and then receding but always retaining the potential to be reactivated. As Chrétien's authority operates at a further remove, it seems to allow greater intervention from continuators, *remanieurs*, and scribes, but still keeps the canonical character of the group in evidence. Anonymous, the 'first continuator' is a composite fiction gathering together under a common 'name' the multiple states and stages of remaniement known collectively as the First Continuation.

Only in T and V, probably dated some time after 1250, does the gap as well as the continuity between Chrétien and the continuations become certified sufficiently for the mixed redaction to add two references to an authorizing *Crestïen*. As we saw in the Introduction, the first mention (I, 1234) accords with his text, since Chrétien's narrator did indeed praise the Grail Castle; but the second (I, 4117–18) invents Chrétien's admiration for the automaton in Alardin's tent. Not often do we catch a writer so blatantly making up his source, though we assume that claims to unverifiable sources are frequently just a literary topos, as in Chrétien's own reference to a book supplied by Philip of Flanders as the source for his story of the Grail. Perhaps we should simply understand with Ferdinand Lot that *Crestïens* is serving here in the guise of authority rather than author (1931: 136). That is precisely how the first allusion phrased his role: 'Crestïen en ai a garant' ('I have Chrétien as guarantor'). At this point in the process of continuation, there seems to be little risk in acknowledging the gap between the first author and the current narrator's *I*.

For medievalists, however, there has been considerable confusion about where Chrétien's text ends and where the First Continuation begins (and ends). Our modern sense of what should belong to an author, what constitutes authenticity, has led to considerable polemics about what should be put to Chrétien's credit (or blame) and what fails to deserve his imprimatur. When Maurice Wilmotte enters the fray to weigh in against Paul Meyer's 1906 identification of Wauchier de Denain as the author of the Second Continuation, the debate is still open on whether or not Chrétien should be given responsibility for the First and Second Continuations (1930: 32–3). Given his evident respect for Chrétien, Wilmotte seems particularly incensed that 'ces obscurs rimeurs' (58) would be given the status of author for continuing 'un grand maître' (68). He concedes parts of the First (the opening, the *Livre de Caradoc*) and all of the Second Continuation to unknowns, while reserving most of the Gauvain Continuation for Chrétien's authorship. Wilmotte continues to recognize Chrétien in the importance given to Gauvain's role, already built into the alternations of the *Conte du Graal*. And he recognizes in much of the writing in the First Continuation 'le *faire* du grand maître, cette aisance du style, ce sens du rythme, ce balancement calculé des deux membres de l'octosyllabe, ces prédilections de vocabulaire, ces jongleries de mots, ces allusions discrètes qui font de lui un écrivain sans rival' (52). To make sense of the style and power of invention demonstrated in the First Continuation, Wilmotte hypothe-sizes an anonymous continuator working from the original author's notes and following his characteristic élan. Subsequent scholars, starting with Lot in 1931, reject that identification, and no one these days contests the end of Chrétien's romance at line 10601 (of Potvin's edition), as attested by manuscripts without any continuations: 'Si li demande qu'ele avoit' (Roach, ed. 9234). But Wilmotte's enthusiasm for the First Continuation as Chrétien's work *par personne interposée*, as it were, confirms the sense of continuity and discontinuity between *Perceval* and the Gauvain Continuation, which is equally reflected in its authorial anonymity, in the manuscript tradition, and in what strikes me as its lively rewriting of the *Conte*, not only at the level of style but in its characteristically decentered textuality.

INTERLACING WAUCHIER DE DENAIN

But the current certainty about where the First Continuation begins does not necessarily apply to where it ends. Without an author's name to lay claim to any particular segment, common agreement follows the alternation of Chrétien's heroes and locates the beginning of the Second Continuation at the point where the narrative finally returns to Perceval. This is a not unreasonable choice inasmuch as it echoes the textual situation in which Wauchier de Denain chooses, almost 12,000 verses later, to identify himself by placing his proper name at the crossroads of the lopsided interlace that connects his two heroes. Shifting identities at the level of character could mirror an earlier shift between continuators:

> Einsint remest o lui Gauvains,
> Dont li contes ne plus ne mains
> Ne conte avant a ceste fois;
> Mais de Perceval lou Galois
> Porroiz le conte avant oïr,
> S'a gre vos vient et a plesir.
> Gauchiers de Dondain, qui l'estoire
> Nos a mis avant en memoire,[19]
> Dit et conte que Perceval,
>
> (IV, 31415–23)

[19] Only T and V localize the moment in the text with a *chi* (here), each associating it with different adverbs, *avant* and *aprez*: 'Gautiers de denet qui l'estoire a mis chi aprez (T)/avant (V) en memoire'. V's *aprez* might suggest that the new author's work is only starting in the final episodes of the Second Continuation (which seems unlikely), but all the other manuscripts agree in using the

(Thus Gauvain stays with him, about which the story will tell no more at this point, but you can now hear the story of Perceval the Welshman, if it pleases you. Wauchier de Denain, who has pursued the story for us, recounts that Perceval . . .)

Corin Corley (1982) has argued, however, that the change in protagonist from Gauvain to Perceval does not necessarily indicate a change in author. Based on manuscripts, rhymes, repeated expressions, etc., he distinguishes a section that straddles the 'boundary' of the First and Second Continuations (4882–10268) and hypothesizes different authors operating across three rather than two continuations before Manessier. In his view, Wauchier's part would begin with the Hunt of the White Stag, that is, after Perceval's visit to the Castle of the Magic Chessboard, which initiates a series of quests as he seeks to qualify for the Chessboard Lady's favors and compensate for his initial failures at her castle (Episode 5, according to Roach's list of episodes found in the Second Continuation).[20]

Corley's hypothesis serves as a model for suggesting why it may be impossible to pin down exactly where Wauchier—assuming we accept his authorship—began, since he gives no indication at the moment of naming. In rereading the Second Continuation, I too have found myself wondering if a different writer might be responsible for the opening series of short episodes that seem rather directionless, despite the repeated efforts to link up with earlier materials in Chrétien's romance. Perceval's meeting with the lady at the Chessboard Castle is the first major episode in the continuation and subsequent episodes seem to get better as they accumulate: by Episode 19 they are more developed, get more out of the constituent elements, common matter and Chrétien matter, create a kind of depth from the interplay and recombinations. Another continuator? Or just a writer who improves? Or the story itself, as the narrator claims (IV, 29202–8, quoted in the opening epigraph)? Perhaps inevitably one has the sense of different hands at work: this is a collective enterprise of writing, as we are reminded by continuing references to sources.[21]

The Second Continuation gives an overwhelming impression of inbetween-ness, of being in the middle of proliferating stories that may and do expand at any

expression *mettre avant en memoire*, which Wilmotte (1930: 69–70) compares with Chrétien's *metre devant* in *Cligès* (4282): not a spatial location in the text but a movement in the mind, which links author/narrator and public: '*Nos* a mis avant en memoire'. See Vial's discussion of *metre avant en memoire*, which he defines as 'conter plus loin, poursuivre la narration de' (1978: 526–9).

[20] Gallais rejects the stylistic argument and insists on the different spirit animating the two continuations (1988–9: 2, 984–5; 3, 1382). See App. 1 for a list of all the episodes identified by Roach in the First, Second, and Third Continuations.

[21] Sources appear as *conte*, *estoire*, even other storytellers, as in L's replacement of *li escriz* with the name Bleheris (perhaps related to Breri, the authority for Tristan stories). See Roach's notes to IV, 29351–7 (539) and Kellermann (1956). In the Second Continuation (IV, 26083–101), the narrator comments on unreliable 'menestrel' who claim to know Perceval's story to make their lies believable. Is this critique of rivals a possible reference to romances like the prose *Perlesvaus* that also claim to continue Chrétien's romance?

point, as the variants testify.[22] But there is also, at some level, a structure that
holds the mass together and moves it forward, like the river of water moving
through the Everglades: the concatenation of episodes tied together by Perceval's
need to reach Mont Dolerous (announced in Episode 1, recalled in 25 and
carried out in 33), to complete the Chessboard quest (opened in Episode 4,
complicated in 5, moved forward in 21 when Perceval regains the hound and stag
head, completed in 26), and, above all, to return to the Grail Castle, which plays
as a leitmotif of Perceval's intentions throughout the narrative until he finally
arrives there in the final two episodes (34 and 35). These interlaced quests
operate like a series of parentheses opened, piled up, recalled, deferred, and
finally, progressively closed, as the later episodes complete the structural impetus
of the opening moves.

How can we tease out of this mass what anonymous (one or two or more?) and
what Wauchier de Denain may be responsible for? If we aim to get a sense of
what the process of continuation is about, trying to tease apart what has been so
assiduously written together seems counterproductive. Throughout this section,
the manuscripts treat the First and Second Continuations as a unit and the only
instance of authorial naming that occurs highlights the open-ended interlacing of
the heroes, identifies authorship with a shift in identities and the fundamental
impulse of writing characteristic of the ensemble. The invented name 'Pseudo-
Wauchier', sometimes used by scholars to designate the anonymous First Continuation, reinforces the way the Gauvain and Perceval Continuations appear to
operate in tandem.

But what of the name Wauchier de Denain: does it give us some information
with which to evaluate his role? Although the proper name serves as a kind of
collector at the interface of extra- and intradiegetic concerns, there is very little
collected by the name Wauchier de Denain. As a translator of some saints' lives
found in the *Vies des Pères*, Wauchier is considered by Wilmotte as too austere
and humbly Christian to author the courtly and frivolous Second Continuation.
On the other hand, Guy Vial considers his authorship of both as perfectly
compatible, given the variety of commissions a medieval writer might expect
(1978).[23] More interesting is the Flanders connection Wauchier offers through
the patronage of Jeanne de Flandre.[24] But even if the attribution is credited by
modern scholars and may have been recognized by some medieval readers in his

---

[22] e.g. T's version of the tournament at the Chastel Orgueilleux magnifies the description with
lists of names and stories (see Roach's app. vii). The author/narrator of the Second Continuation
gives the impression of knowing many stories, to which he alludes along the way: stories of the Glass
Bridge, the Magic Chessboard, the knight in the tomb, etc. Cf. the episode of the Biau Mauvais at
Arthur's court (Episode 17) that recalls the 'loathesome damsel' type.

[23] Cf. Szkilnik's discussion of the verse interpolations where Wauchier names himself in the
course of translating saints' lives into prose, thus showing off his talents as a writer (1986).

[24] On Jeanne's patronage, see Vial (1978), Stanger (1957), Walters (1994), and Roach, IV, 552.
On the last page of ms. L, the lion and arms of Flanders appear in two drawings, which are briefly
described by Roach.

immediate social setting, it seems highly unlikely, given the variants that deform his name across the manuscript tradition, that most scribes or readers would have been able to identify the author or associate much with the name.[25] We might read the name as a reference to an authority, as *Crestiens* functioned in T, but where is authority with so little recognition? The possible referent of the name does not help us read the Second Continuation one way or another.

Reading Wauchier's name within the play of the text is, however, more promising. Its placement at the interlace, about a thousand verses before the interrupted ending, reveals a certain modesty that accords well with the general character of the Second Continuation's 13,000 verses.[26] I would locate that modesty in the deference shown to Chrétien's romance model (which for Wauchier probably included the First Continuation), not only in its reprise of certain key elements from the *Conte*, but most especially in the effort to ask through insistent narrative elaboration the most puzzling and unresolved questions left open by the originating author: what is the relationship between love and the Grail, how is Perceval's relationship to Blancheflor to be understood in light of his quest to return to the Grail Castle?[27] Since there has been no return to Perceval in the Gauvain Continuation, no possible answers have been outlined, except insofar as Gauvain has been allowed to reach the Grail Castle (twice in the Long and Mixed Redactions) without changing his typically amorous character. The second continuator has not tackled the issue head on, and it appears to be Wauchier rather than Perceval who plays the role of the simpleton here, the *nice* who asks the question over and over again but is not quite able to get to an answer: 'What do I do with the girl and the Grail?' Wauchier's obtuseness may well be a match for the consummate cleverness of Chrétien, who typically offers more questions and contradictions than answers.

Readers of the Second Continuation cannot fail to be struck by the prominence given to the Chessboard adventure, in which Perceval fails to win his game against a magic chessboard, then falls in love with the lady of the castle who demands that he bring her a White Stag's head before she will bestow her favors. The illustrator of BN. fr. 12577 chooses to highlight the opening scene of the

---

[25] There is nevertheless a certain consistency for the first name, if not the last (though all of the variations for the latter start with the letter d): E: Gauchier de dondain; L: Gauciers de donaing; M: Gauchier de doudain; P: Gautiers de dons; S: Gauchier de dordan; TV Gautiers de denet; U: Gauchier de doulenz.

[26] Roach's edn. of the Second Continuation picks up the First Continuation at verse 9457 of the Short Redaction and verse 19607 of the Long Redaction (the Mixed Redaction does not diverge radically from the long version at this point—see Roach IV, xv). That means, the Perceval Continuation joins a textual edifice that has already attained a hefty 18,000 to 28,000 verses.

[27] A related and equally crucial question is how Perceval's actions and quest would be affected by his encounter with the hermit uncle. The rewriting of the prose romances clearly takes radical change as the correct response, not only for Perceval but for the entire Arthurian world. The verse continuations seem less certain about how or if Perceval's behavior should change. Cf. Ch. 4 on the issue of violence and, in particular, Manessier's hermit on killing. See also the issue of Perceval's chastity in both Gerbert and Manessier discussed below.

episode with a rubric and a miniature (f. 149v) showing Perceval casually seated with legs crossed, about to move a piece on the chessboard, neatly tilted for our view. While his horse looks on from behind, the empty but open gate of the castle before him suggests the magic quality of the play, since no one is visible to face Perceval despite the engaging gestures of his upraised hand and the forward gaze of his eyes (Fig. 2).[28] For reasons that are not immediately evident, the series of quests for the stag head and the lady's brachet (abducted along with the stag head by another damsel) become explicitly tangled, along with the necessity to go to Mont Dolerous, in Perceval's efforts, highly dilatory, to return to the Grail Castle. The role of Mont Dolerous has some authorization from Chrétien's romance: it is one of the adventures announced at Arthur's court (4724), when the Hideous Damsel's climactic disruption propels the knights in different directions, with only Perceval headed to the Fisher King's. So we may not be surprised that it is precisely the link with Mont Dolerous, reinvented after its role in the First Continuation, that marks the opening and closing moments of Wauchier's continuation (as well as the place for his signature).

With the continuation thus anchored to its originating text, the bulk of the narrative is mapped out by the stages and reflections of the Magic Chessboard adventure, which has no direct precedent in the *Conte du Graal* and bespeaks, from certain points of view, the imaginative excess of the continuation, its discontinuous difference. What I call Wauchier's modesty has struck other readers as the opposite: a blatant diversion from the sense of his predecessor's romance. For Laurence Harf-Lancner, '[c]e roman de Perceval n'est nullement un roman du Graal mais un long conte de fées' (1984: 367). Her analysis usefully identifies the basic module that furnishes the narrative format for variation in six of the twelve episodes linked to the White Stag quest: hero meets fairy defended by giant at tent, fountain, enclosed garden, etc. (371–2). For Harf-Lancner, the two series of adventures, one connected to the Grail, the other to the Chessboard Lady, remain disconnected: Grail story and fairytale fail to coalesce.

And yet the narrative concatenation insists repeatedly on connections (as does the manuscript tradition itself), even if the narrator fails to make explicit any reason for the links between Grail quest and Chessboard adventure. The tie-in is carefully reiterated when Perceval leaves the Chessboard Castle after receiving the sexual favors promised by the lady. The lady herself puts Perceval directly on the 'droit chemin' (28166) to the Fisher King's. And Perceval promises a return after his visit to the Grail Castle, just as he promised to return to Blancheflor earlier in the narrative. The doubling of promises to return may be just the signal that helps explain this fairytale diversion.

The riddle of intertwined quests suggests that the puzzle of Perceval's relationship to love and Blancheflor has been displaced onto his adventure with the Chessboard

---

[28] The rubric above the miniature is given in Old French and translated in *Manuscripts* (1993: 2, 292).

Fig. 2. BN, fr. 12577, f. 149v. Perceval plays with the Magic Chessboard in the Second Continuation.

Castle lady. The continuator can thus experiment with possible outcomes and hold Blancheflor safely aside until the issue of Perceval's sexual involvements may be resolved in another context.[29] Following the comic precedent established in Chré- tien's romance by the Tent Maiden episode and the more courtly developments with Blancheflor, Perceval's erotic gear and potential are kept in good working order, on the back burner, so to speak, until his return to the Fisher King may open the way to working out how the love motivation and the Grail achievement might be con- nected in a romance that differs so substantially from the combination of love and prowess typical of Chrétien's previous romances.[30]

Significantly, Perceval's pattern of failure, the unique feature of his character as hero based on the *Conte*'s Grail Castle visit, plays a key role in the initiation of his Chessboard adventure: he fails to win at chess against the magic board, he fails to keep the lady's dog and the white stag head, just as he fails to keep his focus on the

[29] The return to Biaurepaire occurs in Episode 15 in the midst of Perceval's quest for the dog and stag head, the two tokens that will permit his return to the Chessboard Castle in Episode 26.

[30] We might remember that love and war are successfully juxtaposed in the story of Alexandre and Soredamor in *Cligès*, a kind of dynastic romance that could serve as precedent for Perceval's future.

Grail quest.[31] These failures are important aids for a continuator who wants to keep his narrative from rushing too quickly to an ending. But the association may have ramifications on other levels of meaning, inviting us to speculate about the problematic combination of sexuality and Grail achievement, as well as Perceval's ability to correct failure.

In this respect, Perceval's connections with Gauvain across the interlace of their mysteriously entwined itineraries set up interesting possibilities.[32] In unraveling the puzzle of why the Chessboard adventure takes on such an important role here, we cannot fail to notice a small thread back to Chrétien's authorizing text that passes through Gauvain's adventure at Escavalon and furnishes a number of key elements that will be shifted to Perceval and significantly reinvented by Wauchier. At Escavalon (a name that recalls the fairy island of Avalon featured in Marie de France's *Lanval*), Gauvain dallies with a lady, the sister of his host, who unfortunately turns out to be the daughter of the man he was accused of killing. Once Gauvain is recognized, they are attacked by the townspeople, and Gauvain is forced to use a chessboard as shield, while the lady hurls large chess pieces at the assailants. The resolution offered to the dilemma of hospitality and vengeance obliges Gauvain to set off on his own Grail Castle quest to find the Bleeding Lance—versions of which appear in the various redactions of the First Continuation, along with complicated adventures that feature a seductive lady in a tent (see Chapter 2). In the Second Continuation, Gauvain reappears in Episodes 29–32: the interlace furnishes the final delay in reporting Perceval's return to the Fisher King and the occasion of authorial naming. On his way to find Perceval and the Grail Castle, Gauvain's first adventure is marked by his usual amorous interplay, this time with the Petit Chevalier's sister, who has loved him from afar for some time.

The pattern of these encounters and echoes sets up an expectation that Grail quests and amorous pursuits may have something in common, or at the very least are not exclusive (as they will become once the prose romances rewrite Chrétien's story). When Perceval successfully returns to the Magic Chessboard Castle and unambiguously enjoys the lady's embraces, the second continuator may suggest indirectly through his narrative deployment that the hero will be able to bring together the girl and the Grail.[33] But the *nice*, who may be the continuator rather

---

[31] Chrétien's romance heroes typically follow a pattern of preliminary success, failure (crisis), and a second assent to improved success. This augurs well for Perceval's eventual success at the Grail Castle, although the accumulated differences of this unfinished romance complicate any simple projection of how it might have ended under Chrétien's hand.

[32] Cf. Ribard's 'étymologies séduisantes mais . . . contestables' that connect Perceval and Lancelot as 'personnages-itinéraires' and Gauvain's Escavalon with various doubles of Orcus, the god of the dead in Antiquity (1984: 82, 83).

[33] According to Walters, Wauchier probably envisaged Perceval and Blancheflor's marriage, and the illuminator of Montpellier H 29, who shows a preference for courtly scenes, 'corrected' Manessier's chaste separation by failing to illustrate his part. Walters thus argues for a revisionist dialogue between the images chosen for illustration and Manessier's reduction of Blancheflor's role (1993: 446–52). See Huot (1996: 108) for a critique of her argument.

than the no longer comic Perceval, does not explicitly articulate such a solution.[34] The Second Continuation's replay of Perceval in bed with Blancheflor at Biau Repaire still leaves open (with the narrator's usual discretion regarding the 'surplus') the question of sexual relations between them, though there is a strong hint that they have already been initiated. Perceval takes Blancheflor in his arms and kisses her a hundred times at once, but then the narrator interrupts his description:

> Je ne vos voil mie conter
> Dou seurplus commant il ala,
> Mes s'am Perceval ne pecha,
> Am Blancheflor ne remest mie,
> Qui est plainne de cortoisie
> Que chose qui bien li seïst,
> Por [r]iens ne li contredeïst.
> Einsit menerent lor deduit;
> Petit dormerent celle nuit
>
> (22834–41)[35]

(I don't want to tell you about how it went with the rest, but if Perceval didn't fail [to enjoy the 'surplus'], it wasn't Blancheflor who would refuse: she is filled with courtesy and wouldn't counter anything that pleased him. Thus they shared their pleasure and slept little that night.)

The narrator's ambiguity allows Wauchier the author to continue asking questions through the architecture of his continuation: How will it end? How can the dichotomy between Grail and girl, if it is a dichotomy, be resolved? We modern readers, doubtful of Wauchier's status, are not certain he knows where his story is going, and we are even less sure that he understands where Chrétien's romance might have ended.

But in some sense, Wauchier's modesty as author leads him to replicate *à sa façon* the unfinished character of the master text. He has remained faithful to Chrétien's tendency to maximize the tension of contradictions without eliminating them for the sake of reductive solutions. We may understand his obsessive replay of the hero/fairy/giant module through the White Stag adventures, linked to the Chessboard Lady and intertwined with the Grail quest, as a way of

---

[34] Perceval's characterization as *nice* does not appear to survive after his conversion in the Hermit episode. In the First Continuation, after Gauvain's second Grail adventure, the role of the *nice* tranfers to his son (especially in the Long and Short versions). In TVD, the narrator speaks explicitly speaks of his *niceté*; he reports the son's literal-mindedness, but does not care to linger on it (I, 13621, 13725–58). In Gerbert, Perceval comments at one point on his denseness, a distant echo of Chrétien's characterization (II, 8890–9), and in another recall, the narrator comments on Perceval's taciturnity (9094–7).

[35] On the use of *pechier* as an impersonal verb meaning 'to fail to', see Roach's textual note (IV, 525). My translation echoes his in modern French: 'Mais si Perceval n'a pas manqué [de jouir des faveurs de sa bien-aimée, c'est que] Blanchefleur ne s'y est pas opposée'. T changes this passage to suppress the ambiguity in favor of chastity by omitting 22841–2. Likewise with the Chessboard Lady, an interpolation after 28137 insists on Perceval's vow to preserve his virginity. See Stephens on TV alterations (1996: esp. 61 n. 14).

encoding the failure of resolution between Perceval's multiple desires, while keeping alive the intensity of the questions they pose. Following the *Conte's* example in its own way, the Second Continuation accentuates the role of the *matière de Bretagne*, richly exploited by the Gauvain continuator as well, although neither continuation has completely neglected the Grail story's perplexing Christian connections woven through the Arthurian matter.[36]

In the Second Continuation, the proliferation of storymatter suggests many pieces put together, but the combinations do not always seem to reach a perfect fit, the *molt bele conjointure* Chrétien calls for in the Prologue to *Erec et Enide* where he complains about the corrupted forms and faulty techniques of storytellers who fail to give their material the value it can attain through the art of an author/narrator like himself. Lack of resolution and/or the impossibility of resolution is one of the major issues left by Chrétien's unfinished romance. Here, too, the Second Continuation is strangely related to the problematic ending mid-sentence of the *Conte du Graal*. The puzzle of where, why, and how the Second Continuation ends corroborates and extends the puzzle of if, why, and how the Chessboard adventure predicts a way to tie together love and the Grail for Perceval and Blancheflor.

We know where the Second Continuation ends because both Manessier (V, 42658–61) and Gerbert (I, 7008–14) take pains to signal retroactively that their continuations began at the moment when Perceval put back together the two pieces of the sword, the preliminary test for getting answers to the questions added by the First Continuation during Gauvain's Grail visit(s), which guarantees that the final triumph will be saved for Perceval even if Gauvain achieves a partial success there. But why, we may well ask, did the second continuator stop there? We certainly find no answer in the text or the manuscripts, no explanation like those offered elsewhere in romance: 'he died' or 'he gave the task to another writer'. Wauchier's name placed at the interlace gives no explicit information on ending, although the placement at the Mont Dolerous episode insinuates a movement toward closure as the series of opened parentheses begin to close. 'Et Percevaux se reconforte' (IV, 32594) is the last line of the Second Continuation, as indicated by the manuscript tradition. Wauchier does not seem to have finished, since he is mid-scene even if not mid-sentence, as the two continuators read him by adding subordinate clauses.

> *Et Percevaux se reconforte,*
> Qui de l'avanture a tel joie
> Que je ne cuit mie que j'oie
> Jamés de tel joie parler.
>
> (V, 32594–7, italics added)

---

[36] If the First Continuation's reading emphasizes the Breton thread, it nevertheless launches the association between the bleeding lance and the spear of Longinus. Cf. Robert de Boron's more exclusive focus on Christian connections for Arthurian history.

(And Perceval is comforted, for he has such joy from the adventure that I don't think I've ever heard tell of such joy.)

By insisting on Perceval's joy, Manessier interprets the scene as indicating that the hero has successfully completed his quest and will now go on a sort of post-Grail mop-up for about 10,000 verses to carry out a vengeance plot for the Fisher King.

> *Et Perchevaus se reconforte,*
> Qui parole au Roi Pescheor,
> Mais molt se tient a pecheor
> Quant du Graal ne puet savoir
> La verité . . .

(Potvin, 34934; Williams I, 1–4; italics added)

(Perceval is comforted in speaking with the Fisher King but he considers himself a great sinner since he cannot know the truth about the Grail.)

Gerbert develops Perceval's sense of failure (rhyming *pescheor* and *pecheor*), a specifically sinful failing that requires further effort on Perceval's part in order to bring together the two pieces of the sword without leaving even the tiniest 'osque' (I, 21: chip) in the *soudement*. He thus finds authorization in Wauchier's 'creveüre' (IV, 323558: crack) for his own 17,000-line continuation, which will be notched in between the Second and Third by someone further down the writing line.[37]

As a result the passages from the Second to the Third, or in TV, from the Second to the Fourth to the Third, will take place with a sleight of hand—no narrator, no manuscript rubric or illumination will announce the shift until their authors speak up thousands of verses later. And in each case the transition will occur in the crucial scene at the Grail Castle, as if to look back implicitly each time to the name of the romance given in Chrétien's prologue, a title unlike those of his previous romances, connected not directly to the hero but to the enigmatic object that keeps requiring questions and returns.[38] Did Wauchier stop in the midst of the Grail scene on purpose, unintentionally, unintentionally on purpose, by chance, *par aventure*, according to the logic written into Chrétien's master text and carried forward into the continuations?

In any case, Wauchier participates fully in the general momentum of the series, successfully mirrors the inherent invitation to continue already structured by Chrétien's own plot line, continues its impetus toward and away from closure

---

[37] As Stephens (1996) points out, there are holes in the transition from the Second Continuation to Manessier, since the notch is left uncommented and unfilled. These gaps are smoothed over in TV's transitions from Wauchier to Gerbert to Manessier.

[38] Cf. Busby's suggestion of a 'malédiction narrative' (1998a: 290) that deprives successive narrators of the ability to reveal the Grail's secrets and thus the series of suspended endings at the Grail Castle.

through an implicit call for more storytelling.[39] In the context of this elaborate textual edifice, the location of an author's name at the interlace, at the belated beginning of a return, constitutes a narrative gesture that may be read as a sign of inbetweenness and the uncertainty of ending.

MANESSIER'S CLOSING SIGNATURE

With the Third Continuation, on the contrary, we have Manessier's epilogue and the sureness of ending loudly proclaimed.[40] Logically, Manessier comes next and last in the series, inasmuch as P 1 2 3 constitutes the canonical form toward which the manuscripts tend (as shown by six out of twelve manuscripts plus the Middle High German translation and the French prosification). But variation is as canonical as stability over the whole field: since T and V insert Gerbert before Manessier, I should just as logically follow the order in the maximally cyclic manuscripts and delay Manessier until after discussing the Fourth Continuation, however illogical the numerical order may then appear. Wauchier's non-ending has become a kind of pivot, not unlike his unfinished Glass Bridge, irreducibly bifurcated as it swings back and forth, a single crossing from which two separate roads issue. Forced to choose, I accept the reshuffled order of modern scholarship's terminology and pursue the issues of authorial naming in Manessier before moving back to the Fourth. However much I aim to read with an eye to the experience and expectations of medieval readers, I remain a modern reader looking back, profiting from the perspective offered by multiple readings of the 'same' story written into the manuscript tradition. Going forward and then backward to Gerbert will, moreover, help me move back again toward Chrétien, which is the fundamental impulse of this entire process of continuation.

Manessier's name is for us, as it must have been for most medieval readers not privy to the court of Jeanne de Flandre, only a proper name cited in the text, a way of designating his continuation as the work of a writer who is not Chrétien de Troyes. Who is Manessier after all? His name can only suffer by contrast in the limelight of Chrétien's. Indeed, Chrétien's name is noticeably absent from Manessier's epilogue, though the continuator alludes to it through the link between patrons.[41]

---

[39] Only K gives the Second Continuation by itself, finished with a rapid ending. Among the other manuscripts that include Wauchier, only two out of ten limit the series to P 12.

[40] Verbal repetition emphasizes the act of finishing: 'met a chief' (V, 42642); the verb *finer* reiterated three times (42652, 42656, 42658).

[41] Within his discussion of whether or not Manessier knew the Prose *Lancelot* and the *Queste*, Marx dates the Third Continuation based on the reference to Jeanne de Flandres and the fate of her husband taken prisoner by Philip Augustus at Bouvines (1965: 240–1). The situation is particularly obscured in ms. P's ending, which suppresses Manessier's name and gives Chrétien's instead: 'Si ke crestiiens le tesmoingne' (42641). The epilogue ends in the next line. Since P adds the *Elucidation* and the *Bliocadran* at the beginning, Chrétien's prologue was omitted, with the result that the

> El non Jehanne la contesse,
> Qu'est de Flandres dame et mestresse, ...
> Ai en son non finé mon livre.
> El non son aiol comença

$$(V, 42643-4, 42653-4)$$

(In the name of Jeanne the countess who is lady and mistress of Flanders ... in her name I have finished my book; it began in the name of her ancestor [great uncle])

The omission has the advantage of placing him in Chrétien's position, that of any commissioned writer needful of pleasing a patron. Better to leave out the original, authorizing *actor/auctor/autor* and grab the borrowed prestige of count and countess. In any case, Chrétien is still up front in the prologue and Manessier has waited till the end, like Godefroi de Leigni, to reveal his name as 'final' author (though uncertainty clouds the number of continuators and continuations that lie between him and the first author, and Gerbert's insertion belies the finality of such gestures in medieval practice).

Manessier has written Perceval to the end of his story, laid him in his grave, and set up the epitaph: 'Ci gist Perceval | Le Galois, qui du Saint Graal | Les aventures acheva' (42635–7: 'here lies Perceval the Welshman who completed the adventures of the Holy Grail'). The quest is definitively ended, as is Manessier's task as continuator, and he invites readers to verify what has been written on Perceval's tomb, which sits on four pillars, 'Si com Manesier le tesmoingne' (42641: as Manessier testifies). It can be verified as well in the account of all his adventures written down at Arthur's court during Perceval's last visit there:

> [Manessier] Tant en a aconté et dit
> Con l'on a Salebiere en treuve,
> Si com l'escrit tesmoingne et preuve,
> Que li rois Artus seella.
> Encor le puet on veoir la,
> Tot seellé en parchemin,
> Cil qui errent par le chemin.

$$(42662-8)$$

(Manessier has told all one finds in Salisbury, just as the written testimony, sealed by King Arthur, proves. Those who take that road can still see it there, all sealed in parchment.)[42]

patrons evoked at the beginning and end in other manuscripts are left out in this version (Roach, ed. V, 386). Wilmotte (1930: 72 n. 1 and 73 n. 1) speculates that a verse has been left out after 42652, where Chrétien would have been the subject of the verb *conmença*.

[42] See Séguy's discussion of Manessier's epilogue in which she highlights the way Manessier distinguishes himself from other continuators by his insistence on closing off and definitively ending Perceval's story yet nevertheless responds to the *Conte*'s and the continuations' resistence to ending (2001b). Part of Séguy's argument hinges on assuming that a sealed document can only be read if the seal is broken (which is not supported by many medieval documents whose seals are appended at the bottom and do not seal off the contents), but her main point still stands.

Manessier thus accumulates guarantors for his ending: witness represented by his proper name; superlative value represented by his patroness the Countess of Flanders, whose beauty, virtues, and power stand behind a work done in her name; testimony and proof in the *escrit*, the truthful record signed and sealed in parchment, which can still be ascertained by anyone who wanders on the road to Salisbury. Indeed, Manessier's narrative includes the very scene to which he refers here, when Arthur summons all the knights to retell their adventures, on oath, as they occurred: Lionel and Bohort tell of Calogrenant's death; Perceval enumerates all his exploits from the Grail visit on, giving Manessier the opportunity to recap his entire continuation in Perceval's own words (42337–430). Of course, this authorization of Manessier's text turns out to be wonderfully circular as it anchors its truth in the fiction just read. However much it may refer to outside guarantors, the faithfulness of the account is demonstrated in the narrative itself.

Manessier builds his legitimacy as continuator into the narrative fabric insofar as he returns to Chrétien's romance to pick up and close out loose ends, characters, and actions. But the reference to sealed documents produced at Arthur's court signals how he also updates key aspects to align his verse continuation with prose rewritings of the Grail story. In his version of Perceval's visit to Blancheflor, for example, he removes all ambiguity about their sexual status and thereby corrects Chrétien's and Wauchier's innuendoes, in order to keep his hero in line with the virginity now required for Grail heroes. He sidelines Blancheflor with a perfunctory account of Perceval's return, accompanied by the usual promise of future help (unrealized in the narrative).[43] Here and elsewhere, Manessier's narrative clearly borrows from the *Lancelot-Grail*, where accounts of knight errantry introduced less systematically in the romances of Chrétien de Troyes have now been institutionalized. Like Gerbert, he is writing not only under Chrétien's guiding hand but in competition with the anonymous prose versions of Arthurian romance history.[44] In view of that rivalry, they do not hesitate to name themselves as authors of Grail romances in verse. Their master Chrétien has given them license to make incongruous combinations and pursue contradictions without sacrificing the powerful shock of their collisions. Both Gerbert and Manessier want to take full credit, if only retrospectively, for all the verses they wrote.

In his epilogue, Manessier maps out the entirety of his continuation from the end back to the moment of beginning at the soldering of the sword.

---

[43] Manessier follows the common pattern of (renewed) rescue and quick leave-taking. In his version, Perceval must defend Blancheflor against attack by Aridés of Escavalon (the name Escavalon echoes from the Gauvain section of Chrétien's romance). There is no talk of marriage, and their sleeping quarters remain unambiguously separate with no nighttime wandering from one bed to another (V, 39088–100). Perceval once again declines Blancheflor's request that he prolong his stay and reiterates his promise to return whenever she needs a champion. Blancheflor remains Perceval's 'amie' but that title seems to carry little meaning.

[44] For other examples of their common features, see Ch. 4.

Manessier... l'a finé
Selonc l'estoire proprement,
Qui conmença au soudement
De l'espee sanz contredit.

(V, 42658–61)

(Manessier, who began without contestation at the soldering of the sword, has finished it properly according to the story.)

The act of joining performed (repeatedly) in the romance plot reverberates metaphorically as the textual sign of continuation across the cycle.

Manuscripts M and T emphasize the textual location by adding 'sanz contredit' (42661): they seem to anticipate, just at the moment of fixing the spot so definitely, some possible disagreement about precisely where Manessier has welded his continuation to the preceding text.[45] Of course, the putting together refers directly to Perceval's act of sword repair and undoubtedly designates the scene at the Fisher King's castle, the part actually narrated in the last scene of the Second Continuation. Manessier's textual beginning marks the moment of overlap between his writing and that of the previous author; his verbal gesture resembles the way Godefroi de Leigni designates his own beginning at the moment of Lancelot's imprisonment in the *Chevalier de la Charrette* (7108–10). But in the *Charrette*, finding the right place does entail some confusion, inasmuch as Lancelot is twice imprisoned by Méléagant and the later details identifying the place of imprisonment do not completely agree with the earlier description. Likewise, in the case of Manessier we might hesitate for a moment to ponder whether he refers to the *soudement* at the end of the Second Continuation or in Episode 16 (about 6,000 verses later), when Perceval happens upon a blacksmith who turns out to be Tribüet, the one designated by his cousin as the only blacksmith qualified to repair the sword Perceval received from the Fisher King. When Gerbert's Continuation is inserted between the Second and Third, the task of locating the *soudement*, the moment of welding, doubles (or quadruples), since there are now two solderings of a broken sword at the blacksmith (though carefully delineated as two different swords and two different smiths, father and son) and two sword repairs at the Grail Castle, with and without the imperfection of a crack. Modern editions make our uncertainties about where and which only fleeting, more interpretive game than real quandary, but the smooth transitions of the manuscripts, which obscure all the moments of passage by their continuous writing, remind us that establishing authorship and textual boundaries in the medieval context is no simple affair.[46]

---

[45] The manuscript evidence for Manessier's ending is itself subject to the vagaries of time and accident. By the end, Roach has to shift his base text from E (the model until 40692) to Q, and then for the last 178 lines to M. Few of the manuscripts contain the epilogue. In addition to M and T, more or less the same, Roach's edition also gives the version in U, which specifies that Manessier started at the soldering 'Et l'a parfiné jusques ci' (61: 'and finished it up to this point'), followed by a closing prayer.

[46] The manuscript tradition, as well as Corley's analysis of rhymes in Manessier and the Second Continuation (1987: 240), nevertheless support Manessier's claim.

For modern scholarship, a more persistent moment of confusion appears in Manessier's epilogue, when he says that he is the first to continue Chrétien's unfinished romance.

> Ne puis ne fu des lors en ça
> Nus hons qui la main i meïst
> Ne du finner s'antremeïst.
>
>   (V, 42654–6)

(Since then until now no one put his hand to it or undertook to finish it.)

Lot, who has little respect for 'cet inconnu' who has pillaged the *Lancelot-Grail* with no understanding to put together 'une production misérable' (1931: 127), has suggested reading the verses starting 'Nus hom' with the sense that no one who continued the romance finished it (123). That fits nicely into Lot's argument to disprove Chrétien's authorship of the First and Second Continuations and reject the identification of Wauchier de Denain as author. But it does not offer a convincing reading of the syntax. Perhaps Manessier believes that Chrétien was the author of both the First and Second Continuations, which clearly form part of his model for rewriting, just as they do for the Fourth Continuation.

However we turn those verses, Manessier seems inclined to enhance his own status as author by covering over possible interventions between himself and Chrétien. His narrative is curiously unstable in relation to acknowledging previous continuations. Manessier includes some episodes that link up directly with the Second. For example, when Perceval returns to the Chapel of the Black Hand (Episode 12), he explicitly recalls his previous visit there (narrated by Wauchier in Episode 34). Elsewhere, the Third Continuation denies events that took place in the Second, as when the hero finally begins his return to the Fisher King (Episode 28). The narrator states that Perceval does not know where to find the castle because he has not returned to the Gaste Forest since he left his mother (41847–60), although in the Second Continuation, Perceval returned there to find his sister and learn more about his mother's death (Episodes 18 and 19). Such inconsistencies are not surprising across the vast expanse of the continuations; we find them within as well as between continuations throughout the cycle.

More significant is the way successive continuators shift adventures from one hero to another. Manessier replays an episode at the Castle of Maidens found in the Second Continuation, but substitutes Sagremor for Perceval while turning the adventure into the traditional exploit associated with Perceval's repeated Biau Repaire visits ('save the damsel from an unwanted suitor'). In the First Continuation, a terrible storm forces Gauvain to take shelter in the Chapel of the Black Hand during his approach to the Grail Castle (Section V, Episode 3); Perceval will visit the same chapel in the Second and Third Continuations (Sasaki). Through the words of a priest, Manessier offers an explanation of the adventure (in which a black hand reaches through a window to extinguish the candle) and emphatically stresses its completion here (in anticipation of the total closure proclaimed in the epilogue):

> 'Or est l'aventure afinee
> Et vos l'avez a chief menee.
> Jamés nul mal n'i avendra
> Ne plus faire n'i covandra;
> De tout estes venuz a chief.'
>
> (37545–9)[47]

('Now the adventure is finished and you have brought it to an end. No more evil will ever happen here and there is no more to accomplish. You have entirely achieved the adventure.')

Chapter 2 will follow the way Perceval's adventure with the Tent Maiden passes to Gauvain in the First Continuation and again in Gerbert, then briefly moves back to Perceval in Manessier. These shifts carry forward the way Chrétien has interlaced the two heroes so that their itineraries are at once different and the same, separate and imbricated. The ramifications of that narrative strategy suggest that Chrétien's romance invites us to read across the interlace, in order to interpret Perceval's and Gauvain's stories, on one level, as part of a set of experiences that pass back and forth between them, so that what happens to one necessarily affects the other. The continuators have grasped that potential, which may operate directly in the plot or indirectly on a more symbolic plane, as demonstrated in the way they share adventures between Perceval and Gauvain, sometimes bringing the two heroes closer together, ultimately moving them apart (under the influence of the prose versions). Under Chrétien's guidance, the technique of the interlace has thus become not only part of the aesthetic design of romance but a cognitive category, as readers reflect, recognize parallels, make comparisons, and so on, guided by the narrative arrangement to discover possible meanings inscribed by its patterns.

COLLECTIVE AUTHORSHIP AND GERBERT

The argument pursued throughout this study explores to what extent we should apply the same logic of reading across the interlace to the authors themselves, as part of the contradictory impulse fundamental to these stories: they are one and other, a unit yet disparate, continuous but fragmented. Authors, continuators, redactors, interpolators, scribes, and compilers, individually identified often enough to make us aware that we should not assume, as Manessier's epilogue seems to, the absence of different hands even where anonymous writes silently: all these contributors work together to build collective authorship. Perhaps

---

[47] The priest thus corroborates Manessier's concern to finish off loose ends, as he expresses it in the epilogue. Cf. Gerbert's similar desire explored below.

Manessier himself acknowledges that plurality through occasional forays of his narrating voice into the first-person plural. Although the first-person singular dominates the majority of his interventions, there are a number of interlace formulas phrased in the first-person plural addressed to the public *vous:*

> Mais de lui atant *nos* teson,
> Si *vos* conteronz sanz arest
> De Gauvain, qui an la forest
> Antra, si com oï avez.
>
> (36364–7, italics added)[48]

(But we will now stop speaking of him; we will tell you without stopping about Gauvain, who entered into the forest, as you have heard.)

The change from the narrator's *je* is particularly striking here, since it follows by three verses a comment that prepares a switch in narrative focus: 'De lui ne sai que je vos die' (36360: 'I don't know what to tell you about him').

In her analysis of first-person singular and plural as used by contemporary narrators, Marnette notes that romance is the genre (along with the *lai*) where the narrator's *I* appears most frequently (35–6). She suggests that the infrequent *nous* is used to associate the narrator with his public, by alluding for example to their shared knowledge (57). But in the example quoted above, the public's *vous* is clearly differentiated from the narrating *nous*. In the context of the continuations, interlace formulas in the first-person plural may also suggest the duplicated role of narrators speaking for multiple authors who pass on their collaborative task of storytelling across the interlacing of heroes and the relay of writers.

Among all the verse continuators, Gerbert most readily acknowledges his participation in the collective project of the Grail story, while at the same time inscribing the specificity of his own authorship. Analysis of how he does so further illustrates the process of writing and reading across the interlace to reveal the particular character of successive authors through their narrative choices within the common matter. Gerbert functions as a pivot between the second and third continuators, just as he is the figure who carefully points us back to Chrétien, so this discussion will appropriately take a ring structure that opens and closes with issues related to interlaced authorship, the interplay of *je* and *nous*, authors/narrators and the story that sometimes speaks itself ('Li contes dist'), in order to frame a detailed analysis of the passage where Gerbert links his name to that of Blancheflor and offers his own version of the return to Biau Repaire, his new answer to the issue of Perceval's relations with the fair sex.

When Gerbert's narrator begins to describe Biau Repaire, he alludes directly to previous descriptions. The first indication that 'we' have already described the

---

[48] See also 37141–4, 39360–3, 39576–7, 40402–3, 40975–9. Not all the interlace formulas use the first-person plural, however. Some look more like prose romance formulas: e.g. 'si raconte l'estoire' (35051). Chrétien's narrator occasionally uses the first-person plural, as in *Erec* (1242): 'Or devons d'Erec parler' ('now we should speak about Erec').

castle and its surroundings accurately reminds 'you' the readers that both Chrétien and Wauchier offered detailed descriptions of Biaurepaire, first as devastated by Clamadeus's assault, later restored after Perceval's rescue.

> *Autre fois* l'*avons* devisé.
> Quant Perchevaus l'ot avisé,
> Bien a reconut le païs.
> Mais Gornumans fu esbahis,
> Car ainc puis n'i avoit esté
> Que Clamadeus avoit gasté
> La terre et le païs d'entor.
> Mais ore est de si riche ator
> Con *vous* par *mon* dit le savez
> Et autre fois oï l'*avez*
> Deviser et la grant richece
> Et de la vile la noblece,
> Si seroit anuis du retraire
> *Autre fois*, por che *m'*en veil taire.
> Si *parlerai* de Percheval.
>
> (I, 6211–25, italics added)

(We have already described it [Biaurepaire]. When Perceval saw it, he recognized the country. But Gornemant was amazed, since he hadn't been there since Clamadeu had devastated the land and the country around it. But now it was as rich as you know from my account and you have already heard described the city's richness and nobility, so it would be annoying to tell it again, for this reason I want to keep quiet about it and speak instead of Perceval.)

When Gerbert adds that the reader, unlike Gornemant, has already heard about the restoration 'par mon dit' the shifting character of *je* asserts itself, since the narrator now refers to his own description in the preceding verses (6192–210) and simultaneously assumes into his first person the earlier description from the Second Continuation. The narrating voice confidently controls what he will or will not repeat, as his first person places his work in the context of a collective enterprise that serves to enhance his own contribution.

If this continuator is indeed Gerbert de Montreuil as generally agreed upon by scholars, his particular authorial inspiration seems acutely attached to, even triggered by the specific inventions of other romancers, hence his reprise of Jean Renart's *Roman de la Rose* in his *Roman de la Violette*.[49] Gerbert's art is

---

[49] Gerbert's place name continues the northern France connection already implicated in the literary patronage of the Grail story from Philip of Flanders to his grand-niece Jeanne. See the introduction to Mary Williams's edition (1922) for a brief discussion of the identification with Gerbert de Montreuil (based on linguistic evidence, versification, and style) and bibliographical indications (I, v). See also Amida Stanton (1942). The *Violette* is dated 1227–9 and dedicated to Marie, Comtesse de Ponthieu, who is praised in both prologue and epilogue; the author names himself at the beginning of the epilogue (Buffum, ed. 1928).

not mere imitation but rather reinvention that seriously replays and rethinks his predecessors (cf. Keller). Gifted bricoleur, he takes obvious pleasure in using elements from a variety of sources, including his own narrative, to come up with something new based on the 'already said'.[50] Gerbert points to the writers who have contributed to *Perceval*, when he expresses his interest in continuing the Grail story in verse when all other poets (*chascuns trovere*) have abandoned it (6999). Referring to other writers through their failure to keep writing is, of course, an opportunity to insist on his own authorship and highlight his reading of Chrétien through the First and Second Continuations.

Gerbert's connection with the first author is reinforced when he gives Chrétien's death as the reason for the unfinished state of his romance:

> ... Crestiens de Troie
> ... de Percheval comencha,
> Mais la mors qui l'adevancha
> Ne li laissa pas traire affin.
>
> (I, 6984–7)

(Chrétien de Troyes began [the story] of Perceval but death which overtook him didn't allow him to finish.)

One ending has prevented another (cf. Leupin), and Gerbert is acutely conscious of the difficulty of reaching the proper end, not only for Perceval and his quest but for those who tell the story 'qui onques ne fu trais a fin' (5527: which was never brought to an end).[51] Like the many adventures from which no one can return (until the hero against reason does so),[52] this narrative constitutes a kind of black hole from which no one has emerged to finish it. But just as a knight prays for victory over villainy, Gerbert prays that God give him the strength to reach the end of Perceval's story (7002–3).

These repeated messages about an unfinished story fortify the argument that Gerbert is writing without knowledge of Manessier's ending. Leslie Stephens, however, suggests the possibility that Gerbert's continuation was written to supplement and improve Manessier (1996: 56). Her analysis makes a strong, if not entirely persuasive, argument and demonstrates how Gerbert can be read as anticipating and playing with Manessier, just as a linear reading of T invites. But we cannot entirely disentangle what should be credited to Gerbert's authorship

---

[50] We can see him combining his own material as well as Chrétien's in the elaborate episode with the Red Knight's sons, which features a minstrel hero who plays off against 'Tristan menestrel', a tale included earlier in the Fourth Continuation. Cf. Kjaer (1990).

[51] Gerbert's insistence on Perceval as the only one who finished ('il assoma', 6675; 'il seus assoma', 6678) the Grail adventures, 'Si con trovons es escriptures' (6676: 'as we find in the writings') may have a polemical thrust. Is this a put down of the prose versions? See also 6675–81 (cf. II, 13993).

[52] These include Lancelot from Gorre in the *Chevalier de la Charrette*, Gauvain from the 'borne de Galvoie' in the *Conte*, the knights who encounter Mont Dolerous in the continuations.

and what belongs to a talented redactor of T (or its model) who has pieced together all four continuations and carefully smoothed out inconsistencies.[53]

Nevertheless, Gerbert's uncertainty about finishing is clear: he did not wait for an epilogue to place his name in the game and guarantee his authorial recognition with or without an ending. We might compare his highly unusual gesture with Wauchier de Denain's naming *in medias res*.[54] But the comparison immediately points us in the direction of Gerbert's difference, his correction, if not of Manessier's ending, then more certainly of Wauchier's signature and his reading of Perceval. Two features of Gerbert's self-naming call for special commentary in this respect: where he names himself and why he does so so excessively, repeating his proper name an unprecedented five times. Like Wauchier, Gerbert has delayed the moment of naming but he has not done so for as long as his predecessor. We are about a third of the way into his continuation when Perceval returns to Biau Repaire. Blancheflor's appearance on a richly caparisoned mule leads irresistibly to the question, 'Que diroie de sa biauté?' (6353: what shall I say of her beauty), and Gerbert answers in his own name:

> Autre fois l'avés escouté
> Dedans le conte par avant,
> Mais tant puis dire, bien m'en vant,
> Que onques clerc, ne lai, ne moigne,
> Si con Gerbers le nous tesmoigne
> En son conte que il en fist,
> C'onques nus si bele ne vit.
>
> (6354–60)

(Another time earlier in the story you have heard about it but I can say this much—and of this I boast—that no cleric, lay person, or monk ever saw a more beautiful woman, as Gerbert testifies for us in the story he composed.)

Like Manessier, Gerbert serves as a witness; his proper name guarantees with a hyperbole the description found in Chrétien and expects the collusion of the reader in making the connection ('le *nous* tesmoigne').[55] The verse following the

---

[53] See e.g. Stephens (1996: 65 n. 20) on Ivy's evaluation of the T redactor.

[54] Curiously, there is one work in Chrétien's repertoire where he signs his name at the midpoint. His translation of *Philomela* (mentioned in the prologue to *Cligès*) survives in the anonymous 14th-cent. *Ovide moralisé*, where the translator/redactor frames it by repeating the name Chrétien before and after the story. Within the narrative and added as a kind of interjection, an unusual signature appears: 'Crestiiens li Gois' (734). Although scholarly agreement accepts Chrétien's authorship, no explanation of the singular form his name takes here has prevailed (nor is it impossible, given the context, that the name was added by the 14th cent. editor when he updated Chrétien's text). See Levy (1931) and Kay (1997: esp. 20 nn. 67 and 69).

[55] The description is not found, however, in the Second Continuation. Wauchier passes over any description of Blancheflor, except for a brief statement of her beauty (22653). Her gaze takes precedence, as the narrator plays with her recognition of Perceval (22662–711). Once Gerbert names Chrétien in the authorial frame placed around Blancheflor, the two romancers become mutually authorizing.

proper name identifies it as that of the author: 'En son conte que il en fist'.[56] The previous verse sets off the role of author against all the male aficionados of female beauty represented in their entirety by three categories: the regular clergy, the laity, and monks. The combination of *je/il*, traditionally operating in prologues and epilogues, is slipped in here as the name Gerbert, placed in a subordinate clause, intertwines the author/narrator with his character Blancheflor.[57]

This gesture may seem incidental until the authorial name returns with particular insistence as Perceval takes leave of Blancheflor at the end of the episode.[58] In describing her sorrow that Perceval will not stay longer, 'Si con preudom fait od sa feme' (6979: 'as a worthy man does with his wife'), the narrator assures us that Blancheflor loves Perceval so much that she grants him anything he requests (6982–3). In the next verse, Gerbert cites Chrétien de Troyes as his authority and thus begins a long authorial intervention (6984–7020) during the course of which his name appears four times, always highlighted at the beginning of a verse:

> Si con la matere descoevre
> **Gerbers**, qui a reprise l'oeuvre,
> Quant chascuns trovere le laisse,
> Mais or en a faite sa laisse
> **Gerbers**, selonc le vraie estoire;
> Dieus l'en otroit force et victoire
> De toute vilenie estaindre
> Et qu'il puist la fin ataindre
> De Percheval que il emprent,
> Si con li livres li aprent
> Ou la meterre en est escripte;
> **Gerbers**, qui nous le traite et dite
> Puis enencha que Perchevaus
> Qui tant ot paines et travaus
> La bone espee rasalda
> Et que du Graal demanda
> Et de la Lance qui saignoit
> Demanda que senefioit;
> Puis enencha le nous retrait
> **Gerbers**, qui de son sens estrait
> La rime que je vois contant;
>
> (6997–7017, emphasis added)

---

[56] Chrétien likewise identifies his authorship of previous work in *Cligès* with the verb *faire*: 'Cil qui fist' (1).

[57] Gerbert's gift for such intertwinings also appears just before, when Blancheflor's garment is identified as coming from 'Blanchepart la roïne' (6351). This provides a link with the First Continuation (I, 15182, 15277), in the intercalated story of Guerrehés: the Swan Knight, King Brangemor, is identified as the son of Guingamor and the fairy queen Brangepart.

[58] Cf. the play on Perceval's name, explained in the previous episode at Gornemant's castle, during the encounter with the old woman (see Ch. 5).

(...just as **Gerbert**, who has resumed the work, reveals the storymatter when every [other] poet abandons it. But now **Gerbert** has composed his laisse, according to the true story. May God give him strength and victory to eliminate all villainy and reach the end of Perceval's story which he undertakes to tell according to the book where the matter is written. **Gerbert**, who recounts it for us from the moment when Perceval had so much pain and trouble resoldering the good sword and asked about the Grail and asked what the Lance that bleeds signified, from there on **Gerbert**, who from his understanding extracts the rhyme that I am telling, recounts it to us.)

Gerbert's name is repeatedly associated with the authority of his text, the truthfulness or authenticity of his version, based on his source (6997–8, 7001, 7006–7). Given this insistence on his fidelity, we are forewarned: Gerbert's claim comes precisely to underscore the difference from the written sources he cites, as we can verify if we remember (or return to) 'Crestiens de Troie' and the Second Continuation. In the *Conte du Graal*, we read that Perceval did not dare ask for leave from Blancheflor for she would refuse to grant it: 'Congié prendre s'amie n'ose | Car ele li vee et desfent' (2922–3). Gerbert repeats the same verb *oser* (present in all the manuscripts)—'Rien nule n'en ose escondire | Car tot quanqu'il dist li otroie' (6982–3: 'she dares refuse him nothing for she grants all that he says')—and thus links these two passages, while reversing who dares what and affirming Blancheflor's submissiveness rather than her dominance (though even in the *Conte* she ultimately yields to Perceval's promise of return). The specifics of textual detail lead to the larger issue involved in the lovers' relationship.

What Perceval dares or dares not do with Blancheflor is one of the major questions that Chrétien's romance leaves open. As Gerbert maintains, Chrétien's narrator has indicated more than once Blancheflor's willingness, but always in the context of her encouragement and desire to reward Perceval's prowess on her behalf. For example, when he requests her *druerie* as a reward for service in battle against Enguigeron, she modestly downplays the worth of the love bond he requests but does not want to refuse him:

> 'Mais s'ele [her *druerie*] vos ert escondite,
> Vos le tendriiez a orgueil;
> Por che veer ne le vos weil.'
>
> (*Conte*, 2110–12)

('But if it was denied to you, you would take that as an act of pride and for this reason I don't want to refuse it to you.')

Her reception after his victory is accordingly tender (2354–62): 'De l'acoler et del baisier | Ne li fait ele nul dangier' (2358–9: 'she doesn't begrudge him any kissing and embracing'). The Second Continuation continues in the same vein, allowing ambiguity to cover with modesty what comes out more clearly in Perceval's encounter with the Chessboard Lady. Gerbert's romance, on the contrary, offers an adamant rebuttal of any 'sorplus' (I, 6561) in the relationship between Perceval and Blancheflor, now tied to his own authorial name. Like

Manessier, Gerbert is writing under the influence of the prose romances and
cannot allow any sexual taint to sully his Grail hero.[59]

Gerbert will accomplish the same task of preserving Perceval's chastity as
Manessier but with more inventiveness, when his hero returns to Biau Repaire.
In general, Gerbert is a closer reader of Chrétien, more attentive to the verbal
texture and sequential arrangement of his model, more intent on picking up each
of the major episodes from the master text in order to reinvent them through
elaborate variations in the more ample format of his continuation.[60] Unlike
Manessier, he is not writing post-Grail achievement and so is less rushed to get to
the end, as befits his in-between status. Indeed, this tendency toward amplification may have contributed to Gerbert's failure to reach an ending.

As an excellent reader of his predecessors, the fourth continuator understands
how serious the status of the lovers' relationship remains to the outcome of
Perceval's quest. In order to finish the romance, Gerbert must resolve the
connection in a way that places a new return to Biau Repaire in the series
(including the usual bedtime visit) but reimagines its impact. When Perceval
tries to understand what sin, 'pechié' (5128), still prevents him from achieving
the Grail, he remembers his promise to marry Blancheflor left unfulfilled.[61] In an
earlier episode, he helped his cousin get satisfaction from a knight who failed to
fulfill a marriage pledge (1736–2379). Like Chrétien's *nice*, whose pattern of
learning typically requires repetition and delay, Gerbert's Perceval realizes after a
few more episodes that this is in fact a distorted mirror of his own problem with
Blancheflor.[62] The two-step process allows Perceval to correct first someone else's

---

[59] Gerbert's narrative self-consciously retains the convention of Blancheflor's nighttime visit by
showing her in debate with herself: should she visit his bed since 'aler i sueil' (6533: she's accustomed
to doing so)? But Gerbert goes to even greater pains to raise and clarify the issue of their virginity. He
thus forces the earlier narrators' discretion or ambiguity in the direction of denial. Chastity is
emphatically maintained during the nighttime visit—'Car du sorplus n'i ot il point' (6561: 'For
there was no surplus [i.e. intercourse] at all'). And after Perceval and Blancheflor marry, they both
agree to forgo the pleasures of consummation for the rewards of virginity (6809–955). Gerbert
makes the 'correction' particularly apparent when he sums up their wedding night by rewriting *Erec
et Enide*. Where Chrétien uses the rhyme words to emphasize Enide's transformation from maiden
to 'new lady' ('pucele . . . dame novele', 2103, 2104), Gerbert affirms: 'Pucele i coucha voirement |
Ensement pucele en leva' (I, 6954–5: 'she went to bed a maiden and likewise a maiden she arose').

[60] The signature of the master text implicitly written into the narrative order is thus made explicit
in Gerbert's continuation. A similar relationship can be discerned between the *Folie Tristan d'Oxford*
and Thomas's version of *Tristan and Iseut*, inscribed episode by episode in the fool's account.

[61] In the *Conte*, 'uns pechiez' (6393) was already associated with Perceval's failure; here it is
doubled in relation to both his mother and Blancheflor. See the Fisher King's announcement in the
opening scene of Gerbert's continuation (I, 28–55). Later at his mother's grave Perceval removes the
first sin (2741), while the other is yet to be discovered. Larmat argues that the personal sin attached
to Perceval by the *Conte*'s hermit has been elevated in Gerbert to the social dimension as the sin of
the whole knightly caste, the sin of pride and vainglory (which takes us back to one of the issues
raised in Chrétien's prologue). Nevertheless, Gerbert's text firmly attaches the second sin to
Perceval's unfulfilled marriage promise.

[62] The episode after his marriage with Blancheflor also deals with a forced marriage that Perceval
needs to remedy. Thus a whole cycle of episodes reinforce Gerbert's lessons on marriage and sex (cf.
the issue of sodomy, Perceval's clerical criticism, etc.). The comic aspects of Perceval's *niceté* have
shifted elsewhere in the Fourth Continuation, for example, to the 'Tristan menestrel' episode.

mistake and later his own. As soon as he realizes and confirms his insight with Blancheflor's uncle Gornemant (5127–77), he sets off to remove his sin, fulfill his marriage pledge to Blancheflor, and keep his Grail status intact by keeping his chastity safely guarded in a *mariage blanc* (6042–77). Gerbert's reinvented Blancheflor anticipates Perceval's desire to put aside desire and suggests they both keep their virginity in a spiritual marriage to which the hero readily consents. As they pray together, a voice gives a lesson on proper sex in marriage, commends Perceval's choice of virginity, and announces his future honor—to be revealed by five generations of his descendants, as long as he does not renounce his Grail quest (6882–943). How the virginal hero's posterity will be generated remains moot.

Gerbert's return to Biau Repaire thus steps out of the series of rescue operations that characterize Perceval's interactions with Blancheflor and firmly establishes his new reading of their relationship. As we look back from this episode, which Gerbert now allows us to do, since his authorial intervention designates the moment of transition (7008–20), we can appreciate to what extent the fourth continuator has strongly taken over and redefined the *Perceval* Continuations in order to reconnect with the *Conte du Graal* (however paradoxical this may appear, given his deference to the *Queste*'s conception of the Grail hero). Gerbert does so in part by restoring the religious focus that so inexplicably intertwined with Arthurian matter in Chrétien's unfinished romance. In the Fourth Continuation, clerical perspectives have penetrated both the narrator's and the characters' speech (although without the kind of hegemonic control associated with the hermits' explanatory discourse in the *Queste*). We may wonder if the multiplication of Gerbert's name as frame for the Blancheflor episode operates as an echo and response to the Second Continuation's timid act of authorial naming and its veiled suggestion that love and marriage, sex and the Grail may not be unimaginable.

In any case, the series of episodes leading from the Grail Castle to Biau Repaire establish a pattern that puts religious concerns back into play, corrects any expectation that Perceval will engage in amorous pursuits, and systematically follows the threads of Chrétien's plot to lead Perceval along an itinerary that reimagines the places of his past. Gerbert's first episode takes place at the wall of the 'Paradis Terrestre' where Perceval breaks his sword and extends his quest by seven years; the next one has Perceval refusing a lady's offer of her favors and serves as lead-in for Gerbert's blacksmith episode to repair the broken sword. A quick pass by Mont Dolerous recalls the episode where Wauchier named himself; it leads to the false marriage episode, followed in turn by a *pucele* (really a devil in disguise) who tries to trade Grail secrets for sex to no avail. With Perceval's return to his mother's manor in the next episode, Gerbert restarts Chrétien's sequence and moves in order from home to Gornemant to Blancheflor.

The opening moves of Gerbert's narrative have thus consolidated his *prise de pouvoir*, but in case we have not sufficiently divined the change in orientation, his authorial intervention now explicitly pinpoints where he started and what he has added:

> Gerbers, qui nous le traite et dite
> *Puis enencha* que Perchevaus
> Qui tant ot paines et travaus
> La bone espee *rasalda*
> Et que du Graal *demanda*
> Et de la Lance qui saignoit
> *Demanda* que senefioit;
> *Puis enencha* le nous retrait
> Gerbers, qui de son sens estrait
> La rime que je vois contant;
> Neïs la luite Tristrant
> *Amenda* il tot a compas;
> Nule rien ne vous en trepas.
>
> (I, 7008–20, italics added)

(Gerbert, who tells us [Perceval's story] from the moment when Perceval had so much pain and trouble resoldering the good sword and asked about the Grail and asked what the Lance that bleeds signified, from there on Gerbert, who from his understanding extracts the rhyme that I am telling, recounts it to us; even Tristan's wrestling match he improved with art; I leave out nothing for you.)

Any possible confusion about where Gerbert's writing begins has been eliminated: the action of putting back together (*resalda*) is firmly attached to Perceval and the test for asking the requisite questions about Grail and lance (*demanda . . . demanda*). The narrative move forward from the 'beginning' at the end of the Second Continuation is carefully demarcated and underlined by the repetition of 'Puis enencha' around the verses that frame the textual location. The certainty reassuringly attached to the moment of beginning contrasts with the uncertainty of finishing, acknowledged in the preceding verses (7002–4). There is no mention of the gap in the newly soldered sword which, as Leupin points out (1982), stands both for the possibility and impossibility of ending. But the missing element remains in play in the ongoing impetus to add more to the story.[63]

That additional impulse is explicitly noted here by reference to the account of 'la luite Tristrant', Tristan's wrestling match with Gauvain, which intervenes between the episode in which Perceval escorts his sister to the 'Chastel as Puceles' (from the Second Continuation) and his return by chance to Gornemant's castle, last visited in the *Conte du Graal*. Elaborately told over 1,600 verses, the Tristan interlude starts at Arthur's court then moves to Mark's for a tournament in which twelve Arthurian knights accept Tristan's challenge to fight disguised as minstrels.

---

[63] This is dramatized in the Gornemant episode, where Perceval recounts his failure and repeats the key words, *resalder* and *osque* (5111–19, 5175). See the analysis of the ivory barrels and the spectre of deathless narrative that looms like the deathless knights (Ch. 5).

During the mêlée they eventually meet up with Perceval and the narrative thread of his quest resumes. Among all the episodes recounted between his opening verses and this point in the narrative, Gerbert has chosen to highlight the one example of interlace in the first third of his continuation. By displacement, he thus recalls the alternations between Perceval and Gauvain that characterize the master text.[64] Gerbert reintroduces the interlace at the end of the Tristan episode (I, 4789–868), when Perceval and Gauvain renew the quests they first announced in the *Conte* (Perceval off to find the Grail Castle and Gauvain to Montesclaire):

> De Gavain et de Percheval
> M'orrez d'ore en avant conter.
> De Percheval premierement
> Vous dirai ore une partie,
> Ainz que de Gavain rien vous die.
>
> (4862–6)[65]

(You will hear me narrating about Gauvain and Perceval from now on. First I shall tell you a part about Perceval before I say anything about Gauvain.)

Gerbert accents the familiar rhythm of a typically decentered Grail romance, where multiple heroes share the plot line in lopsided segments. And like Chrétien, he underlines the art with which he has made his particular contribution to the twists and turns of the tale: 'Neïs la luite Tristrant | Amenda il tot a compas' (7018–19). Curious choice of verb: *amenda*. Gerbert has attached, amended, 'repaired' the tale, perhaps even better than Perceval has repaired the sword, since (as he claims) nothing is left out in his retelling. The repetition of 'Gerbert' in verses 7008 and 7016, framing the narrative identification, makes the author's name synonymous with the action of putting together. Given the accent on Gerbert's particular contribution, the mention of 'la luite Tristrant' not surprisingly follows a statement that the verse-making comes from his own head: 'Gerbers, qui de son sens estrait | La rime que je vois contant'.[66] The key word *sens*—wisdom, understanding, sense, wit—recalls Chrétien's use of the term in the *Charrette* to distinguish his writerly contribution from the 'matiere et san' furnished by his patron Marie de Champagne.[67] Gerbert's own art is constantly refueled by the textual detail furnished by his predecessor's writing.

---

[64] Similarly, in the First Continuation, the interlace alternates the adventures of Gauvain and Caradoc, then Gauvain and Guerrehés.

[65] The interlace will be recapped later in Gerbert by the insertion of Gauvain's 1,700-verse Tent Maiden episode between Perceval's visit to the castle of the Red Knight's four sons and his continued progress toward the Grail Castle on 'the road from which none have returned'. See Ch. 2.

[66] According to Kjaer (1990), there is no known source for 'Tristan menestrel', which was probably Gerbert's invention. Kjaer studies the correlation between this episode and Gerbert's larger purpose.

[67] Although the pain and travail mentioned here belong to Perceval (7010), the motif of hard work finds an echo in two of Chrétien's prologues: 'sans ne paine que g'i mete' (*Charrette* 23: 'the understanding and pain that I put into it'); 'Fors sa painne et s'antancïon' (*Charrette* 29: 'except for his pain and his attention'); 'Dont avra bien salve sa paine | Crestïens, qui entent et paine' (*Conte* 61–2: 'then Chrétien, who focuses his intent and takes pains will have safeguarded his pain').

Equally curious in this passage is the return of a narrating *I*. We are accustomed by Chrétien's prologues and epilogues to the interplay of *je* and *il* in the authorial moments of naming. But here their intertwining seems unsettling; the equivalence of the two may be in question. Is it Gerbert in his persona as narrator who says *I* in these verses or perhaps an editor/scribe who spliced his continuation in between the Second and Third, thus realizing Gerbert's worst fear, his loss of power over the ending (cf. Kjaer 1990: 357)?[68] Such are the uncertainties written into the shifting narratorial voice across the canvas of the continuations that it is difficult at any number of points, especially in ms. T, to identify specific connections between successive authors and a narrator who continues to address us through the same pronoun, whatever changes in referent it may conceal. The unusual repetitions of Gerbert's name may be a protective act of authorial self-naming or the product of another writer's hand designating his written source, just as the name 'Crestiens' appeared twice as reference and authority in T's Mixed Redaction of the anonymous First Continuation. Interestingly, this whole passage of authorial naming was introduced by the designation of Gerbert's own source: 'Ce nous dist Crestiens de Troie' (6984). Chrétien's proper name in full (unlike his signature in the Prologue to the *Conte*) here stands for and designates his unfinished romance, repeatedly rewritten into manuscripts as the fixed starting point for the continuations.

Gerbert's (or the editor's?) repeated use of *nous* (6984, 7008, 7016) during this passage participates in creating uncertainty about who speaks. The first instance, just quoted, places the current author/narrator on the same side as the readers in relation to Chrétien, the first author. The second and third uses appear as more or less parallel restatements of the same idea: 'Gerbers, qui nous le traite et dite... Puis enencha le nous retrait | Gerbers'. These verses may repeat the pattern established in l. 6984 or instead differentiate between Gerbert as written source and the anonymous scribal narrator who identifies with the readers.[69] The ambiguity stands unresolved in the absence of any way to determine if the passage has been re-engineered by a redactor to fit together four continuations (as we can observe in a number of T's interpolations) or simply reflects the way Gerbert wrote it. The act of welding, so carefully clarified to fit retroactively into the transition from the Second to the Fourth Continuation, reappears after further analysis as less certain, paradoxically at the very moment when the author's name repeatedly claims his due.

---

[68] Cf. Walters's discussion of the way Chrétien's five romances have been interpolated into Wace's *Roman de Brut* in BN, fr. 1450: the scribe-editor has made various cuts, including most of the prologues with Chrétien's name, but he retains the *Cligès* prologue where Chrétien presents himself in the third person and enumerates his previous works. 'Cette façon de se présenter convient bien à quelqu'un qui introduit un texte, tel un jongleur ou un copiste' (1985: 306). See also Nixon (1993: 23–5).

[69] Cf. the discussions of *nous* in the verse where Wauchier de Denain's name appears. According to Lot (1931: 124), *nous* indicates that it is not the author naming himself, but for Vial (1978: 524–6) *nous* does not eliminate that reading.

In any case, Gerbert willingly associates his work with that of others. Consider the play in his narrative voice which moves between a personal narrator, *je* or *nous*, and an impersonal style of evocation that appears in the verse following this long authorial intervention: 'Li contes dist que Perchevaus' (7021: 'the story says that Perceval'). The formulas of the story more or less telling itself, so characteristic of the prose romances, appear in Gerbert (as in Chrétien's master text), with and without personal pronouns. Gerbert's verbal formulas for the interlace offer numerous examples of how he mixes narratorial perspectives (italics added below highlight the interplay of voices):

> De Gavain et de Percheval
> *M'orrez* d'ore en avant conter.
>
> (I, 4862–3)[70]

(You will hear me tell about Gauvain and Perceval from now on.)

> Un poi s'areste, ce *me* semble,
> *Li contes* chi de Percheval
> Et de la Lance et du Graal,
> Si *vous* raconte une aventure
> De Gavain qui molt fu dure.
>
> (II, 12376–80)[71]

(The story of Perceval and the Lance and the Grail stops here a bit, it seems to me, and tells you an adventure of Gauvain that was very difficult.)

> De lui *lairons* en tel maniere
> un petitet, . . .
> Or dist *li contes*, c'est vertez,
> que li chevaliers, toz armez,
> chil a le Cote Maltaillie, . . .
> tot ensi, va querre le roi.
> Mais *ne me veil* chi traveillier
>
> (III, 16552–3, 16556–8, 16562–3)

(Let's leave him thus for a bit . . . Now the story tells, it's true, that the fully armed knight, the one with the ill-fitting coat of mail, goes off just as he is to find the king. But I don't want to go to pains here.)

These references to the *conte*, which may designate either the current tale unfolding or its source (or both simultaneously), regularly dot the landscape of the *Perceval* Continuations. Like Chrétien, Gerbert's authorial intervention

---

[70] Cf. Chrétien in the *Conte*: 'Des aventures qu'il trova | M'orrés conter molt longuement' (4814–15: 'of the adventures he encountered you'll hear me tell for a long time').

[71] See also II, 14074–5, 14078–9. Cf. Chrétien in the *Conte*: 'De Perchevax plus longuement | Ne parole li contes chi, | Ainz avrez molt ançois oï | De monseignor Gavain parler | Que rien m'oiez de lui conter' (6514–18: 'The story here speaks no longer of Perceval; rather you will have heard much about my lord Gauvain before you hear me tell more about him').

stresses his fidelity to the authenticating source: 'Si con la matere descoevre' (6998: 'as the storymatter uncovers'); 'selonc le vraie estoire' (7001: according to the true story); 'Si con li livres li aprent | Ou la meterre en est escripte' (7006–7: 'just as the book where the matter is written teaches him').

BACK TO THE STORY AND CHRÉTIEN

Estoire, meterre, conte, and *livres*—these terms pick up and recall Chrétien's own claims, staked out in the prologue and reiterated through the narrative, that he is telling a story based on a book given to him by his literary patron, a story authorized by a source that exists outside the current author, although we have access only to what Chrétien claims to write under its authority.[72]

> Crestïens, qui entent et paine
> Par le comandement le conte
> A rimoier le meillor conte
> Qui soit contez a cort roial:
> Ce est le Contes del Graal,
> Dont le quens li bailla le livre.
>
> (62–7)

(Chrétien, who takes pains at the count's command to rhyme the best story ever told in a royal court: This is the Story of the Grail of which the count gave him the book.)

The punning on *conte* is too well known to require analysis here. Its exuberance is frequently read as downplaying the (hypothetical) source, not to mention other authorities included (the count, religious discourse, etc.).[73] But it may be interesting to consider here Michel Stanesco's suggestion in 'Le texte primitif' (1993: 53–5) that we should give more importance to the role assumed by the notion of source in a culture where authors operate, as Paul Zumthor (1978) and Daniel Poirion (1986) have demonstrated, on 'text fragments' that reproduce a model located elsewhere, where the value of authorship is located not in mere production but in reproduction, the grafting of one text on another. That is certainly the model of authorship operating in the continuations, whose repeated claims on *le conte, l'estoire, le livre,* sometimes line up with a specific written source (Chrétien or a previous continuation), but more generally imply a kind of stable, continuing authority, that conveys authenticity on the whole textual edifice by virtue of the common, unidentified, unverifiable source constantly invoked from Chrétien's *Conte du Graal* to Manessier's conclusion.[74] Such a source is no

---

[72] Zink points out that there is no indication in the prologue of how Chrétien's romance relates to the *livre* (1987–8: 18).

[73] See e.g. Dragonetti (1980: 101–32, esp. 116–23).

[74] In Manessier, consider e.g. 'si con li contes afiche' (35116: 'as the story shows'), 'si con li livres le retret' (104: 'as the book describes it'); or references to 'l'estore' (35049: 'the history/story'), 'si con

doubt fictitious at some level and difficult for modern readers to accept, but for medieval readers and writers the shared fiction of what Stanesco calls 'le texte primitif' provides a sustaining element for continuity across the continuations, which plays in contrast, as well as in tandem, with the discontinuities of named authors and their differences.

If we pass from the level of abstraction back to the level of practice, it is nevertheless true that one real source operating throughout the continuations is Chrétien's own originating text, not exclusively to be sure, but most effectively for each of the continuators as the concrete point of departure for their own narratives. Chrétien's *Conte* is the common reservoir where they find material for reinvention, a common center that guarantees continuity through its own decentered nature. As suggested by the notion of centrifugal intertextuality, however far away we are carried by the forward thrust of the continuations, we are also invited back again and again to the master text to see where we have come from and where we are supposed to be going. This is the essential rhythm, the push-and-pull logic of the dialogue between Chrétien and his continuators. If we now follow that force field back to its source, how does Chrétien's name (re)appear in the text as an authorial signature, seen through the insights and byways written into the continuations?

Chrétien's own source references throughout his corpus provide a context for situating his work in the *Conte du Graal*. The terms used in prologues and epilogues to designate a source or refer to his own writing reveal significant overlap in the two sets. In *Erec* (13, 19), *conte* designates his source; in *Cligès* (8, 22, 43) and *Perceval* (63, 66), his own work.[75] In *Cligès*, *estoire* refers to a source (23); in *Erec* (23), to his current romance. *Le livre* as used in *Cligès* (20) and *Perceval* (67) identifies a source; in the *Charrette* (25), it refers to Chrétien's romance.[76] Two other terms are more restricted and refer only to Chrétien's work: *romans* in *Yvain* (6805), the *Charrette* (2), and *Perceval* (8); *uevre* in the last verse of *Cligès*, which announces, 'Ci fenist l'uevre Crestien' ('here ends the work of Chrétien'; NB the rhyme with the previous verse's 'lien' makes it clear that this is not a scribal explicit—cf. Gerbert 6998). The interchangeability of *conte*, *estoire*, and *livre* ensures a seamless passage between the common reservoir and

l'estoire le raconte' (42430: 'as the history recounts it'). In his *Perceval* edition, Busby's description of the totally contaminated and hopelessly intermingled manuscript tradition offers a kind of practical equivalent or expression of this underlying logic (xl–xlviii). See particularly the passage where he quotes Micha imagining a scene in which multiple scribes pass around squires of different versions of the romance without concern that they are mixing different strains in the production of new 'copies' (xli–xlii). The same story accommodates, includes, transcends all the microchanges, the *mouvance* of transmission. See also van Mulken (1993: 41–5).

75 In Godefroi's epilogue to the *Charrette* he uses the term *conte* (7110) and *romanz* (7101) to designate Chrétien's work; the last *conte* (7112) is more ambiguous and could refer to either the source or Chrétien's text.

76 Manessier uses *livre* (42652) to designate his continuation and makes no claim about a written source in relation to his patron, as Chrétien did. Gerbert uses *livre* to refer to a source (7006), as in the *Conte*.

an individual author's input, as Chrétien both stakes out his particular invention and acknowledges multiple authorizing elements. He has explicitly set up the dynamic that both he and his continuators follow.[77] The sources may well be largely fictitious; the already said or told is unlikely to look exactly or even much like what we are reading. But the references create an aura that plays around the edges of the writing to problematize ever so slightly where any particular author's work starts or ends within the common matter, the common models so many writers and storytellers share.

Chrétien thus opens the *Conte du Graal* with a piece of shared knowledge, a proverb that introduces the parable of the sower as a figure for the third person author named in verse 7. 'Crestiens' elaborates the scene of sowing and reaping to structure his relationship both to the romance that follows and to the patron from whom he expects the appropriate harvest, the reward for his commission royally carried out:

> Ki petit semme petit quelt,
> Et qui auques requeillir velt,
> En tel liu sa semence espande
> Que Diex a cent doubles li rande;
> Car en terre qui riens ne valt,
> Bone semence seche et faut.
> Crestïens *semme et fait semence*
> D'un romans que il *encomence*,
> Et le *seme* en si bon leu
> Qu'il ne puet [estre] sanz grant preu,
> Qu'il le *fait* por le plus preudome
> Qui soit en l'empire de Rome.
> C'est li quens Phelipes de Flandres...
> Crestïens, qui *entent* et *paine*
> Par le comandement le conte
> A *rimoier* le meillor conte
> Qui soit contez a cort roial:
> Ce est li Contes del Graal,
> Dont li quens li bailla le livre.
> Oëz coment il *s'en delivre*.

(1–13, 62–8; italics added)

(He who sows little, reaps little, and the one who wants to reap much scatters his seed in such a place that God will give it back to him a hundred fold; for in worthless land, good seeds dry out and fail. Chrétien sows and seeds a romance that he begins, and he sows it in

---

[77] The pattern is corroborated in the narrative of the *Conte du Graal*, where references to a source, which recur at intervals throughout the romance, are particularly keyed to descriptions, just as descriptions frequently elicit the first-person interventions of the narrating voice: sources linked to descriptions, e.g. 2806–7, 3262, 4616–17, 7680; first-person narrative interventions and descriptions (frequently cut short), e.g. 1566, 1569, 1805, 2678ss, 3928ss, 4150–1, 4620, 6987, 7728–9.

such a good place that he cannot be without great profit, for he does it for the most worthy man in the empire of Rome, that is, count Philip of Flanders... Chrétien, who takes pains at the count's command to rhyme the best story ever told in a royal court: this is the Story of the Grail of which the count gave him the book. Hear how he carries out the task.)

Some of the matter may be borrowed but the rhetorical display and wit we recognize as Chrétien's. Without a common noun to designate the author, his proper name is here associated with verbs: figurative action, *seme et fait semence*, then *seme* again, this time connected directly to romance writing, which will be modulated through a series of verbs: *encomence*, *fait*, *entent*, *paine*, *rimoier*, *s'en delivre*, verbs that catch the various facets of his role and recall authorial actions described in his other prologues. Since naming himself in his first romance as 'Crestiens de Troies' (9), Chrétien has signed prologues or epilogues with one proper name unmodified, as if we should be able to distinguish the work of the master. He has indeed already sown quite a few seeds that will bear fruit, especially among later romancers who will multiply his words by a factor far exceeding 'cent doubles' (4). A metaphor of multiplication furnishes a particularly apt epigraph for a romance that will subsequently generate vast quantities of writing, rewriting, and continuation.

Is Chrétien's proper name here simply a notation to align this new work with previous ones and give it his authorial stamp, or does it have a greater weight that requires evaluation? In the romance that follows, acts of naming have serious consequences for each of his heroes.[78] Perceval has to guess his name at the moment of his greatest failure, signaled retrospectively by his cousin's comment that 'Perceval the Welshman' (3575) is now 'Perchevax li chaitif' and 'Perchevax maleürous' (3582–3: the wretched and unfortunate Perceval). The now triply named Perceval begins to grasp the change only when the Hideous Damsel arrives at Arthur's court to repeat the message. Gauvain, on the contrary, is sure of his identity and always gives his name when asked. Yet inexplicably, he withholds his name at the Roche de Champguin just before learning Ygerne's (8742), the clue that identifies his grandmother, mother, and sister. One of the great mysteries left by the unfinished romance is what Chrétien would have done with the recognition scene Gauvain was engineering for Arthur's whole family in the last verses written by the originating author. However obscurely, naming is fraught with meaning in the romance proper and may be so in the prologue as well.

Entwined by Chrétien's verses, the names of author and patron become mutually defining. We do not know if Count Philip turned out to be as generous in remuneration as Chrétien was in praise. Was Philip persuaded by the game of rhetoric to translate sublime charity, which lives in God (48–50), into the

---

[78] Many scholars have examined the importance of names in the *Conte*. See e.g. Sargent-Baur (2001) and Walter (2004, esp. the chapter on 'Les Noms secrets'). On Perceval guessing his name, see also Ménard (1995) and Amazawa (1998).

material compensation that passes from patron's hand to writer's purse? Philip's documented history only furnishes us the date *ante quem* for the unfinished romance: his death at Acre in 1191. Should we wonder if that death or Chrétien's own (as Gerbert claims) occasioned the suspension of the writing: lack of patron, lack of prospect for the reward sought, lack of author? Or might we discover here a socio-political subtext, the perennial triangle of Flemish politics that appears in the subtle interplay between Flanders, linked in v. 12 to the 'empire de Rome' (currently in German hands) and the allusion to a 'cort roial' (65) which could apply, not to Flanders, but rather to the French or English monarchies?[79] With no sure biographical or social context, we have by necessity to stick to the text, to see how Chrétien's name plays off against other names, other signs.

Words play a key role here as Chrétien juggles levels of meaning, using words figuratively and then signaling their literal sense, moving back and forth between parable and straight talk, textual quotation and commentary. His own usage creates an expectation of meaning on several different levels, requiring interpretation, incurring risk.[80] Appropriately, the first of Philip's virtues concerns speech:

> Li quens est teus que il n'escoute
> Vilain g[ap] ne parole estoute,
> Et s'il ot mesdire d'autrui,
> Quels que il soit, ce poise lui.
>
> (21–4)

(The count is such that he doesn't listen to evil speech [nasty jokes] or foolish words, and if he hears someone speaking ill of others, whoever it may be, it pains him.)

The description evokes several categories of words escaping from proper control, anticipating Keu's repeated verbal abuse, roundly criticized by the king and ultimately punished but not repressed. Ironically, Perceval's failure to perceive the seneschal's sarcasm not only procured him the desired red arms but also saved an apparently disarmed Arthur from the Red Knight's aggression.[81] Keu may speak out most inappropriately but his 'vilain g[ap] ne parole estoute' often serve a useful function where politeness shows itself to be less effective. In Gauvain's part of the romance, the uncourtly speech of the Male Pucele, also condemned by characters in the story, will ultimately be revealed as a significant critique of Arthurian chivalry and its 'coutume de Logres' (cf. the mother's opening description of knights as the angels who kill, 399–400).[82] Perhaps *vilain gap* have their use after all, at least in certain circumstances. Of course, Perceval is the primary

---

[79] Cf. Cazelles's social reading of *Conte* (1996), as well as possible links with Henry II and Aliénor d'Aquitaine's court noted in the *Erec* coronation at Nantes (Schmolke-Hasselmann 1981).

[80] Cf. Bäuml (1980) on the expectation of meaning carried over from Latin written tradition into early vernacular narrative (esp. 254–5, 263–4).

[81] Perceval's action also saves the romancer from repeating the *Charrette* scenario, where Arthur's failure to act against an unknown knight's aggression allows havoc to ensue.

[82] See the discussion of violence in Ch. 4.

center of comic play tied to verbal pitfalls. The *nice* talks too much or too little; he fails to understand the plain sense in the words of advice given by his mother and Gornemant de Gohort. His literal-mindedness, paradoxically and grotesquely useful in the encounter with the Red Knight, is at once hilarious and dangerous. This is a new kind of hero who leaves death and destruction in his wake: his widowed mother dead, the Tent Maiden persecuted, countless knights killed, the Fisher King unhealed, his land laid waste, orphans and widows unprotected.

Perceval's example, indeed everything in this text points our attention to words and what they do, how they respond to each other and to other levels of reference and meaning. The mirror play of the romance's two heroes is set up in part by the narrator's reprise of particular words, words linked to objects like the bleeding lance that crosses over from Perceval's to Gauvain's quest, like the red color that further connects blood shed on snow and Blancheflor's rosy cheeks. What about less obvious repetitions like the *eschaces* (trestles) of ebony holding up the Fisher King's table (3267 ff.) and the *escace d'argent* (silver prosthesis) of the *escacier*, the one-legged man who remains silent when Gauvain passes by at the Castle of Ladies (7651 ff.)?[83] Chrétien's word play engenders expectations, sets up puzzles, asks questions. Who is authorized to interpret and by what criteria? We need to determine how much belongs to the letter of the word, its literal and figurative meanings held 'an la letre' (IV, 29206), as the second continuator expresses it in medieval terms that emphasize the word's written inscription on the manuscript page.

Words matter: the trick is to figure out when and how. If he wants compensation, a writer must convince his patron of the sincerity of his praise, and praise of Philip constitutes the bulk—fifty verses out of sixty-eight (10–60)—of this fairly sizable prologue.[84] It comes in the form of a proof: 'je proverai' (16) is the first of only two verbs attributed to *je* in the entire prologue.[85] This authorial *I* named 'Crestiens' (7) will prove that Philip is superior to Alexander, a challenging verbal and logical feat inasmuch as this well-known model from Antiquity has already appeared in romance as a synonym for generosity.[86] In order to

[83] Cf. Méla's review of Dragonetti's *La Vie de la lettre* (1983).

[84] This is also true in the one other prologue where Chrétien praises a patron, although in the *Charrette* critics disagree about where exactly the praise starts and stops.

[85] The other (48) is linked to his citation of St Paul and will be analyzed below.

[86] The expression 'valt mix' (14, 17, 57), repeated three times, will frame this virtuosic proof. The QED of the question and answer that closes the demonstration—'Ne valt mix cil...? | Oïl, n'en doutez ja de rien' (57–60: 'Isn't it worth more? Yes, don't doubt it at all')—serves as a transition to Chrétien's second act of self-naming and the final paronomasic play on *conte* that closes the prologue by wrapping back around to the beginning. Hunt relates this proof to logical demonstration (1971: 367–8) and sees a correspondence between the picture of Philip offered in Chrétien's praise and that found in his contemporary historians (372–4). Dragonetti, on the other hand, reads the necessity to prove as a coded hint that there may have been a gap between praise and reality. He sees reflected ironically in Chrétien's praise how the chroniclers highlight Philip's reputation as a lover of tournaments, associated with prodigality and waste (1980: 104–6f.).

establish his bona fides, the author introduces as part of his proof not only biblical quotations but models of exegesis for deciphering their meaning. The added weight of Scripture will thus tip the scales and heighten the truth value of the romancer's good words.

This is an astounding first in the context of Chrétien's overwhelmingly secular corpus. It anticipates the enigmatic difference of his last romance, not least in the way his examples of biblical reference play out so distinctly in the prologue's rhetorical display. The opening metaphor of the sower has already introduced, without directly identifying them, a number of New Testament references (2 Corinthians 9: 6, 8; Matthew 13: 3–23; Mark 4: 3–20; Luke 8: 5–12).[87] Chrétien has wittily combined and reinterpreted them to divert their meaning from a parable of hidden discourse on God's word, reserved for those who understand (as Jesus explains to his disciples), to the writer's hopefully remunerative relationship with his patron. In this transfer, the worthy Philip has become the fertile soil where Chrétien's word, boldly occupying the place of God's, will certainly multiply to good profit. The ethical and spiritual thus entwine with aesthetic and material dimensions.[88] The transposition, which carries considerable if indirect praise for the romancer's own words, has both humorous and serious overtones: a joke (*gap*) containing sense and nonsense.

The issue of words not immediately understandable, stories that reserve their meaning for some and deny it to others—the crux of the discussion linked in three of the four Gospels to the parable of the sower—places the burden of what we do with Chrétien's word seeds directly on our shoulders. These are the very problems that have for centuries preoccupied readers and rewriters of the enigmatic *Conte du Graal*. Indeed, the principle of continuation functions here (and in the cycle as a whole) not only within the narrative sequence but in the mode of interpretation as well. Commentary, added explicitly through the voices of narrators and characters, or more often implicitly through continued narrative development, engages readers in their response to the text as much as successive authors working in relay. Not surprisingly then, the first merits discerned in Philip include his ability to stop some kinds of speech (by avoiding it) while encouraging others (like romance writing) through patronage.

---

[87] See the notes in Poirion's Pléiade edn. (1994*a*: 1325–6), Raugei (1993: 206–8), as well as Luttrell's (1983) and Hunt's articles (1971, 1994) on the prologue. Luttrell identifies not only the biblical references already cited here but possible links to the *Glossa ordinaria*, Psalms 7: 9, Colossians 3: 12, and I John 3: 17 (2–3).

[88] Cf. Haidu (1986: 433–8). Already in *Yvain*, as Haidu points out (1983), Arthur plays a Solomonic role in deciding the outcome of the duel between Yvain and Gauvain. The ethical and political dimensions that characterize the seriousness of Chrétien's romances from the beginning become more insistent in the *Conte* with the explicit mixing of religious concerns. The equilibrium between these different domains is easily upset, as Jehan Bodel's fabliau demonstrates: *De Brunain la vache au prestre* offers a more blatant and jaundiced view of how the basic Christian parable of multiplication can be comically inverted and perverted across material and spiritual realms, as the peasants' and the priest's cows swap back and forth.

As he elaborates the count's virtues, in contrast to Alexander's vices, Chrétien moves more directly into a discussion based on biblical references used as proof texts for Philip's superiority. Like the giving that distinguishes the count's largess, Chrétien is writing 'selonc l'evangille' (29: 'according to the gospel'). First, on the literal level: loving justice, loyalty, and holy Church, Philip is generous, giving secretly, without hypocrisy or guile (25–30). The description leads to a biblical quotation: 'Qu'el [l'evangille] dist: "Ne sache ta senestre | Les biens quant les [fera] ta destre"' (31–2: 'for the Gospel says, don't let your left hand know the good things/deeds your right hand performs'). After embroidering the conceit (32–6) to play up the secrecy of Philip's giving, known only to God and his recipient (a significant addition not in the Bible), Chrétien moves on to allegorical exegesis. Why, he asks, does 'l'evangille' (37) say the left hand should not know what the right hand gives? The passage quoted comes from Matthew 6: 2–4, where Jesus criticizes hypocrites in the synagogues and streets who ostentatiously display their good deeds for praise. Speaking to the multitude in the Sermon on the Mount, Jesus rephrases the critique as an instruction on how to give alms properly, in secret, so that God will reward the deed. The New Testament context is thus particularly pertinent to Chrétien's dual purpose, both praise and pitch.

This passage of the prologue deftly combines biblical quotation and paraphrase, as Chrétien bends Scripture to his proof, fitting it into his web of words. His commentary will proceed from authority: 'selonc l'estoire' (39). *Estoire*, story, history, must in this context refer to the biblical text, although in Chrétien's usage *estoire* typically refers to Celtic sources whose oral traditions escape us except for the written traces left in Geoffrey of Monmouth, Wace, romances, lays, and so on. Romance sources are here extended to include biblical tradition, as Chrétien's narrator momentarily takes the voice of a preacher (anticipating Perceval's hermit uncle and Gerbert's Perceval), using quotes, paraphrase, question and answer, exhortation—all the rhetorical devices of a good homily. In constructing an allegorical explanation that equates left with vainglory and right with charity (39–47), the romancer moves from the passage in Matthew (from which he has faithfully extracted the notion of vainglory, though the word itself does not appear there) to another biblical quotation, for which he cites St Paul:

> . . . qui vit
> En carité selonc l'escrit,
> Sainz Pols le dist et je le lui,
> Il maint en Dieu, et Dieu en lui.
>
> (48–50)

(he who lives in charity, according to the Scriptures—St Paul says it and I read it in him—lives in God and God in him.)

The source references here are not the vague allusions to story matter typically seen elsewhere and introduced at the end of the prologue in the word play on *conte.* These are precise references to a written text, *l'evangille*, *l'escrit*, the Bible, the book par excellence of the Middle Ages. Chrétien is already combining in his prologue two types of sources related to two types of matter, Arthurian and Christian, that will reappear in his romance with all the enigmas encoded in that unexpected combination.[89]

This is a rare opportunity to see how Chrétien manipulates a source we can actually check. Precise reference, yes, but not precisely to St Paul, since the quotation as worded comes from 1 John 4: 16. Much speculation has addressed Chrétien's apparent mistake: similar ideas were famously expressed by St Paul (1 Corinthians 13); St Paul was used as a term for a set of books including St John; St Paul was the patron of knights; Chrétien does or does not know much about the Bible, has first- or only second-hand knowledge, and so on.[90] Nancy Regalado's work on misquotations in Jean de Meun's *Rose* demonstrates how useful such 'mistakes' may be for forcing the reader back to other texts, forward to further reflection on meaning (1999). We may legitimately wonder if Chrétien's misquotation is part of a game to make us ask how words are used, as they shift between figurative and literal meanings: the sower of seeds, the givers who may be liberal in fact but not in the appropriate spirit, the count who becomes a *conte* and whose largess produces writing that reveals secrets hidden away in the patron's heart and viscera, known in theory only to God, but trumpeted here in order to praise Philip's virtues. Shifted to the mouth of another, such praise becomes proof, not of 'vaine gloire' (40), but of true charity.

Having at this point recognized a variety of voices and styles at play in Chrétien's 'molt bele conjointure', we should consider yet another source, the rhetorical tradition and matter of Antiquity also contributing to the prologue. Any liberally-trained contemporary of Chrétien would have been able to recognize the richness of his mastery, the rhetorical skill displayed in his exordium cum encomium. In an effort to debunk any connection between prologue and romance (presumably as a counterweight to Urban Tigner Holmes and Sister Amelia Klenke's allegorical Christian interpretations), Tony Hunt (1971) suggested that the humanistic tradition from Cicero to John of Salisbury could have provided Chrétien with many of the components used here, from the figure of the sower through the humbling of Alexander and the exaltation of Philip (in the person of Alexander's father). Hunt later conceded many of Claude Luttrell's 'strictures' to his argument (1994: 154). In particular, Luttrell demonstrated that the Classical tradition on giving reached twelfth-century humanists through Seneca, whose critique of Alexander's liberality for the sake of self-glorification

---

[89] Crossovers of vocabulary may be comic (e.g. tent as church), but may also appear in a serious vein (e.g. the talk of penitence and confession in the midst of Arthurian adventure, when Perceval's hermit episode is surrounded by Gauvain's adventures). On the combination of oral and written traditions, cf. the General Prologue to Marie de France's *Lais*.

[90] See e.g. Hunt (1971: 374 n. 2), Gouttebroze (1995, 1996), Raugei (1993), the note on St Paul in Pickens's edn. (1990: 452).

anticipates Chrétien's, while most of his contemporaries gave Alexander more mixed reviews than the romancer's thoroughly negative contrast to Philip's laudatory portrait (1983: 6–7). For Luttrell, Senecan ethical material combined with proverbial and scriptural allusions set up a powerful, if not exactly transparent, matrix for the romance that follows, whose meaning he locates in Christian charity.[91]

Once we enter into the spirit of play with which Chrétien invests it, the prologue appears as complex and ambiguous as the romance it introduces, with many tantalizing threads connecting the two. Hunt's initial caution that we are reading not theology but eulogy (1971: 359–61, 374–5) still serves as a useful reminder that Chrétien may occasionally borrow the language of religious discourse but his *Conte du Graal* should by no means be reduced to a tract illustrating Christian doctrine. Medieval churchmen were never fooled into thinking that tears shed for romance heroes were acceptable signs of Christian piety. And yet the new role played by religious teaching in Perceval's story, interwoven problematically with more traditional Arthurian concerns, is explicitly anticipated by a new kind of discourse introduced into the prologue, a discourse that insistently calls attention to different levels of meaning, reading, and understanding. Normal expectation might place vernacular romance in the realm of amusement not edification, but Chrétien's prologues insist that meaning may be found in his fictions (cf. Calogrenant's own call to listen with both heart and ears, before beginning his tale in *Yvain*).[92] Does Chrétien expect readers to submit his text to the kind of allegorical exegesis demonstrated here on some biblical verses? Surely such an approach is too reductive for the rich ambiguities and contradictions of Chrétien's writing, the constantly shifting play among different levels of literal and figurative meanings. Even here in the prologue, the examples of textual transposition and manipulation are more subtle and varied than the simple equivalence offered for right- and left-handed giving.

Nor does his play always follow a hierarchy from the literal to the figurative.[93] The generosity Chrétien most insistently calls for in his opening gesture translates spiritual charity back into the financial reward he expects to receive from his literary patron. As if to say that Philip (and the readers) must not after all forget the letter in its most concrete and material sense, its obvious as well as less obvious meanings. Perceval himself has a hard time paying attention to the letter—witness his 'dialogue de sourd' with the knight in the opening scene or later with his mother intent on giving him family history and good counsel on

---

[91] Likewise, in *La Destre et la Senestre*, Sargent-Baur (1992) aims to read *Perceval* as a romance on charity.

[92] See Baumgartner on the relative rarity of such play with figurative and literal levels within contemporary fiction (2003: 110). See Haidu's discussion of different kinds and uses of allegory in the introduction to *Aesthetic Distance* and in his explanation of 'adjutorial allegory' (2004: 242–5).

[93] Cf. Kay's remark on Jean de Meun's Genius whose literalism collapses the courtly agenda (2000: 92). Much work needs to be done in comparing the interplay between allegorical and literal senses in the *Roman de la Rose* and the Grail romances.

how to treat young ladies and recognize churches. I described Perceval as too literal-minded when he ignored Keu's irony, but the *nice* is also and often too distracted from the letter to pay it proper attention, distracted from others' intentions to his own hungers and desires. Not too literal but insufficiently literal, Perceval must learn to listen rather than shape meaning a priori to his limited focus.[94] His unfinished education reflects the progress he makes, slowly, painfully, in attending to the value of his own and other people's words. Both progress and regression are expressed in the transformations of his proper name.

What is invested in the letter of a name and, first and foremost, in the proper name of Perceval's author? Roger Dragonetti reads Chrétien's name as a pseudonym, an oxymoron expressing his double nature, the Christian from pagan Troy, which sets in motion the play of the signifier throughout the *Conte* (1980: 20–2).[95] 'Troie' may be absent from this prologue, but the matter of Antiquity is abundantly present, encapsulated in the name 'Alexandres' played off against 'Phelipes de Flandres' at the rhyme (13–14). Sarah Kay (1997) looks at the Christian in 'Crestien de Troies' and speculates that it may be a common noun masquerading as a proper name, a pseudonym shared by a number of writers who subordinate their individual identity to a collective one and call for some Christian perspective on their writing.[96] Her argument puts into question common assumptions about what fits together in an author's corpus, the modern tendency to separate secular production from religious writing, even though medieval authorship frequently crosses what later centuries consider exclusive domains (cf. the debate about Wauchier de Denain as author of the Second Continuation). We may not be persuaded by the argument for anonymous 'Crestien', but Kay does demonstrate the advantages of looking at so-called

[94] Perceval's problem with the letter is also tied to his unfamiliarity with the courtly context in which his mother's and Gornemant's advice necessarily operates—a lack of familiarity that serves as a powerful tool for critiquing the violence tied to the chivalric order (see Ch. 4). Cf. Larajinha on the difficulties of perception in the *Conte* related to the ironic structure of the bipartite romance: she too argues that Perceval's misunderstandings of the letter are more complex than mere literal-mindedness (1998: 179).

[95] See also Steele (1993) on the alterity of the pagan heritage as part of Christian identity in medieval usage of the term *clergie*, Chrétien's name linked to the myth of the Franks as descended from Trojans, and Christian empire as a continuation of the Roman empire.

[96] I would also suggest, in light of the *Conte*'s exceptional anti-Jewish invective included in two characters' speeches, that Chrétien's proper name also calls attention to the Christian of Jewish Troyes. Troyes was an important political, cultural, and literary center as one of the two capital cities of Henry the Liberal, the count of Champagne (see Benton and Putter). But 12th-cent. Troyes, at the crossroads of trade between northern and southern Europe, was also well known in the Middle Ages as a center of Jewish life and learning, the home of Rashi (Rabbi Solomon ben Isaac, 1040–1105), the foremost biblical and Talmudic scholar of the Middle Ages, and the site of his academy (Rashi's grandsons were contemporaries of Chrétien). Without becoming involved in biographical speculation about Chrétien as a possible Jewish convert (Holmes and Klenke 1959), I plan to pursue in a future project possible parallels between *Perceval*, the cycle of continuations, and contemporary Jewish and Christian biblical exegesis, in order to examine more deeply the link that has been repeatedly suggested (but without substantial investigation) between Chrétien's narrative and 12th-cent. exegetical interest in the literal level of Scriptures.

'pagan' and 'Christian' works in relation to each other, particularly in the case of Chrétien de Troyes whose *Conte du Graal* is itself a study in heterogeneity.[97] According to the logic of Chrétien's name, we should pay attention to the multiple traditions evoked in the prologue, neither dismissing any of them a priori, nor giving any of them priority on principle.[98]

The comparison between Alexander and Philip gives a clear sense of hierarchy: Philip is better than Alexander. This is not only a matter of degree but a difference in quality: Philip's Christian charity is superior to Alexander's vainglorious liberality (Hunt 1971: 368–9; Luttrell 1983: 6). Does this proof foreshadow the superiority of Perceval's Christian chivalry over Gauvain's Arthurian chivalry? That is certainly the reading offered by the *Queste del Saint Graal* which puts 'chevalerie celestiele' above 'chevalerie terriene'. The same model has been followed to varying degrees by modern critics.[99] But we may have serious doubts about what exactly Perceval's chivalry would have looked like if Chrétien had continued his story after the hermit episode. His romance does not privilege Christian values as exclusively as the prologue does. Rather than maintaining the heroes' difference, the *Conte*'s two parts entangle them in ways that move Perceval and Gauvain closer together despite their disparate starting points—and the first two continuations will maintain that trajectory of convergence across their alternating rhythm.

The humanists' view of Alexander and his father, Philip of Macedonia, the pair operating behind the proper names highlighted in the prologue's judgment of Count Philip and Alexander, allow for a variety of evaluations. Historically, father and son are both located on the pagan side of the equation, but the ethical tradition still finds a good exemplar to contrast with a bad one, when it is so inclined. If Alexander comes out with the short stick in this comparison, in the vernacular literary tradition as a whole he appears repeatedly as the hero of his own eponymous romances. In other heroes' romances, his name is frequently invoked as the quintessence of largess, as in Chrétien's own *Erec et Enide* (2265–6, 6665–8), which furnishes a witty subtext for this new contrary proof of Alexander's vices. This larger context suggests that the comparison here is more

---

[97] See Kay's promising comments on possible connections between *carestia* in Chrétien's lyric poem and *caritas* in the *Perceval* (1997: 24–7).

[98] In Chrétien's romances, the range of proper names used in comparisons, references, and so on, includes names from Antiquity, as well as biblical and Breton ones. The glossaries of proper names in the continuations indicate that the field of Antique names remains unused except for Wauchier's mention of Alexander and Rome.

[99] Cf. Berthelot's reading of Chrétien's prologues: she associates the *Conte* with the choice between 'l'autorité, profane ou spirituelle' (1991: 40 n. 40). Haidu rejects the spiritualizing mode in modern criticism (1986: 432–41), while Frappier offers a moderate version of the polarization in his three part hierarchy: Perceval, Gauvain, and bad knights (1972a). Saly's reading of the two heroes and their reversed symmetries according to a typological scheme informed by biblical exegesis, rejects the notion that Gauvain is devalued by the comparisons between the two heroes (1994b). Cf. Maddox's chapter on *Perceval* (1991a): he offers a view that recognizes difference and underplays the hierarchy between the two orders represented by Perceval and Gauvain (see Ch. 4 below).

the work of circumstance (a limited truth in praise of his patron) than absolute truth to be applied to his two heroes. Context is an important component of any word's meaning, as the romance demonstrates by putting into action the relative value of *vilain gap*, depending on context, despite Philip's condemnation as reported in the prologue.

If we return to the passage where Chrétien comments on the quotation from Matthew, we should note more closely how he places it in context, covers over the shift between different New Testament passages with his blanket claim of fidelity to 'l'estoire' (39). Although he seems to go back to the same biblical text first designated by 'l'evangille', Matthew supplies only the sinister explanation; the right hand's gloss derives from a second passage, identified only after the fact by the name St Paul and Chrétien's affirmation that 'I read him/it', although in fact he could not read these particular words in Paul, even if the same general idea can be found in his writing. Two biblical passages are joined to comment on each other: this is typical in exegetical interpretation designed to elucidate, fill in holes, add layers of meaning, by bringing different parts of the biblical text into dialogue. But Chrétien's textual joining across an unexpressed gap also mirrors his own narration in a romance that conjoins without warning the stories of Perceval and Gauvain.[100] These combinations create surprising puzzles, even when the author/narrator appears to be offering satisfactory explanations. Interpreters will have to pay close attention to the unexpected intersections of words, events, situations: they will have to play with, in, and beyond the letter of the text, as Chrétien has demonstrated, once his sample exegesis, too deceptively simple, is placed in context.[101]

By destabilizing the hegemony of any single sign system, including the dominant discourse of Christianity explicitly displayed here, Chrétien implicitly claims a freedom to play with words, even religious words, and their possible meanings, in the fictions of romance. In the extradiegetic world of the writer, the patron was present to caution, if not limit, the intradiegetic wit.[102] In the romance that follows, there is much written to remind us of all the weight involved in the free play of words, spoken and unspoken, for good and for evil, especially when the Good Word of the Gospel has been invoked.

As his opening metaphor claims, Chrétien's romance sows the seeds that grow into the very particular textuality realized by the whole architecture of the four continuations. For each of the four continuators, *Perceval* serves as 'le texte primitif' that shapes and confers authenticity on writers who share its common matter. This powerfully generative textuality, contiguous yet discontinuous, continuous yet

---

[100] Cf. Rider (2001) on Chrétien's use of enigma rather than allegory, as he combines biblical texts in his parable of the sower.

[101] Putter discusses the formation of a public, associated with Henry the Liberal's court at Champagne, capable of responding to the subtleties and allusions of Chrétien's romances. In his view, Chrétien reflects as well as shapes the ideal of the clerical knight (1995: esp. 264–6).

[102] On the issue of problematizing religious discourse among Chrétien's contemporaries, see Koziol (1995) and Van Caenegem (1995).

contradictory, is rooted in the interplay between the *Conte*'s two parts, through which its two heroes constantly but enigmatically rewrite each other. The continuators may not have Chrétien's notes, nor should we read their words as his. But, as I demonstrate in the following chapters, across the accumulation of their successive additions, through their collective hindsight and wanderings along the routes traced by Perceval and Gauvain, the verse continuations maintain a dialogue with Chrétien that helps us better understand crucial issues inscribed in the *Conte du Graal* under his authorizing signature. The verse continuators in general have understood Chrétien's mixed signals about the interplay of literal and figurative levels of reading and writing. Even if occasionally Manessier and Gerbert may show some allegorical tendencies that reflect the influence of the prose versions, they do not write an overall program of allegory like the *Queste*, where hermits control meaning cast as biblical history and Christian truths.[103] The continuators return to the thorny problems posed by the *Conte*—questions about society and the individual; love, sex, and family ties; chivalry, violence, and religion—but they do so within the ambiguities of romance as constructed by Chrétien's model. Contradictions and competing values, amplified to the breaking point in the Vulgate Cycle, are maintained as complementary tensions in the verse continuations. Like Chrétien, the continuators do not force resolution. Their narratives continue to inscribe a figurative potential rather than turn romance into allegory. Indeed, narrative continuation itself appears as a mode of exegesis and commentary; the intertextual dialogue linking successive segments of the *Perceval* Continuations to the *Conte* thus provides us with a model to follow in our own interpretations.

And the name Chrétien de Troyes conjures up not only the new puzzle of how to understand the Grail story's religious connections but also how to read them interwoven with the traditional elements of love and combat that have become synonymous with Arthurian romance as invented by Chrétien himself. Since the advice Perceval receives from his mother, Gornemant, and his uncle, sets out an agenda for educating him (as well as the readers) precisely in the three domains of love, chivalry, and religious practice, we can follow that itinerary by focusing next on how Perceval and Gauvain interact with the fair sex, whether they be ladies in need of help or the heroes' own mothers.

---

[103] The limited tendency toward allegory can be seen in an episode borrowed from the *Queste*, when Gerbert's Perceval arrives at an abbey and sees (through a grill) a man on a bed wearing a crown who receives communion. He is convinced that 'tout est par senefiance' (II, 10336), which provides a lead in to the lay brother's account of Evalac and Joseph of Arimathea. The scene also reinvents elements of Perceval's visit to the Fisher King in Chrétien (e.g. aspects connected to Perceval's family through the figure hidden in the back room, sustained by the single host carried in the Grail) and thus expresses implicitly the contest between prose and verse, allegorical and literal readings of the model text.

2

Telling Tales, Of Maidens in Tents

Without Contraries is no progression.
William Blake, *The Marriage of Heaven and Hell*

The test of a first-rate intelligence is the ability to hold two opposed ideas in
the mind at the same time and still retain the ability to function.

F. Scott Fitzgerald, *The Crack-Up*

The enduring interest of Chrétien's Grail romance can be explained at least in
part, I think, by his gift for creating mysteries. He invents artfully constructed
puzzles whose solutions escape us while giving us no escape, no easy outlet to
assume correct answers cannot be found simply because they do not exist.
Without the release of meaning assured or denied, we are left in the tension of
the quest. The particular enigmas posed by Chrétien in *Le Conte du Graal* are
byproducts of the radical innovations he practices in his last romance. While the
mysterious object designated as the Grail has often garnered the lion's share of
attention, it is by no means the only source of enigma in Chrétien's unfinished
romance. Among the most startling differences that characterize the *Conte* is a
redefinition of the hero, doubled in the figures of Perceval and Gauvain and recast
as a perpetrator of violence, as well as the adversary of evildoers. By moving flaws
and misdeeds into the behavior of heroes, Chrétien now deals with problems at a
deeper level than in his previous romances, where evil is typically displaced onto
the other.[1] What, he seems to ask, about the mixture of good and bad in 'the best
and the brightest'? The question, once raised, operates in a wide range of
situations, sexual, political, social, and religious. If many of these are already
staples of romance, some (and especially some combinations) are unexpected. We
have already wondered, along with Wauchier de Denain, if a failed hero will
achieve the Grail quest and return to his beloved Blancheflor. If we continue to
inquire about the relationship between the girl and the Grail in Perceval's plot line,

---

[1] On the figure of evil in romance, cf. Jameson (1975–6). See also Vincensini's analysis of
Melusine's son Geoffroi as an example of the knight's 'trois excès irrémédiables' (2005: 17), based on
Dumézil's mythical view of the warrior's *furor*. In Chrétien's previous romances, the heroes do of
course have certain character flaws and make mistakes (Erec's uxoriousness, Yvain's failure to keep
his promise to Laudine, etc.), but they are not accused of treasonous murder like Gauvain in the
Conte, nor do they cause the deaths associated with Perceval's otherwise innocent actions (leaving his
mother, kissing the Tent Maiden, failing to ask the Grail questions).

we should certainly add a query about Gauvain: what is the ladies' man doing in the midst of all this, in a romance entitled 'the Story of the Grail'?

TEXTUAL INTERCOURSE AND HUMAN DEVELOPMENT

All four continuations of *Perceval* stand as testimony to the readers' desire to ask and find answers to such questions; the textual accumulations pay tribute to the fascination exercized by Chrétien's enigmatic, but compelling puzzles. Confronted by this enormous intertextual panorama, we look for ways to line up two heroes, the girl and the Grail, across the continually shifting responses to Chrétien, as continuators and scribes add to and re-sort, rewrite, and respond to 'le vieux Perceval'. A recurrent thread may serve to guide us through the maze, a tantalizing tale told (and retold) in installments across the compilation, repeatedly signalled by a maiden in a tent. A young woman alone, isolated on the edge of the social space in her temporary pavilion, the movable locus amœnus of love, first appears in Perceval's story as if conjured up by the advice received from his mother about churches and damsels.

The episode can be briefly summarized, but it will cast a long shadow across successive continuations. On his way to Arthur's court, the first comical adventure the naïve Perceval blunders into takes place in a beautiful tent, which (based on his mother's description) he mistakes for a church, until the presence of a sleeping damsel redirects his religious impulse to a more amorous vein. Perceval's youthful bluntness stops at the most elementary and simplest of satisfactions: kisses, a ring, meat pies. But the damsel's jealous friend mistakes their innocence for lust and numberless knights pay for the mistake with their lives, as the damsel herself suffers relentless torment, until Perceval encounters her once again and corrects the misprision. So begins a series of erotic adventures in the intermediary spaces of mobile pavilions—neither court nor forest, somewhere between the civilized life of courtly society and the uncivilized life of savage nature. They will reappear in each of the *Perceval* Continuations, though with greatest effect and consequence in the First and Fourth.

Chrétien's own use of the tent setting reaches back to evoke a rhetorical set piece from the antique romances, the descriptions of tents associated with the movement of armies and heroes at war, now modulated through the kind of faraway love story told in Marie de France's *Lanval*.[2] In each case (except the last), the golden eagle that commands the top of the pavilion plays the role of telltale sign inviting us to connect, as well as distinguish, the significant stages of a wandering itinerary that engages the violence of amorous and martial pursuits, so

---

[2] On the rhetorical tradition associated with tents, see Baumgartner (1988) and Castellani (1993). On Chrétien's varied vocabulary for the tent, see Eskénazi (1993).

frequently intertwined in the problematics of romance. In the First Continuation, Gauvain will have his own startling encounter with a tent maiden who is already in love with him without ever having met him. It is a story told first by the narrator as a seduction (with Gauvain seduced rather than seducer); thousands of verses later Gauvain himself narrates it as a rape.[3] In both cases, whether voluntary or involuntary, sex leads to fatal encounters between Gauvain and the damsel's father and brothers. Following an itinerary already set in motion by the *Conte du Graal*, the tale thus shifts to the second of Chrétien's heroes, the one whose reputation is constantly linked to courtly dalliance.[4]

In his continuation, Gerbert will elaborate an even more extensive episode based on the First Continuation's model, while at the same time mixing in elements that circle back to Chrétien and Perceval. This time the tent functions as ambush: a damsel and her brothers (hidden nearby) plot the death of Gauvain as revenge for another brother's death at his hands. Twenty knights have already died in the trap, but Gauvain is saved when he makes the sign of the cross and discovers a knife hidden in the bed. His enemy disarmed, Gauvain takes his pleasure in spite of her. This appears to be the dramatic moment represented by the illustrator of T (Fig. 3) when he places a man and a woman together in a bed under a tent whose decorative top emerges from the square frame of a miniature whose corner is neatly notched for the capital M (for 'Messire Gauvain') to fit snugly into the column of text. The two appear at first glance to be lovers, their heads brought close as if ready to kiss, their side by side position typically represented vertically (the point of view is doubled, simultaneously looking from the side and above). Gauvain's head bends down slightly toward the woman's upturned face; their naked shoulders emerge from the drapery of the bed covers. Closer inspection reveals a knife laid across the bed, which angles down from Gauvain's extended arm and hand. The large knife remains menacingly poised over the woman's body and suggests both her initial aggression and his sexual revenge, all neatly capped by the umbrella of the tent.

Paradoxically, Gauvain's act of rape transforms the lady into his *amie*, according to Gerbert's text, and the illustrator seems to have caught the rich ambiguity of the moment, as it visually combines the acts of love and rape. Forced to switch

---

[3] In Thomas Hahn's introd. to the 15th-cent. *Jeaste of Sir Gawain* (1995), he connects the story of Gawain's encounter with the Tent Maiden, which the English romancer borrows from the 1530 French prosification, to the loathly lady stories in which the quest to discover what it is that women want most is traditionally initiated by a seduction or a rape. The suggestion deserves further reflection in light of the twists and turns of the Tent Maiden model through *Perceval* and the continuations, with their repeated oscillations between rape and seduction, delightful sex and violent aggression, male and female points of view, as we shall see in the analyses that follow.

[4] In the Second Continuation, there are a number of episodes that include a tent but none of them coalesce around a Tent Maiden adventure as examined in this chapter. The omission may correspond to Perceval's more successful engagement with the Chessboard Lady. To follow the Second Continuation's occasional use of the tent as a familiar feature of romance, see Roach's summary descriptions of Episodes 9, 13, 21, and 22 (in the introd. to vol. IV). App. 1 offers a quick overview of Roach's divisions.

Fig. 3. BN, fr. 12576, f. 201v. Gauvain and the lady of the tent in Gerbert's Fourth Continuation.

poles from avenger to victim, this tent lady considers herself chastened by the trick; the deceiver once deceived is ready to assume a new role as beloved and even defender. Shortly after leaving the tent, Gauvain unknowingly takes refuge at her father's castle and is forced to recount his adventure as required by custom. Only the daughter's wily and extemporaneous deceptions save her new lover from her father's wrath and send the hero on his way.

Finally, in Manessier's continuation, the tent episode returns briefly to Perceval's storyline. In one short episode, when the chaste hero crosses himself, he unmasks a devil temptress disguised as Blancheflor. Manessier has extracted the erotic overtones of Perceval's relationship with Blancheflor from their encounter at Biaurepaire and rerouted them to this earlier episode, where they take on a completely negative cast. The false Blancheflor tries to seduce Perceval by welcoming him into her bed. On the point of succumbing to her naked charms,

Perceval is saved only by making the sign of the cross. When the devil jumps out from under him, picks up bed and tent, and disappears, Perceval thanks God for saving him (V, 38010–179).[5] The Christianization of the Grail story, reflected back into the verse continuations by way of the Vulgate Cycle, thus surfaces distinctly and distinctively in both Gerbert and Manessier. The eroticized space of the tent, no less than the lady's chamber, has become the site of conflict between Christian values and secular Arthurian ideals.[6]

This quick overview suggests what is both fascinating and frustrating when dealing with *Perceval* and the continuations. Intentionally or not, Chrétien has discovered the mesmerizing power of the unfinished—at least if properly laid out and suspended. He has set into motion a story whose continuation and ending we desire as much as the medieval writers and readers who preceded us. Although many romancers, continuators, interpolators, and editor-scribes continued Chrétien's story, they nevertheless discontinued a number of trajectories inscribed in his romance. We moderns may be more susceptible to the disconnects than a medieval public, more disturbed by the apparent failure of the verse continuations to live up to our expectations, especially since those expectations are often formed by later and more recent versions of the quest for the Holy Grail. The more we grasp the extent of Chrétien's greatness as an inventor of romance, the more we may feel disappointment that the continuators cannot duplicate his unique genius, however much they imitate the master's work. In the *Conte du Graal*, Chrétien does what seems impossible by the standards already put into place by his own, as well as contemporary and preceding romances. He has introduced figures, materials, and issues previously beyond or outside the normal reach of romance. In so doing, Chrétien poses an extraordinarily problematic task for subsequent romancers confronted by the continuities and discontinuities operating in his *Perceval*.[7] Closer analysis of the continuators' efforts to cope with, by rewriting, the puzzles invented by Chrétien may not resolve all the mysteries, but the process may offer a firmer grasp of what eludes us.

---

[5] This is one of the episodes shared (with variations) by both Manessier and the *Queste del Saint Graal*. In the *Queste* (1967: 108–11), Perceval is similarly tempted by a damsel in a tent, who turns out to be a devil in disguise. When he happens to see his sword, Perceval makes the sign of the cross, the devil disappears, and Perceval punishes himself for his momentary weakness in succumbing to seduction by wounding himself in the thigh. A hermit subsequently glosses the episode's *senefiance* (112–15). Manessier's version demonstrates that, like Gerbert, he has welcomed in this area the univocal vision of the quest for the Holy Grail (Corley1986: 581–5). The tent motif returns again briefly in another episode of the Third Continuation, when Perceval saves a woman kidnapped from a tent during her lover's absence (a variation on Perceval's more innocent adventure in the *Conte*).

[6] McCracken follows a similar shift between heroes and value systems in the *Perlesvaus*'s rewriting of the blood drops on the snow: connected by a nexus of motifs to the Tent Maiden episode, this scene moves in the 13th-cent. prose continuation of the *Conte* from Perceval's story to Gauvain's experience of the Grail, now interpreted as a reenactment of the mystery of trans-substantiation. McCracken's analysis shows how the violence represented in the Tent Maiden episode connects the order of chivalry to the sacrifice of women (1998a). See also the discussion of chivalry and violence in Ch. 4.

[7] Beate Schmolke-Hasselmann (1980a) notes a kind of hiatus in Arthurian romance production after Chrétien: until 1200, only the First and Second Continuations fill the gap.

Dante hailed the twisted but beautiful byways of romance as one of its essential features; modern critics have likewise recognized the interlace as a characteristic technique of the prose romances (Vinaver 1971: 68–98). Chrétien's initial use of interlaced episodes finds an equally enthusiastic response among the verse continuators who imitate the irregular and lopsided rhythms of their model. The Tent Maiden adventures supply such a thread to guide us through the labyrinth of narrative amplification and lead inexorably to a set of problems: the sexuality of the individual and the couple, the erotic as a place where love and violence meet in human development, the confrontation between sexual needs and desires, on the one hand, and the bonds of family and society, on the other. Read together across the two parts of Chrétien's romance and on into the continuations, these episodes placed in the liminal space of tents explore the problematic continuum linking love, seduction, and rape, as well as the violence intertwining amorous and martial pursuits. Above all, this network of interconnected stories problematizes the role of retelling as the quintessential act of Arthurian romance. They force us to ask about the effects of representation, when tales of love and prowess are encoded into the memory of narration.

Fundamental to my analysis of this series and others is the notion that narrative architecture determines the structure of interpretation, as it aligns and superimposes characters and situations. Of course, isolating a single feature is as impossible as picking up an individual stitch in a sweater: the more you pull at it, the more you find it connected to all the threads knit together to form the whole, as the continuators' own rewritings of Chrétien constantly remind us. They may not always meet our expectations when they pick up the threads of his romance, but they are extremely careful readers of Chrétien, who practice the same kind of *inventio* as their master. They do not read or rewrite one episode at a time isolated from its extensions and connections, any more than Chrétien does. Just as Chrétien's (re)appropriations of his own material offer indirect commentaries that help us fill in what the narrator leaves unstated, so the continuators' returns to what is inscribed in the *Conte* may lead us to a better understanding of the possibilities and issues put into play by the originating author.

CHRÉTIEN'S CRISS-CROSSING ITINERARIES

In the *Conte du Graal*, the two scenes in which Perceval first encounters the damsel in the tent and then rediscovers her transformed by the Orgueilleux's jealousy are located within a series of associations that spread through the Perceval section and on into Gauvain's adventures. These episodes mark Perceval's trajectory out from his mother's manor in the forest and out again from his disquieting experience at the Fisher King's castle. They reverberate throughout the series of male/female encounters wherever there is a potential for erotic interaction, from the kind of locus amœnus associated with the tent in a clearing near the forest (cf. the pastourelle's *mise en scène*) to the castle-enclosed privacy of the lady's chamber. Thus, in Perceval's storyline, we move from his mother's advice on what chivalric and courtly conduct permits when meeting damsels, to the Tent Maiden, and then to Blancheflor, first as she appears in person at Biaurepaire, then as a *semblance* evoked by blood drops on snow. When Gauvain's storyline picks up where Perceval's stops, it moves not only forward in a linear pattern but backward in the opposite direction through successive associations with Perceval's own experiences. Gauvain meets first the Pucele aux Petites Manches, then the sister of the king at Escavalon, next the Male Pucele, and finally, unexpectedly, he moves 'back' to mothers who are now doubled across the generations from grandmother to sister.[8] All these encounters, in various assortments, will supply materials for reinvention of the Tent Maiden episode in the Gauvain Continuation and Gerbert.

Already in Chrétien, what is striking about these criss-crossing trajectories is the degree to which two heroes who begin at the antipodes in terms of their character and experience—Perceval the naïf and Gauvain the ladies' man—nevertheless end up more or less in the same boat, erotically speaking. In the unfinished state of Chrétien's romance, both Perceval and Gauvain have a series of encounters whose erotic potential remains unrealized. Both heroes fall short of the kind of passionate connection represented by the model of Lancelot's *amour passion*. According to their tendency to converge and diverge, it may be that Perceval and Gauvain, who already have more in common than appears on the surface, have still more to learn from each other's experience. Or is it the readers who have more to learn by learning how to read the double helix of their intertwined fictions? Henri Rey-Flaud has argued that Perceval represents in Chrétien's romance 'le devenir humain', the typical pattern of human development (1980). We need to complicate our view of that pattern of becoming as it reflects through the very different personalities and starting points of both heroes. Perceval and Gauvain operate in Chrétien's romance not only as two separate instances of human development but also as one multifaceted, composite identity strangely staged across two intermittent itineraries.[9]

Daniel Poirion has analyzed Perceval as a hero of failure, failed actions, and missed opportunities—a kind of anti-hero (though Poirion does not use the term) whose fear of *impuissance* is tied to the double taboos of his mother and Gornemant (1977). What are these taboos? In her parting advice, Perceval's mother asked him to remain, for her sake, in the first innocent stages of love

---

[8] Many scholars have identified and studied analogues between the Perceval and Gauvain sections—see e.g. Haidu (1968) and Saly (1976). See Laranjinha (1998) on the play of ironic contrast between the Perceval and Gauvain sections.

[9] Rey-Flaud's analysis of Gauvain and Perceval as doubles of each other (1999: 30–8) resembles the argument I make here but does so from a psychoanalytic framework. See also Kay on the notion of the double in epic and romance, discussed according to Girardian and psychoanalytic terms, as well as MacCannell's 'regime of the brother' (1995: 165–72).

and renounce the 'surplus', the euphemism for ultimate pleasure frequently invoked in courtly diction.[10]

> 'Dames et puceles servez,
> Si serez par tout honerez;
> Mais se vos alcune en proiez,
> Gardez que ne li anuiez
> De nule rien qui li desplaise;
> De pucele a molt qui le baise.
> S'ele le baisier vos consent,
> Le sorplus je vos defent,
> Se laissier le volez por moi.'
>
> (541–9)

('Serve ladies and maidens and you will be honored everywhere. But if you court one, make sure that you don't annoy her with anything that displeases her. A man who kisses a maiden receives much. If she grants you a kiss, I forbid you the rest, if you are willing to leave it for my sake.')

Gornemant's advice reiterates much of the mother's general counsel on the practice of chivalry and religious observance, but specifies in particular that Perceval should avoid talking too much: he should especially stop mentioning his mother as the guiding voice of his conduct.

> 'Ne ne parlez trop volentiers:
> Nus ne puet estre trop parliers
> Qui sovent tel chose ne die
> Qui torné li est affolie, . . .
> —Or ne dites jamais, biax frere,
> Fait li preudom, que vostre mere
> Vos ait apris rien, se je non.'
>
> (1648–51, 1675–7)[11]

('Don't be too quick to speak: no one who's too talkative can fail to say things that frequently make him look like a fool.' . . . 'Never say, fair brother,' says the worthy man, 'that your mother rather than I taught you anything.')

Poirion connects these inhibitions—no surplus in love or language—to the kind of censorship inscribed in courtly ideology. It is language itself that patrols the boundaries of the courtly. The salacious lies beyond what is properly said or described in courtly discourse, yet there is at the heart of romance a constant

---

[10] In his discussion of the links between sexuality and the parable of the sower, Rider points out that in medieval texts sexual restraint is a commonplace of maternal advice to sons (2001: 257–61).

[11] Huchet has explored the mother's and Gornemant's complementary interdicts from a Lacanian perspective. For Huchet, the mother's 'désir de l'Autre' has definitively blocked Perceval's sexual development at the oral stage: 'L'extraordinaire du *Conte du Graal*, c'est d'arrimer à la mère la question de l'impasse sexuelle' (1980: 78). The banishment of the mother from Perceval's discourse will be addressed in the next chapter.

flirtation with unspeakable sex, the surplus, sexual matters at the limits of what you can and cannot say in a courtly mode. Romance situates itself at this boundary, discretely titillates and hints at sex, while idealizing and ennobling it within the context of 'courtly love' (an expression I hesitate to introduce but it serves as a useful shorthand for a preoccupation with the art of love, whose parameters are continually explored and debated in a large variety of forms and texts from the twelfth century on). Long before Kathryn Gravdal raised the issue in *Ravishing Maidens: Writing Rape in Medieval French Literature and Law*, I believe Chrétien's last romance intentionally forced his reading public, medieval or modern, to ask what happens as we move along the continuum linking desire, seduction, and *jouissance*.

This is not to say that Chrétien's *Perceval* calls for a rejection of courtly love as a mere simulacrum of rape. Nor is it, in my view, a clerical argument for rejecting sex in all forms. I agree with Poirion's suggestion that the later Grail romances' push toward greater chastity and more exclusive focus on religion and purity constitute a misreading of Chrétien's romance (a strong misprision in Bloom's sense or, in their view, a necessary correction of Arthurian values[12]). But I would like to nuance Poirion's view that the romance pushes Perceval to escape the constraints of courtly ideology, which exercises 'sur le désir une fatale contrainte au détriment de la naturelle joie d'amour' (1977: 164). A questioning of *courtoisie*, yes, but I would argue as well for a significant interrogation of what constitutes the 'natural'—and how it needs to be refined.

As demonstrated by Perceval's first appearance in the romance, the 'natural joy of love' may still be somewhat suspect. Consider possible parallels between Perceval's behavior with the Tent Maiden (with its grave consequences) and the falcon's early morning attack, then abandonment of the goose whose blood dropped on the snow and occasioned Perceval's later reverie on Blancheflor. Both involve a male and female conjunction in a most aggressive form but not without displaced links to more erotic encounters. At the very least, the comparison serves to introduce an important theme in the romance: the relationship between nature and nurture, a topic the romance stages as a non-disjunctive opposition, mutually imbricated terms working together. The 'devenir humain' suggested in the patterns of Perceval's and Gauvain's development recalls the well-known proverb: 'reculer pour mieux sauter'. That is, Perceval's starting point in nature, isolated in his forest refuge, requires a process of learning that involves more than simply arriving at Arthur's court. He must be civilized into *courtoisie*, the courtly and the courteous (the realm in which Gauvain is already a master). But the linear movement forward involves risk, the risk of losing something valuable in the process. If it is in the nature of human development to unfold in a progression, at critical junctures we cannot avoid moving back to rediscover, reintegrate, correct, and move beyond. To continue moving forward, both

---

[12] Haidu (1977) describes the dynamic of how the Christian establishment responds to the problematic celebrity of Chrétien's romance.

Perceval and Gauvain must loop back to recover certain values eradicated or neglected by Arthurian ideology.[13]

Emerging from the forest, Perceval started below the courtly, the reasonable; he needs to learn and then, to a certain extent, unlearn and relearn *courtoisie*. Likewise, if Gauvain is to assume fully the status of hero rather than merely serve as standard measure for the hero—that is, if he is to step outside the role he has played in Chrétien's previous romances—he needs to go below and beyond the measure of the reasonable, the measure of courtly and chivalric conduct. Each hero must acquire the advantages and overcome the constraints of the other. They must regress, as well as progress.[14] 'Reculer pour mieux sauter' may indeed be the key figure not only in human development, but in Chrétien's romance as well. How does this look in terms of the series of erotic encounters outlined above? We need to follow more closely the specifics in each hero's trajectory as recorded in the *Conte du Graal*, in order to situate the continuations' responses to the complexities of their common model.

PERCEVAL AND THE TENT MAIDEN: SIMULATING RAPE

Judging by the narrator's *mise en scène*, interest falls first and foremost on Perceval's sexual development: these episodes are seen primarily from the male characters' point of view; although the woman does express her resistance and innocence, we know little of her own desires.[15] When he finds a lady sleeping in the tent he mistook for a church, Perceval's repeated claims to follow his mother's advice (the first sign of his menacing foolishness, from the lady's point of view, 687–8) produces both a caricature of rape and a kind of *impuissance*.[16] The 'sex' is both explosive and inhibited: climbing on top of her struggling body, Perceval kisses the damsel three, seven, or twenty times (depending on the manuscript). When he notices her emerald ring, desire is rerouted. Earlier, after forbidding him the 'sorplus', his mother told Perceval that he may accept such tokens as a gift:

[13] Cf. the looping pattern formed in the continuations once Gerbert is inserted in the ensemble (see Ch. 5).

[14] Ribard (1980–1: esp. 108) offers a similar analysis of the interplay between Perceval's and Gauvain's itineraries. In particular, he argues that Gauvain must undo his former identity in order to reconstruct a new one and thus motivates Gauvain's refusal to give his name at the Roche de Champguin.

[15] Sargent-Baur suggests that the Orgueilleux has placed his lady in the luxurious tent in a sort of 'elegant concubinage' (1992: 183): the scene allows us to read male desire reflected on her from inside and outside the romance. Later when Perceval rediscovers her riding along with her dress in tatters, the description of her exposed body peeking through the holes even as she tries modestly to cover herself (3719–45) may also be calculated to foreground erotic associations that are simultaneously undercut by the evident misery of her situation. On readers and male desire, see the feminist analyses of Krueger (1993), Burns (1993), McCracken (1998a), and Gravdal (1991).

[16] Cf. Dietmar Rieger's overview of rape in medieval French literature and his assessment of Perceval's negative example: 'le quasi-viol balourd de la demoiselle de la tente' (1988: 247).

> 'Mais s'ele a anel en son doi
> Ne a sa corroie almosniere,
> Se par amor ou par proiere
> Le vos done, bon m'ert et bel
> Que vos em portez son anel.
> De l'anel prendre vos doinz gié
> Et de l'aumosniere congié.'
>
>   (550–6)

('But if she has a ring on her finger or an almspurse at her belt, if for love or in answer to your plea, she gives it to you, then it's fine with me if you take away her ring. I give you permission to take her ring or almspurse.')

Perceval's memory is selective, controlled as it is by impulse: he has remembered the endpoint and not the if-clause, so he helps himself to the 'gift', with his mother's permission, despite the lady's physical and verbal resistance, which clearly but ineffectively points back to the condition that distinguishes gift from theft.[17]

Perceval's appetites continue to control the scene and next recall the hunger that originally motivated his desire to enter the 'church': famished after a night spent alone in the forest, Perceval was planning to ask God for something to eat.[18] Now finding some meat turnovers under a white napkin, Perceval helps himself and washes them down appreciatively with wine. Promising to reward the lady at some future point and ignoring her distress, Perceval then exits, having momentarily exhausted the sum total of permissible desires. As he pointed out to the damsel before prying the ring off her finger, he has been mindful of his mother's prohibition.

> 'Encor me dist, fait il, ma mere
> Qu'en vostre doit l'anel presisse,
> Ne que rien plus ne vos fesisse.'
>
>   (712–14)

('And she also told me, said he, that I might take the ring from your finger but do nothing more to you.')

Memory of his mother's words has been partial, not totally repressed: desire has been acknowledged, channeled, and limited. The narrator will later affirm during his first night at Biaurepaire, that, in fact, Perceval knows nothing of further

---

[17] Thus, through selection and omission, Perceval has and has not followed the letter of his mother's advice (cf. the discussion of Perceval's literal-mindedness in Ch. 1). Selective hearing has been one of Perceval's characteristics since the opening scene, not only in his willingness to contravene his mother's instructions (e.g. his readiness to confront what he thinks are devils, when he hears the knights in the forest) but also in his considerable delay in hearing (i.e. responding to) the knight's repeated query about knights and damsels who may have passed nearby. Perceval has indeed heard the question but his own desire to find out about the knight's armor and arms takes precedence. For further analysis of this passage, see Ch. 4.

[18] The playful move from spiritual to material levels of meaning echoes the prologue (see Ch. 1), but is here exploited for more obviously comic effect.

pleasures, specified as 'deduit | de pucele' (pleasure of a virgin, 1939–40)—a suggestive phrase that will reappear in Gerbert (13760). On the whole, what we see in the tent is a kind of innocent violence, operating at the elemental level of physical appetites.

As seen through the eyes of the Orgueilleux de la Lande, however, the encounter signifies sex beyond control or inhibition. Of course, he has not actually seen anything: his view is an interpretation based on the report given to him by his frightened lady. Once she describes how Perceval took her ring and stole her kisses, she inadvertently triggers in her lover's mind the usual *gradus amoris* with precisely the romantic connotations that escaped Perceval. The Orgueilleux's jealous rage immediately assumes the stages of love have run their course from kissing to the final act of love-making. His retelling to each knight who subsequently appears at the poor lady's side offers a caricature of Perceval's initial adventure (3840–83).[19] With great crudity and exaggeration, the Orgueilleux uses the discourse of misogyny to emphasize his view of excessive female sexuality: 'Feme qui se bouche abandone | Le sorplus molt de legier done' (3863–4: 'a woman who yields her mouth very easily gives the rest').

It is worth noting here that retelling is already an integral part of the episode and, even more significant, that retelling risks transposing as travesty the actions reported. Correction of that travesty occurs once the hero's own erotic interests have been firmly—if ambiguously—situated elsewhere with Blancheflor. By vanquishing the jealous lover in combat, Perceval proves the veracity of the damsel's version and corrects his own deficient grasp of past events. Whatever the risks involved, retelling, indeed multiple acts of retelling, may be required to gain a deeper, clearer understanding of the past and the future. Appropriately then, the restoration of harmony between the Orgueilleux and his beloved serves as prologue to the second stage of Perceval's relationship with Blancheflor, when his meditation on the three drops of blood against a background of white snow demonstrates his ability to recognize and reflect on his lady's *semblance*. This image constitutes a kind of visual retelling of his love relationship with Blancheflor: Perceval can now represent her to his mind's eye, make her present in her absence, become present himself to his own desire, even as he becomes absorbed in the love meditation, 'Si pense tant que il s'oblie' (4202: 'he thinks so much that he forgets himself').[20]

But Perceval's reverie is repeatedly interrupted by emissaries from Arthur's court, which has set out to find the 'fair unknown' and celebrate his achievements. When celebration turns to crisis, both Perceval and Gauvain must leave the court, Perceval to correct his failure at the Grail Castle, Gauvain to counter an accusation

---

[19] For the initiated public, these scenes also offer a caricature of Erec's quest with Enide in the position of bait, represented in Chrétien's first romance, as well as a variation on the custom of Logres described in *Le Chevalier de la Charrette*.

[20] According to Rey-Flaud, Perceval's emergence as subject depends on a momentary loss of self (1980: 22). Haidu, on the other hand, argues that Perceval is never able to attain subjectivity (2004: 103).

of treason. Is this another faulty retelling? We never find out, but the seneschal Guigambresil's complaint that Gauvain has killed the king of Escavalon's father forces Arthur's nephew to defend his honor in a judicial combat at Escavalon. The narrator explicitly announces that he will speak at length of Gauvain before returning to Perceval. Unexpectedly and without explanation, Chrétien's double-stranded and decentered romance requires us to leap from Perceval's to Gauvain's plot line. As I suggested earlier, we can best grapple with that strange juxtaposition if we locate both on the common trajectory of human development and read Gauvain's story as, in some sense, a continuation of Perceval's.

TOO LITTLE AND TOO MUCH FOR
THE LADIES' MAN

Gauvain's first encounter with the opposite sex is incongruous: the consummate ladies' man meets a young girl in pigtails, apparently well below the age of eligibility even by medieval standards. She is the Pucele aux Petites Manches, the maiden with sleeves so small they appear to be written on her arms. The narrative firmly places her in the family context as beloved daughter and bratty younger sister (at least from her older sister's point of view). As her 'proper' name suggests, she constitutes for Gauvain a brief return to the innocence of youth. A hero whose amorous desires and love service are always on high here takes a touching and sweetly comic turn (recalling the broader farce of Perceval's opening adventure in a minor and decidedly more courtly key). As Jeanne Lods points out (1978: 378), Gauvain treats the *pucele* with dignity, honors the woman to be in the amorous young girl who recognizes his worth when others heap scorn on him (since he has so far failed to join in the tournament at Tintagel, which has interrupted his journey to Escavalon). At her request and with a large sleeve fabricated by her father fixed to his lance as a love token, Gauvain dominates the next day's fighting as the little sister's champion, avenges the slap she received from her older sister, and teaches both the lady and her knight a lesson about *vantardise* and *vaine gloire* (cf. the prologue). At day's end, Gauvain promises to remain in the *pucele*'s service and return whenever she sends for him, even when his hair turns gray and white (5604–10)—which we may recognize as a charming parody of his promise to Lunete in *Le Chevalier au Lion*. At the moment of departure, moving completely outside the mode of typical courtly gestures, the *pucele* impetuously kisses his foot to make sure that Gauvain will never forget her. Is it too early for the young maiden, too late for Gauvain? In any case, the maiden's intervention gently moves Gauvain back to youth, before or beyond the reasonable stance of avoiding the tournament for fear that it might interfere with his judicial obligation. The episode constitutes a youthful phase for the mature hero that puts him in parallel with the young Perceval (re)learning the art of chivalry. If Gauvain is to evolve beyond the fixed norm he represents in

Chrétien's other romances, then he must take this first step into character evolution and open-ended heroic action.[21] After all, Lancelot did not let prudence negate action when he decided to rescue his amorous hostess, even at the risk of endangering his quest for the queen.

With the sister of the king at Escavalon, we see another angle: going too far too fast with an inappropriate object of desire. Gauvain's hostess is the daughter of the slain king; the guest is the unrecognized enemy she has been instructed to treat like her brother. When a vavasor identifies Gauvain and rallies the citizens of Escavalon against him and the sister, the discourse of misogyny (5840–65) once again travesties an innocent encounter (innocent at least in the couple's eyes).

> 'En cele n'a de feme rien
> Qui het le mal et le bien aime; . . .
> Mais tu iez feme, bien le voi,
> Que cil la qui siet dalez toi
> Ocist ton pere, et tu le baises!
> Quant feme puet avoir ses aises,
> Del soreplus petit li chaut.'
>
> (5855–56, 5859–63)

('In the one who hates evil and loves good there's nothing of woman . . . but you are a woman, I see well, who kisses the man, seated there beside you, who killed your father! When a woman can have her pleasure, she worries little about the rest.')

The surplus, that useful catch all word so often carrying the trace of unnarratable desire, has here been attached to the kind of vengeance the lady should be seeking: not kissing and embracing but tearing Gauvain's heart from his chest literally, not figuratively (5844–9).

In this episode, 'normal' courtly dalliance generates violence, first through the vavasor's interpretive words, then through actions, as the townspeople begin their attack against the tower. The situation may seem dire but the comedy of an unarmed Gauvain using a chessboard for his shield, while the unjustly maligned lady heaves large chess pieces as missiles, recalls the comic elements of Perceval's early encounters.[22] On a darker note, however, the episode anticipates a thread that will be elaborated in the continuations, where combats continue to escalate the violence embedded in erotic encounters that violate limits imposed by family ties, social order, and institutions. Within the *Conte*, the temporary resolution of Gauvain's quarrel at Escavalon for the first time seems to offer some rationale, as yet unclear, for including Gauvain in a story of the Grail, which at first seemed to belong to Perceval alone.

The compromise reached with Gauvain's host now obligates the second hero to quest for the lance that bleeds, the mysterious object preceding the Grail

---

[21] Cf. Ribard's play on Gauvain's name and the 'borne de Galvoie' as doubles: Gauvain must go beyond himself (1984: 85–6).

[22] See Haidu (1968) on comic and ironic distantiation typical of Chrétien's discourse.

cortege, which was also supposed to provoke a very specific question from Perceval. Gauvain's task is rather different—bring the lance to Escavalon, or return after a year of questing. But the configuration of episodes creates enticing, if enigmatic, echoes across their two trajectories.[23] Gauvain and the sister parallel Perceval and Blancheflor as gateway encounters to Grail adventures. As we saw in Chapter 1, the Second Continuation's Chessboard Lady adventures respond to that implicit suggestion. Chrétien himself reinforces the associations by switching plot lines once again, just as Gauvain sets off on his quest. The recall of events at the Grail Castle undoubtedly triggers the return to Perceval, whose visit to his hermit uncle confirms the connection between his mother and the Grail quest but leaves unclarified the link to Blancheflor and the shape of future action.

GAUVAIN AND THE MALE PUCELE: THINKING ABOUT RAPE

When the narrator returns to Gauvain after the five-year time warp of Perceval's hermit episode, he picks up the second hero's story exactly where he left it, but that story now grows considerably more complex—perhaps under the influence of Perceval's, although there is no direct indication of how these new adventures may relate to either heroes' Grail Castle quests. Fragments of episodes are interlaced through an extended series of adventures with the Male Pucele, the Evil Maiden (the pun on 'male' may not be incidental). There is no tent here, but her proper name, the Orgueilleuse de Nogres (or Logres, in some manuscripts), invites us to see through the role reversals a set of variations on Perceval's encounter with the Tent Maiden and the Orgueilleux de la Lande. Gauvain spots her sitting alone in a meadow, gazing in a mirror. He hastens toward her until checked by sharp words. She knows what he is thinking: raptus, which in medieval usage runs the gamut from abduction to rape, under the assumption (related to the Orgueilleux's) that once a woman has been seized, the 'sorplus' easily follows.

> 'Or me dites, amie bele,
> De coi vos fustes apensee,
> Qui si tost m'avez amembree
> Mesure, et ne savez por coi.'
> —'Si faz, chevalier, par ma foi,
> Que je sai bien que vos pensez.'
> —'Et coi?' fait il.—'Vos me volez
> Prendre et porter ci contreval
> Sor le col de vostre cheval.'
> —'Voir vos avez dit, damoisele.'

> (6692–701)

[23] Cf. Sasaki's examination of how the motif of the lance is linked to the Chapel of the Black Hand, an episode that develops later across three continuations (1984).

('Now tell me, fair friend, what were you thinking of when you so quickly told me to remember moderation and you don't know why?' 'Yes I do, knight, by my faith, for I know exactly what you are thinking.' 'And what?' says he. 'You want to take me and carry me away on your horse.' 'You've spoken truly, damsel.')

The boisterous impulsivity momentarily reminds us of Perceval, but in contrast to the *nice* who was at first unaware of his desire (or unaware of different levels of desire), Gauvain has characteristically been in frequent contact with his. We may nevertheless be surprised to find him acknowledging as true a desire to grab this beautiful lady and ride off with her.

Significantly, one of the stories interlaced with the Male Pucele's is that of a rapist, Greoreas, who violated the custom of Logres that protects women traveling alone (the same custom that led to the death of the Male Pucele's beloved, as she will later reveal).[24] As executor of the king's justice, Gauvain severely punished Greoreas by making him eat for a month with the dogs (7109–25)—a punishment designed to underline the animal instincts he failed to curb. In his encounter with the Male Pucele, Gauvain becomes aware of and controls his own desire for raptus. Does he acknowledge implicitly, or at least lead readers to discover in this paragon of courtliness, a fellowship with Greoreas at the level of common appetite?[25] The echoing sound of their names may express some expectation of kinship—extended to Guigambresil and Guiromelant as well. Gauvain's actions, however, assert a fundamental difference in his ability to exercise contol over the basest part of his 'normally' human nature. Throughout an increasingly bizarre series of encounters, Gauvain listens to and humbly accepts the harsh speech of the Male Pucele, demonstrates a humility and patience that strike us as something new in a man who elsewhere exhibits a bit of the vainglory typically associated with knights in the panoply of medieval vices. More overtones of Lancelot chastened, all the better to be exalted by love service? Such a reading is extrapolated by Wolfram von Eschenbach in *Parzival*, when the translation/adaptation elaborates Gauvain's impulse of lust as love. Within the *Conte*, this relationship may offer a new take on the virtue of *carité* extolled in Chrétien's prologue to praise his patron Philip of Flanders. In Gauvain's dealings with the Male Pucele, the spiritual rather than the material sense of charity is foregrounded in Gauvain's unrewarded actions on her behalf, even in the face of her 'vilain gap ne parole estoute' (see Chapter 1).

In this odd couple, the Male Pucele remains in control and that means no touching. Gauvain may not even help her mount; she is repelled by the very idea. Here finally is the story of a woman's desire, as we eventually learn it, along with Gauvain, from her own account.[26] The sting of her uncourtly language is, in fact,

[24] Adventures cast in the mold of the custom of Logres are endlessly repeated and problematized throughout the *Conte du Graal* (see Ch. 4).

[25] Huchet (1980: 91) also links Greoreas to Perceval through the Tent Maiden episode.

[26] The narrator has also made us privy to some of Blancheflor's desires earlier in the other plot line, depite his primary focus on the male point of view. Kay analyzes the narration of woman's desire as counternarrative (1995: 146–7).

a tool, an expression of her double desire for revenge and death. Unceasing love for her beloved, a knight killed by Guiromelant, drives her to seek death by forcing a series of defenders to turn on her, so she hopes, and kill her. If she has thereby sought an end to her suffering, she has simultaneously used her beauty and her tongue to punish these knightly escorts, representatives of chivalry, which according to Gornemant is the highest order (1635: 'Le plus haute ordene'), whose values should operate in her defense but have instead made her the hapless victim of any knight stronger than her beloved.[27] Mutatis mutandis, the deadly trap she has reenacted countless times resembles that of the first Orgueilleux. Her transformation and healing, revealed when she retells her past, emerge unexpectedly in response to Gauvain's willingness to do the impossible at her request. By jumping back and forth across the Gué Périlleux, he accomplishes (albeit with some awkward scrambling the first time across) what no knight before him had ever done.[28] Expecting to send him to his death, the Male Pucele has instead led Gauvain unreasonably beyond normal limitations—and led herself back to human society.

In this light, it may not be surprising that the interlaced series of encounters with the Male Pucele leads Gauvain to, out from, and back again to the Roche de Champguin, the queens' enchanted castle, where the ladies' man meets his mother, grandmother, and sister. Gauvain and mothers are here pushed beyond the normal and the normative for Arthurian romance, thus offering another opportunity to explore the unreasonable conjunction of sexuality and mothers in Chrétien's 'Story of the Grail'. Paradoxically, Gauvain finds what Perceval was seeking and then abandoned (too soon?). Gauvain finds what he was not seeking, since he thought his mother and grandmother long dead and did not even know of his sister's existence. It remains to be seen what Chrétien might have done with their recognition scene, which Gauvain has purposely delayed by untypically withholding his name before he knows who these ladies are (8350–3). Chrétien's romance breaks off before Arthur's court hears the message summoning them to witness Gauvain's juridical combat against Guiromelant (who has added a second accusation of treasonous murder against the king's nephew). What would Chrétien have made of their grand reunion? Unfortunately, he has himself abandoned the narrative conjunction too soon for us to know.

When the first, unknown continuator picks up the thread to complete the adventure left dangling on an incomplete sentence, he makes nothing at all of the belated meeting of mothers and sons. Given the suspense created in Chrétien's fragment, we cannot help but feel cheated by the continuator's failure to meet

---

[27] Cf. the mother's advice on protecting women (*pucele* or *dame*) in need (532–42), echoed by Gornemant (1656–62). Both women offer a critique of chivalry made all the more poignant by their personal suffering.

[28] Gauvain earlier encountered the Male Pucele by daring to pass beyond ' "la bosne de Galvoie | Que chevaliers ne puet passer | Qui jamais puisse retorner" ' (6602–4: "the boundary of Galway that no knight can pass beyond or return from"), despite Greoreas's warnings.

head on the implications of their reunion. But perhaps the problematic conjunction of mothers and sexuality cannot be approached directly in romance. Perhaps it can only be broached indirectly through displacements, as successive continuators return to and reinvent Chrétien's matter. In one of the last scenes written by Chrétien, Gauvain sits with his sister, quietly delivering the message and ring from her would-be lover Guiromelant, while his mother and grandmother comment on what a beautiful couple the two of them make together. The grandmother wishes them married and hopes her granddaughter will please the man who has put an end to the castle's enchantment as much as Lavinia pleased Eneas. The mother responds by hoping they will be like brother and sister, with a love so strong they become as one flesh (9047–64).[29] Once the unconscious irony embedded in these remarks has been allowed to make its effect, the narrator is quick to reassure us that, as soon as all the recognitions fall into place, the love between Gauvain and Clarissant will be only and appropriately that of the brother and sister they really are: the literal level of their kinship will remove any indiscretion in the figurative play embedded in the biblically and classically phrased wishes.

The scene of courtly dalliance observed, however incorrectly, by the mothers[30] recalls the advice Perceval's mother gave him regarding sex and the single girl. At that point, Perceval was urged to stop in the early stages of love: only kissing and exchanging gifts. No longer dealing with inexperienced adolescents like Perceval, these mothers envision the next appropriate step: nuptials leading to sexual fusion as one flesh. Their wishes for the couple imply no incompatibility between love and marriage, but rather a desirable combination and natural progression—naturalized in romance at least, if not in the society contemporary with Chrétien. But the normal continuation of life-cycle events may also become problematic in the world of romance: consider the variety of roles that marriage has already played in *Erec*, *Cligès*, and *Yvain*. In the *Conte* thus far, disruption has been the prevalent mode, which has led a number of modern scholars to speculate that the romance's unfinished state is more structural than accidental, integral to an underlying design resistant to *achèvement*. See Bloch (1983: 206–7), Pickens (1977: 285–6), Ribard (1976: 315–21). Nevertheless, on the level of the syntagm, the mothers' speculation as well as the narrator's comments imply there is more to

---

[29] On the biblical allusion embedded in this phrase (left out of Guiot's copy) and the issue of incest, see Gouttebroze (1995). Cf. Poirion on the mythic background and overtones of incest (1973, 1986, as well as notes to his Pléiade edn.). Régnier-Bohler's analysis of the sister in relation to the dissemination of knowledge and the hero's identity, explored in a number of Grail romances, concludes that '[n]ulle jonction incestueuse n'est mise en œuvre dans les récits arthuriens qui font appel à la figure sororale' (1995: 25). Gouttebroze (1983) offers a psychocritical approach that takes off from Lévi-Strauss's reading of Perceval as an anti-Œdipus but he too rejects the notion that incest is at the heart of the *Conte*.

[30] Although the mode of interpretation here goes in the direction of love and union, their misreading of Gauvain and his sister's tête-à-tête recalls that of the vavasor in Escavalon when he found Gauvain with another sister. In the course of his adventures, Gauvain seems caught in a series of misalliances, which often work out to surprising consequences.

be written in order to work out how lovers and mothers may be integrated in a story of the Grail that involves interlacing heroes. Medieval continuators will respond to that apparent call for literary if not sexual generation.

The next chapter will explore further the complexities linking sons and mothers, mothers and lovers in these stories. In anticipation, I would suggest that the anomalous importance of mothers in both heroes' itineraries might be tied to Chrétien's exploration in this romance of many different types of love marking different phases of human development, from filial and maternal love to sexual love to love of God, the prologue's *carité*.[31] Wider in scope than Chrétien's previous studies of love, the *Conte du Graal* delineates the importance of differentiating and following appropriate stages, rather than claiming, as the *Queste del Saint Graal* will, the incompatibility of earthly and divine love. Perceval did not, could not return for his mother's authorization to move on to the next stage, as he intended when he left Blancheflor, promising to return with his mother alive or dead. Has that promise been forgotten by the narrative, as Perceval himself seems to have forgotten, or does Gauvain's own experience substitute for, intertwine with, and move forward the stages of Perceval's progress in love? Has the ladies' man actually made any progress beyond the naïf, as his success on the 'Lit de la Merveille' (7805) seems to suggest?[32]

This is where Chrétien's abandonment, intentional or unintentional, forces us to move on to the continuations. If *impuissance* marks both Perceval and Gauvain in *Le Conte du Graal*, we may well ask how they measure up in the hands of continuators. The results are definitely mixed. Perceval's adventures with the Chessboard Lady, as narrated in the Second Continuation, resemble the kind of episodic flirtation we more readily associate with Gauvain and suggest a certain potency, but the status of his relations with Blancheflor remains unclear (as we saw in Chapter 1).[33] Perceval's subsequent image shows no integration of sexuality. Writing under the influence of the *Queste del Saint Graal*, the last two continuators present a Perceval who is totally and unambiguously chaste, despite several returns to Biaurepaire and eventual marriage with Blancheflor. On the other hand, by shifting the Tent Maiden adventure into the plot of the second hero, the First and Fourth Continuations move Gauvain into the realm of *puissance* to explore the possibility of succession, literal and figurative, inscribed in Chrétien's last unfinished episode.

---

[31] The hermit assures Perceval that his mother's love, operating in the spiritual realm of prayer, has continued to protect him even after her death. The notion of love moving hierarchically from the creature to the creator is at least as old as Plato's *Symposium*. Cf. how Gauvain's relation with the Male Pucele begins with intimations of rape and then moves to charity, relocating the erotic connection and offering an enticing model for Gerbert's Tent Maiden episode.

[32] Although the Bed of Marvels seems to have been dislocated from any amorous adventure, we may wonder if it points to the erotic elsewhere as a possible thread to be developed (as the mothers' hopes seem to suggest). The bed's link to enchantment and violent attack recalls Lancelot's experience with a series of beds in the *Chevalier de la Charrette* (see Sarah White 1983).

[33] Wolfram, on the other hand, has no problem making Parzival's relationship with Condwiramurs a fruitful one, with the birth of twin sons and eventual reunion.

THE FIRST CONTINUATION'S GAUVAIN:
CONFESSING RAPE

As he picks up Gauvain's story without returning to that of Perceval, the first continuator confirms Gauvain's independent status as romance hero.[34] In a complex and elaborate narrative development worthy of Chrétien, the anonymous romancer invents a Tent Maiden episode that reveals the intricacies, as well as conflicts, involved in conjoining erotic and family relations. The basic outline of the adventure emerges in William Roach's division of the First Continuation into six large sections, each containing multiple episodes (see Appendix 1). The two major parts of the Tent Maiden episode are embedded in what Roach identifies as the second and fourth sections. The first part appears as an amorous interlude framed by Arthur's siege of Bran de Branlant's castle (T, 2546–987). The built-in continuation (doubly motivated since, as the hero departs, we are told that the damsel is pregnant) will not be realized until Gauvain encounters her brother Bran de Lis a second time. The entire 'romance' of Caradoc (almost 6,000 verses) is then inserted between the two widely separated halves of the episode. The second part begins in section IV. On the way to Chastel Orguelleus to rescue one of Arthur's knights, Gauvain finds himself obliged to retell his earlier adventure and concludes it with a final combat against Bran de Lis.

Gauvain's retelling of the past takes the readers by surprise: not only is his version almost twice as long as the narrator's (567 and 367 verses, respectively); he transforms the original events in a way that plays off the Orgueilleux's distorted retelling in the *Conte du Graal*.[35] A short return to Chastel de Lis at the end of the Chastel Orguelleus section (pp. 340–5) furnishes an epilogue, during which the lovers' son is kidnapped. The story is picked up again and continued briefly at the end of the next section, as Gauvain's now grown-up son reappears defending a ford, while his lady waits in a nearby tent. When Gauvain encounters him there, combat leads to recognition, and the episode has come full

---

[34] Perceval does, however, make a brief appearance in the Long and Mixed versions of the First Continuation during the long tournament episode narrated in the *Livre de Caradoc*. In the series of marriages that mark the triumphant end of that episode, Perceval is rather surprisingly married to Alardin's sister, whose only name is the 'pucele du paveillon' (I, 4201–2; II, 9553): another maiden, another tent, in this case belonging to her brother Alardin. The redactor of ms. T has 'corrected' this unacceptable marriage by omitting Perceval's name, retaining only the epithet used along with it in manuscripts EMQU (II, 9554–5), and deferring identification of the 'buen meschin': 'Nel weil nomer a ceste fois' (I, 5975: 'I don't want to name him at this point'). Though subsequent continuators either ignored or declined to credit this marriage (neither the tournament nor the marriages appear in the Short Redaction), it stands as another testament to the conviction among numbers of Chrétien's 12th-cent. readers that Perceval's involvement in the Grail quest does not disqualify him from the pleasures of love and marriage.

[35] There are also some touches that recall Calogrenant's recital of shame in *Yvain*, suggesting the continuator's general familiarity with Chrétien's romances.

circle back to the originating space of the tent.[36] By putting together as well as separating and coordinating this series of stories, the first continuator orchestrates a complex *conjointure* of the sort we might expect from Chrétien—and he does so by following the diverse strands of the Tent Maiden associations spun out across both parts of the *Conte du Graal*.

To make sense of this complex narrative structure requires more detailed analysis of specifics. The series is initiated when, recuperating from a wound that has kept him confined for months, Gauvain rides out to test his strength and enjoy a beautiful springtime morning (cf. the opening of the *Conte*). He happens upon a tent set up near a fountain (2593–4): the time and place of love seem perfectly joined for adventure. The idea of the tent as a female space, which turned out to be a highly contested illusion in Chrétien, is here realized and synchronized with the action. The change is cued immediately by the image of a young woman sitting up rather than sleeping on her bed. This physical change in her placement also entails a dramatic shift to the *pucele*'s point of view and her own expression of desire. Like the fairy who acts out her *amor de lonh* for Lanval, this young lady has long been in love with Gauvain and wants nothing more than to consummate that love as soon as she verifies that the knight is indeed Gauvain.[37]

As the initiator of love, the *pucele* steps outside the normal constraints of courtly standards, as she makes quite clear in her own words by insisting on the literal, not simply conventional, meaning contained in standard formulas of greeting. With Gauvain, for example, before she knows who he is, she rejects his gallant salutation, 'ma dolce amie chiere' (2621: 'my sweet, dear friend'), and insists on being properly designated as a maiden, *pucele*. Responding to his corrected greeting, she then replies, 'may God keep my lord Gauvain and you afterward' (2630–1). The unexpected phrase provokes an explanation that leads Gauvain to volunteer his name without waiting to be asked. She demands verification of his identity by matching his face and portrait, then allows Gauvain to satisfy her longstanding desire:

> D'amor, de jeu, de cortoisie
> Ont puis ensamble tant parlé
> Et bonement ris et jüé,
> Tant qu'a perdu non de pucele,
> S'a non amie et damoisele.
>
> (2715–19)[38]

---

[36] In the romance's last section, the action veers off again to follow the adventures of Gauvain's brother Guerrehes. This story also involves retelling something the knight would prefer to keep to himself. The First Continuation thus faithfully retains the general character of the *Conte* with its multiple heroes and decentered tale (Bruckner 1993a).

[37] Elements of this episode reappear in the Prose *Lancelot*, where Gauvain manages to penetrate a castle in order to find the castellan's daughter, guarded by her twenty knights, who awaits the occasion to consummate her love for Gauvain. As in the Tent Maiden episodes in the First Continuation and Gerbert, love-making triggers considerable combat. See Kennedy's edn. (I, 507–14).

[38] The narrator's words echo the description of Enide the morning after her wedding night (*Erec* 2103).

(Of love and play [love-making] and courtesy they then talked so much together and laughed so well and played so much that she lost the name of maiden and is now named beloved and damsel.)

Here the initial stage of courtly play passes quickly and effectively to the 'sorplus'. Shortly after Gauvain departs, having arranged to come back and take her with him later, her father and then her brother arrive at the tent. Each time, in her now post-virginal state, the damsel forthrightly rejects the designation of *pucele*:

> 'Vo fille sui, ce n'est pas gas;
> Mais pucele ne sui je pas. . . .
> [Mesire Gavains] Mon pucelage me toli;
> Piech'a jel vos avoie dit
> Que il l'aroit sanz contredit.'
>
> (2735–6, 2740–2)

('It's no joke, I am your daughter but I'm not a maiden . . . My lord Gauvain took my maidenhood; I've told you for some time that he would have it with no gainsaying'—cf. 2803–9, with the brother.)

This damsel speaks consistently with neither evasion nor euphemism; she does so without consideration for who may be listening or what consequences her speech act may entail.

These repeated transgressions of normal courtly conduct and discourse recall those perpetrated by Perceval and the Male Pucele. Here again the play is both comic and lethal. The damsel's father and brother, guardians of her virginity, direct their anger against Gauvain. This is now an affair among men, responsible for any offense against their lineage.[39] Despite Gauvain's offers of reparation and marriage, the ensuing combats multiply the offense: the father is killed and the death of an uncle recalled as additional incitement to vengeance. When the combat between Gauvain and the damsel's brother is interrupted and postponed for a future meeting (in consideration of Gauvain's previous wound), the narrative leaves open a space for expectation to build across more than 6,000 verses. In this account, there are many family members but no mothers, until the erstwhile maiden, as announced at the end of this segment, gives birth.

The second part of the episode takes place at Bran de Lis's castle, a social space where the problematic of sexuality and family relationships—absent for Perceval's Tent Maiden but already inscribed in Gauvain's adventures at Tintagel and Escavalon—will play out with a new twist. Gauvain's retelling unexpectedly transforms a tale of female desire into a story of rape. Forced to explain to Arthur why he has suddenly armed for combat in some unknown castle, Gauvain relates how he came upon a damsel sleeping in a tent and forced himself upon her in spite of her resistance. As in the Orgueilleux's account, female desire is obscured and misrepresented: Gauvain's own desire for appropriation replaces and covers

---

[39] Cf. the biblical account of how her brothers avenge the rape of Dinah (Genesis 32).

over the woman's desire repeatedly expressed by her with uncharacteristic direct-
ness in the narrator's first account.[40] A similar scenario was enacted with the
damsel's brother, or rather brothers, since they are now doubled in Gauvain's
version. As represented by Gauvain, they appear unable to believe that the man
they have surprised in their sister's tent, guilty of such a vile, base act ('garçonerie',
10115), the work of a churl ('oevre de garchon', 10113), could possibly be
'Mesire Gauvain' (10107).

Ironically, the rape story told by a man constitutes a return to courtly ideology,
even if it is *courtoisie* as defined by a violation of its code.[41] Unlike the maiden's
original action and discourse, Gauvain's reported act of rape designates a transgression that stays within the expected bounds of the courtly, erotic system. It has
already been anticipated by Greoreas's violation of the custom of Logres and
Gauvain's own admission that he wanted to carry off the Male Pucele, even though
single women unaccompanied should be respected by all self-respecting knights.

Gauvain's readiness to marry his *amie* would lead to a normalization that puts
the woman's desire back into the social institution of marriage, but his repeated
offers are rejected in favor of vendetta. Even when the damsel places herself and
Gauvain's 5-year-old child in the midst of their ferocious swordplay, only the
intervention of King Arthur can settle the quarrel between father and uncle.[42]
The reconciliation does not include marriage; there is succession, but not
legitimacy. She who acts upon her own desire bears fruit in the first continuator's
reinvention: she produces a son who leads to yet more stories. But Gauvain is not
about to become a family man. Indeed, he refuses to participate in the quest
when his son is mysteriously kidnapped, though he does eventually encounter
him—as he will encounter others in *Le Bel Inconnu* and *Gliglois*, where they
appear as the Fair Unknown (cf. Perceval's original appearance at Arthur's court),
whose origin ultimately receives the imprimatur of their father Gauvain. Arthur's
nephew retains his erotic appeal, as well as his availability, and his *amie* Guilorete
remains at Arthur's court, one in a series.[43]

[40] Frappier (1958: 339) argued that Gauvain lies in order to protect the woman's reputation, less
endangered by rape than willing sex, an idea vehemently rejected by Gallais (1988–9: 4, 2261–4).
Other interpretations depend on speculation about the textual editing of successive versions: see
Bruckner (1987–8: 255–8), Van Coolput (1986: 23–8, 32–3), and Gallais (1964b; 1988–9: 4,
2265–83). On the positive and negative trajectories of Gauvain's reputation, see Busby (1980), esp.
on the Pucelle de Lis episode in the Short version (160–70) and the summary view of Gauvain's role
in the Grail romances (233–5, 238). Cf. Leupin's non-mimetic reading of the two versions (1979).

[41] In the pastourelle tradition in northern France, the issue of *courtoisie* also involves both class
and appropriate manners, and the shepherdess serves as the counterpart of the courtly lady of
troubadour and trouvère lyric.

[42] At this point, the continuator seems to echo (with variations on significant elements) the
Guiromelant episode where he picked up Chrétien's unfinished romance.

[43] The Tent Maiden is named by the narrator as Guilorete only at the moment when she arrives
at Arthur's court (12678). Earlier in the narrative, well before the Tent Maiden adventure, Guilorete
was mentioned in passing as an *amie* who sent Gauvain a penant for his lance, a love token that
increased his prowess (811–16). Only retrospectively can this Guilorete be identified with the Tent
Maiden.

GERBERT'S GAUVAIN: ACTING OUT RAPE

The First Continuation's riffs on the Tent Maiden episode thus present a multifaceted view of Gauvain and the woman in the tent. Gauvain's potency is a measure of the partial success he achieves in his Grail Castle visit—and a measure, too, of the first continuator's own power to reconnect and reinvent a wide range of Chrétien's materials. Gerbert demonstrates a similar capacity. If the First Continuation moves from voluntary sex to rape, Gerbert starts with rape, as if Gauvain's travestied retelling gave rise to Gerbert's variations. From rape the continuator moves back to the realm of love relations, all set within the conflicting claims of family. In some sense, Gerbert's retelling seems to revel in the 'illegitimate'. There is no succession of any kind but a temporary delight in the 'joie d'amour' generally denied in this more chaste and repentent vision of the Grail knight. The tent adventure's two separate parts are now joined in one elaborate episode, as the locus moves from tent to castle, and then from lady's chamber to the nearby forest. In his continuation, Gerbert gives us only one major episode for Gauvain, 1,698 verses for the lady's man (12379–14077), surrounded by more than 15,000 verses focused on the chaste Perceval. This is indeed a kind of interlude that plays on all the meanings of the term.

Passing a difficult ford, Gauvain spots a tent in the middle of a meadow. This tent (sans eagle) is a trap, where he will be offered hospitality by a damsel apparently playing a role similar to that of the First Continuation's Tent Maiden. But this one offers love as a test, the *assag* familiar in troubadour lyric: if Gauvain agrees to share her bed, naked but chaste all night, she promises to grant him the full measure of her charms in the morning. 'Si porrez de moi vo bon faire | Et vostre cors du mien refaire' (II, 12449–50: 'then you can do as you will with me, and your body with mine'). Her words and, especially, the narrator's seek to enflame Gauvain's desire:

> Gavains comencha a esprendre
> Et plus et plus quant il l'entent....
> Mais quant plus la dame regarde
> Plus l'esprent Amours et alume.
> Cele qui bien set la costume
> D'engignier home et de sozprendre
> Le regarde por mieus esprendre...
>
> (12458–9, 12464–8)

(Gauvain begins to burn with desire more and more as he listens to her.... But the more he looks at the lady, the more Love burns and lights his fire. The lady, who knows well the custom of deceiving and surprising a man, looks at him all the better to arouse his desire...)

The language of desire is insistent, but menacing in the narrator's foreshadowing: a hidden knife puts into question which body will be penetrated. The tension between language and act is intensified, when Gauvain is described as forcing on the maiden the 'ju d'Amours' (12627: game of love): 'Weille ou non, sosfrir li estuet | Le ju de mon seignor Gavain' (12638–9: 'willing or not, she must suffer my lord Gauvain's game'). The love game of the First Continuation has been turned radically inside out.

This deeply ironic distortion of courtly discourse recalls once again the problem of language. Where the Orgueilleux and the vavasor in Chrétien's *Conte* masked innocence with misogynistic tales of lust, the narrator here dresses up rape in courtly diction. Later Gauvain himself will describe his action as discretely as possible, using the expression the lady herself introduced: 'Mon bon en fis dont ele ot ire' (13195: 'I took my pleasure with her, which caused her distress'). It is the girl's father who calls a spade a spade: 'Ma fille avez despucelee' (13244: 'you've deflowered my daughter').[44] His charge echoes the direct language of the First Continuation: the Tent Maiden's boast, her father and brother's accusations.

Gerbert's constant transpositions put into question the link between word and referent, meaning and language. They create a kind of blur that makes it difficult to identify the referent or fix signification. Chrétien's own usage prepares and anticipates the problem of slippage which the continuators will exploit in their distinctive ways. In the *Conte du Graal*, the status of the first woman in the tent is ambiguous in the discourse of narrator and characters. There is no simple linear progression in the words that identify her as *damoiselle*, *pucele*, *amie*, and the pejorative *feme*.[45] The choice seems random, shifting, reflecting changing points of view, the uncertainty about what goes on in the tent with Perceval and the Orgueilleux.[46] But where Chrétien's text is voluntarily ambiguous (cf. the doubtful status of sexual relations between Perceval and Blancheflor), the continuators' word play tends to pin down meaning, even as it floats and transforms itself.

Gerbert's narrator initially flirts with uncertainty in designating the woman in the tent. She is a *damoisele* (12399), a *dame* (12422, 12425, 12464, 12569), a *pucele* (12623), but also an *anemie* (12556). Given the religious discourse frequently invoked in this romance, as well as the narrator's repeated warnings about her game of deception, we begin to wonder if she is the Enemy, a figure of the devil anticipated by the Satanic figure of the Male Pucele.[47] Bloiesine's subsequent metamorphosis into Gauvain's *amie* recalls, even as it performs a

---

[44] When he later threatens Gauvain, 'Onques mais deduis de pucele | N'achata onques hom plus chier' (13760: 'a man never bought so dearly the pleasure of a virgin'), his expression 'deduis de pucele' echoes farther back to Chrétien's romance and the description of Perceval's ignorance about sex, described by the narrator during his first night at Biaurepaire (see above).

[45] *damoiselle*: 671, 679, 759, 787, 3780, 3846, 3965, 3986, 4010; *pucele*: 682, 687, 697, 717, 723, 751, 3715, 3836; *amie*: 767, 786, 3787, 3885, 3939, 3998, 4050; *feme*: 3860, 3863, 3868.

[46] Similarly, the Male Pucele elicits a range of commentary on how she should properly be designated: 'pucele n'est ele pas | Ainz est pire que Sathanas', says the boatman before the Castle of Ladies (7455–6: 'she's not a maiden, rather she's worse than Satan'). Cf. Gauvain and Guiromelant's discussion of her name (8631–40).

[47] Cf. the episode in Manessier, when a devil is disguised as Blancheflor (see below).

variation on, the Male Pucele's own transformation.[48] Although this damsel's truth-telling will be limited by the necessity to continue playing the role of deceiver for her family, for the readers and the couple, there is no further doubt about her status in relation to Gauvain.

Gerbert's continuation thus reinforces and recontextualizes the associative strands of Chrétien's text from the Tent Maiden to the Male Pucele, as well as the reinterpretations already inscribed in the First Continuation. Retelling is now integrated into the episode as instant replay. Attacked by the damsel's brothers and cousins, Gauvain escapes to a nearby castle, which turns out to belong to her father, Urpin de la Montaigne Irouse.[49] The custom requires Gauvain, however unwillingly, to recount his day's adventure. The recognition that inevitably ensues entails the same guest/enemy problem introduced at Escavalon. When the damsel herself shows up escorting her dead cousin and brother, her impromptu trick to protect the unarmed Gauvain from attack places him in her 'prison' overnight. Like Poe's purloined letter ostentatiously left in the open the better to be concealed, the lady's reprise of a common motif of courtly love allows her to take the 'prisoner' to her chamber, a locus amœnus ironically located under the watchful eye of her family.[50]

If Gerbert's Gauvain remains a figure synonymous with sexual conquest, Perceval's characterization in the Fourth Continuation bears rather the imprint of Grail heroes from the prose cycle. A sober knight dispensing sermons as well as swordfights, he has become a combination of knight and *clerc* who speaks the religious discourse of repentance.[51] Even when Perceval finally marries Blanche-flor, husband and wife remain virginal; unconsummated marriage suffices to remove the sin of a promise too long unfulfilled. In the sexual domain, this Perceval voluntarily chooses the *impuissance* inscribed in Chrétien's romance. Is it by accident that the editor who interpolated Gerbert between the Second and Third Continuations interrupted Perceval's success at the Grail Castle and deferred

---

[48] Like Guilorete, this Tent lady is named only toward the end of the episode (13893), in this case just as Gauvain is about to kill her father, allowing her to plead for his life without revealing her real relationship with Gauvain. Earlier, having chastised herself for her failed deception, the lady awakened Gauvain to warn him of her approaching cousins who plan to kill him. As she informs him, she does not want Gauvain killed, even though in going to bed with him she would have liked to pull out his heart with her bare hands (12673–5). Note the verbal echoes between her words and the *Conte*, where the desire to pluck out Gauvain's heart appeared as a kind of leitmotif, expressed by the vavasor at Escavalon (5847–54), Greoreas the rapist (7096–7), and Guiromelant, who without knowing that he is speaking with him, expresses the desire to extract Gauvain's heart from his chest, even if his sister should try to intervene (8769–71).

[49] His name recalls villainous characters in Chrétien's *Yvain* (Harpin de la Montagne) and Thomas's *Tristan* (Urpin le Velu).

[50] More specifically, they are observed by the damsel's chambermaids, Joliete and Violete (cf. Guilorete in the First Continuation and Gerbert's own *Roman de la Violette*), who guard the door and enthusiastically endorse their mistress's taste for the pleasures of love. The prison of love was also exploited as a double entendre in the *Chevalier au Lion* when Yvain turned himself over to Laudine as her prisoner.

[51] Cf. Putter (1995) on the convergence of knights and *clercs* at the court of Champagne.

it once again until Manessier's reprise? By contrast, Gauvain's own *puissance*, no longer operating in the Grail quest (as it did in the First Continuation), finds its customary locus in love affairs with no ultimate effect on the main plot line.

Gerbert's variation on the Tent Maiden adventure constitutes a momentary return to the discourse of courtly love, with all the dangerous allure spelled out in language and action. Along with Gauvain we enjoy the interlude, contained and subtly controlled within a more religiously inspired value system.[52] Inside the locus amœnus we see fun; outside we recognize the traditionally negative tropes for woman as deceiver and sex object. Yet misogynist discourse, which creeps into the First Continuation through the brother's criticism, remains surprisingly absent from Gerbert's tent episode. Indeed, Bloisine is given almost the last word, when she advises her father against the temptation of despair, though he has been defeated by Gauvain and left without any hope of avenging his sons' deaths or his daughter's rape. One final recall serves to silence these events all together. When Gauvain meets up with Arthur's court, after leaving Urpin de la Montaigne Irouse, he reports Perceval's adventures but says not a word of his own (14055–68). In light of recent experience, Gauvain had already resolved (13312–19) to tell no more tales 'Dont alcuns averoit contraire | Et moi torneroit a meschief' (13176–7: 'from which some might risk reprisals and for me turn to misfortune').

RETELLING LOVE STORIES: WRITING FORWARD AND BACK

We may thus be reminded again of the paramount role of retelling, whether by the characters, the narrator, or successive authors. Representation involves contextualization, point of view; it implies ideology, a variety of competing ideologies that claim to orient the tale. As we look back over this vast edifice of retelling, what finally emerges from the multiplicity of interwoven tales of sexuality and social relations, love and violence? Consider first how the shifting relationship between the two heroes appears with greater clarity in the dialogue between Chrétien and the four verse continuations. The widening gap that gradually separates them and returns Gauvain to his incidental role as secondary hero in Gerbert and Manessier underscores by contrast the intensity of their interdependence and intertwining in 'le vieux Perceval'. By the end of Manessier, Perceval has achieved the Grail quest; he has been crowned king at the Grail Castle and passed the kingdom along to his descendants.[53] He has returned as promised to Blancheflor and in two out of

---

[52] The episode known as 'Tristan the minstrel' offers another major digression into the usual romance conjunction of hero, love, and combat. App. 1 shows where it fits in the arrangement of episodes.

[53] That descendance passes through nieces in Manessier; in Gerbert (I, 6880–943), the voice that explains about proper sex in marriage and urges Perceval to guard his virginity also announces five future generations but without specifying exactly how they will be produced.

eighteen manuscripts he has even married her. But the two strands of his story in Chrétien's romance have not really been connected, just as the link with Gauvain's adventures has ultimately been severed. If the First Continuation seemed to confirm Gauvain's newly acquired status as romance hero (not just secondary foil), we will have to look elsewhere in subsequent verse romances of the thirteenth century to find Gauvain in the starring role (for example, *La Vengeance Raguidel* and *L'Atre périlleux*). In the later continuations, as in the great Arthurian prose cycles, literary tradition appears to have reinstated the stock character of Gauvain, confining him to his role within the constellation of Arthur's court: he remains the king's nephew, a figure seen positively or negatively, seducer or rapist, according to the ideological pressures put into play. He is still the ladies' man, not the marrying kind, and never the founder of a lineage, despite unrecognized sons who may pop up here and there.

Retelling the story of the Tent Maiden across the competing trajectories of two heroes and successive continuations has nevertheless kept in play the complexities and anomalies inscribed in Chrétien's romance. In the First Continuation, when Gauvain contradicts the narrator to retell his own adventure with a willing *pucele* as forced rape, there is no effort in ms. T to motivate the disjunction: it is left to readers to play out the implicit contrast. Modern scholarship may eliminate the contradiction by hypothesizing initially separate tales and successive layers of rewriting, but we must still account for how readers, medieval or modern, make sense of the narrative syntagm that writes these tales together.[54] In the accumulation of multiple versions and variations, sex emerges as a kind of knot or nexus linking polarities in a continuum, with love at one end and its opposite, rape, abuse of power and desire, at the other. Gerbert's version of the tale, the last significant one in the series, suggests the distance between the two poles may be short and subject to reversals. But the direction of transformation is not one way. The Orgueilleux's verbal travesty of Perceval's initially 'innocent' act, Gauvain's own encounters with rape as criminal act (Greoreas's) or blocked desire (his for the Male Pucele), stake out in the master text a whole range of possibilities subsequently tried out in the continuations as they respond to the logic of and/ both characteristic of the *Conte* (even if the last two succumb in part to the reductive reading of the *Queste*).

The initial questions posed implicitly by Chrétien thus remain unsolved: what is the relationship between love, sex, and the Grail, between Perceval and Gauvain, between lovers and mothers? With the hindsight gained by the continuations' rewritings, we may be in a better position to speculate on the arc of the *Conte du Graal's* unfinished trajectory. I suggested earlier the need to read Perceval's and Gauvain's storylines as segments of a composite human development requiring the difference of two human types (according to the logic of and/

---

[54] Cf. biblical criticism based on the identification of separate strands (J, E, P, etc.) or methods of exegesis that seek to discover meaning in the complex, contradictory text produced by the redactor. Cf. Ch. 5.

both) to play out the complex interactions of nature and nurture, the leaps forward and back. What future criss-crossing between the two heroes is inscribed *in potentia* in Gauvain's last episode? The disrupted society at the Roche de Champguin mirrors the Grail Castle's afflictions once Perceval fails to ask the appropriate questions: the destructions of war and exile leaving widows and unmarried girls, lords absent or incapacitated, men and youths unknighted. Gauvain's successful achievement of the test linked to the marvelous bed has already ended the paralysis of enchantment and set into motion a restoration of social life at the castle. Five hundred *valets* have been knighted; the mothers project marriage for Clarissant and Gauvain.

Even if plenty of loose threads and strange time warps keep us uncertain, the impetus of the story seems to lead in the direction of families re-formed or formed anew within a reinvigorated society. In previous episodes, mothers and fathers (or father figures) have been strangely dislocated, separated from each other across the social space of romance. Yet possible lines of reconnection have been intimated. Perceval's hermit episode outlines the Grail lineage connecting two brothers and a sister: Perceval's mother, his uncle the hermit, and the Fisher King's father. The Fisher King himself is connected to Perceval's father by a common wound in thigh or hip (discrete locations used to cover some sexual disjunction). Perceval's mother has died and he has given her up,[55] yet her prayer for his well-being continues, according to the hermit (6403–8), to exert a salutary grace over her son despite the effects of his sin (the mysterious *pechié* connected to her death, 6392–402, 6409–14). Just as this father figure reorients Perceval's quest and reconnects it to his mother, Gauvain's own storyline foregrounds a meeting with mothers planning marriage for their newly-recognized lord (though not thoroughly recognized since he has concealed his name). The marriage these mothers mistakenly project for Gauvain will, of course, concern his sibling—not just Clarissant (whom the First Continuation marries off to Guiromelant) but perhaps Perceval himself, Gauvain's brother in arms, his strangely twinned co-hero. (The thematic of siblings, though not pursued here, is as insistent in Chrétien's romance as that of parents and children.) In a sense, Gerbert confirms such a reading, when he interprets the implications of Perceval's promise to return to Blancheflor as a promise of marriage left unfulfilled, another sin to be confessed and repaired.[56] But, of course, the intervening influence of the highly successful prose cycle reroutes Gerbert's reading through the *Queste*'s strong misprision and allows Perceval to combine marriage and the Grail only in the form of a sexless *mariage blanc*.

Contrary to the univocal spirit of the *Queste del Saint Graal*, the concatenation of elements, the multiplicity of threads knit together in the *Conte du Graal*, require any

---

[55] As Perceval, echoing Luke 9: 59–62, says to his cousin: 'the dead with the dead and the living with the living' (3630).

[56] Manessier by contrast reads less boldly when he composes a simple repetition of Perceval's return to rescue and then once again abandon Blancheflor.

successful resolution to function not only in the spiritual dimension but solidly in the social and sexual dimensions as well, however unexpected such a scenario may appear to readers (and however uncertain any resolution remains in the unfinished state of Chrétien's romance still poised between success and failure). When the mothers at the Roche de Champguin hope for marriage and a couple joined as one flesh, their biblical language suggests an ideal capable of integrating a constellation of experiences across the spectrum of human desire, including love, sex, and marriage within a complex unifying vision, one that fits the biological and sexual needs of men and women into a social dimension that prepares for their recognition and celebrates their potential for generation.[57] Of course, actual as well as fictional human experience demonstrates how difficult it may be to realize such a vision, how easily the elements can be separated and problematized. The nature of the violence, the catastrophic disruptions repeated from one location to another, as well as the overlapping sets of advice Perceval receives from his mother and two father figures (Gornemant and the hermit), nevertheless suggest there should be no radical discontinuity among the individual, social, and spiritual dimensions, even if there is as yet no clearly successful implementation of their possibly harmonious inter-action in the romance as written. As written by Chrétien who, willy nilly, has avoided the anticlimax of endings in preference to the desire for ending, the invitation to continue rewriting the patterns of romance across the rise and fall, the steps forward and back of human development, *puissance* and *impuissance*.[58] It may not be surprising that the Grail quest initiated by Chrétien continues to figure in our own century the ultimate achievement that eludes our grasp and fires our imaginations, in whatever domain that compels our quests. In this medieval and literary domain, we need to follow the tangled knot of sexuality into the next chapter in order to explore further the problematic conjunction of mothers and lovers and sons.

[57] Cf. the examples of problematic isolation offered earlier in Chrétien's corpus: the eponymous couple in *Erec et Enide* mirrored by Mabonagrain and his lady, as well as the hidden couple, Fénice and Cligès, who must be reintegrated into society. Cazelles's reading of Chrétien's *Conte du Graal* insists on its social dimension, too often obscured by interpretations focused on the religious and spiritual possibilities evoked by the Grail (1996). See Ch. 4.

[58] Cf. Balsamo's Lacanian reading of Perceval as the personification of 'a perpetual, unremitting stagnation of desire' (1993: 281).

3

Sons and Mothers, Mothers and Lovers

His own life was no longer a single story but part of a mural, which was a
falling together of accomplices....

> *Only the best art can order the chaotic tumble of events. Only the best can
> realign chaos to suggest both the chaos and the order it will become.*

Michael Ondaatje, *In the Skin of a Lion*

Rewriting Chrétien's *Conte du Graal* has been a growth industry ever since the
twelfth century and Chrétien himself may be thought of as the first rewriter in
question, since with it he significantly revises romance—his own previous
romances, as well as the newly forming genre.[1] That process is intensified within
the narrative insofar as the Perceval and Gauvain sections are constantly rewriting
each other: the interlaced adventures of both heroes set up a pattern of recall and
variation that invites us to connect their storylines and read across their corresponding differences. Within this unexpectedly doubled and decentered world,
some of Chrétien's boldest innovations focus on themes and materials that
previously fell outside standard romance matter. The Grail, with its mysterious
Christian and spiritual overtones, has captured the fascination of countless
readers and rewriters, but another, less debated innovation deserves our attention
as well. In Chrétien's other romances, mothers appear incidentally, if at all; they
are part of the furniture; their presence or absence does not seem relevant to the
major concerns of characters, narrator, author, or readers. Chrétien's rewriting of

---

[1] I use the term genre here and elsewhere not in the sense of a set of fixed, well-defined literary
archetypes functioning outside chronological development (as in the Classicizing categories that
characterize critical debates in the French 17th cent.), but as a useful, cognitive category: readers and
writers in the Middle Ages recognized distinct types that function together in dynamic interaction
within the literary system. The contemporary terminology found in texts and manuscript rubrics
(*roman, lai, vers,* etc.) may not always correspond to the divisions medievalists try to establish, but
they do reflect differences among the available literary types. Writers pick and choose among them
and, especially in the case of romance, hybridize, with the expectation that audience response will be
able to appreciate the interplay. Cf. Jauss (1982), the conclusion to *Shaping Romance* (Bruckner
1993b), and the introd. to *Companion to Medieval French Literature* (2008). In cultural and political
terms, Haidu defines romance as a moment of evolution and even revolution (2004: 96–8), which
'addresses the problematics of violence, sexuality, and even the family, from the perspective of a new
form of governance and civilization' (personal communication, 4 July 2006). Haidu disconnects
Chrétien's works from 19th- and 20th-cent. notions of romance and reconnects his 'perspectival
novel' with the complexities of fictionality and subjectivity (2004: ch. 5). On the issue of violence
and the romance tradition, see Ch. 4.

romance in the *Conte du Graal* suddenly makes the irrelevance of mothers, alive or dead, a problem calling for attention. To grapple with the significance of this shift, I focus in this chapter on the topic of mothers and sons and lovers in the context of the family and Arthurian society, as they appear in Chrétien and the verse continuations. The progressive erasure of the mother, which we can literally chart in Perceval's speech and adventures, mirrors the general pattern already in place in Arthurian society and pointedly represented as such in the *Conte*. The isolation and marginalization of mothers, linked by the characters to the transition from Utherpendragon to Arthur, from father to son, has become institutionalized during Arthur's reign, setting a pattern for romance.

Although significant mothers may have been in short supply in Chrétien's previous romances, they play important roles in contemporary *lais bretons*. The plots of anonymous lays like *Doon*, *Tyolet*, and *Tydorel* or those of Marie de France's *Yonec* and *Milun*, offer a variety of triangles, frequently involving mortal and fairy lovers, their sons and spouses, which play off suggestively in relation to the stories of Perceval, Gauvain, and the First Continuation's Caradoc.[2] The dialogue on this theme set up between Chrétien's unfinished romance and the Gauvain Continuation forms a powerful matrix that reveals how the conjunction of mothers and sons is tied to a set of contradictory forces: the interplay of nature and nurture through the stages of education and separation, mutual protection and destruction, alternating marginalization and restoration of mothers, the criss-crossing alignments of the family on vertical (or generational) and horizontal planes (siblings, lovers, spouses), and finally the sexuality of mothers and sons, which introduces issues of chastity and fidelity both within and across generations. Analysis of these facets will reveal the specificity of Chrétien and his first continuator, the anonymous voice who responds most immediately to the *Conte*'s suspended potential, while at the same time highlighting obvious and less obvious connections between them.

If the later continuations find no place in a chapter focused on mothers, that absence is not without significance. Wauchier's concentration on the Chessboard Lady and Perceval's quests on her behalf shows continuing concern with the hero's sexuality but bespeaks as well his shift away from any attention to maternity and mother–son relationships in favor of engagements between lovers, as the Chessboard Lady stands in (potentially) for a future return to Blancheflor, once the Grail quest has been achieved. The influence of the prose romances short-circuits any such development, as the *Queste*'s focus on chastity and, more stringently, virginity for the Grail hero effaces mothers and replaces the notion of motherhood with patrilinear descent.[3] In a sense, the turn away from mothers, despite the *Conte*'s radical turn toward them, is already prepared in the First

---

[2] See e.g. Maddox (1991a), Braet (1981), and Régnier-Bohler (1980).

[3] McCracken analyses how mothers are sacrificed and replaced by spiritual fathers in the later Grail romances (1999). Cf. the role of the Lady of the Lake as surrogate mother in the Prose *Lancelot* (see below).

Continuation. Though the story of mothers resurfaces in the aftermath of Gauvain's affair with Guilorete and then again in the story of Caradoc, in both cases, the mothers' move to stage front is only temporary and leads once again to their marginalization. The persistence or disappearance of certain themes inevitably reveals the dialogic character and changing emphases that bring together Chrétien and the four continuators. Mothers, and especially their links to sexuality, remain difficult issues in the realm of romance.

Generational relations and stresses operate as significantly on the structural and intertextual levels as they do on the level of content in the *Conte du Graal* and its subsequent continuations and rewritings. In this light, Chrétien's romance functions as the 'mother text' both formally and semantically. First, in contrast to the romancers of the Vulgate and Robert de Boron cycles, who not only rewrite but displace and disperse Chrétien within their own series of texts, Grail heroes, father figures, and mother surrogates, the verse continuators retain Chrétien's romance as their own beginning. However miscellaneous and disconnected their inventions may strike modern readers, the manuscripts themselves attest to a process of generation and *remaniement* that constantly realigns first, second, third, and fourth continuations as the textual offspring of 'le vieux Perceval', whose integrity is for the most part unobscured by later additions. Thus canonized, the mother text remains literally present, just as mothers are surprisingly present and active in the stories of Perceval and Gauvain. Indeed, Chrétien's *Conte* is the mother text even before the continuations and the manuscript tradition make it so, precisely because of the unusual presence of Perceval's, Arthur's, and Gauvain's mothers. Their insistent presence necessarily leads to questions not only about these particular mothers, but about the general category of mother in the Arthurian world.

The mothers and sons who appear in the *Conte du Graal* and the Caradoc episode of the First Continuation reveal a nexus of problems clustered around the mother as a site of contradictions and oppositions, an incitement to the sons' search for reintegrations.[4] Much is at stake in the mothers' isolation within and from Arthurian society, as in the uneasy links connecting mothers and sexuality. These issues intertwine in the complexities of Chrétien's narrative and set up a series of analogical relationships between mother and son, mother and society, tradition and text, and ultimately text and reader, that suggest many more questions than they supply answers, as is typical in this romance. As earlier chapters have demonstrated, the play of resemblances between the Perceval and Gauvain sections constantly teaches its public a lesson in non-mimetic reading.

---

[4] Cf. Sinclair's overview of how the female body, and in particular the mother's body, is constructed in the 12th and 13th cents. at the conjunction of theological doctrine and natural science: 'Any kind of resolution of the problem posed by the acknowledgement of the power of the female body and the woman as individual subject proves impossible to resolve in a coherent way. The differing ideologies and beliefs that framed the maternal body are here seen in conflict, producing an image of the female body and its potential influence that is contradictory and convoluted, open to different types of construction and reading in different social and textual contexts' (2003: 40).

The interplay suggests that we move from signifier to signified by recognizing, gathering together, and sorting through all these connections across the gaps of their differences. We thus find ourselves in a kind of Fun House, a Hall of Mirrors at once enjoyable and disquieting. As we try to find and analyze all the reflections, we have the illusion of moving forward toward meaning. But we frequently find ourselves caught in the circular paths of a labyrinth: the more we look, the more resemblances and refractions we find, as the play of *semblances* seems to multiply beyond our control and the unfinished state of the text leaves us paradoxically with no exit.[5] The romance's lure is, nevertheless, irresistible, so we moderns, like the medieval continuators, continue to rewrite Chrétien through interpretation and retelling.

Choosing the appropriate interpretive mode for the *Conte du Graal* is itself open to dispute and has significant ramifications for the kind of questions and answers sought and found. Robert Sturges argues for resisting the allegorical impulse at once invited and undermined by Chrétien's romance, in order to encounter fully the conflicting perspectives inherent in the literal level, as understood by biblical and classical exegetes of the twelfth century. Sturges recommends a kind of metonymic interpretation: seek the appropriate and practical contexts that will illuminate puzzles posed for the characters as well as the readers of the *Conte* (1991: 42–7; cf. Stanesco 1981). This advice tallies with my own sense that we have not yet fully encountered the literal bodies of mothers still waiting at the margins of Arthurian society. Let us look for them and try to understand their problematic presence.

PROTECTING MOTHERS: CONNECTIONS AND CONTRADICTIONS

Separation, protection, and education are intimately bound together in Perceval's family experience; the same themes resurface refracted through the scattering of Gauvain's family between Arthur's court and the Castle of Ladies. As scholars have remarked, the characters' retrospective accounts tie the withdrawal of both families to the same moment in the past, the troubled transition from Utherpendragon's reign to that of Arthur. These passages allude to materials represented in Geoffrey of Monmouth's *Historia* and Wace's *Brut*; they constitute a departure from Chrétien's previous tendency to isolate his heroes' adventures from the march of Arthurian history, another significant anomaly of this romance (usefully explored by Sara Sturm-Maddox 1984). The contrast between the two families' responses suggests the play between the realistic and the fabulous that lies at the heart of Arthurian tales, neither entirely true nor entirely false, in Wace's own

---

[5] Cf. Rider (1998) on the role of enigma in Chrétien's romance and Méla on the role of the *semblance*: 'L'identité ne s'appréhende qu'en sa possible altérance' (1979: 11).

expressive phrase. With the father wounded, Perceval's family withdraws to a nearby forest and establishes a manor and farm; with the aid of 'un clers sages d'astronomie' (7548: a clerk wise in astronomy), the old queen has an enchanted castle built to await the arrival of their liberator. These initial givens will lead to quite different insights into the question of isolation and protection.

Is Perceval's mother overly protective? Has she in effect imprisoned him in the forest by depriving Perceval of knowledge about the past, his lineage and identity? These are some of the questions that emerge in critical discussions, usually answered with quite negative judgments of the mother and offered from a variety of social and psychoanalytic perspectives.[6] The *Conte du Graal* itself, as well as a number of important intertexts, suggest more nuanced responses are needed. The two-generational, biographical frame of *Cligès*, borrowed from the Tristan model, offers a good background against which to measure Perceval's entrance into Arthurian society. The arrival at Arthur's court of a young man seeking to be launched on his knightly career is repeated twice, with variations for Alexandre and Cligès. The underlying pattern of the 'bel inconnu' will function in numerous Arthurian romances, but at this point in Chrétien's corpus, the role of the mother in such an initiation is insignificant: fathers send their sons to Arthur's court for training and knighting with the best.[7] Perceval's family is at first no exception to this pattern, except in terms of destination. But when both older sons, newly knighted, are killed on their way home, their father's death from grief brings about a more significant permutation.

Should we expect Perceval's mother to fill the role previously played by the father, as the Lady of the Lake does in the Prose *Lancelot*, an intertext that lovingly rewrites Perceval's 'enfances'? The Lady of the Lake successfully plans and executes Lancelot's smooth transition into knighthood, despite the disruptions caused by the death of his father and the loss of his patrimony to the unjustified aggressions of King Claudas. Her difference on this point should not obscure what they do and do not have in common. Apparently it has seemed as unlikely to the thirteenth-century romancer as to Chrétien that a widowed mother could achieve such a feat. It is not so much a question of love as of resources and perhaps even vraisemblance within the mixed economy of Arthurian fiction (cf. de Combarieu 1984). Human mothers who are widowed do not typically have magic to fall back on, as does the Lady of the Lake, however attenuated her fairy status appears in the prose romance.[8] As a genre, romance

---

[6] See e.g. Balsamo (1993), Huchet (1980), Holzbacher (1998).

[7] See Baumgartner's comparison of Jaufre and Perceval in relation to the pattern of the Fair Unknown (1977). Caradoc's father starts him learning letters at the age of 5 plus and then sends him off to Arthur's court for the next stage.

[8] To the Lady of the Lake's tender white magic, we might compare the black magic of the giant mother in *Jaufre*, who offers a parodic version of the opening sequence in *Perceval*. When her giant husband dies and leaves her with two young sons to protect on the land taken over by her husband's depredations, the mother resorts to the help of the black knight, a figure of the devil, finally defeated by the highly moral hero Jaufre.

offers a mix of the marvelous and the realistic, the historical and the fictional. Chrétien's romances demonstrate in general a judicious restraint in deploying the resources of magic where they may have maximum effect (*Erec*'s 'Joie de la Cort', *Lancelot*'s future cemetery, *Yvain*'s fountain). Realism, while not a totalizing system as it will claim to be in the nineteenth-century novel, represents one of the literary effects used by Chrétien, in counterpoint with the pleasurable release of magic when necessary (cf. Nykrog 1973). The *realia* included in his romances invite contemporary readers to recognize and reflect on facets of their own experience refracted through the displacements of fiction.

In the *Conte du Graal*, it is Arthur's mother Ygerne in the more fabulous part of the romance who has access to magic, thanks to that unnamed *clerc* who can be none other than Merlin, the very enchanter responsible for the trick of illusion that led to Arthur's birth. But Perceval's mother offers Chrétien the opportunity to represent within his fiction a contrasting response as well, one shaped by the human realities of death and destruction, unmitigated by the supernatural. An artist capable of painting in a few quick strokes the tenderness of a father for his young daughter, Chrétien demonstrates equally sensitive insight into the fearful love this mother bears for her son, her anxiety at his delayed return, her joy when he finally reappears. Her decision to keep Perceval ignorant of the past is presented as a realistic response to the deaths and losses they have endured. Given the state of her resources as described (and Perceval's 'natural' affinity for knighthood, bred into him from both maternal and paternal lineages), the mother's decision to remove any mention of knighthood provides a second layer of protection for Perceval, a double of their refuge in the forest. Though her solution will not resist further developments of the plot, the stratagem works until Perceval's chance encounter with five knights, when the adolescent is strong enough to protect himself, as he will soon demonstrate with the Red Knight.

Equally important, the mother's actions or omissions appear not simply as a way to manage her situation but rather as an aggressive and radical rejection of knighthood itself. 'Tu as veü, si com je croi, | Les angles dont la gent se plaignent, | Qui ocïent quanqu'il ataignent' (398–400: 'You saw, I think, the angels people complain about who kill as many as they reach'). Through her voice, Chrétien contests the very system that is at the heart of Arthurian romance, strips it of any romantic or idealizing trappings and reduces it to its essence of violence (cf. Gravdal 1991 and Krueger 1993). That violence is vividly represented on the magnificent first folio of the *Conte du Graal* in BN, fr. 12577 (Fig. 4), one of the latest and most elaborately illustrated manuscripts in the tradition (Huot 1996: 106). In this lavish fourteenth-century copy, six roundels placed in the leafy borders and spaced around the bottom and right-hand margins contain three-quarter figures of knights, armed with helmets and shields, their swords aggressively raised. They frame a two-part miniature, illustrating four scenes which take over most of the highly decorated page and visually anticipate the important opening movements of a romance whose first verses appear in two short columns below.

Fig. 4. BN, fr. 12577, f. 1. Perceval says goodbye to his mother, who then falls down and dies (left top and bottom). On the top right, Perceval kneels before the first knights he has ever encountered; on the bottom register, he kills the Red Knight.

On the left top and bottom, two successive moments in Perceval's leave-taking: crossing the drawbridge out from his mother's manor in the forest, Perceval turns back to say goodbye; his mother stands in the doorway and gestures toward him. Echoing the very first scene in which Perceval practices with his hunting equipment on a beautiful spring morning, the illustrator shows Perceval with three javelins (as well as bow and arrows in the bottom image), even though according to Chrétien's narrator his mother has persuaded him to tone down his Welsh wildness by taking only one javelin with him. On the bottom left, she falls down (and dies), while her son continues to ride off, facing onward and ignoring her fall. Unwittingly, Perceval's mother has become the first victim of his encounter with knights and knighthood. On the miniature's top right, the naïve youth is shown earlier in the very scene that provokes his departure: holding his three javelins, Perceval kneels before knights on horseback, tightly grouped together, their colorful shields held out and their lances in vertical counterpoint. They are the first knights the young boy has ever encountered. A gesture of prayer visualizes his misunderstanding, since he has taken them for the angels his mother told him about, and their leader for God himself, so great is his splendor. The mother's falling body traces a line extending from the bottom left corner and intersecting with this scene, as it gives spatial expression to her ironic reprise of Perceval's language: these angels do indeed kill her through their effect on her son.

On the bottom right, Perceval himself enacts the deadly gestures of chivalry, when he kills the Red Knight and grabs the cup he has stolen from King Arthur (a cup that proleptically looks like a ciborium, the form used by the illustrator to represent the Grail as seen through the eye of the continuations in a manuscript that ends with Manessier). Perceval wields his javelin like a lance, which does not correspond to the description given later (Perceval actually throws his javelin into the Red Knight's eye), but it correctly anticipates how Perceval himself will become a formidable opponent in combat, once he has been instructed by Gornemant de Goort in the finer points of the chivalric code. In this miniature, Perceval is shown dressed in red; the Red Knight shines brightly in an orange that echoes the color inside the open door of his mother's manor. Though her son still wears the Welsh clothing she made for him, the color suggests that Perceval will replace and become the Red Knight, as he effectively does once he dons the dead knight's armor and continues the acts of violence associated with those angels who kill all they encounter.

Characteristically, Chrétien's last romance engages what normally does not fit into the purview of romance writing. The mother's severe critique of knighthood appears more typically in the realm of religious discourse and may not ultimately be compatible with the demands of the romance genre.[9] But her point of view is

---

[9] Cf. the Lady of the Lake's highly moral and idealized view of 'l'ordre de la chevalerie' (*Lancelot*, ed. Micha 1978–83: 7, 248–56). In *Le Conte du Graal*, religious discourse may itself be problematized insofar as it introduces its own level of violence in the anti-Jewish invective of the Veuve Dame and the knight penitent, another disturbing anomaly found in Chrétien's last romance and vigorously developed by subsequent rewriters like Robert de Boron and the anonymous author of *Perlesvaus*.

no less formidably expressed here. While the romance as a whole privileges the point of view of its male heroes, by including their identities as sons Chrétien highlights family connections in Arthurian society and makes it possible to include the Veuve Dame's perspective. As in previous romances but with greater insistence in the *Conte*, Chrétien's ambivalent handling of chivalry and the Arthurian ideal seems designed to debunk and give new definition to that ideal.

The mother–son nexus plays an important role in this dual task. The mother's ironic and passionate outburst against the mortal violence of knights, combined with Perceval's foolish equation of knights with angels, lead to deeper questions about the role of protectors, whether in the form of mothers or knights. We can laugh at Perceval's naïveté because we know that knights are neither devils nor angels, but that comic polarization introduces more searching questions about what knights really are and do. Perceval's teachers—his mother, Gornemant, and his hermit uncle—consistently include in their advice a responsibility to protect the weak, especially women in need of help, though Gornemant includes men as well.[10] The women who need protection are categorized as widows and orphans, ladies and young maidens. With the addition of the clergy (highlighted in the hermit's discourse), these are the very categories of people deserving protection according to the Peace and Truce of God movements, as well as Carolingian tradition.[11] Yet Perceval's first act of violence in pursuit of knighthood is against his widowed mother, and all the members of his maternal family that Perceval encounters in his wandering fit into the category of those needing (but often failing) to receive his protection. Ironically, Perceval will learn later from the hermit that, by commending him to God, his mother has continued to protect him during his five years of fruitless adventures. From the Christian point of view, it is not Perceval's prowess that protects but rather the grace of God obtained through his mother's prayer. The question of who is protecting whom in Perceval's family as in Arthurian society becomes more complicated as the narrative unrolls.

THE SIN OF THE MOTHER

According to his cousin and uncle (6392–402), unbeknownst to Perceval, 'le pechié . . . De ta mere' (3593–94) led to his failure at the castle of the Fisher King.

---

[10] There is general agreement in the advice Perceval receives from all three, although each one highlights areas that reflect their specific identities as mother, knight, and hermit. The progression of the figures themselves parallels to a certain extent the typical phases of an aristocratic youth's upbringing in the 12th cent.: from the mother's nurturing to the father's instruction and then on to further training by the clan, in order to complete the process of socialization. The three advisers thus outline for Perceval a certain pattern of social integration that plays through and against isolated pockets—the mother's manor, the hermitage in the forest—that mark the Arthurian landscape.

[11] Other critics (e.g. Le Rider 1978) have already made connections between Chrétien's romance and the Peace and Truce of God, initially organized in southern France by church institutions, but taken over by secular powers in Normandy and Flanders by the 11th cent. and imposed by royal decree in the kingdom of France by the mid-12th (Bisson *c*.1982–9).

That hidden causation, twice revealed, contradicts the more apparent and comic cause given in the linear presentation of events—that is, the advice from Gornemant not to speak too much. The adverse consequences (to lesser and greater degrees) of Gornemant's otherwise well-meaning advice are insistently developed by the doubling of Perceval's misapplications, first at Biaurepaire, then at the Fisher King's. The contradictory explanations are further complicated by the overwhelming paradox of Perceval's situation: he must leave his mother to achieve the Grail; he cannot leave his mother and achieve the Grail (cf. Méla 1984: 89). Perceval cannot arrive at the castle to ask the questions without causing his mother's death and thus incurring the very sin that prevents him, according to his maternal relatives, from asking the healing questions. The and/ both logic of Chrétien's romance suggests we need to explore how Gornemant's advice and the 'sin of the mother' may be related, may even express the same idea in contradictory ways. As he demonstrates in the prologue, Chrétien invites readers to pursue meaning through interpretation on different levels.

What is the relationship between Perceval's mother and Gornemant de Goort, the father figure who initiates his education as knight?[12] Despite the substantial agreement in their parting counsel, there is one point on which Perceval receives contradictory advice from them, and it is precisely in the area of speech. The mother encourages what appears to be Perceval's natural tendency to ask questions, when she advises him to ask the name of any companions he makes and seek the advice of *preudomes* (557–64). Gornemant is more concerned with controlling Perceval's tongue, as he tries to refashion the rustic youth whose repeated evocations of his mother's teachings are clearly comic and inappropriate for an Arthurian knight. Gornemant's removal of the mother from the boy's speech, replaced by 'the one who put on his spurs' (1687), the more acceptable social referent, corroborates the isolation of mothers that seems to have become the pattern in Arthurian society. Perhaps this is the sense in which we can understand the overlay of explanations for Perceval's silence: he has sinned against the mother by accepting Gornemant's advice to remove not only the clothes she sewed for him but her very name—which in the context of this romance is defined by her function as widow and mother since she has no proper name of her own.[13] Just as Perceval is the widow's son, 'li fix as la veve feme' (74), until he guesses his name, she is and remains 'la/ma/ta/sa mere'.

The fault or faults repeatedly signaled in the text by the narrator as well as the characters compel us to ask who is responsible and what that responsibility entails. Gornemant, Perceval, and his mother are all on the line. Gornemant's

[12] The form of Gornemant's surname most commonly used, 'Goort' or 'Gohort', is the version based on Guiot's copy. In ms. T, Gornemant's name is given as 'Gornemans de Gorhaut' (1548, 1892): see Huchet's play on that form in relation to the 'pays de Gorre' in the *Chevalier de la Charrette*, as he discusses Gornemant's links to the mother and the 'Nom du Père' as well as links between the doubled heroes (1980: 80–2).

[13] Cf. Baudry's discussion of widows in Old French literature, starting with *Perceval* (1998).

teachings are essential to Perceval's development as a knight, and Blancheflor speaks highly of him to Perceval in the next episode (1893–1907). Yet her glowing description of the riches and worth of this *preudome* strikes an odd note when she juxtaposes them against her own destitution. Her people are starving, her land laid waste, and she is under siege by an unwanted suitor. Why has Gornemant not come to her aid, especially given his advice to Perceval to help men and women 'desconseillez d'aucune rien' (1659: 'in need of protection for whatever reason')? Such a criticism is not voiced by his niece and may not be relevant to the intermittent realism that characterizes romance. After all, the best explanation for Gornemant not to have done anything for his niece is so that Perceval can come to her rescue. But Chrétien was not obliged to make Blancheflor Gornemant's niece. If, on the narrative level, the family connection serves to link two juxtaposed episodes, on the level of *sens*, uncle and niece are caught in the same pattern of destruction and isolation that Perceval's quest should ultimately aim to overcome.

When Perceval learns from his cousin (3591–4) that many bad things will happen to him and to others because of 'le pechié . . . De ta mere', the word *pechié* remains ambiguous: it can mean sin or misfortune in Old French. The religious connotation is unmistakable in the hermit's discourse but the cousin's language, like that of the Hideous Damsel, leads repeatedly in the direction of misadventure, what happens, misfortune: 'Perchevax li chaitis! | Ha, Perchevax maleürous, | Come iés or mal aventurous' (3582–4: 'Perceval the wretched! Ah, unhappy [unfortunate[14]] Perceval, how unlucky you are now'); 'De che que si t'es mescheü' (3603: 'from what went wrong for you'). The linguistic ambivalence invested in *pechié* is nevertheless sustained, since she connects the fault to Perceval for having caused his mother's death: 'De ta mere t'est avenu, | Qu'ele [est] morte del doel de toi' (3594–5: 'it came to you from your mother since she died of grief because of you'). In the cousin's formulation, Perceval is responsible and his mother is the victim, even if misfortune takes some of the blame.[15]

But the issue of responsibility also taints the Veuve Dame through interpretations that discern an incest myth, like that of Œdipus (Poirion 1973), a story known to contemporaries from the *Roman de Thèbes*. In Poirion's reading, the ambiguous syntax of 'le pechié . . . De ta mere' becomes the sin of, not against the mother, that is, incest with her brother, glimpsed through gaps in the history of Perceval's maternal lineage (Poirion's edition, 1994a: 1316–18). Moreover, Perceval's mother attracts criticism in the psychological as well as the mythical mode, when she is blamed for her son's misapplications of her advice. Problems of individuation and separation that we observe in Perceval's move from adolescence into adulthood are issues that recur in the dialogue between critics and

---

[14] The Old French *maleürous* still conveys its astrological underpinning: 'born in an evil hour'.
[15] The sin of matricide as a sign and trigger of violence will be treated less ambiguously in Manessier: see the brief discussion of the Black Chapel episode in Ch. 4.

text.[16] Disentangling what Perceval's upbringing has done to him and what he does on his own initiative is not easy, when we consider that Perceval's naïveté may be the effect of youth, the lack of a certain kind of courtly education, the result of temperament, or a combination of all three. Repeated efforts to differentiate, understand, and finally reconnect the son and his mother constitute crucial stages for characters as well as readers.

NATURE AND NURTURE

Standing at the juncture of nature and human nature, Perceval's mother invites us to question and cross over the apparent oppositions between nature and nurture, or nature and culture, court, and society.[17] The mother's particular circumstances dramatize this interplay insofar as she serves as the head of an isolated social unit living in the forest (cf. the solitary hermit) but maintaining an agricultural economic base. Hers is a displaced and reduced society that has banished all talk of knighthood but has not excluded culture in a number of senses. Perceval may be foolish but he is no wildman or savage.[18] We might compare him with Voltaire's *Ingénu*, in which both the story and its hero argue for the importance of nature properly cultivated by education and training. Just as Voltaire's comic *conte philosophique* suggests that it is as important to start with good primary material as it is to avoid spoiling it, the opening *sentence* of Chrétien's prologue (1–12) reminds the listening public that choosing the right field or person to cultivate is as important as sowing good seed, if you want to get a high yield.[19]

Perceval's mother assures her son of the quality of his inheritance from both father ('N'ot chevalier de si haut pris', 416: 'there was no knight of higher worth') and mother ('de chevaliers nee | Des meillors', 423: 'born from the best knights').

---

[16] The problem in sorting out responsibility between Perceval and his mother seems to occur even among the most careful and sensitive readers of the romance. For example, Sturges describes the mother as a teacher of allegoresis or over-interpretation because Perceval takes her statement that angels are beautiful creatures as the basis for concluding that knights are angels (1991: 47). But the mother makes no such equation. Here as elsewhere, Perceval exercises his own faulty reasoning to arrive at a problematic interpretation of signs.

[17] The ambivalent views of nature, human nature, and esp. feminine nature, available in medieval culture are briefly summarized in Desclais-Berkvam's ch. 5 (1981) on nature and *norreture*. See also Krueger's chapter (1993) on the *Roman de Silence*, whose plot, characters, and narrator play extensively on the proper and improper uses and claims of nature and nurture. Haidu explains the use of adjutorial allegory and demonstrates how *Silence's* use of nature and nurture undermines the principle of exclusive disjunction (2004: 242–53). In their introd. to *Framing Medieval Bodies* (1994: 4), Kay and Rubin recall Mary Douglas's critique of Lévi-Strauss and suggest that the European Middle Ages correspond to the kind of society where body and spirit operate as a more fundamental opposition than that between nature and culture.

[18] Chrétien's exploration of madness in *Yvain*, with its potential to effect a clean slate, nevertheless offers interesting parallels to Perceval's characterization. Just as temporary insanity allows Yvain to reconstruct his fractured identity, so Perceval's youthful ignorance leads to his unwitting reconstruction of Arthurian chivalry, exposing its faults as well as its promise. See Ch. 4.

[19] See also the brief description of Soredamor's pregnancy and Cligès's birth, which introduces the same metaphor of seed sown and grown to fruit (*Cligès* 2359–64).

The information she is finally forced to share with him about his lineage stresses the common geographical origin of both families as well as the superiority of the mother's line. We learn nothing more about the father, his name or lineage, after the mother's account (a blank the verse prequel *Bliocadran* and other prose rewritings will seek to fill), but Perceval's wanderings will lead him to significant further revelations about his mother and her family (Pickens 1977, Maddox 1994). Rosemarie Deist suggests that 'Perceval represents in essence one heritage' (1995: 3), which seems to be the case in Chrétien's romance insofar as the mother's lineage, especially as figured by the maimed Fisher King, conflates and stands for the male and female lines that combine to produce Perceval. The priority given to the mother's line in representing both deserves more notice, especially in the context of twelfth-century social developments.[20] On the other hand, Perceval's name, which he guesses at the critical moment when learning about his failure at the Grail Castle, does not explicitly tie him to either lineage.[21] When his cousin states that he is no longer 'Perchevax li Galois' (3575), as he surmises, but rather 'Perchevax li chaitis ... Perchevax maleürous' (3582–3), the transformation of his *sornom* highlights the result of his own actions, even as it hints about the timeliness of the moment lost.

What more can we infer about the mother's nurturing? Perceval's actions as well as his explicit references to her teachings suggest a large margin of freedom: he roams the forest at will, has learned physical skills like horseback riding and javelin throwing that lay the foundation for his rapid rise to expertise in manipulating knightly arms. He has kissed his mother's serving girls ... In short, all his physical systems seem properly primed, exuberant, and ready to go. His capacity for exercising his own will seems equally well developed, if undisciplined. The very first time Perceval refers to his mother's instruction (in a monologue reported by the narrator in direct discourse, 114–22), he rejects the religious behavior she recommends for dealing with devils (making the sign of the cross) and prepares for more violent action with a javelin. Perceval may appear to be attached to his mother's words as he frequently and comically repeats them, but he is just as ready to disregard them when they do not suit his purpose or ignore them, as when he summarily dismisses the mother's long discourse on their family history (489–95) by a peremptory call for something to eat, and insists on his intention to depart 'cui qu'il em poist' (495: 'no matter whom it grieves').[22]

---

[20] See Bloch (1983: 64–91), Schmid (1986), and Spiegel (1993).

[21] Following the lead of Roger Dragonetti, Méla plays on the sounds and syllables of Perceval's name: he supplies the missing link to the father by reading *Perce-val* as an act of penetration into the valley where the Grail Castle lies (1984: 86). Of course, both medievalists are preceded in this game by the continuator Gerbert de Montreuil (see Ch. 5). On the interplay of *nom* and *surnom*, see Kelly (1994).

[22] Haidu points out the cruelty of Perceval's words, coming just after the Veuve Dame's explanation that he is her sole remaining joy. In his view, the irony cuts at her expense: the mother's isolation of her son has necessarily produced Perceval's unfeeling disregard (1968: 127–8).

Indeed, the romance continually foregrounds in a variety of direct and indirect ways not so much what Perceval has been taught, as how he processes information, instruction, advice, and sensory data from inside and out. His own appetites and desires come first but they do not completely filter out input from his interlocutors, even if the delay in responding may be considerable. Perceval does eventually help get an answer to the first knight's question. He does want to return to his fallen mother, once he has obtained the coveted arms; he does want to ask the necessary questions about the Grail and the lance. What Perceval lacks, as Michel Stanesco suggests in the vocabulary of Hugh of St Victor and John of Salisbury, is 'assiduitas operis' (1981: 292–3). Perceval's deficiencies in the area of understanding have been extensively explored and debated. Scholars disagree on whether or not Perceval makes any progress beyond his initial starting point.[23] Does his *sornom* 'le Gallois' continue to tag him throughout with the craziness reputedly assigned to the Welsh? Playing the fool may be the price of providing a critique of Arthurian society. In any case, the mother's choice to withhold certain information about Perceval's family plays a dual role: while on the one hand, it creates a deficiency that will have to be corrected, on the other, it favors the development of certain character traits in Perceval that may provide the key to his future success, however problematic they may appear in certain circumstances. Contradictions follow the steps of both mother and son, as nature and nurture interact.

The Veuve Dame and Gornemant agree that Perceval should not be blamed if he is ignorant in certain areas. Both express optimism about his capacity to learn what he needs. The passage where Gornemant explains his views—and receives corroboration from the narrator—is particularly useful in situating the complex interaction of nature and nurture in the process of education:

> 'Ce qu'on ne set puet on aprendre,
> Qui i velt pener et entendre, ...
> Il covient a toz les mestiers
> Et cuer et paine et us avoir;
> Par ces trois le puet on savoir.'
>
> (1463–4, 1466–8)

('One who wants to work hard and attentively can learn what he doesn't know, ... It's necessary in all crafts to have passion [lit. heart] and effort and experience; by these three can one learn.')

When Perceval then begins to manipulate lance and shield as if he had always been exposed to wars, tournaments, and knight errantry, the narrator motivates his astounding progress by expanding Gornemant's remarks:

> Car il li venoit de nature,
> Et quant nature li aprent
> Et li cuers del tot i entent,

---

[23] See e.g. Haidu (1968), Frappier (1972a), Stanesco (1981), Sturges (1991).

> Ne li puet estre rien grevaine
> La ou nature et cuers se paine.
>
> (1480–4)

(For it came to him by nature and when nature teaches him and he puts his whole heart into it, nothing can be too hard for him where nature and heart take pains.)

As Perceval's mother told him, if it had pleased God to keep his father and friends alive, 'Chevaliers estre deüssiez, | Biax fix' (412–13: 'You should have been a knight, fair son'). Inheritance bountifully supplies Perceval's natural aptitude for knighthood; Gornemant briefly provides the nurturing. By so doing, he may well function as a father figure, although fathers in romance do not usually train their own sons past a certain age: they send them off to lords, kings, or even vassals, for initiation into knighthood (as in the case of Melian de Lis in the Gauvain section). The key term in Gornemant's and the narrator's commentary is *cuer*: Perceval's own heart must furnish the will and desire to put both nature and nurture to good use.

Heart: the medieval site of courage, love, memory—there is no word more powerful to trigger associations between Lancelot and Perceval, especially as the Prose *Lancelot* expands its commentary on the role of the hero's great heart in a number of significant passages that mark his growth under the Lady of the Lake's tutelage and anticipate his later role in the Arthurian world.[24] Linked to Lancelot's heart and equally important for his pursuit and attainment of extraordinary achievements is his particular capacity for *joie* (Baumgartner 1985b: 18–20). The Lady of the Lake's protection is crucial for nurturing these aspects of Lancelot's nature, given the disastrous circumstances of his father's death and the transformation of his mother into 'La Reine aux grandes douleurs'. If the problem for both romances is similar (how to raise a joyous, optimistic, large-hearted boy in the face of his family's destruction and exile?), the later intertext throws back a useful light on the *Conte du Graal*.

Perceval's mother does not have the resources of magic, but in the cultivation of joy, the romance's first image of Perceval suggests that her results rival those of the Lady of the Lake. Despite the potentially negative tag that initially marks him as 'li fix a la veve fame', Perceval first appears in a springtime opening and responds with joy to the joyous singing of the birds, just as troubadour poets do in countless lyric songs.

> Et maintenant li cuers del ventre
> Por le dolç tans li resjoï,
> Et por le chant que il oï
> Des oisiax qui joie faisoient;
>
> (86–9)

(And now the heart in his chest rejoiced because of the sweet season and the song that he heard which the birds sang for joy.)

---

[24] See e.g. in the *Charrette*, 4664–8; in the Prose *Lancelot*, 7: 73, 195, 248.

The adolescent Perceval's joy is less focused than the lover's, to be sure, and that aspect of his development will remain more dispersed than Lancelot's. But both romance accounts suggest implicitly that temporary ignorance about the family's unhappy past plays a necessary and nurturing role in allowing the youths to develop their hearts and their 'natural' tendency to joy. In Perceval that joy has comic overtones: he makes people laugh, as he did 'la pucele qui rit' ('the maiden who laughs'), a figure who suggests that his comic exuberance plays as significant a role in his achievements as his failures.[25]

The mother's upbringing has not repressed Perceval's joyous disposition; he is indeed the only source of joy remaining to her, as she explains in language that recalls the lover's joys, transposed into the mother's life and idiom.

> 'Vos estïez toz li confors
> Que jou avoie et toz li biens,
> Car il n'i avoit plus des miens;
> Rien plus ne m'avoit Diex laissiee
> Dont je fuisse joians ne liee.'
>
> (484–8)

('You have been all the comfort and all the good that remained to me for I have no other family. God left me no others for whom I could be joyous and happy.')

His mother's love, her joy expressed in his, has allowed Perceval to develop, in Chrétien's metaphor, as fertile land to be sown and cultivated, unspoiled material ready for the enrichments of socializing and education but also ready to point out, if indirectly and unconsciously, the shortcomings of the civilized world, in this case the less-than-ideal ideal of Arthurian society.

Misunderstanding habitually precedes and fuels his quest for understanding, as Perceval's learning curve remains open-ended. Learning how to fight like a proper knight is surely the simplest of Perceval's tasks. Despite Gornemant's desire to keep him at least a month, Perceval leaves his castle the very next day, enough improved in terms of prowess and chivalric behavior to achieve all the martial tests he will subsequently be called upon to master. Unfortunately for him, progress in this romance is not necessarily linear and his mistakes past and future will require more than martial skills to correct them. The removal of his mother from Perceval's speech, the price paid for his socialization, begins a process of erasure that culminates, once he learns of her death, in Perceval's abandonment of his quest to return to her. That may seem a logical response, as Perceval's proverb maintains: 'Les mors as mors, les vis as vis' (3630: 'the dead with the dead and the living with the living').[26] Yet the returns of the mother's

---

[25] For a brief comparison of the comic aspects of these two heroes in Chrétien's romances, see Bruckner (2005: 143).

[26] In the notes to his edn., Poirion identifies this phrase as a proverb (1994a: 1353 n. 1). Holzbacher calls it a biblical injunction and cites Matthew 8: 22 and Luke 9: 60.

death in each of Perceval's encounters with family informants, the repeated calls for him to recognize and atone for the 'sin concerning the mother', suggest that something more is required of him. If the mother's presence in the narrative is short, her absence remains present throughout Perceval's adventures and casts its spell on Gauvain's as well.

THE MARGINALIZATION AND RESTORATION OF MOTHERS

The Arthurian effacement of mothers, reenacted in Perceval's plot, finds a miniaturized echo in Gauvain's first conversation with the old Queen, who asks him about King Lot's and King Urien's sons, about King Arthur and the present Queen (i.e. Guenevere, who remains unnamed in their conversation). Without revealing his own identity, Gauvain names all the sons (including himself and his brothers), describes Arthur's good health, and praises at length the Queen's goodness: 'de li toz li biens descent' (8188: 'from her all good things descend'). The mention of descent may remind us by contrast that Guenevere herself is not a mother.[27] Although Arthurian romance generally does not give voice to this issue, Wace's account explicitly mentions that she and Arthur could not have children ('ne porent anfant avoir', 1118). Mothers are not at Arthur's court, and it does not occur to Gauvain to ask or comment about them. He is not looking for mothers. Later, when he discovers from Guiromelant the identities of Ygerne and his mother, he exclaims (again without revealing his own identity):

> ... 'Gavain, biax sire,
> Connois je bien, et bien os dire
> Que il n'ot mere icil Gavains
> Bien a passé vint ans al mains.'
>
> (8753–6)

('Gauvain, fair lord, I know well, and I dare say that this Gauvain hasn't had a mother for at least twenty years.')

Chronology and common belief assign both generations of mothers to the grave. As elsewhere, the fabulous aspects of the romance hint of Celtic matter reinvented and many have connected the Castle of Ladies not unreasonably with the Other World of Celtic myth.[28] That being said, we are nevertheless required by

---

[27] See McCracken's discussion of adulterous queens and maternity (1998b: chs. 4 and 5).

[28] More recently however, the *Conte du Graal* has attracted 'orientalizing' interpretations. Reichert, for example, argues that the romance in general and the figure of the forsaken mother in particular is informed by the 'matière d'Orient' coming from Spain; she thus contrasts Perceval's and Gauvain's mothers from a point of view informed by Islamic mysticism, alchemy, and Sufism (2006: *passim* but esp. the last chapter on *Perceval*; see her introd. for a discussion of other scholars like Gallais, Visconti *et al.* working in this mode).

Guiromelant's assurances to accept that these mothers are alive and well—and why not, if Arthur himself, according to his mother, is still a mere child, only a hundred years old and not a day over? Time in this romance is extremely malleable and given to strange leaps and warps. The narrator uses exact chronology only when it suits his purpose. The resources of enchantment keep these ladies frozen in time and place, waiting for their designated champion, whose identity as son and grandson does not seem incidental to the task of liberation that awaits him.

The elastic lives of Arthurian mainstays furnish a useful foil for the characters whose deaths are to be considered no easily forgotten fiction. Realism and enchantment alternate and combine. Perceval's brothers and father are dead; he has himself caused the death of his mother, in the view of his cousin and uncle. Although Perceval's faux pas often make us laugh, they may have lasting and dire consequences. If the Tent Maiden's fortunes were ultimately restored, the death of the mother is irreversible, irreversible at least in the linear chronology of a human life. But perhaps not in the spiralling patterns of Chrétien's romance. Perceval is as much a creature of fiction as Gauvain, and their two stories intertwined invite us to read their connections across the gaps of plot and characterization. In this respect, fiction and historiography intersect, at least in twelfth- and thirteenth-century usage: the necessity to read the *Conte* in both its linear and nonlinear patterns across the imbricated itineraries of two heroes may be compared with the use of both typological and biographical grids for con-temporary history-writing and genealogies (Spiegel 1983). While on one level, medieval readers may distinguish between chronicle and romance, many of their features are shared (the use of the marvelous, combinations of chronology and patterning, etc.) and demonstrate their common origin (Zumthor 1972: 346–51, Kelly 1974). In the pleasures of fiction, the medieval public may see its own image reshaped for experimentation, but the techniques and displacements of narrative must first be recognized to gain their full effect.

In the *Conte*, the pattern of interlace suggests that Gauvain unconsciously and unexpectedly takes up Perceval's abandoned quest for the mother, not only for the sake of his own family and Arthurian society, but for Perceval as well. Gauvain must literally meet his mother (and grandmother and sister) in another place and perhaps (but this part has not been written in Chrétien's unfinished romance) reintegrate those mothers into their appropriate family and social networks. This is a pattern we have seen elsewhere in Chrétien's romances: the isolation and reintegration of Mabonagrain and his lady in *Erec*, the interruption of the lovers' paradisiacal interlude in Jean's tower in *Cligès*. The arrested development of the incomplete society gathered around the mothers at the Roche de Champguin, where young men and old await knighting, widows suffer exile, and orphan maidens hope for suitable husbands, is to be restored by the champion of the Bed of Marvels. We may wonder if that restoration will extend to Arthur's realm and forecast the healing of the Fisher King's *terre gaste* as well. With the knighting of five hundred men, the restoration at the Castle of Ladies has only just begun.[29]

However Chrétien intended to complete his romance, the pattern of Gauvain's adventure, already inscribed with so many reflections of Perceval's own, suggests that Gauvain encounters actual mothers who are still living in a marginal place, so that subsequently Perceval himself might recognize what he has so far failed to understand. He can of course no longer retrieve his dead mother. But before learning of her death, he promised Blancheflor that he would return either to place his mother as a nun at the convent of Biaurepaire or, if she was dead, establish yearly prayers there for the good of her soul—a good intention lost in subsequent adventures and a possible link between maternal, filial, and sexual love articulated within Arthurian society. Perceval left his mother without turning back when he saw her fall, so strong was the press of his desire for knighthood and arms. But just as he appeared oblivious of the knight's questioning but made sure he received the information sought once the youth's own questions were answered, just as he appeared unconcerned about Arthur's cup, though he eventually made sure that Yvonet returned it to the king, just so this son intended to return to his mother. Indeed, he repeated that desire both to Gornemant and Blancheflor. In that light, his quick dismissal of her death is all the more surprising; his abandoned quest to take her back to Biaurepaire, dead or alive, reveals how far he has become enmeshed in the typically Arthurian omission of mothers.

In the Blood Drops episode, Perceval began to show a new capacity to connect past and present through an act of reflection, the ability to remember his beloved in another *semblance*, making an equation between two different representations of the same person.[30] Perceval fails to make such connections with his mother, despite repeated invitations to do so, if not with her actual person, at least with her family and lineage whose members tie Perceval to the Grail Castle through uncles and cousins, male and female. Perceval expresses no link between his desire to return to the Fisher King with the earlier desire to find his mother. His ignorance before visiting the hermit provides sufficient motivation for the gap; once the hermit informs him that he is Perceval's uncle and that his mother, the Fisher King's father, and he are brothers and sister, we might expect such a connection to surface, but the potential is left unrealized, when the pattern of interlace fails to return to the first hero before Chrétien stops writing.

---

[29] The First Continuation will pick up this hint when Gauvain's visit to the Grail Castle brings about a partial restoration. See Saly (1976) and Maddox (1991a) on Gauvain's potential for success. Critics who read the romance with a psychoanalytic grid tend to see in the *Conte*'s return to mothers a dangerous regression (e.g. Gouttebroze 1976, Huchet 1980). But Gauvain's coming-and-going after his victory, as well as the imminent arrival of Arthur's court, appear ready to abolish a custom that would maintain the Castle of Ladies as an isolated unit and make of its liberator a prisoner. Cf. Köhler (1960) and Maddox (1991a) on customs in Chrétien.

[30] Cf. Schwartz's analysis of this stage in Perceval's development and her interpretation of the Blood Drops scene as a foreshadowing of Perceval's return to the Grail Castle (1996: esp. n. 32).

The effacement of mothers in the Arthurian world is curiously paralleled in the critical tendency to gloss over too quickly Perceval's explicit quest to find and return to his mother—perhaps a mirror of that moment when Perceval himself drops the quest in the face of death.[31] The reading suggested here does not deny the importance of fathers, whose absence, doubling, and displacement also requires interpretation. But my focus in this chapter seeks to restore and examine the significance of mothers so insistently represented in Chrétien's last romance. Although Perceval's progress in assuming a quest for the castle of the Fisher King may also constitute a metaphorical quest for the absent father, it is more emphatically represented in the romance as embedded in a kind of maternal quest that can be achieved only by seizing the opportunity to ask questions about objects, people, and their family connections, illuminated in as yet mysterious ways by questions of spirituality.

Perceval's final scene in the unfinished romance shows the hermit uncle implicitly and explicitly suggesting such connections for Perceval, as he confirms the mother's continued existence and protection on another plane of spiritual life, the Other World of Christianity. A hermit properly highlights the links between Perceval's mother and religious teachings, but it remains for Perceval himself to demonstrate in his future conduct that he has understood the lesson that, in some sense or *semblance*, his mother can still be and still needs to be found in his own words and deeds. Based on the trajectory of the unfinished *Conte*, it would appear that grown sons, properly separated from the maternal sphere through the stages of education, knighthood, and social participation, still need to reintegrate mothers (in person or in memory) into their adult lives and into the life of their societies. Lineages grow not simply through the line of sons succeeding fathers but through a complex interweaving of maternal and paternal lines.[32]

MOTHERS AND SIBLINGS: FROM THE *CONTE* TO THE FIRST CONTINUATION

Gauvain's adventure suggests that, when possible, it is not enough to find the mother's family. Find the mothers of the family as well—and the sisters, potential mothers of future narratives. Indeed, judging by Gauvain's particular pattern of

[31] Many critics tend to replace the puzzle of the mothers' presence by a search for the absent father (e.g. Gouttebroze 1976, Braet 1981, Bloch 1983, Méla 1977, Maddox 1991b). Though there are good medieval precedents for playing out Perceval's implicit desire for the father, as evidenced by the prequel *Bliocadran*, the *Perlesvaus*, and Robert de Boron's rewritings, the text of the *Conte* continues atypically to highlight mothers.

[32] Cf. Sinclair's notion of the genealogical matrix and her analysis of the role of mothers in the *chansons de geste*, esp. their importance as 'supportive supplement' (2003: 277) in 'texts that reveal the ethical slippage of the paternal structure' (266). See esp. her discussion of *Parise la Duchesse* (228–41) and the conclusion.

adventures, his main focus appears to be the world of siblings: the two sisters in the tournament episode, the brother and sister at Escavalon, his own sister Clarissant, and of course his brothers, the sons of King Lot he enumerates, including Engrevain li orgueillous, who spoke out in the tumult of Arthur's court urging Gauvain to defend the honor of their lineage in the face of Guigambresil's accusation of treasonous murder.[33] The anonymous Gauvain Continuation, which in light of this thematic we might label both sibling and son of Chrétien's narrative, will offer as its final set of episodes the story of Guerrehet and the swan-boat: the brothers' stories seem to exercise an attraction over each other that reflects the underlying patterns of Chrétien's own romance. The 'only child' Perceval (whose grown-up brothers are long dead and erased from his memory until the mother's account recalls them) finds in Gauvain a brother-in-arms with whom he shares his status as romance hero, most unexpectedly for the reader no doubt but as if in response to a deep need in Arthurian society for the companionship and rivalry of siblings explored through the interwoven threads of this interlaced romance, decentered by the alternation of two heroes.

The reappearance of brothers and sisters in the First Continuation's story of Caradoc and his mother highlights in retrospect how parents and siblings intersect in Chrétien's romance, particularly at the Roche de Champguin, where the mothers do not seem to be seeking their sons any more than the sons their mothers. The interrupted communication between the generations that Donald Maddox explores in the *Conte du Graal* and other family romances ('Lévi-Strauss in Camelot') operates just as significantly across the gender gap. Gauvain's refusal to give his name when asked by Ygerne parallels the Veuve Dame's family secrets withheld from Perceval: in both cases, the interruption prevents (at least momentarily) the discovery of family connections. In this episode, Gauvain's extended incognito allows the suspense to build and the queens to speculate on a possible match with Clarissant. As we saw in the last chapter, Gauvain's mother formulates with unconscious irony her hope that their future union might mirror the closeness and affection of brother and sister (9060–73).

At the same time, Gauvain himself plays the role of go-between for Clarissant and Guiromelant, whose amorous relationship, along with its complications for Gauvain, catches the lion's share of attention and narrative development as the first continuator picks up the threads of Chrétien's narrative. When Arthur marries the lovers before satisfying Gauvain's demand that he be cleared of the treason charge, the king's nephew sets off for a new set of adventures involving the Grail Castle and Escavalon, followed by the piquant variation on the

---

[33] As Perceval's mother recommends, you can know a man by his *surnom*: Engrevain's cameo appearance here plants the seeds of much future rewriting. Readers of the Vulgate Cycle know what an important role will be played by the rivalry between Gauvain's brothers and Lancelot, the undying hatred Gauvain will harbor against his friend once the queen's defender has become the killer of Gaheriet and Guerrehet.

encounter with a Tent Maiden discussed in Chapter 2. At the suspended conclusion of that episode, the biographical romance of Caradoc begins: it will occupy over 5,600 verses, about a third of the total in ms. T's version of the First Continuation. If we were disappointed earlier that the continuator seemed to make so little of mothers and sons during the reunion of Arthur and Ygerne, Gauvain and Norcadés (as his mother is named there: I, 285), we can see in this narrative development an indirect response to Chrétien's treatment of the theme that throws back new light on the earlier story and reconfigures its components (cf. Kennedy 1986).

As the son of Arthur's niece, Caradoc is quite literally the next generation of heroes, whose story from birth to fully accomplished knight catches up with and threads through the tapestry of Arthurian romance.[34] Chronological time and fictional time once again enmesh, as Caradoc interacts with the standard and still vigorous heroes of Arthur's court. The list of knights who participate in the big tournament scene (which occupies a third of the Caradoc section in ms. T) reads like a who's who of Arthurian romance and indicates in particular how carefully the continuator was reading the *Conte du Graal*. Caradoc's introduction into the narrative of Gauvain's adventures replicates the interplay between the Perceval and Gauvain sections in Chrétien's romance: his story will weave together elements taken from both heroes' connections to their mothers, primarily by reinventing the role of enchanter, sibling relationships, and 'le pechié de la mere'.

THE SEXUALITY OF MOTHERS

William Roach's edition of the *Perceval* Continuations reminds us that when we read Caradoc's story in T we are reading directly or indirectly the work of a *remanieur* who has made a visible effort to integrate and reconcile various redactions of the Gauvain Continuation and 'le vieux Perceval'. Perhaps continuators first needed to escape the centripetal pull of the *Conte*'s multiple reflecting surfaces to play out and forward the threads of plot still left dangling. But the linear march of this voluminous narrative operates as much under the spell of Chrétien's complicated fiction as our own interpretive rewritings. Inevitably, the textual thread leads back to the question of mothers, now entangled with the issue of sexuality: the troublesome *surplus* moves from the separate realms of mother's advice and son's courtly adventures into the imbricated love stories of both generations. The problematic of protection functioning between mother and son permutates into an exploration of mutual destruction and revenge.[35] The First Continuation thus acts as a kind of polarizing lens that

---

[34] McCracken (1998a) follows mothers and sexuality into the Grail quest's second generation as represented in the Prose *Lancelot*.

[35] Using the trifunctional schemes of Durand and Dumézil, Gallais views the Caradoc section as the foundation of the entire First Continuation, although it finds its place in the center: the

magnifies to the extremes of good and evil certain elements left implicit in the *Conte* (cf. critical speculation about the mother's sin of incest). In the so-called *Livre de Caradoc*, the restoration that eventually takes place will require the intervention of the son's beloved as a reconstructed figure of the mother, now virginal, faithful, and life-giving.

The initial view of mothers in the Caradoc romance seems to take off from certain hints and unexplored references in the Gauvain section of *Perceval*. The veiled allusion to Merlin may recall Ygerne's problematic status as Arthur's mother: was she unfaithful to her husband the Duke of Cornwall, if Utherpendragon appeared to her in her husband's own form?[36] Does Ygerne's doubtful role as wife and mother spill over onto Guenevere's status as wife unable to become a mother? Enchanters seem to play both a positive and negative role in these machinations, as attested by Merlin's ambivalent reputation. Wace also mentions Arthur's sister Anna, presumably Gauvain's mother: the sibling theme appears again to start off another series of speculations, which surface in the Vulgate Cycle when stories about Arthur's sister Morgan and the incestuous engendering of Mordred enter the intertextual dialogue and culminate in Mordred's treachery and Arthur's fatal wounding at Salisbury, as recounted in *La Mort le roi Artu*. From Clarissant's marriage in the First Continuation to the sacrifice of Perceval's sister in the *Queste* and Morgan's frustrated love turned into vengeance across the Prose *Lancelot* and the *Mort*, when sisters enter the already complicated arena of mothers and lovers, more problems emerge in the writing of romancers who follow the traces of Chrétien's work. What about the arrested sexuality of all those widows and unmarried girls waiting for husbands at the Roche de Champguin and the future *terre gaste* of the Fisher King? Typically, there are more questions than answers at this point, but the explicit references to Wace's *Brut* and the intensified use of the *matière de Bretagne* in this part of the *Conte du Graal* set up a fertile field that will be fruitfully cultivated by the anonymous romancer in the Caradoc section.

The 'aventure merveilleuse' (I, 3080) the narrator offers as Caradoc's story begins with the marriage of Arthur's niece, Ysave de Carahés, to Caradoc, king of

---

self-contained romance of Caradoc is 'placé sous le signe de la mère—et de la mauvaise mère (nocturne, déceptrice, attachée à sa vengeance, cruelle, frustrante—on pense encore une fois à la Reine de la Nuit)...sous le signe de l'"oralité" et de la (mauvaise) mère, dont le héros doit "se libérer"' (1988–9: 4, 2370, 2690). While Caradoc is named in a list of knights in *Erec* (1689), the elaboration of his story in the First Continuation (which explains his epithet 'Briebraz') has given many medievalists the impression that the first continuator offers a miscellany of Arthurian tales. Two important elements from his story appear elsewhere: in two lays, the chastity test connected to the horn (see below), and the beheading contest, now identified with Gawain in the 14th-cent. *Sir Gawain and the Green Knight* (Busby 2006: 223–4).

[36] Ygerne's story was available in Geoffrey's *Historia* and the *Roman de Brut*. Wace also indicates that many stories were circulating orally, which he refrained from recording. Cf. the allusion to the tale in the *Roman de Silence*'s final scenes, when Silence's cross-dressing and Eufeme's adultery are unmasked.

Nantes.[37] While we know nothing about Ysave's feelings at this point, we learn immediately that an enchanter named Eliavrés loves her so much that he cannot be separated from her (3103–8). For three nights, he keeps the newly wedded wife for himself and substitutes three different animals in the husband's bed. Caradoc is conceived the third night; his birth is greeted with great celebration and not a hint of scandal. At a suitable age, he is sent to Arthur's court to be knighted and claims as his first feat the challenge to participate in a beheading contest. When it is his turn to submit to the blow of the ax, the unknown knight takes him aside and reveals his identity as his biological father. Without saying a word at Arthur's court about the revelation, Caradoc returns to Nantes to tell his surrogate father the truth about his mother's adultery. At the son's request, the mother is imprisoned in a tower to prevent further infidelities. While the trysts nevertheless continue, the narrator puts off pursuing the mother's story for over a thousand verses, in order to follow the son's adventures, which initiate his love for Guignier and demonstrate his excellence as knight.

In a variation on the custom of Logres, Caradoc saves Guignier from an unwanted suitor, Alardin, when her brother Cador is unable to protect her. The brother and sister relationship will continue to play throughout the rest of the story, while the friendship that forms between Alardin du Lac and Caradoc further connects his adventures and fairy matter. The description of Alardin's tent, for which 'Crestiens' (4118) is cited as guarantor, includes an animated sculpture that plays a magic harp whose strings go out of tune and break if any girl entering the tent claims falsely to be a virgin (4118–26). Although the harp plays no further role in the story, it points to the major theme of the whole section—the relation between fidelity and female sexuality—and specifically anticipates the drinking horn of the final episode that reveals the infidelities of wife or *amie*.[38] Caradoc's beloved Guignier, who will be his wife before the end of the story, is presented from the start as the epitome of truthfulness and fidelity:

> Et avec che c'ot de biauté
> Ot ele tant de loiauté
> Car c'ert cele c'ainc ne tricha
> Vers son ami ne ne falsa.

(3679–82)

[37] The mention of Nantes is an evocation par excellence of the *matière de Bretagne*: Erec's father was also king of Nantes, as was the husband in *Tydorel*. By this point in the narrative, Arthur has distributed quite a few nieces in marriage as part of peace accords. The category of niece is a conveniently unlimited set of usually negligeable female characters through whom relationships to Arthur's court can be multiplied at will. In this case, the category serves to place Caradoc in a position parallel to Gauvain's but one generation removed.

[38] Cf. Brodman (1991a). In exploring the link between the drinking horn and Caradoc, Baumgartner (1984) reveals common threads that reinforce the lines of attraction between his 'intercalated' story and that of Chrétien's doubled heroes. Both horn and Grail, sent to disrupt the Arthurian court, function as magic objects associated with production and reproduction; both Caradoc and Gauvain belong to a type of male figure whose power of seduction represents a destabilizing element in Arthurian fiction that must be controlled by linking it to the knight's prowess.

(And she had as much loyalty as she had beauty for she was the one who never deceived or betrayed her beloved.)

The contrast with Caradoc's mother could not be established more forcefully, although the importance of love as the basis of their relationship introduces retrospectively an unanswered question about the way Ysave's marriage was arranged without regard for her own feelings or attachments.[39]

After the long tournament episode that emphasizes the traditional romance coordination of prowess and love,[40] the narrator intervenes at length to explain that he has delayed as long as possible but must finally return to Ysave despite his disinclination to do so (6004–32). He is most apologetic that he must speak ill of a lady: we shouldn't generalize her misconduct and think badly of ladies in general (6016–17). He takes comfort finally from the fact that his story will end well because of Guignier: one bad woman will spoil everything; one good woman will redress the situation. The narrator plays unmistakably on a favorite medieval topos, Eve the sinner redeemed by Mary the Virgin Mother. That underlying pattern will become more explicit in the events that follow, as the mother's sexuality becomes a destructive force threatening to kill her son. While the narrator's explicit remarks provide a frame that demarcates who is innocent and who is to blame, the story he tells provides a more complicated and ambiguous picture of where multiple faults lie.[41]

With Ysave in the tower, the discretion that formerly guarded the lovers' secret is abandoned. Everyone can hear their joyous uproar. When Caradoc learns from the king what is going on, he lies in wait until he catches the enchanter with his mother. In a tit for tat, the king takes vengeance on Eliavrés by making him sleep with three different animals and then banishes him from the country. When he

---

[39] Given the way romance fictions play with contemporary social realities, medieval debates on the role of consent in marriage, as well as conflicts between the church's and the aristocracy's points of view, are usefully recalled here. See e.g. Duby (1981) and Natalie Zemon Davis's introd. to the English trans. (1983), as well as Adams's argument for reading the romance hero who integrates love, sex, and marriage as a figure invented by clerics forced by papal policies to renounce marriage and accept celibacy (2005: esp. 76–106). A number of contemporary stories seem to justify the wife's involvement in a love relationship by her mistreatment at the hands of her husband (e.g., *Eracle*, *Guigemar*, or later *Flamenca*). While the circumstances are obviously different, the mother's later imprisonment in a tower provides a suggestive link. Cf. Szkilnik (1989: 269 and n. 2).

[40] The whole elaborate pageant rewrites *Cligès* and *Partonopeu de Blois* with its grouping of three heroes (Alardin, Perceval, and Cador), who furnish a counterpoint and enhance the performance of Caradoc, the major winner of the entire tournament. With its accumulated allusions to both sections of the *Conte du Graal*, the amplification magnifies the general pattern of multiplying heroes that characterizes *Perceval* and its continuations. The links that connect prowess and love are clearly articulated, when each member of the trio is matched to a suitable *amie*. Alardin's lady turns out to be Aguigenor, the daughter of Guiromelant and Clarissant—Gauvain's sister did indeed become a mother. The three marriages celebrated at the end anticipate Caradoc and Guignier's union and at the same time underscore what was missing in the match between Ysave and the king.

[41] In different redactions, the narrators' express different attitudes toward Ysave and Eliavrés (Gallais 1964a: 198–203; 1988–9: 2, 643–6). This is also true for different readers: see e.g. Loomis's vehement condemnation of the mother (1965).

comes to say farewell, the queen asks the enchanter's help to take vengeance on their son. This is the first time we have direct access to Ysave's own point of view, expressed here in direct discourse. In the face of Eliavrés's hesitation, she is adamant in her desire to show Caradoc no more pity than he has shown his parents. She wants to avenge Eliavrés and hurt Caradoc because he has deprived them of their joy: 'Il nos a tolu nostre joie | Si que jamais point n'en arons' (6244–5: 'he has taken our joy away from us so that we shall never have any more').[42] Let the punishment fit the crime: 'Vivre le ferai a dolour' (6258: 'I'll make him live in pain'), responds the enchanter.

Given the biblical overtones already introduced with the *Eva/Ave* opposition of the female protagonists, we are not surprised to find a snake playing a major role in this betrayal. Ysave tricks Caradoc into opening a box from which a snake jumps out and entwines itself around his arm, beginning a slow and painful process by which Caradoc will be sucked dry of all vital fluids. Believing that Guignier can no longer love him (echoes of *Ille et Galeron*), Caradoc slips away from everyone and leads a miserable life in the forest near a hermit to whom he has confessed all that happened.

> De son pere se rent copables
> Et vers sa mere trop pechables.
> Bien regehist qu'a bon droit fust
> Se molt de mal encore eüst
> Qu'il nen a, et por che s'en fuit;
> Car jamais joie ne deduit
> Ne velt toute sa vie avoir,
> Des qu'atant que sara por voir
> Que sa penitance soit faite
> Por la honte qu'il lor a faite,
> Dont molt sovent pleure et sozpire.
>
> (6889–99)

(He sees himself guilty toward his father and very sinful toward his mother. He fully confessed that it would have been right if he had even more suffering than he had and for this reason he fled, for he never wants to have any joy or pleasure his whole life long until he knows truly that he has done penance for the shame he caused them, for which he often cries and sighs.)

The detailed account of his confession and the weight of the son's sense of guilt translated into indirect discourse demonstrate that Caradoc has at this point followed Ysave's charge that he confess the sin against his father and mother ('Del pechié qu'eüs de ton pere | Et de moi qui sui toie mere', 6371–2). But his suffering

---

[42] Rossi (1980) reads this joy as lust rather than love and judges the romance to be anti-courtly, but similar loves appear with positive overtones in *lais* like *Yonec* and *Tydorel*, where the fairy lover likewise produces an offspring the husband fails to provide. In this respect as in others, Szkilnik emphasizes the king's weakness and Eliavrés's creativity.

and contrition, emphasized in the last line quoted above, will continue for a considerable amount of time before Cador locates him in his forest hiding place.

The interplay with Perceval's situation is unmistakable here. Both have committed a sin against the mother and, while Caradoc's may appear less dire and more justifiable than Perceval's, his more extensive atonement seems to make up for Perceval's negligence, as well as the brevity of his three-day visit with the hermit. The narrator has articulated only unqualified condemnation of Ysave, but her son recognizes that his conduct toward her and his real father merits the suffering he now endures. When he later meets with his mother and releases her from imprisonment, he asks and receives her forgiveness:

> Carados, qui molt s'umilie
> Et doucement merchi li prie
> Por le mal que il li ot fait.
> Ele l'en quite le mesfait,
>
> (8075–78)

(Caradoc greatly humbles himself and gently begs her forgiveness for the evil that he did to her. She pardons his wrongdoing.)

Mother and son are now 'quits', even, their mutual transgressions balanced and canceled out.

Their reconciliation is achieved through the intervention of Cador and Guignier, brother and sister, friendship and love, tirelessly dedicated to Caradoc. Once Cador locates his sick friend after a two-year search, his next task is to convince Ysave to save him. Cador offers her a lesson on proper maternal chastisement which should only hurt 'un poi' (7545, 7548) and should be followed by motherly solace (7543–50). Both mother and son have been guilty of excess in their treatment of the other. The mutual protection they owe each other has been replaced by mutual destruction. Sins have been committed on both sides of the generation gap. Ysave reveals that she has blamed herself for the martyrdom her son has suffered because of her (7567–72). That very night she obtains the recipe for Caradoc's cure, when Eliavrés once again returns to share her bed. It is as if the pleasure and punishment of mother and son are inextricably tied together: if the parents are permitted their joy, then the son may once again be restored to his.

If the mother's sexuality is thus tacitly admitted, it is quickly defused, not only by redefining motherhood in the virginal Guignier, but by eliminating the offending relationship. Once Caradoc sees that his mother is released from her imprisonment, the narrator assures us that 'ainc puis ne mefist al roi' (8085: 'she never again did wrong toward the king'). The mother's liberty and point of view acknowledged, no obstacle remains to the normalization of their family—and a return to the normal status quo ante of Arthurian romance in which mothers are marginalized. The paradoxical motherhood of a virgin will replace the now repentant mother Ysave; the line of inheritance will pass unchallenged from surrogate father to ever loyal son, and the mother may disappear from the story (cf. McCracken 1999). That denouement is prepared by the biological father's instructions, passed along by Ysave to Cador, for undoing what he calls his own 'pechiez' (6234).

THE GOOD MOTHER AND THE BELOVED

The restoration takes full advantage of Guignier's desire to offer her own life, and more specifically her own body (6601–4, 7711–14), to save the man who had earlier risked his to free her from Alardin. She matches all the conditions set for the cure, which requires a maiden equal to Caradoc in beauty and age 'et que ele amast Karados | Tot autretant come son cors' (7599–600: 'and she must love Caradoc as much as she loves herself'). She must be placed in a vat of milk with her bare breasts exposed above the top. A naked Caradoc should occupy another vat placed four feet away and filled with vinegar. She should tempt the snake to come take hold of her breast and when he leaps to do so, Cador must kill him with a sword. As prescribed, so carried out. The snake begins to fry in the vinegar, as Guignier shows him her breasts and praises their white and tender qualities that contrast so enticingly with Caradoc's thinness (7900–18). This is a wonderful turn around on the serpent tempting Eve with the pleasures of round fruit. Duped by the innocent maiden's allurements, the snake jumps and Cador, standing by with naked sword ready, cuts off his head—along with the tip of Guignier's breast.[43]

Illustrated manuscripts of *Perceval* and the continuations, which consistently focus on the Caradoc section, especially highlight this scene, which appears in M, S, and U.[44] In BN, fr. 1453 (S), a Parisian manuscript from the early fourteenth century, the two lovers appear as elegant figures, posed naked in their respective tubs, each one framed by the white drapery pulled back over their heads, with their gestures highlighted against a diapered gold background (Fig. 5). Guignier's naked breasts are on full display to attract the snake curled up Caradoc's arm. Its head, poised above Caradoc's hand, peers appreciatively in Guignier's direction, while her outstretched hand and slightly tilted head gesture alluringly in its direction. Caradoc's free arm, held against his chest, indicates that he too is attentive to his beloved's sacrifice on his behalf, as their bodies curve toward each other. In the beautifully symmetrical design of the miniature, they all wait in suspense, like readers who may gather closely round the miniature to see the image announced by the rubric. The snake will soon make its leap, but for the

[43] Is this an echo of *Yvain* when the hero is obliged to cut off the tip of the lion's tail when he saves him from the dragon's attack? Le Menn traces variations on *La femme au sein d'or* from a fifteenth-century saint's life to modern Breton songs.

[44] At an unspecified moment in the plot, Caradoc appears alone with the serpent in T (Busby 1993c: 1, 370–1). By contrast, only one manuscript represents Perceval's mother: the opening illustration of BN, fr. 12577 (U), described earlier in this chapter. All four images of Caradoc can be seen in *Manuscripts* (1993: vol. 2, figs. 111, 174, 334, 389). Cf. Brodman (1991b) on the iconography of Terra Mater and Luxuria.

Fig. 5. BN, fr. 1453, f. 85. The rubric announces that Caradoc bathes in a tub, as does his beloved, and the snake entwines around the knight's arm.

moment action remains suspended, so that we may contemplate this picture of perfect loyalty and love.

A virginal Guignier immersed in milk appears as the very image of the good mother, pure and white, who will fool the snake eager to suckle at her breast and give Caradoc new life at the very moment when he was about to die, sucked dry by the bad mother's serpent.[45] *Eva/Ave:* the replacement of the evil mother by the

[45] See Desclais-Berkvam on the tangible links between mother and child through the consumption of maternal milk (1981: 52). The *Livre de Caradoc* offers a displaced reference to contemporary ideas on mother's breast milk across the reconfiguration of virginal Guignier's immersion in milk as cure for her lover/son. It also seems to anticipate Melanie Klein's reworking of Freudian theory to offer a classic example of the infant's violent fantasies of good and bad mothers (Segal 1973).

virgin mother gives a new twist to the links between mothers and religion that appeared in Perceval's story.[46] The lovers will henceforth carry the mark of their experience inscribed on their bodies, Caradoc on his arm, for which he will be known as Briebras (you can know a man by his *sornom*, says Perceval's mother!), and Guignier on her breast, whose tip will be restored in gold by a magic shield given to Caradoc by Alardin.[47] Arm and breast, particularly representative body parts for each sex. Guignier's breast has undergone a kind of circumcision that purifies and redeems her female sexuality, just as Caradoc's shortened arm bears the imprint of his sin and redemption.

The remaining episodes, which follow their happy union in marriage, continue to emphasize the theme of fidelity in contrast to the opening representation of the mother's infidelity. When Caradoc commands Guignier to keep the golden nipple a secret known only to husband and wife, he sets up the possibility for a scenario like that of the wager romances, *Guillaume de Dole* or *Le Roman de la violette*. But the Caradoc section concludes more rapidly with a variation on the *Lai du cor*, in which every member of Arthur's court, from the king on down, is revealed to have either a wife or *amie* who has deceived him—all, that is, except Caradoc.[48] Paradoxically, the anomalous fidelity of Guignier in this episode looks as problematic as Ysave's infidelity looked to her son when Caradoc first learned of it at Arthur's court. The couple's triumph leads ironically to their separation, when Guignier is quickly removed to protect her from the queen's hatred. With her life-giving powers focused on Caradoc (cf. Iseut and Tristan), the virginal mother will produce no new generation; the prognosis for successfully integrating sexuality and motherhood in the same figure, or even the same romance, remains problematic.

If we look back from the Caradoc section, the possible links between motherhood and sexuality, as they appear only in the hints and interstices of Chrétien's romance, are thrown into relief. Perceval's widowed mother spoke of sexual issues in the instructions given to her departing son. Chastity and control of her own

---

[46] Gallais sees in Ysave's name a combination of Eve and Yseut (1988–9: 3, 1784). During the cure, the narrator tells us, all the hermits who dwell in the forest nearby sing a mass and make a procession around the *pucele* calling on Jesus Christ and praying God to destroy the snake without hurting either Caradoc or Guignier (7919–28). Spirituality and sexuality enter into an uneasy alliance through the exercise of control and sacrifice.

[47] Leupin's analysis of 'la faille' establishes a link that goes from the initial fault of the parents through the beheading contest and Caradoc's shrunken arm to Guignier's severed nipple (1982).

[48] In the *Lai du cor*, Biket focuses on the relationship of the couple rather than on the chastity test, according to Rider (1985). As Schmolke-Hasselmann indicates, in moving the *lai* into his romance, the continuator reduces the size of the tale and shifts the main focus to Caradoc's jealousy: his anxious doubt, signaled in the way he looks at Guignier before she drinks, is quickly put to rest by her reassurance (1980b: 109–12). Baumgartner (1984: 65–6, 69) traces associations between the drinking horn and the Grail, both associated with the production and reproduction of life, which she ties not only to the hero's capacity to seduce but his 'vocation à maîtriser et à s'approprier le monde sensible, ses richesses, ses sources de vie' (66). In this respect, Caradoc resembles other heroes, like Lanval and even Gauvain, whose troubling talent for success based on love more than prowess may require putting them at some distance from the Arthurian court (67–8).

sexuality are not in question, although her fidelity to the lineage of the father and chivalric descent is repeatedly questioned by critics who fault her for suppressing information or speculate on incest with her brother. Maternal affection in the *Conte du Graal* is represented without sexual overtones, except insofar as the language of affection (like *carité*) transcends any boundaries separating love for family members from love for the opposite sex.[49] But where there are mothers, questions of sexuality and sex still wait in the wings. Just as the Lady of the Lake plays an important role in managing the early stages of Lancelot's love for the queen, the maternal role in the *Conte du Graal* includes preparation for Perceval's future encounters with love, at least up to the point of marriage.[50] Her advice draws a sharp line between admissible foreplay (kissing and exchanging gifts) and forbidden *sorplus*. The way Perceval comically follows his mother's advice, first with the Tent Maiden, then with Blancheflor needs no further analysis here. But uncertainty still clouds the lovers' chastity after the innocence of their first night together in Perceval's bed. His status as a hero whose relationship to love differs radically from that of Chrétien's previous romance heroes constitutes another of the *Conte du Graal*'s significant anomalies (cf. his flirtation with the Chessboard Lady in the Second Continuation). Problematic sexuality continues to shift back and forth between mothers and sons, sons and lovers, across the dialogue linking Chrétien's Grail story and the continuations.

A number of feminist analyses have suggested that Chrétien's corpus gives less and less importance to women characters, especially the hero's feminine counterpart (Lefay-Toury 1972, Gravdal 1991, Krueger 1993). It might be argued that Perceval's connection to Blancheflor appears to play a less central role in the overall plot precisely because it remains as yet disconnected from his problematic and unresolved relationship with his mother and her family, the unifying thread that appears throughout the Perceval episodes as written by Chrétien. The significant insertion of the mother into the romance's concerns displaces the importance normally given to the hero's beloved alone. I suggested earlier that Perceval's newly developing ability to make connections between Blancheflor and her *semblance* provides a model for what he needs to do in relation to his mother. He can take that task a step further by pursuing the potential relationship between the two women who play such significant roles in his development, from both the vertical viewpoint of lineage and descendance and the horizontal

---

[49] Huchet, however, reads the mother's expression of joy in Perceval and her prohibition of the *sorplus* as a sign of a devouring desire that prevents the son's sexual development (1980). The question is to what extent we are justified in reducing *Le Conte du Graal* to the patterns of Freudian and Lacanian theorizing that claims to release hidden meanings in the text. However useful such comparisons may be, this critical gesture is subject to the same kind of misreading found in interpretations that replace Chrétien's romance with reconstructions of Celtic myth or allegories of Christian theology.

[50] The intertwining roles of fairies, mistresses, and mothers appear more ambiguous in the tradition of Breton *lais* and need to be carefully treated in the case of the Lady of the Lake (cf. Paradis 1984; Baumgartner 1985b).

perspective of an individual's assumption of his role in society. Perceval and the reader need to ask more questions not only about different *semblances* of the same person but the different, contradictory roles of the female person, as she appears in relation to the individual, the family, and society, in the romance text as in the world of authors and readers.

What about Gauvain's own notoriously wandering sexuality, his irresistible *courtoisie* and charm always available for another encounter, as represented by Chrétien in the episodes with the Pucele aux Petites Manches and the sister at Escavalon, and then developed in the First Continuation with the Tent Maiden adventure (especially in the two contradictory versions of their meeting included in T)? Should we relate Gauvain's escapades to the questionable role of mothers and wives in Arthur's family, or to the questionable role of Arthur as father and uncle? In the amplifications of the Vulgate Cycle, these issues are made explicit and the answers take a negative turn; the *Queste* sacrifices mothers, replaces Perceval by an unquestionably virginal Grail hero, and totally discredits Gauvain. As we saw in Chapter 2, when the Third and Fourth Continuations deal with the heroes' sexuality, the *Queste* also casts a shadow on their inventions.

The issues linked to mothers and sons and lovers may have been purposely obscured in the *Conte du Graal*, isolated in order to explore the ideal of an Arthurian kingdom suspended in time between two moments of destruction that mark its beginning and end. Both moments are attached to a problematic engendering and an interrupted passage between the generations; both are explicitly but enigmatically recalled and anticipated in Chrétien's last romance. Is this a temporary and beneficial ignorance, as I have suggested Perceval's mother secured for him by remaining silent about their past? Does it represent, like the pockets of isolation eventually eliminated in *Erec* and *Cligès*, a potentially destructive ignorance when prolonged too long? What is definitely included in the *Conte du Graal*, in the conversation reported between the two queens, shows them optimistically going beyond the stage of advice given by Perceval's mother, in order to plot the marriage of Clarissant and Gauvain and so plan the next generation. Through the voice of the narrator, the romancer has promised to surprise them. If we could only know exactly how. Of course, even Chrétien's finished romances contain loose ends, gaps, holes—his is an art that has no *horror vacui*, unlike many romancers who follow in his tracks, filling in, explaining, interpreting. But the unfinished state of the *Perceval*, its insistence on the need to formulate questions and return to previous sites, leave us more dissatisfied than usual with the tantalizing potential inscribed.

Multiple connections between mother and beloved, motherhood and sexuality, sketched out as possibilities in the *Conte du Graal*, remain to be realized in writing and rewriting. Like the Grail procession, mothers repeatedly parade before our unaccustomed gaze in Chrétien's romance, waiting for our astonishment to produce questions. They are still waiting, their enigma still beckons, inviting our efforts to understand not only their metaphorical, but also their literal presence and absence in Arthurian romance. Just as Perceval, thinking to find the inhabitants of the Grail Castle outside, found himself precipitated off a suddenly closing drawbridge, so we find ourselves jumping into the unknown from the suspended ending of Chrétien's romance. Stories, like lives, are always finished and unfinished; they end and do not end. We plunge into continuations of one sort or another. But the textual tradition remembers the mother text. Chrétien's romance and the manuscripts that repeatedly locate it as the beginning of rewriting and continuation keep placing these mothers before us, allow us to return to them again and again to formulate questions that, we hope, correspond to the surprising and difficult facts set before us.

4

Violent Swords and Utopian Plowshares

Et conflabunt gladios suos in vomeres,
Et lanceas suas in falces.

Isaiah 2: 4

And they'll beat swords into plowshares and
    plowshares into swords,
and so on and so on, and back and forth.
Perhaps from being beaten thinner and thinner,
the iron of hatred will vanish, forever.

Yehuda Amichai, 'Sort of an Apocalypse'

VIOLENCE AT THE HEART OF ROMANCE

When Chrétien begins writing romances, he aligns his work with a nascent vernacular tradition that first appeared toward the mid-twelfth century. Writing romance ('mettre en romanz') is first a linguistic and cultural transformation, a choice to put the riches of the Latin written tradition at the disposal of a lay public. The earliest French romances are called 'antique romances' precisely because they are translated from Latin and Greek classics and thus claim a high pedigree despite their vernacular language. *Le Roman de Thèbes*, *Le Roman d'Eneas*, *Le Roman de Troie*: these titles evoke the conjunction of history and epic; they conjure up stories of war, when Œdipus' two sons destroyed each other at Thebes and the Greeks annihilated Troy as prologue to the founding of Rome by fugitive Aeneas. The link between violence and the highest forms of art captured in our founding myths is a truism of Western civilization. The price of art's metamorphosis is dearly bought in blood in and out of fiction.[1]

---

[1] See Heng's analysis of 'the critical nexus of violence lodged at the very genesis of medieval Arthurian romance' (2003: 49) in her chapter on Geoffrey of Monmouth's *Historia*. For a meditation on the value and exorbitant cost of the humanist tradition that does not look at the Middle Ages but nevertheless resonates with the problems dramatized by the *Conte du Graal*, see Steiner's T. S. Eliot lectures (1971). Of special interest for the themes of this chapter are his views on the relations between violence and high culture (29); the character, dangers, and necessity of utopian vision, with its linking of hope and transcendence (71–3 and 91–3); and the undermining of 'binary cuts' that orchestrate the values of Western civilization from the 'post-culture''s point of view (81–2).

The founding moments of romance, which transpose into a contemporary medium the epic traditions of Antiquity, address twelfth-century problems of violence no less pressing for the aristocratic public claimed in the prologues of *Thèbes* and *Troie*. Medieval romance is entertainment to be sure, but not without its serious side, even when Chrétien de Troyes gives it a new twist by apparently abandoning the matter of Rome for the matter of Britain, frivolous stuff with its marvelous tales of Arthur and his knights of the Round Table (whatever historical claims Geofflrey of Monmouth may make for this legendary king of Britain[2]). A master of rhetoric, as subtle as he is complex, Chrétien soaks up all the models available to him and boldly reinvents them through his art of *conjointure*, which sets a benchmark for numerous romancers who follow in his wake. Within his own corpus and particularly in his last romance, Chrétien anticipates, shapes, and challenges a whole romance tradition, still in formation when he is writing in the latter half of the twelfth century. This chapter examines how his 'Story of the Grail' participates in a dialogue about violence that takes offl from *romanz* to intersect with biblical visions of destruction and restoration. As we shall see, his complex interrogation of violence will reverberate significantly in later rewritings of the Grail quest.

From the enigmatic title calling attention to the serving dish whose story the author/narrator announces in the prologue with great fanfare (but what does the story of a deep, wide dish have to do with knights of the Round Table?) to the hermit's authoritative explanation that opens more mysteries than it solves, questions linked to transformations are what this 'Story of the Grail' seems to be about. And while there is much room for disagreement about the Grail, few readers would argue with the suggestion that Chrétien's *Conte du Graal* poses the problem of human violence and the creation—or rather, the restoration—of a just society. Yet this may seem a polemical claim to those familiar with the plethora of difflerent critical interpretations generated by this romance. In the early 1980s, Harry Williams summarized more than fifteen widely divergent views published since 1928, and the list continues to grow.[3] Brigitte Cazelles sums up the majority of those interpretations, which see the *Conte du Graal* 'as a turning point in the development of medieval romance' and read it as 'offlering to its audience a spiritualized ideal of a new kind of chivalry governed by a universal vision of chivalry's redemptive mission in the world' (1996: 1). In contrast to that critical trend, Cazelles offlers a 'social reading' of the romance, which she anchors briefly in the social history of contemporary France but follows primarily within the narrative representations found in the *Conte* (see below). Her approach is a valuable reminder that Chrétien's romance engages the social and political problems of his time, though it does so indirectly through the displacements of

---

[2] On the move between history and fiction in the 12th-cent. historiographic tradition, see Rollo's analyses of William of Malmsbury, Geoffrey of Monmouth, Wace, Benoît de Sainte-Maure, Gerald of Wales, and William of Newburgh (1998).

[3] For an updated list of readings that includes spiritual, Celtic, and more recent psychoanalytic (Lacanian and Jungian) approaches as well, see Burgwinkle (2004: 91 and n. 9).

fiction. My own reading struggles with the atypical interaction of the social and the spiritual as represented in this romance world, the incongruous conjunction that offers verse continuators and prose romancers such a difficult model for reading and rewriting. Concerned with tracking in the *Conte*, and in its dialogue with the continuations, the explorations made possible through fiction, I rarely take my readers directly back to the world outside romance. But Chrétien's play across the boundaries of romance and history invites his public, both medieval and modern, to follow the implications of his works into the problems of contemporary society in which they participate as both mirror and shaper of the historical text. I hope that this examination of violence as represented in the realm of fiction will invite my readers to take the next step in deepening our understanding of medieval society's efforts to grapple with a problem that has become no less pressing today.[4]

Just as the symbol of the Grail has come to represent in modern Western society an ideal solution as yet unfound, so in Chrétien's originating work any hope for a final resolution remains enigmatically suspended, as the romance continues to orient our hermeneutic search without offering up the object of our—or the heroes'—quests. But if Chrétien gives no easy solution to the enigmas posed, he has not left us without resources to explore the nature and parameters of violence represented within the problematic of an Arthurian ideal confronted by its failures, as well as by the rival and possibly incompatible ideal of Christianity. Christian practice and belief, which served as backdrop in previous Arthurian romances for knights who regularly went to mass on their way to encountering marvelous adventures, here moves into the foreground precisely because it not only deepens the critique of courtly values; it offers a vision and mode of change.[5]

'The good old days' topos that opens the *Vie de saint Alexis* is typical of a negative model of change widely available in the Middle Ages: an expectation that any transformation represents a falling away from a primary moment of truth and value, crystallized in Christian beliefs based on the Fall and original sin redeemed by the coming of the Messiah, or in the myths of Antiquity that situate an original moment in the past designated as a Golden Age. The popular figure illustrated by the Wheel of Fortune presents change as cyclical with every rise countered by a fall and vice versa. But the twelfth century also offers some

---

[4] For more direct approaches to the question of violence in medieval society, see Haidu's work on the interplay of literary and historical co-texts, and esp. his discussion of the debate in contemporary historiography about the prevalence of violence in the Middle Ages (2004: 16–22). Among historians see e.g. Bennett (1998) and White (1998).

[5] This is, of course, not the first time that a critique of courtly values appears in Chrétien's corpus: the gap between the Arthurian ideal and knightly practice has been a constant in his romances, as his heroes aim to bring values and performance into alignment. *Le Chevalier au lion* marks an important stage, insofar as it teaches the impulsive Yvain how to put his knightly prowess in the service of others. Although some later Grail romances will use the Christian point of view to formulate a more explicitly negative evaluation of Arthurian chivalry (see below), other romances follow Chrétien in finding a critical perspective from within a courtly and secular value system, as can be seen, e.g. in the Prose *Tristan* as reflected through the figures of Kahedin, Daguenet, and Dinadan.

positive views of change, Augustinian and Chartrian models that allow hope for improvement or advancement.[6] Eschatological schemas, intellectual progress, moral enhancement, conversion, education, endless cycles, or the entropy of decadence: what kinds of change does Chrétien's romance describe or imply through actions performed, character development, or voices that speak within it?

One of the most unsettling enigmas of the Grail story is the interlacing of Celtic and Christian elements, which raises the question of how a Christian vision afflects the nature of any transformation *in malo* or *bono* represented in the context of Arthurian romance. The commonplaces of Grail criticism include many difflerent Christian interpretations: they posit a celestial chivalry that transcends the terrestrial one, or recontextualize the Grail within the Passion story or the ritual of the mass—often confusing or conflating the *Conte du Graal* with later continuations and rewritings. Always the clever trickster, Chrétien himself invites readers to set offl in this direction with the prologue's New Testament quotes and sample of allegorical exegesis, Perceval's Easter conversion, and the hermit's explanations profflered in terms of sin, confession, and penitence.[7] But the matter of Britain remains central to Chrétien's *Conte*, even as religious elements take on a new role within it. The byways of his romance remain multiple, interlaced, and elusive. In order to probe the transformations envisaged or realized within this atypical confrontation of ideals, I follow here a less frequented path, one that intertwines romance and Old Testament waste lands, viewed through Isaiah's utopian vision of change.[8]

'Your land is desolate, your towns burned down, your fields—strangers lay them waste before your eyes' (1: 7). Echoing the curses of Deuteronomy (28: 15–68), the succession of destructions and restorations enumerated in the history books (especially the latter part of Kings and Chronicles), expressions of grief in Psalms (137, for example) and Lamentations (cf. 5: 3 'We are orphans, we are fatherless; our mothers are like widows'), Isaiah describes Israel's punishment for sins and wrongdoings in a manner familiar to readers of the *Conte du Graal* who have read the descriptions of destruction around Biaurepaire, heard the predictions of disaster that will befall the Fisher King's realm since Perceval failed to ask the questions. In conjunction with his dire warnings, the prophet also holds out

---

[6] See Delcourt (1990) on Augustinian and Chartrian models in relation to romance. On the notions of progress and decadence in the Middle Ages, see also the preface and collection of essays edited by Baumgartner and Harf-Lancner (*Progrès* 2003).

[7] Cf. Kay's argument for interpreting the signature 'Crestïen' as a kind of pseudonym inviting us to read across the boundaries of the courtly and the religious (1997).

[8] In his discussion of Hugh of St Victor's *Didascalicon* as 'a manual for Christian learning', Signer points out that Hugh 'understood the reading of the Bible as pertaining to things of this world rather than heavenly life' (2005: 84). In exploring the parallels between the Old and New Testaments' three-part structure, Hugh aligns Isaiah with the Gospels as an evangelist who announces the coming of Christ (85): his prophetic vision thus appplies to what has already happened in history. Hugh's understanding of Isaiah is consistent with the foundational role of history and the literal sense of Scripture (which he conceives primarily as the *sensus historicus*) in his educational program. In some sense then, we can say that the spiritual and historical concerns of the *Conte* intersect in this biblical reference.

the promise of future restoration not only for Zion but for all peoples, when 'they will hammer their swords into plowshares, their spears into sickles. Nation shall not lift up sword against nation and there will be no more training for war' (2: 4).[9] This biblical model—whose recall for a courtly public might be triggered by a number of elements in Chrétien's romance to be identified below—outlines a scenario that offlers the hope of change for the better, even as it recognizes the certainty of change for the worse before any future renewal takes place. It phrases a vision of peace in the vocabulary of *homo faber*'s gift for making weapons of war, as well as tools of agriculture—or, to borrow a phrase, civilization and its discontents.

If you want to beat swords into plowshares, you have to explore the categories of violence and the possibilities for change, and that is exactly what this romance does. The process of growth and change is easily recognized in Perceval's *Bildungsroman*, but many scholars have considered Gauvain to be a more static character, already fixed in Chrétien's earlier romances as the exemplary foil for the knightly protagonist who must surpass him. I have argued, along with others, that Perceval's story is complemented and enriched by Gauvain's own unexpected itinerary, his new role as a second, problematic hero in formation, or rather, re-formation. Structured through the complexities of two heroes, two interlocking parts, the *Conte du Graal*'s open-ended exploration of swords and plowshares does not solve all the problems raised, but it uncovers crucial factors that any future solution will have to incorporate, if it is to succeed. Clearly, the paradoxes of human nature and the nature of human society are inextricably intertwined in this problem of violence.

WHAT IS A LANCE?

The romance's opening scenes are designed to make us focus, through the naïve and fresh eyes of Perceval himself, on the definition and use of arms and armor. An

---

[9] For the sake of convenience, biblical quotations are given in translation from *The Jerusalem Bible*. Friedman points out the likelihood that much of Isaiah, Micah, Hosea, Proverbs, and the Solomon-to-Hezekiah sections of Kings and Chronicles, date from the reign of Hezekiah, *c.*715–687 BC (1989: 213; cf. 152 on the literature of exile). Rider's discussion of the prologue traces the link from Matthew back to Isaiah (2001: 254). Raugei (1993) concludes that there is only limited evidence in his works for direct knowledge or use of the Bible, based on her inventory of biblical material in Chrétien's corpus through direct allusions, names, etc. In her view, Chrétien's romances reflect rather a general familiarity with the Bible from clerical education and medieval culture. In email exchanges with Prof. Frans van Liere, Calvin College (15, 16, and 20 Sept. 2006), I have verified that Isaiah 2: 1–5 has a textual parallel in Micah 5 and was part of the liturgy for the first Sunday of Advent in the Roman Missal. Van Liere adds: 'I think it's safe to conclude that the text from Is. 2: 1–5 would resonate among medieval audiences, either through the liturgy, or through preaching' (20 Sept. 2006). It should be remembered, moreover, that the kind of public gathered together at the court of Henry the Liberal and Marie de Champagne would include clerics along with well educated and less educated lay people. See Benton (1961) on Henry's court and literary personnel; Putter on the converging roles and interests of 'knightly clerks' (a 'monstrous' combination 260) and 'clerical knights' (1995). For other explorations of links between Chrétien and biblical material, see e.g. Gouttebroze (1995, 1996), Laurie (1971, on Classical, Celtic, and Christian echoes), and Mickel (1972, on *Erec* and a commentary on Psalm 44).

adolescent boy who has grown up in complete isolation from the court goes out into the forest on a beautiful springtime morning, the time of change and renewal, to practice throwing javelins. This is no mere sport, though it is a pleasurable sport for the boy. Perceval's three javelins are weapons used in the pursuit of food, and he is training himself in the pragmatic art of hunting, when suddenly he encounters knights for the first time in his life. Astounded by the beauty of their arms glinting in the sunlight, Perceval interrogates their leader and demands definitions for each item inventoried. What are you, what is that, and that, and that? Were you born that way? Who fixed you up that way? When he is given an explanation of the knight's lance and hauberk, the adolescent Perceval insists on the superiority of the thrown javelin and piously hopes that God will keep such defenses from the animals he pursues, doe or stag (198–207, 269–76).

This encounter of ignorant boy and glamorous knight figures the meeting of opposites: javelin and lance, wild Welshman and courtly *chevalier*, the savage life of the forest and the civilized life of the Arthurian court. Its importance is signaled in the opening miniatures of manuscripts BN, fr. 12576 and 12577, discussed in earlier chapters (see Figs. 1 and 4). Properly aligning this series of oppositions defines the fundamental difference that characterizes *courtoisie*, the courtly ideal typically proposed by romance. As Perceval will be taught repeatedly by his mother, his cousin, his mentor Gornemant de Goort, the Hideous Damsel, and his hermit uncle, the order of chivalry was founded as a means of protecting orphans and widows, damsels in distress, the helpless young and old, in short, the weak of every category against the strong.[10]

While Perceval's javelins connote hunting, the pursuit of noncourtly prey, the knight's lance stands for courtly combat carried out according to a regulated code of conduct.[11] Their exchange about the lance thus reveals most significantly what is at stake here, both in the nature of the categories implied and the quality of Perceval's understanding. Once the naïve boy takes in the knight's appearance as a whole (his armor is so brilliant and beautiful, Perceval concludes he must be God accompanied by angels), his questioning pinpoints the lance as the first object of interest, perhaps in large measure because it resembles the javelins he holds. When the knight identifies the object, 'ce est ma lance' (197: 'this is my lance'), Perceval asks if that means he 'lances' it, i.e., throws it like a javelin: 'Dites vos, fait il, c'on la lance | Si com je faz mes gavelos?' (198–9). The knight is at pains to negate Perceval's literal interpretation of the word itself: 'Naie, vallet, fait il, tu iez toz sos! | Ains en fiert on tot demanois' (200–1: 'No, boy, says he, you're so silly;

---

[10] The biblical phrasing that identifies the victims of violence with the poor, orphans, and widows can also be found in the letters of Peter the Venerable (see Smith 2002: 19). In the Prose *Lancelot*, the Lady of the Lake gives her 'adopted' son a more developed exposition on the institution and history of the order of chivalry, including the *senefiance* of each piece of equipment: shield, hauberk, helmet, lance, sword, and horse (1978–83: 7, 249–56).

[11] Cf. Le Goff and Vidal-Naquet's discussion of arms in contrasting sets to analyze Yvain's use of bow and arrow in *Le Chevalier au lion* (1979).

rather one strikes with it directly').[12] Judging by Perceval's later reaction to the Red Knight's unchivalric use of his lance, turned to strike Perceval with the flat of the wooden haft, this succinct explanation probably escapes the novice's understanding. Perceval does not learn the proper use of this weapon until Gornemant's later demonstration of how to charge on horseback with the lance extended (see especially 1442, 1454, 1492). According to the historian Jean Flori (1998: 93–5), the use of the lance as a horizontal thruster—i.e., held horizontally by a knight on horseback, the iron tip used as the point of impact against an opponent with the aim of wounding and/or unseating him—was a fairly recent invention of chivalric culture in this period. The lance as weapon for jousting (preceding combat with swords) thus constitutes a new technique designed precisely to define a difference: the set of knights distinguished by a code of chivalry. The lance serves as a well-chosen synecdoche for a developing ideal.

The difficulty of putting that chivalric ideal into play—and maintaining the opposition that grounds it—appears repeatedly in the unfolding events of the romance. It is certainly no accident that Gornemant's instructions in the art of chivalry include not only the use of lance and sword but most especially the granting of mercy and the control of one's tongue. Perceval's meeting with Gornemant immediately follows his violent confrontation with the Red Knight, the hostile challenger of Arthur's authority (another scene vividly figured on the first folios of manuscripts T and U). His horse, vermillion arms, and armor now belong to Perceval and apparently define him as a knight. But that definition is one of the great questions posed by the romance. The meeting between Perceval and the Red Knight is decidedly unchivalric: neither one pays much attention to the other's words, as each one focuses on his own goal. In the case of Perceval, this means getting the Red Knight's arms, which he believes King Arthur has granted him, thanks to a sarcastic intervention from Kay the seneschal (whose irony completely escapes the literal-minded naïf). When the exasperated Red Knight uses the butt end of his lance as a club to give Perceval a blow on the shoulders, Perceval kills him with a javelin thrown straight into his eye. In Fig. 1, the illustrator of ms. T acutely represents the moment just before the tip of Perceval's javelin, lined up precisely with the visor of the Red Knight's helmet, penetrates, carrying forward the motion implied by its horizontal thrust across the image. So much for the protection of armor and the niceties of chivalric combat. In the scene on the bottom left, an earlier moment shows Perceval arriving at Arthur's court and asking a fellow to point out which one is the king. The illustrator shows how carefully he (or the organizer of the workshop) has read Chrétien's text, since we can clearly see Yvonet holding his knife (cf. the attribute identifying a saint), just as the narrator indicates, while the king and queen appear among

---

[12] The use of the verb *ferir* problematizes this explanation, since the same verb is used indiscriminately by characters and the narrator to designate a variety of violent actions that entail hitting, whether by lance, javelin, or sword. See vv. 201, 228, 270–1, 2671, 4304, 5109, 5517, 5678–9.

their companions at table (lower right). The complex juxtaposition of these two scenes, set side by side, below the initial meeting between Perceval and the five knights, seems to anticipate the whole arc of the narrative leading up to and after the Red Knight's death, since only Yvonet will follow Perceval to see what happens and thus be available to hear his exasperation and offfer help. In case we missed the metaphoric reduction of uncourtly knight to hunted prey, Perceval's frustrated attempts to separate the body from its armor lead him to exclaim:

> 'Je cuidoie de vostre roi
> Qu'il m'eüst ces armes donnees,
> Mais ains avrai *par carbonees*
> Trestot esbrahoné le mort
> Que nule des armes en port.'
>
> (1134–8; emphasis added)

('I thought your king gave me these arms, but I'll sooner have this body cut into pieces and grilled than put on a single piece of this armor.')

If Perceval himself seems oblivious of the deliciously black humor, his representation of a body chopped into bite-sized pieces and grilled like shish kebab signals to what extent he is incapable at this point of registering the difference between dead animals and dead people, incapable of recognizing the violent disproportion between provocation and response.[13] Chrétien's romance never explicitly criticizes this particular act of violence, although continuators and Wolfram von Eschenbach will see in Perceval's deed a failure of chivalry that calls for correction.[14] Here, on the contrary, Arthur develops a growing admiration for the unknown who may be a bit wild-eyed but whose prowess delivers the king from the Red Knight's shameful threats and then sends to his court a stream of vanquished knights as prisoners.[15]

At issue (at least in part) is who benefits from knightly deeds of arms. Appropriate violence may aim to keep the abuse of the strong in check, but what exactly is deemed appropriate and from whose point of view? As we saw in the last chapter, Perceval's mother responds to her son's ecstatic first vision of

[13] In the notes to his edn. (1994a: 1335), Poirion comments on the dissymmetry in this confrontation between a 'chasseur sauvage' and a 'gibier chevalier', while emphasizing Perceval's failure to distinguish between inside and outside, accident and substance. I would add that other oppositions at stake here include born and made, natural and not (or un-) natural, all made ripe for re-examination by the romance's insistent play.

[14] In Gerbert's Continuation, an elaborate episode takes Perceval to the castle of the Red Knight, whose four sons seek vengeance for their father's death (II, 10614–12305). In Wolfram's *Parzival*, the Red Knight is named Ither of Gaheviez and genealogically connected to Arthur's and Parzival's families. Parzival regrets his wrongful killing and must atone for it, as well as his mother's death (1980: 242, 253, 282, 295, 370–1).

[15] This episode implicitly raises a difficult issue: do certain situations call for noncourtly violence? Because of his uncourtliness, Perceval accomplishes what Arthur's knights have failed to accomplish, i.e. eliminate the imminent danger posed by the Red Knight. Cf. the discussion of the prologue's 'vilain gap ne parole estoute' in Ch. 1.

creatures more beautiful than angels with her own well-founded view of their destructive bent: 'Tu as veü si com je croi, | Les angles dont la gent se plaignent, | Qui ocïent quanqu'il ataignent' (398–400: 'You have seen, I think, the angels people complain about, who kill all they encounter').[16] The conflation of religious concepts and vocabulary with the deadly actions of killers is jarring, but powerful. The narrator exercises his gift for gallows humor with both mother and son, each comic thrust emblematic of their differing points of view. The Veuve Dame's family experiences exile and mutilation in the civil war attending the passage from Utherpendragon's to Arthur's reign; the subsequent killing of her two older sons soon after being knighted and her invalid husband's death from grief, give ample testimony to the truth of her negative assessment and justify, from her perspective, the removal of Perceval from knights and knighthood, despite his hereditary and natural inclination to find his place among the highest ranks of chivalry. Her solution is imperfect, temporary, and, in the end, no real solution to the issues raised by her critique (though it does offer a kind of secular equivalent to the withdrawal from society represented by monastics and hermits elsewhere in the narrative). But her founding act of separation is precisely what allows Perceval and the romance public to (re)investigate the nature of chivalry, its failures as well as its potential.

COLLAPSING OPPOSITIONS

The specific mechanism of failure highlighted in Perceval's encounter with the Red Knight may be termed a category violation, that is, the opposition between courtly and noncourtly weapons has collapsed because the opposing terms have crossed over, obscuring their difference: a lance is used as a club, a hunting weapon kills courtly prey. Even more disturbingly, the category of perpetrator—the clear distinction that should obtain between the heroes and villains—is, in this romance, radically violated when Perceval is repeatedly shown to be the one who does violence against the weak, however unwittingly. His mother's death, the caricature of rape forced on the Tent Maiden and her subsequent punishment at the hands of her beloved who kills countless knights in pursuit of Perceval, the Fisher King left unhealed and the numberless orphans, widows, and exiles who will suffer as the rich king's lands are devastated and his knights die—the victims seem to accumulate faster than the vanquished knights who announce Perceval's good deeds on behalf of his beloved Blancheflor. How does this excess of violence, intended or unintended, figure in the portrait of a youth who is expected to be the best knight in the world, according to a prophecy announced at Arthur's court by 'la pucele qui rit' ('the laughing maiden')?

---

[16] Cf. the Male Pucele's own critique of knighthood as she describes to Gauvain the violence she suffered as victim of the custom of Logres (see Ch. 2).

'Vallet, se tu vis par eage,
Ce pens et croi en mon corage
Qu'en trestot le monde n'avra,
N'il n'ert ne on ne l'i savra,
Nul meillor chevalier de toi;
Ensi le pens et cuit et croi.'

(1039–44)

('Young man, if you live long enough, this I think and believe in my heart, there will not be in the whole world, neither will there be nor will anyone know of any better knight than you. This is what I think and feel and believe.')

This is an extravagant prophecy, hyperbolic in its wandering clauses, emphatic in the repeated affirmation of the maiden's belief—and confirmed by the fool's recall of another prophecy that this maiden would not laugh until she saw the one who would have 'de chevalerie . . . toute la seignorie' (1061–2: 'complete lordship over chivalry'). Based on what we have seen thus far, Perceval is indeed someone who makes us laugh in relation to such preposterous claims, which the romance paradoxically sets out to realize through a series of disastrous failures, as well as astounding successes.

Moreover, Perceval is not the only hero in the romance who seems to cross over unexpectedly into the category of perpetrator. Accusations accumulate against Gauvain, twice summoned to justify himself against charges of treasonous murder and accused of imposing a punishment exceeding the bounds of justice even against a rapist (cf. Delcourt 1990: 247). Those accusations may or may not be justified. In its incomplete state, the romance does not allow its heroes to exonerate themselves fully.[17] Perceval corrects his unintentional abuse of the Tent Maiden, but in the romance's suspended ending he has yet to return to the Grail Castle to repair the damage against the Fisher King and his people; he has yet to atone for what his uncle identifies as the sin against his mother.[18] For his part, Gauvain twice prepares for a judicial combat to demonstrate his innocence, but so far has not been given the opportunity to do so. Nevertheless, his triumph as redeemer at the Castle of Ladies, which takes place between the two accusations, warrants the second hero's superiority in courtly virtues.[19] The positive and negative qualifications explicitly enumerated for successful completion of that marvelous test include prowess, wisdom, courage, and loyalty, while excluding cowards, traitors, perjurers, the covetous, and those with any evil vice of avarice or foolish, flattering speech (7553–62, 7585–604). The host's description provides retrospective proof of Gauvain's good intent and good deeds, once his successful abolition of the enchantment is proclaimed. He may indeed have

---

[17] The anonymous author of the *Queste del Saint Graal* amplifies Gauvain's negative role to the point that his wickedness disqualifies the king's nephew from the Grail quest.

[18] Gouttebroze identifies a repeated kernel in multiple episodes of the *Conte* (calamity/intervention of the hero/prosperity), which he reads as an indication of Perceval's eventual success at the Grail Castle inscribed in Chrétien's romance (1983: 52).

[19] Similarly, Lancelot's role as redeemer for the prisoners in Gorre plays as counterpart to the shame of riding in the cart, illustrated most explicitly when the two rumors about him collide in the Orgueilleux's challenge (2566–600).

killed—death, as the Veuve Dame indicates, is often associated with knighthood, whatever mercies the chivalric code introduces—but the notion of justice is not incompatible with all violence in this romance world, especially when self defense or defense of the weak is at stake.

Gauvain's curious adventures call attention to another mechanism for putting into question the clear distinction between courtly and uncourtly weapons—or for that matter, between weapons of war and tools of peaceful agriculture, the more radical opposition envisioned by the prophet Isaiah. When Gauvain arrives unrecognized at Escavalon, where Guigambresil has summoned him to answer for the king's death, he finds himself caught in a trap: brother and sister have unwittingly extended hospitality to the family enemy and welcomed him into the very chamber of the dead man's daughter. As soon as Gauvain is recognized by a vavasor, both he and the sister find themselves under attack by the enraged townspeople. The lady quickly helps Gauvain arm himself but he has no shield. A chessboard will do the trick, along with his sword Excalibor (usually associated with Arthur but here in the hands of his nephew). Gauvain easily defends the door of the tower, as the lady joins the fray, throwing large chess pieces like missiles against the angry mob. The scene offlers a riotous burlesque of courtly engagements, as Gauvain plays the role of doorman ('portier', 5989, 5997), and the combatants include numerous peasants and bourgeois, as well as the sister, even though ladies are more typically cast in the role of helpless victim in need of defense.[20] If the category of combatants seems to take a ride on a merry-go-round, the category of weapons increases exponentially to include the very tools of agriculture Isaiah's prophecy associates with peace.

> Lors veïssez vilains engrez,
> Qui prenent haces et gisarmes;
> Cist prent un escu sanz enarmes,
> Cist prent un hui et cist un van....
> N'i a si malvais qui ne praigne
> Forche ou flael ou pic ou mache.
>
> (5936–9, 5944–5)

(Then you could see angry peasants grabbing axes and pikes; this one takes a shield without straps, that one takes a door and this one a winnow. No one is such a scoundrel that he doesn't take a pitchfork or a flail or a pick or a club.)

These are not swords turning into plowshares, but pitchforks, picks, winnows, and flails joining in with clubs, axes, halberds, shields without straps, and even doors, to become weapons of destruction in the hands of townspeople who first attack Gauvain and then the tower itself.[21]

---

[20] Compare Gauvain's equivocal identity at the tournament. The accusation that he is a merchant avoiding taxes is linked precisely to the signs of his knightly status: the multiplication of horses and shields brought along on his journey.

[21] The description of the town's *métiers* begins with an enumeration of those who make helmets and hauberks, saddles (in ms. A: lances) and blazons, bridles, spurs, and swords (5766–9).

What can we make of this topsy-turvy world? In *How the Mind Works*, the cognitive scientist Stephen Pinker reminds us that the human brain is compelled to organize: 'without categories, mental life would be chaos' (1997: 307). He is quick to point out, however, that some categorizing may appear useless and illogical. Pinker takes his example from Jorge Luis Borges's description of a Chinese encyclopedia article that divides animals into those that belong to the Emperor, embalmed ones, trained animals, suckling pigs, mermaids, fabulous ones, stray dogs, those included in this classification, those that tremble as if mad, innumerable ones, others, those that have just broken a flower vase, and those that resemble flies from a distance (307). We may wonder if the same illogic applies to the apparently senseless explosion of the weapons category in Chrétien's romance. But the *Conte*'s enigmas, however much they disorient us, constantly suggest that they are not meaningless nonsense but rather puzzles to be solved (if we can). It does not require much digging here to discern a pattern that demonstrates how anything and everything may become a weapon, from the mob's heterogeneous collection of objects to the human body itself demonstrably used for violence over and over again in the narrative. Not just lances and swords, but hands and feet, and most especially words, words spoken with or without sarcasm, and even words not spoken at all may wound and brutalize.

Confronted with such evidence, we might simply agree with the criticism of Perceval's mother. Her family's history teaches the lesson of moral entropy:

> 'Malvestiez, honte ne pereche
> Ne dechiet pas, qu'ele ne puet,
> Mais les buens dechaoir estuet.'
>
> (432–4)

('Evil, shame, and laziness do not decline since they cannot but the good must fall.')

Is the romance only a straightforward demonstration of her maxim that the good, even the best, must inevitably degenerate, while *Malvestiez*, already at rock bottom, stays the same? We should first look deeper and see if this shift in categories may yet hold out some hope of improvement. Isaiah has warned that change for the worse is certain, but he has not abandoned the possibility of renewal. His prophecy is meant to act not as an impossible utopia outside of time but as a lesson in how to redirect the movement of history away from the inevitable regressions toward transformations, improvements that move closer to a vision of peace. Chrétien's exploration of the Arthurian ideal, offered as a model for imitation while yet in need of repair, seems to follow a similar thrust.

Hints of possible links between the *Conte* and Isaiah's prophetic vision begin to surface in the strange episode that precedes Gauvain's arrival at Escavalon and serves as prelude to it, since Gauvain's aborted hunt leads directly to his meeting with the new king, out hunting in the forest.[22] This is surely among the most

---

[22] Likewise, Perceval meets the Fisher King while he is fishing, the only form of hunting the wounded king can enjoy. Finding, exploring, and contrasting the many parallels between the Perceval and Gauvain sections is an important facet of criticism focused on this romance—e.g.

obscure and least satisfyingly explicated scenes in the entire puzzling romance.[23] Critics have recognized fragments of the Celtic marvelous, which in stories like Marie de France's *Guigemar* or Chrétien's own *Erec et Enide* use a magical white animal to introduce the hero's most significant adventures. Here the hunt of the white doe seems strangely out of joint. First of all, Gauvain is on his way to a judicial combat, accompanied by seven horses, two shields, and seven squires—including Yvonet who helped Perceval disentangle and then don the Red Knight's armor. When he spots some beasts grazing near a forest, Gauvain decides to go hunting on his best horse and with a lance 'molt roide et fort' (5667: 'very stiff and strong') brought along for use in combat against the king of Escavalon.[24] When a chivalric lance thus functions as a weapon of the hunt, we can observe a replay of the same category violation featured in Perceval's encounter with the Red Knight, here played in reverse.

In pursuit of the does, Gauvain 'laid his lance across the neck' of one of them: 'si li mist | Sor le col sa lance en travers' (5678–9). What exactly does that mean? Did he use his lance as a horizontal thruster? Did he 'lance' it, in the way Perceval threw his javelin into the eye of the Red Knight? Difficult to determine from the syntax, the gesture strikes us nevertheless as strangely familiar, since the narrator used the same expression, *en travers*, to describe how the Red Knight struck Perceval with a lance whose iron point he carefully turned away: 'si l'en done tel colee | Par les espaulles en travers' (1104–5).[25] That heavy but essentially harmless blow led to Perceval's deadly response. In this case, the doe jumps like a stag ('come cerf', 5680),[26] and Gauvain gives chase. He would have caught it

Haidu (1968: 200–59), Vial (1987: 9–12)—although it has too infrequently led to deeper analyses of Gauvain's part and its impact on Perceval's.

[23] Saly offers an interesting commentary of this episode, picking up some of the same clues I analyze but leading into a typological reading of Perceval's and Gauvain's stories in relation to each other, against the mythical background of the Sovereignty theme seen in contemporary Irish tales (1994b).

[24] Hunting is of course a courtly pastime, although it is not often that Chrétien's heroes engage in it. In *Erec*, Arthur's entire court (minus Erec) goes out hunting on 'chaceors', armed with 'ars et . . . saietes' (73–4: 'hunting horses, bow and arrows'). 'La chasse, leur [les chevaliers] plaisir favori, leur fournissait l'occasion d'affronter, dans les vastes forêts, des animaux sauvages encore nombreux en Europe occidentale, avec l'arc mais aussi avec la lance et l'épée' (Flori 1998: 131). Contemporary usage varies, as Flori indicates, but in this romance the lance is clearly identified with its 'proper' use as a weapon of courtly combat. Cf. debates about theories of origin and the length of the bleeding lance carried in the Grail procession, since the size of lance typically used as a horizontal thruster could scarcely be held upright at its midpoint, '[e]mpoignie par le mileu' (3193), as this one is. Diamond suggests that, overall, bow and arrows used in hunting mark an advancement over the spear in the repeated march toward and declines from greater civilization found in cultures all over the globe (1999).

[25] Does this blow on the shoulder caricature the act of knighting? Cf. the three actions by which Gauvain knights 500 *valets*, first tying on their right spur, then their sword belt, and finally the accolade: 'si lor dona la colee' (9186). When Gornemant knights Perceval, he ties on his right spur, according to the custom of that time (as the narrator explains, 1624–8), places his sword belt around his waist, kisses him, and then lectures him on the order of chivalry. No accolade is mentioned.

[26] The cross-gendering introduced by the comparison recalls the male/female conflation in *Guigemar*, in which the wounded doe who pronounces a prophecy for the hero also carries antlers.

but, when his horse unexpectedly went lame, he was forced to abandon the pursuit. Is this an anticipation of the interrupted tête-à-tête with the sister at Escavalon? A recall of the sparrowhawk and the abandoned goose whose three drops of red blood against the white snow led Perceval to lean on his lance and meditate on the *semblance* of Blancheflor, an episode that so frequently attracts critical attention? The association has led many readers to recognize an intricate nexus of red and white operating throughout the romance whose network includes the bleeding lance that precedes the Grail at the Fisher King's castle.[27] Multiple connections and overdetermination are typical modes in Chrétien's romances, but another less obvious and still loose string requires attention.

Gauvain's horse has thrown a shoe, and they will need to find a blacksmith to repair it (5684, 5697–702). That blacksmith does not turn up in Gauvain's plot line, but it may be no accident that such an apparently gratuitous detail has already appeared in Perceval's story (and will return in both the Third and Fourth Continuations). According to his cousin, Perceval, too, will be looking for a blacksmith, although his will have another task: to reforge the sword given by the Fisher King, a sword destined exclusively for Perceval and yet destined to break at a moment of great peril.[28] Both heroes experience significant equipment failures that require the intervention of an iron worker. Perceval's cousin gives quite detailed instructions about who the blacksmith must be in Perceval's case: only Triboët can repair the sword 'qui unques d'ome ne traist sanc | N'onques ne fu a besoig traite' (3656–7: 'which has never drawn a man's blood, nor was ever drawn in need'). Is this the kind of sword, one never connected to violent action, that can be beaten into a plowshare? Is Triboët a blacksmith who can beat weapons into agricultural tools or, in the Vulgate translation, *lanceas* into *falces*, that is, lances into pruning hooks, sycthes, or sickles? Could he or some other blacksmith help shoe Gauvain's horse and even transform the bleeding lance destined to destroy Arthur's kingdom?[29]

The wise vavasor at Escavalon who reports the prophecy attached to the lance describes it as crying tears of bright blood from its tip:

---

[27] The beauty of a woman's face connected to great acts of devastation, as well as great poetry, has a long history in Western civilization, as indicated in the introduction to this chapter.

[28] Ms. T has an interpolated passage in which the sword breaks during the combat between Perceval and the Orgueilleux de la Lande (3926a–t). The gift of this sword, sent by one of the Fisher King's nieces, immediately precedes the appearance of the bleeding lance. The whole passage (3133–84) contains a mystifying amount of detail regarding the sword's history, its physical appearance, what the Fisher King observes, etc. These veiled hints invite future elaboration, which continuators will not fail to appreciate when they introduce the test of the broken sword as another qualifying action for the Grail hero.

[29] In counterpoint, we might think here about the role of blacksmiths in mythic traditions both classical and Celtic, from Vulcan (who makes arms for Aeneas) to the many-talented Lugh (blacksmith, goldsmith, king and warrior, father of Cúchulainn with the formidable spear). Cf. the many theories that try to explain the origin and symbolism of the Grail and the lance, summarized by Frappier (1972a: 193–212).

'La lance dont la pointe lerme
Le sanc tot cler que ele plore;
Et s'est escrit qu'il ert une hore
Que toz li roiames de Logres,
Qui jadis fu la terre as ogres,
Sera destruis par cele lance.'

(6164–9)

('the lance from whose tip form tears of bright blood that it cries. And it's written that one day the entire kingdom of Logres, which in the old days was the land of the ogres, will be destroyed by this lance.')

Sufflering and violence are thus woven together into the very fabric of Arthur's kingdom, from its past, as sounded through the rhyme words 'Logres' and 'ogres', to its future, written in prophecy. The lance itself seems to mourn its destined role in the destruction, expressed in the doubly resonating image of its tears of blood. By the terms of an agreement that permits him to leave Escavalon after the fiasco of his reception, Gauvain himself is caught in paradox, required to seek the lance that will destroy his uncle's kingdom. Inexplicably at this moment, Perceval's and Gauvain's separate quests converge in the direction of the Fisher King's castle, though the intersection remains unexplained and unwritten in Chrétien's romance. The *Queste del Saint Graal* will extrapolate from this prophecy a connection between Grail quest and catastrophe for Arthur's kingdom, but Chrétien's *Conte du Graal* still remains suspended between prophecy and realization, with an escape clause for Gauvain's quest, represented as impossible and limited to a single year.

ISAIAH'S UTOPIAN VISION IN ARTHURIAN GARB

One prophecy may recall another, and the prologue has given us a model for using biblical comparisons. A look back to the opening movements of the romance reveals further links to Isaiah's precedent. Perceval's questions about arms and armor during the first episode play in counterpoint to the knight's repeated efflort to find out if a party of five knights and three damsels has passed by. Although Perceval appears to ignore the questions, once his own queries have been satisfied, he suggests the knight will find the answer he seeks from the widow's harrowers, who break up clods of soil nearby in order to sow the plowed fields. Here we are at the crux of Isaiah's vision. Perceval has been living in a world from which knights and all they represent, even their very name, has been banished, a world whose economy is based on peaceful agricultural production as represented by the mother's harrowers.[30] In the cross-currents of Perceval's new

---

[30] Baumgartner suggests that Perceval's sin against his mother may have been his rejection of the heritage she prepared for him: 'ce royaume de paix qu'elle lui offrait, . . . ce val où vivre en harmonie avec soi, avec la nature, au rythme des grands cycles vitaux que la mère avait su préserver, dans la joie

and old worlds, we find juxtaposed the very implements and domains aligned in Isaiah's prophecy of swords beaten into plowshares.

This vision should not be taken too literally. Indeed, deciding how literally to interpret is one of, if not *the* major task of Perceval's development, of any properly human development. It reflects the dilemma of Chrétien's readers in every one of his romances but here more crucially than ever. The author/narrator has set the stage for this scene and its metaphorical overtones from the opening words of his romance.[31]

> Ki petit semme petit quelt,
> Et qui auques requeillir velt,
> En tel liu sa semence espande
> Que Diex a cent doubles li rande;
>
>   (1–4)

(He who sows little reaps little, and anyone desirous of a large harvest should scatter his seeds in such a place that God will give it back to him a hundred fold.)

Chrétien is himself one who plows and sows, not literally of course, but with words that plant seeds for growth and change in his patron, as in the society which finds pleasure and food for thought in his romances.[32] His aristocratic audience could hardly envision Perceval joining his mother's harrowers in their work, and we do not expect Chrétien to put forward a social argument in which the first estate would take up the tasks and identity of the third, literally speaking.[33] But he does seem to invite us, however enigmatically, to ponder how and if his contemporaries (and ours) might change weapons of war into tools of peaceful culture. He has sown that question throughout the romance by constantly foregrounding violence and weapons, although, paradoxically, the narrative gives very little space to actual descriptions of fighting, since the narrator repeatedly refuses to waste time describing combat (e.g. 2228–33, 2678–80, 3928–9).

If agricultural implements can so readily become weapons of destruction, such transformations, however deadly, may at least presage the possibility of change for the better, since the process of change itself is so obviously unavoidable. Can we accept the widow's realism and yet remain hopeful? In the unfinished Story of

---

perpétuelle de la reverdie, et dont le graal sans doute est le signe sensible' (1999: 112). Deist analyzes the role of the forest refuge in relation to Perceval's past—the mother's isolation from aristocratic lineage—and future—the hermit uncle's reconnection of Perceval within a web of aristocratic filiations (2003: 138–51; see also the section on Gornemant that picks up these elements, 195–203).

[31] As we saw in Ch. 1, the maxim recognizable here has both New Testament and Classical roots; the same idea is widely disseminated in medieval culture in the form of proverbs. See Raugei (1993: 206–8), Luttrell (1983), and Hunt (1971).

[32] The metaphor equating plowing and writing (with a stylus) is a commonplace of ancient and medieval thought. Dragonetti (1980: 68) cites Isidore of Seville as an example.

[33] But Heyworth argues for reading *Perceval* as a rehabilitation of 'a labor ethic to unite the religious, commercial and humanistic spheres of medieval culture' (2000: 19).

the Grail, Chrétien has left open the possibilities for comedy and tragedy, failure and success, optimism and pessimism. As we shall see, the verse continuations will generally play out the positive view, the *Queste del Saint Graal* and the *Mort le roi Artu* the negative. But first, in order to pursue further how Chrétien dramatizes the problem of violence in relation to the problematic of change, we need to examine more closely the *Conte*'s characteristic interplay of setting up and undermining oppositions between different categories of weapons. The collapse of categories witnessed so far does not necessarily mean that there is no possibility of making viable distinctions. Chrétien's romance does not encourage that degree of nihilism. Though he may puncture the comforts of illusion, the dreams of escapist fantasies, this author counts on the power of fiction and imagination's flight to explore and enlarge the realm of the possible, even if our inventions must answer to the constraints of human nature, conceived in medieval terms.

RE-READING OPPOSITIONS

Then what is to be gained by setting up oppositions and then undermining them—lance versus javelin, real fighting versus war games (as tournament or chess)? I would argue that Chrétien is not suggesting there is no significant difference between weapons properly used for hunting and those used in combat according to a code of chivalry. The efforts to channel, control, and regulate violence constitute necessary and worthwhile steps any society needs to take, and history shows that all societies do so in one way or another (Van Creveld 1991: 80–94). At one level then, the value of these oppositions and distinctions is indisputable. But given the possibility that anything and everything can be used as a weapon added to our inclination to do so, the classifications that would establish difference are ultimately part of the same open-ended set: lance & javelin & chessboard & fist & word & so on. We forget at our peril that violence is part of human nature, even in heroes, that the use of violence to curtail violence frequently escapes the bounds of control. Lest we forget, Gauvain's name linked to a series of accusing and criminal knights sounds an insistent aural reminder: Guigambresil, Greoreas, and Guiromelant.

The creation and collapse of categories should ultimately help us grasp the paradox of human nature, its unchanging changeability, which requires us paradoxically to sit on both sides of opposition, as reflected in the and/both logic of Chrétien's romance. As long as we operate under heaven, *soz ciel*, any solution to violence—a problem that has philosophical and theological, as well as historical dimensions—can only be provisional. We are always on the way up or down around the Wheel of Fortune, in the microcosm and the macrocosm, individually as in society as a whole, though of course for any given individual or society, it matters where we are located in the patterns of history, the alternation of restorations and destruction. It matters how much or how little violence prevails. In that light, we might consider Isaiah's prophecy again not only in terms of its immediate call for change but in terms of its placement within the Old and New Testaments. The Bible as a set of books recognizes the cyclical aspects of human history, but it situates those cycles within an overarching linear development. Isaiah's vision of peace and restoration thus calls for action in history even as it sounds that call within and across the pattern of Israel's past and future, its repeated rise and fall across the march of biblical history. Just so, in the *Conte du Graal*, Perceval's and Gauvain's quests are located within the larger framework of Arthurian history, its rise and fall.[34] This is another striking anomaly in Chrétien's last work, which re-inserts romance into the framework of history from which *Erec et Enide*, his first Arthurian romance, had excerpted it. His public already knows that Arthur's reign—whatever value it may possess as an ideal—cannot, did not, will not last. It is not a permanent solution, and perhaps none exists inside the human frame.

Yet the biblical trust in the direction of history orients Christianity's views on solutions that move into and out of this world. Christ's Passion and the Day of Judgment, repentance and grace, all these themes are reflected in the romance as well. They represent actions or interventions that open a space for sudden trans-formation, a leap to a different level of experience. They appear in the characters' Christian greetings to each other, as they do in the repetitions of the credo by Perceval's mother and the knight penitent who leads Perceval to his Easter encounter with the hermit. When Perceval remembers that he has forgotten God during five fruitless years of adventures that failed to lead him back to the Grail Castle, when he has confessed and repented and experienced the Easter renewal of life, he is ready to set out once again, a more complete knight prepared to undo the wrongs done.

Christianity's radical model of change through conversion thus supplements and enriches the gradual model of change built into education, the *Bildungs-roman* of Perceval's development.[35] But this Perceval is quite unlike Galahad, the hero of the quest for the Holy Grail who will take shape as a figure of Christ in the thirteenth-century prose romance. Chrétien de Troyes does not appear to make an argument for renouncing the world. His romances tend to reject solutions that lead to withdrawal from society at large (cf. *Erec* and *Cligès*). They initiate instead a process of restoration *soz ciel* through defamiliarization or 'making strange', a device dear to the Russian Formalists of the early twentieth century.[36] In this romance, defamiliarization aims especially at our understand-ing of arms and armor, knights and knighthood, which are suddenly changed by being removed from their expected roles and viewed from a new perspective. Defamiliarization becomes a process of education by putting into question

---

[34] See Ch. 5 on structural parallels between the Bible and the *Perceval* cycle.

[35] Cf. the discussion of Gornemant's views on nature and *norreture* as complementery forces in education in Ch. 3.

[36] See e.g. Victor Chlovki's 'L'Art comme procédé' in the collection of essays translated by Todorov (1965).

typical responses and assumptions; it requires reflection and opens the way for rethinking, transformation, difference. Continually problematized in the *Conte*, the category of weapons is presented in a strange light: disarming likened to the extraction of food from a shell, remedial lessons in jousting, a lance that bleeds, swords that break, a knight with two shields mistaken for a merchant, a game-board used for a real fight, and knightly arms unsuitably juxtaposed with palfrey and nag. Examples multiply as the first part's approach to the familiar material of romance is renewed through the unfamiliar eyes of Perceval and finds its complement in the second part when even the standard bearer of Arthurian romance, the stock character Gauvain moves into what is for him the unfamiliar territory of the evolving hero.

The matter of Britain is itself a common device for defamiliarization in romance, as it opens different windows on the world, disrupts or enlarges the constraints of common experience based on *realia*, adds new dimensions for change. The *merveilleux* of Breton storytellers supplies much of the source material for Arthurian romance and contributes more than a little to its charm. Gauvain's disenchantment of the queens' castle at the Roche de Champguin, where he meets Arthur's mother and his own, is the most successful restoration presented in the *Conte*. The castle frozen in time and awaiting its savior operates in the dimension of the marvelous, as it recalls the Other World of Celtic myth. Yet it remains within easy travel distance from Arthur's court. This episode, as well as others in the romance, suggests a dynamic interplay between the marvelous and the quotidian.[37] On the one hand, most human activity takes place in the day to day where we have to solve the problems of human nature and its tendency to violence. On the other, different levels of reality available in the play of fiction may help us conceive and invent new possibilities to widen the scope of what is possible within the ongoing movement of daily life. Gauvain's success at the Castle of Ladies is thus celebrated with a resumption of social life figured in the knighting of five hundred *valets* (some grown gray-haired during their long wait for a new lord).

But that triumph is quickly bypassed, as the hero picks up his journey with the Male Pucele and jumps over the Gué Périlleux—the Perilous Ford no one has ever crossed. Another marvelous success to designate an extraordinary hero?[38] In

---

[37] Of course, what constitutes the real may differ between people as between epochs: what is realistic or *vraisemblable* shifts between Chrétien's time and ours. The Christian marvelous and the Breton *merveilleux* suggest that the boundary between the real and the supernatural, the fantastic, the magical, etc., may be effaced or moved around in different contexts, especially where the interplay between history and fiction sets 'the rules of the game'. Cf. Harf-Lancner's analysis of images of the fantastic (a mix of Christian and Breton *merveilleux*) in the manuscript illustrations (1993), as well as Rollo's analysis of magic and sorcery as a metaphor for the power of language and writing in 12th-cent. texts (2000).

[38] In Perceval's story, the prophecy of the 'pucele qui rit' (1039–44), as well as the Grail Castle adventure, work similarly to mark him for an extraordinary future. In Chrétien's romances, an adventure out of the ordinary series traditionally designates the hero (e.g. the 'Joie de la Cort' in *Erec*, the furture cemetery in *Lancelot*); its doubling here may reflect the difficulty of moving Gauvain out of his role as the standard bearer and into the role of hero who surpasses the

any case, it leads most significantly to a meeting with Guiromelant who hates Gauvain because Gauvain's father killed Guiromelant's and Gauvain himself killed his cousin. We have come full circle with the second hero, since this takes him back to the similar accusation of treasonous murder he had to confront in the crisis scene at Arthur's court, where his story began unexpectedly some 5,000 verses into what appeared to be Perceval's romance.[39] The problem of violence is not simply that of individuals and their actions; it involves families and clans, communities and the multiple individuals tied to them.

Perceval's own triumph at Arthur's court was similarly interrupted as soon as word of his failure at the Fisher King's castle caught up to him. The marvelous restoration anticipated did not take place. Perceval failed to ask the questions about bleeding lance and Grail—why does it bleed? whom does it serve?— questions that focus precisely on the fundamental opposition between war and peace called into play by Isaiah's vision and the romance's own interrogation. What does this weapon of violent destruction have to do with a dish carrying food, symbolized by the single host it contains, the bread of Christ's body?[40] Defamiliarization robs us of our certainties and introduces questions. In the romance's opening scene the naïf asks many questions, but paradoxically in the course of the action he learns to remain silent at the wrong moment. He makes progress, but not all changes are positive; some inevitably tend toward the worse, require correction, further improvement. Perceval must still learn how to ask questions appropriately, at the right moment, in order to heal the javelin-pierced Fisher King, restore life to his lands and to those exiles who became strangers like Perceval and his mother, the exemplary widows and orphans repeatedly offered protection by the chivalric code in romance and Mosaic law in the Bible, by Carolingian and Capetian kings, as well as the Peace of God movement in medieval France.[41]

UNENDING QUESTIONS

In Perceval's Grail adventure, the key to transformation, healing, and restoration is not prowess in combat. Although it may still be necessary to defend the weak against the strong even in the best possible society, arms alone will not supply the necessary solution to mutability and violence. More significant is the ability to

standard. Saly's analysis of the inverted symmetries between the two heroes sets up a pattern in which their failures and successes appear to be coordinated (1994b).

[39] See the discussion of looping as a characteristic move in the narrative architecture of the *Perceval* Continuations (Ch. 5).

[40] The First Continuation will answer that question by interpreting the lance as the weapon used by Longinus to pierce Christ's side, but the *Conte* insists on the Celtic associations tied to the lance, which resist integration into a Christological reading (cf. Walter 2004).

[41] On the Peace and Truce of God movements, see Bisson (*c.*1982–9), Haidu (2004: 22–32), and Bennett (1998: 137–8).

ask the right question at the right moment.[42] Although the romance has guided us to the basic categories in the interplay between violence and sustenance, destruction and production, it cannot give all the answers for all time in all places for all people. Given the moral entropy described by Perceval's mother, individuals as well as societies will have to engage in repeated quests for restoration: only *Malvestiez* remains itself. At different points in history, specific human societies may be closer or farther away from biblical or Arthurian ideals, but the romance reminds us through the examples of its double heroes that men and women have the power to (re)educate and convert themselves, reverse downward trends: 'les buens dechaoir estuet' (434) rhymes with the verb 'puet' and suggests, beyond the mother's disillusioned view, that the good may fall but, like Perceval and Gauvain, they may also, given enough time and narrative, improve, correct shortcomings, restore health to a king or a queen, renew their lands and societies. This utopian vision, tempered by realism, by the risk of failure as well as the possibility of hope, may be one of the meanings associated with the prologue's praise of *carité*, love, generosity, compassion, charity which is God.

The doubling of heroes in the *Conte*, like the confrontation of Philip and Alexander in the prologue, is not incidental to the process of conversion and compassion. It suggests in a different way the changeability of the human species and our need to diversify approaches: particular improvements will work for some, not others, sometimes, not always. In all likelihood Gauvain and Perceval will arrive at different destinations, however much their paths intertwine and intersect. Restorations *soz ciel* will in any case never be permanent. So the romance continues to force us to work for new questions, new answers, however temporary their solutions may be—as witnessed by the four verse continuations that line up in Chrétien's wake, along with the multiple prose rewritings in the Middle Ages, modern retellings in narrative and film, critical bibliography that continues to pile up. Some rewriters are more inclined to emphasize the upward trend, others the downward spiral, but all must respond to the complex movements inscribed in Chrétien's double vision.

Paradoxically, eliminating weapons altogether may be the least likely solution to the problem of violence, since that seems impossible within the parameters of human nature as we know it in Chrétien's romance.[43] In some sense, such a

---

[42] Stanesco discusses the importance of the question over the answer in medieval thought and the idea of too much *taciturnitas* as a sin, a notion that resurfaces in the 13th cent. (2002: 166–9). His analysis of Perceval's failure to ask the questions during his first visit to the Grail Castle also emphasizes the positive value of such a delay: the possible gain in reflexivity through maturation, the necessary reticence in moving from appearance to being (177). We might also compare this move from violent to verbal solutions to the reconciliation at the end of *Le Chevalier au lion*, when Yvain's aggression against Laudine's fountain is followed by Lunete's word play. See Bruckner (2006b), as well as Cheyette and Chickering's analysis of *Yvain*'s ending in light of contemporary conflict resolution between feuding nobles (2005).

[43] When Bernard of Clairvaux preaches the Second Crusade, his effort represents at least in part a recognition of the inevitability of human aggression, as well as a desire to turn the violence of Christian knights away from internal feuding and against the 'infidels' in the Holy Land. Backman connects the crusades with the Peace and Truce of God movements, which he sees as the precursor for crusading zeal: 'The passion for crusading arose from a passionate desire for peace' (1995: 278).

solution may not even be desirable, since acts of creation require a certain degree of violence: a plowshare is precisely the forward thrusting part of the plow that cuts through and breaks up clods of earth, so that seed can be sown and grown.[44] But we still need to learn better how to make distinctions, curb excessive and inappropriate violence, turn some swords into plowshares, some lances into scythes. At any point in history we will find ourselves closer to or farther away from Isaiah's utopic vision, but with no less obligation to work (asymptotically) toward its realization in the lives of individuals and societies.

Education remains a constant, and the educational process of defamiliarization is not unrelated to the collapse and explosion of categories I spoke of earlier. If you can envision a Chinese encyclopedia's apparent miscellany as a logical set, perhaps you can make a creative leap as bold as Gauvain's across the Perilous Ford and jump into a new category that includes swords *and* plowshares, as well as metamorphoses between them that may work toward more productive culture and civilization. Is Gauvain's own efflort to use a lance as an instrument of the hunt a promising first step in this direction, however unsuccessful? Apparently the time was not right for Gauvain, as it was not for the sparrowhawk. Like the romance public, he still requires the intervention of a blacksmith to reforge iron. Heroes for the twelfth as for the twenty-first century, Perceval and Gauvain both fail yet continue to quest.

In any case, we should not expect the process to reach its endpoint down here in the space of mutability, any more than the *Conte du Graal*, given to surprising leaps in every facet of its unorthodox structure, has found an ending under Chrétien's hand. When we reach his last incomplete sentence, there is inevitably a sense of let-down: no final epiphany, no answers given to all the questions raised. Willy nilly, that appears to be Chrétien's enigmatic strategy for being in the middle, here under heaven where there may be no final answers for the issues raised.[45] The necessity remains to keep finding and asking questions, to keep imitating the movement of the quest itself in order to find some change for the better glimpsed through Isaiah's vision and the romance's fiction.

This story does not, cannot end, even if it has a series of endings. Indeed, the shifting sequence of endings (or temporary endpoints) offlered by the successive accumulation of continuations offlers a powerful measure of the *Conte*'s success in translating the argument, however indirect, for continually renewing an unfinishable quest. Their interplay with Chrétien's romance suggests tantalizing confirmations and caveats to the way *Perceval* satisfies, in its distinctive way, the propositions offlered by Michael Wood to define 'the genre of the unfinishable work' (2007: 1394):

---

[44] Cf. Guézennec's discussion of 'la violence, puissance vitale' (2000: 100) at the end of her exhaustive inventory of violence in the *Conte du Graal*.

[45] For more on the middle, see Ch. 5.

1. A work devoted to its own unfinishability can end only when we are no longer interested in its ending.
2. Such a work can end only some time after it has already ended. (1401)

Do these fit *Perceval* with or without the continuations? We might answer yes and no: along with countless medieval readers and writers, we moderns are surely not uninterested in the *Conte*'s ending, and yet we may not be interested in or satisfied with the endings we have been given or in any of the endings we might possibly invent. We have become invested to a large extent, thanks to the architecture of its quests, in the *Conte*'s not ending. Both of Wood's propositions insist in diffllerent ways on a space and time outside a work's parameters, as designated in the Kafka aphorism that furnishes the point of departure for his speculations and the last of his three propositions: '3. There are works whose whole ambition is finally to enter the secret space between the last day and the last day of all' (1401).[46] If Kafka's parable conjures up an eschatological perspective, the distinction between the last day in a series (or a series of successive last days?) and the day that ends succession all together, the last day of all, the *Conte*'s utopian anticipation of a day when swords will be transformed into plowshares falls into a similar kind of waiting. Waiting for the day the Messiah arrives, waiting for the end of violence, for restoration or redemption, figures an expectation (with or without hope), places us firmly in that 'secret space', attached to an unfinished sentence that is not yet the ending, can only be defined by the ending's indefinite abeyance, not here, yet here, the and/both of Chrétien's non-ending.

Such a reading of *Perceval* tends to agree with interpretations of its unfinished state as integral to its coherence. Given the issues addressed, its fragmentary character constitutes a logical whole, whatever the author's intentions may have been.[47] Making swords into plowshares still appears in the twenty-first century as an ongoing, never finished human activity, an elusive ideal not easily translated into the realities of social practice. The cumulative response of the continuators nevertheless insists that we look for and find an ending, which the Third Continuation duly accomplishes for the verse cycle, after the quest has been lengthily prolonged through the momentum for continuity built into the *Conte du Graal* itself. Manessier's 10,000-verse ending thus constitutes both a betrayal and culmination of the *Conte*'s and/both logic, as he carefully picks up and finishes offl the threads of narrative accumulated from Chrétien through the first two continuators. Although modern critics may prefer Chrétien's suspension of ending to the risk of anticlimax, writers across the European Middle Ages had no problem inventing (and reinventing) a wide variety of endings for his story of the Grail.

---

[46] Wood quotes the full parable at the end of his article (2007: 1401): 'The Messiah will come only when he is not needed, he will not come until one day after his arrival, he will come not on the last day but on the last day of all' (*Hochzeitsvorbereitungen auf dem Lande* (Frankfurt: Fischer, 1991), p. 67).

[47] In dealing with works 'located in the space between the last night and the last night of all', Wood dismisses the issue of the 'accidentally incomplete or intentionally open-ended but without a conceivable term of expiry' (2007: 1396).

Before considering specifically how Manessier's conclusion handles the problems of violence represented by 'le vieux Perceval' in contrast to the French prose tradition, it may be useful to return briefly to the place where this chapter began, the 'translation' of epic tradition into Old French romance. The violence sung in Virgil's *Aeneid* ('Arma virumque cano', as the famous opening line puts it[48]) ends abruptly with an act of mercy denied. About to spare his enemy Turnus, Aeneas sees the belt of his dear friend Pallas and sends his killer down to the shades below. The *Roman d'Eneas*, its medieval counterpart, adds a new ending for the epic by narrating the happy realization of Anchises' prophecy. The marriage of Eneas and Lavinia, who have fallen in love with each other according to the twelfth century's typically Ovidian inspiration, will produce a great lineage linked to the future founding of Rome. In his final Arthurian romance, Chrétien probes deeply both the promise of future redemption and restoration and violent failures of compassion. His double vision takes us back to Virgil's tragic appreciation piercing through Augustan triumphalism, without abandoning the more hopeful view offered by *Eneas*'s innovative rewriting of Latin tradition. In a surprising act of cross-fertilization, the *Conte du Graal* brings together the matters of Rome, Britain, and Christianity, to make us rethink the problem of violence at the heart of romance, as in the human heart. Through the seeds broadcast into the nourishing soil of his readers' hearts and minds, Chrétien effects a kind of creative violence to defamiliarize the world of his public, whether medieval or modern. Subsequent romance tradition demonstrates how difficult it is to occupy both sides of contradiction and thus hold on to the violence of the *Conte*'s and/both logic. In the thirteenth century, romancers and continuators who take up in writing his invitation to cultivate those strange seeds offer radically different answers to the questions left unresolved by the two heroes' interlaced quests for justice and restoration. All their solutions to the problems of violence, chivalry, and religion appear less ambivalent and more simplified than Chrétien's double-stranded projections. If in the broadest sense, the prose romancers no less than the verse continuators write 'continuations' of Chrétien's work, their diverging treatment and degree of separation from his model (suggested by the distinction between centripetal and centrifugal intertextuality described in the Introduction), appear most striking in the way they play out the implications and transformations of his Grail story. In contrast to the dystopic vision of the Vulgate Cycle's closing acts, Manessier's ending, while remaining faithful to some of the contradictory tensions of the *Conte*, will nevertheless offer a positive resolution of Perceval's quest, signaled by kingship and priesthood in a restored Grail kingdom.[49]

---

[48] 'Arms I sing and the man' (1916: 1, 241), in the Loeb Classics translation.

[49] Perhaps the most positive medieval reading of *Perceval* is offered by Wolfram von Eschenbach, who elaborates the *carité* of Chrétien's prologue as the leitmotif of *triuwe*, used as the organizing theme of his *Parzival*. As Wynn describes it: 'The basic meaning of *triuwe* is a capacity for loving in total selflessness, . . . It denotes the bond between humanity and God and declares itself as maternal

GRAIL QUESTS AND THE ENDS OF VIOLENCE

The modern public's perception of the Grail quest as prelude to the disastrous ending of Arthur's kingdom is filtered primarily through the tragic vision of the Vulgate Cycle, reprised in the fifteenth century for the English-speaking world by Malory's *Morte d'Arthur*. The powerful fascination of the thirteenth-century prose cycle, as it culminates in the tragedy of *La Mort le roi Artu*, is attested by the manuscript tradition whose one hundred or so extant copies suggest the medieval equivalent of a Broadway smash hit. If the *Perceval* Continuations' twelve manuscripts bespeak a more modest success—something on the order of an offl-Broadway production—their less well-known but more comic finish to the Grail quest offlers useful insight into medieval authors and readers who may have been more tolerant of contradictions and happy endings, more interested in the continuing exploration than in the endpoint of the Arthurian experiment.

In a gesture that typifies the modern tendency to read the Grail quest through the optic of the Vulgate Cycle, Robert Bresson chose the end of Arthur's kingdom as the appropriate medium through which to meditate on the twentieth century's own catastrophes. *Lancelot du Lac* opens with the camera focused on two knights in single combat; they grasp their heavy swords in two hands and smash them against the opponent's armor. A severed head appears and then blood spurting from the neck of the defeated knight. Other knights gallop through the forest toward their destination. Wild-eyed horses mirror our perspective through the camera's eye, which switches back and forth between the riders and random scenes of violence and destruction. Such is the return of the Grail questers to Arthur's court, as represented in the prologue to Bresson's 1973 film. At the end, nothing is left of Arthur's kingdom but a heap of dead bodies encased in armor.

With its dark blue cast, Bresson's film darkens literally as well as figuratively. His interpretation reduces the inherent ambivalence characteristic of the Vulgate Cycle's fusion, as it knits together Lancelot's story and the Grail quest within the overarching chronicle of Arthur's reign, but the film does highlight an aspect of the *Queste del Saint Graal* that has always struck me as paradoxical. The Grail quest is announced as an adventure whose marvels operate on a new plane: it is not a quest of 'terriennes choses' (earthly things), but the pursuit of God's secrets. We learn immediately, as does Arthur's court (7), that Galahad and the Grail quest, which only he can fully achieve, will put an end to the marvelous adventures that constitute both the bane and the pleasure of Arthurian knight-hood and the romance public. No wonder Arthur expresses reluctance and sadness when he sees the knights of the Round Table swear to join the quest.

---

and paternal love, love in marriage, love among siblings, love between friends, feudal allegiance, and compassion' (1994: 192). Cf. the expanded categories of love represented in the *Conte*, as discussed in Chs. 2 and 3.

He knows already that many will not return to the fellowship of his court. As the *Queste* and its sequel *La Mort le roi Artu* demonstrate, the Grail quest and its aftermath effectively put an end not only to 'les aventures de la Grant Bretaigne' (10: 'adventures of Great Britain') but to the entire Arthurian experiment with a society founded on a secular ideal of chivalry.

The links set up between the Grail quest and the total destruction of the Vulgate's Arthurian kingdom point to a paradox and a question. Why does the Grail, now figured as a holy object, a good thing according to its own claims and the belief of those who participate in its quest, produce a chain of disasters for the society that pursues it?[50] The violence of that textual inscription emerges with particular clarity through the comparative prism offered by the *Perceval* Continuations.[51] Like the *Lancelot-Grail* synthesis, they take offl from Chrétien's originating romance, but find authorization there for a triumphant ending that carries no threat to Arthur's kingdom. The Vulgate Cycle's violent integration of the quest for the Holy Grail and its univocal set of values (which breaks open the multivalent world set up in the Prose *Lancelot*) contrasts markedly with the way *Perceval* Continuations contain the tensions by playing out the enigmatic hints and unfinished threads of Chrétien's romance. In the verse continuations, the Arthurian frame remains the necessary and sustaining tapestry against which Perceval's—and Gauvain's—Grail quests wander along ambivalent and contradictory paths to final achievement and ending, *achèvement* in the fullest sense. Despite Chrétien's brief allusions to the future destruction of Logres, the continuators find it possible to imagine an Arthurian society unendangered by Perceval's 'excentric' and individual quest, a world where violence remains an important topic without invading the process of representation itself.[52]

In the verse and prose cycles, questions about the legitimacy of knightly violence are inevitably caught up in the interplay between Christian and chivalric registers. The question of whether these are two competing or two complementary value systems has ramifications for individual bodies as for the body politic.[53] In their differing views on the relationship between Arthurian kingship

---

[50] Of course, looking back from the *Queste*, the reader is reminded that already in the *Conte*, Perceval's failure to ask the questions produces catastrophe for the Fisher King and his kingdom, which according to the Hideous Damsel is without remedy. But there is no indication that this effect will spill over on to Arthur's kingdom nor does Perceval accept her prophetic claims based on the role of Fortune. Opportunity may knock only once but he nevertheless persists in his quest: Perceval has already shown himself to be the hero of second chances.

[51] In the less spiritual, more secular perspective of the Prose *Tristan*, the Grail quest is also problematized and associated with a sense of paradox and disillusionment, particularly when Tristan regrets his decision to participate and many knights blame Gauvain for initiating it and causing a good many of its fatalities (see Baumgartner 1990: 86–7, 94, esp. n. 10; Van Coolput 1986: 160–1).

[52] Of course, Geoffrey of Monmouth and Wace have already ended the history of Arthur's reign with neither Lancelot nor the Grail quest in sight: Arthur's downfall is tied to Mordred's treachery in their versions. Cf. Chrétien's variation on and deferral of that ending as recorded in the plot of *Cligès*.

[53] Cf. Augustine's *City of God*, with its contrasting earthly and heavenly cities, which continued to model a Christian future throughout the Middle Ages.

and Grail kingship, both the *Perceval* Continuations and the Vulgate Cycle are guided by the possibilities mapped out but left unfinished in the *Conte*. How does the bipartition built into Chrétien's romance through its two heroes, Perceval and Gauvain, represent the relationship between the Grail lineage and Arthur's kingdom, and how does that model afflect subsequent romancers? We can hypothesize a number of possibilities: two polities may operate in opposition, competition, or simply coexist. Reading the *Conte* through Robert de Boron's rewriting, the *Queste* sets up a hierarchy that subordinates the Arthurian sphere to the Grail. But without Robert's pre-history based in the primacy of the Passion story, Chrétien's romance as usual raises more questions than it resolves.

Two studies offer different answers in explicating what the *Conte* tells us about the relation between Arthurian and Grail kingdoms. In *The Arthurian Romances of Chrétien de Troyes*, Donald Maddox projects an ending that would entail the establishment of two new orders. The parallel reigns of Perceval in the 'remote locus' of the Fisher King and Gauvain in Arthur's place, as the 'anterior order' is reconfigured, would represent a continuing contrast between a community in exile living as strangers and pilgrims under the New Law and a replica of the Arthurian order still struggling with and still vulnerable to the evils of this world (1991a: 117–18). In Maddox's view, two polities (more or less equal) mutually coexist. In *The Unholy Grail*, Brigitte Cazelles (1996) puts aside religious issues to elucidate the political and social dimensions. She sees in Chrétien's romance two factions pitted against each other, the Grail lineage and the Arthurian kingdom, two factions who share the same values and whose unremitting antagonism and violence offer no resolution on a higher level. In her view, two polities remain locked in undifflerentiating factionalism.[54]

Both scholars project a continuing duality built into Chrétien's romance, although Cazelles's focus on mutual violence may foreshadow the possibility of a future destruction.[55] She asserts an underlying antagonism between Arthur and the Grail lineage, which forces Perceval to make a choice between them. But he seems

---

[54] Cazelles's reading (see especially her introduction) locates Chrétien's *Conte* in relation to the rivalry between two Philips (the king of France and the count of Flanders), complicated by constant and constantly changing political maneuvering with two other rival factions, the English king and the German emperor. She suggests that the *Conte* should serve as a cautionary warning to those parties, although it is unclear how her emphasis on the *Conte* as a vengeance plot might apply to the relations evoked. On the socio-political struggles between Philip of Flanders and Philip Augustus (or in general, the tensions between aristocratic and monarchical efforts to hold or accumulate power in this period), see Baldwin (1986), Duby (1973), Spiegel (1993), and Haidu (spring 1998–fall 2003: 63–7; 2004).

[55] However, Cazelles sees no hierarchical relationship of transcendence giving the Grail chivalry a superior and redemptive role that corrects and supersedes Arthurian chivalry, such as one finds fully developed in the Vulgate Cycle. I agree with her assessment that Chrétien's romance does not oppose two exclusive orders of chivalry, one discredited, the other raised as a model above the Arthurian ethos, although the religious elements that constitute one of the most unsettling and distinctive features of the *Conte* require us to situate chivalric values vis-à-vis Christianity in an unanticipated and surprising way, given the precedents in Chrétien's four previous romances (cf. Frappier 1978 and Ménard 1984).

oblivious of any such choice, and the specific messages he receives do not spell out clearly any mission of revenge against Arthur. If Cazelles's overall interpretation remains unconvincing, her call to focus on underlying issues of violence that link the Grail lineage and Arthurian kingship deserves further analysis in view of the *Conte*'s brief allusions to its social and political history, before and after the events narrated. These emerge from the characters' own comments: the civil strife after the death of Utherpendragon, which in some unspecified way is responsible for the misfortunes of Perceval's family (442–9), and the bleeding lance, which is tied to the destruction of Logres and the end of Arthur's kingdom (6166–71). Unprecedented in Chrétien's corpus, these references to events known from Geofflrey of Monmouth's *Historia regum Britanniæ* and Wace's French translation, the *Roman de Brut*, situate Arthur within the series of kings of Great Britain. The history of his reign has always been a story with a beginning and an end, even if Chrétien's earlier romances tended to make his public forget that temporal chronology. As we have seen, the threat of violence that frames Chrétien's last, unfinished romance permeates both lineages and both kingdoms, thereby doubling the destruction as well as the hope for restoration.

When the prose romancers of the Vulgate Cycle rewrite and reinterpret Chrétien's *Conte du Graal*, they respond in a very direct way to its specific anomalies and, in particular, to those temporal allusions, which will eventually structure the overall chronology of Arthur's reign in the prose cycle. From the point of view of the *Queste*, the celestial chivalry of the Grail is superior to Arthur's terrestrial chivalry because it claims a difflerent scale of values. Its univocal, triumphantly militant Christian view breaks apart the delicate balance of competing values built up in the complex texture of the Prose *Lancelot* (cf. Frappier 1954). The quest for what is now the Holy Grail prepares and, in a sense, demands the inevitable end of Arthur's kingdom narrated in the *Mort*, which in turn elaborates a further series of specific causes that precipitate the disastrous ending: adultery, clan rivalry, and hatred, Fortune, incest and be-trayal.[56] This quick overview begs the question of how to read the *Queste*'s monologic discourse within the competing and dialogic discourses of the Prose *Lancelot* and the *Mort*.[57] But from the perspective of the *Queste*, we are required to take seriously its claim to offler interpretations and establish truths that preempt all others.

---

[56] In exploring the vengeance stories that seem to lie behind and beyond Chrétien's romance, Blaess suggests that a possible rivalry between Arthur's clan and Lancelot's (linked to the Grail through the person of Galahad) may be hinted at in the *Conte*'s allusions to Ban de Gomoret (Lancelot's father in the Vulgate Cycle) and the bleeding lance's role in the future destruction of Logres (1978: 72–3).

[57] A more complete analysis of the *Lancelot-Grail* would have to question whether or not these romances (even the *Queste*) totally abandon secular values and the Arthurian ideals represented in their seductive byways. If the *Queste* rejects and resolves the contradictory tensions of Chrétien's model, the Vulgate Cycle as a whole tends to reflect the interplay of their ambivalence. Cf. Savage (1977) and Regalado (1985).

And from that Christian point of view (whether it is properly Cistercian in inspiration or not[58]), the performance of Arthur's knights collectively engaged in the quest to end all quests demonstrates, on the one hand, the failure of Arthurian society—as represented by even the best knights of the Round Table like Lancelot and Gauvain—and, on the other, the achievement of a few individuals, the elect—Galahad, Perceval, and Bohort. The election politics in this romance are definitely not by popular vote. Measured against Chrétien's model, several spectacular transformations appear here afflecting the nature of the Grail quest and the identity of the questers. Perceval's desire to return to the castle of the Fisher King and ask the questions he failed to ask during his first visit becomes in the Vulgate Cycle a quest open to and engaging all the knights of Arthur's Round Table, whose objective is a thoroughly Christianized and Holy Grail since Robert de Boron's trilogy, *c.*1190–1210, conjoined Grail history and the history of Britain.

The shift to a quest with multiple questers (who will be ranked by different degrees of success and failure) may pick up and amplify one of the more mysterious and unresolved aspects of Chrétien's romance: the role Gauvain is given at Escavalon to search for the bleeding lance.[59] But the logic that determines the shift from Perceval's individual adventure to the collective enterprise announced in the *Queste* may be more properly understood in terms of the shift from social and political concerns highlighted in the *Conte*—and the *Perceval* Continuations—to the exclusively spiritual focus of this branch of the prose cycle. At Arthur's court when the Hideous Damsel castigates Perceval for his failure to ask questions when opportunity knocked, she spells out the consequences of his failure according to the human and social cost: the rich king's wounds will not be healed, he will not hold his land in peace, and therefore ladies will lose their husbands, lands their proper lords, young girls will remain orphaned and many knights will die—all because of Perceval (4646–83).[60] It is a terrible charge and, when a host of knights volunteer for the two quests announced by the Hideous Damsel, the narrator tells us that 'Perceval redist tout el' (4727: 'Perceval spoke altogether different'). His quest is not to be shared. Despite the Hideous Damsel's assertion that the opportunity has been lost, his objective is solidly focused on undoing the wrong he has (inadvertently) done at the Fisher King's castle.

---

[58] See e.g. Matarasso (1979, esp. 205–41) and Geary (1985).

[59] The unfinished state of Chrétien's romance prevents us from deciphering exactly how Perceval's and Gauvain's quests might have overlapped, although the temporal warp of the hermit episode five years into the future suggests that any possible encounter of the heroes at the Grail Castle would remain conceptual rather than actual.

[60] In exploring the Hideous Damsel as a figure of Sovereignty (alternately beautiful or ugly as a reflection of the hero's readiness or failure to assume kingship), Saly suggests that the well-being of the Arthurian kingdom depends on the drama of the Grail kingship (1994a: esp. 30, 47). In her interpretation, the two polities are seen as intertwined, with the Arthurian in some sense subordinated to the Grail kingdom.

In the *Queste*, the questers for the Holy Grail encounter the kind of violence and social ills outlined in the *Conte* but in some sense their correction is only incidental to the real work of this new quest. The real work is each knight's individual salvation to be obtained—or lost—through the Grail quest itself. In this context, saving one more damsel in distress may be tangential to saving one's soul, especially when that damsel is more than likely a devil in disguise trying to tempt the quester to his eternal damnation, as happens repeatedly in the adventures of Galahad, Perceval, and Bohort. If salvation is necessarily the business of every Christian, then it is a fortiori the primary goal of every Christian knight in the service of the highest and most marvelous adventure of all. So, of course, all the knights of the Round Table will join the quest that has become itself an instrument of salvation. As reconceptualized according to the Christian viewpoint expressed by numerous hermit explicators, it cannot be Perceval's alone.[61] But concomitantly, if Arthurian society has not been designed to save souls (as it clearly was not), and if the body politic is corrupt, then it must be killed in order to save the individual souls that can be salvaged. Hence the logic of Arthur's and his kingdom's disastrous end, the logic of Galahad's election.

The son of Lancelot replaces Perceval, or rather relocates him in a trinity of heroes with a figure for Jesus Christ at its summit. If Lancelot was the flower of Arthurian chivalry through hundreds of adventures recounted in the Prose *Lancelot*, his adultery with the Queen (even confessed and renounced) disqualifies him in the Grail quest, where only his son can properly replace him as the best knight in this brave new world. Inscriptions on chairs, stones, ships, and swords, mysterious announcements, and the events of the quest itself all prove that the virginal Galahad has fittingly donned the singularity that was Perceval's and Lancelot's in Chrétien's romances, while reconfiguring that singularity in the Christian drama of salvation instituted by the *Queste*: the Fisher King is now Galahad's ancestor and will receive his cure from the new Grail hero (8, 10). Lancelot himself will eventually qualify for salvation after a very Christian end, having spent years in repentance at a hermitage, but that salvation will come only after the complete destruction of the society in which he played so important a role. Neither Galahad's saintly death at Sarraz at the end of the *Queste* (once he has seen openly, in a Eucharistic vision, the secrets of the Holy Grail), nor Lancelot's death at the end of the *Mort*, provide a view of how a just society here on earth might replace Arthur's kingdom. The withdrawal to Sarraz and the removal of the Grail from Arthur's kingdom offer, in some sense, a return to Perceval's initial history in the *Conte,* although his family's retreat to the wilderness of the 'forest gaste' (451) is now recast in an Eastern and monastic mode for

---

[61] On the shift between individual and collective, chivalric and spiritual enterprises, cf. Stanesco's comment on the necessary role of the gloss in the *Queste*, where knights are no longer permitted to understand the meaning of their adventures: 'L'aventure chevaleresque était individuelle, la glose est une parole collective' (1998: 1268).

its knightly trio of heroes.[62] Protective isolation elevated to Christian virtue counterbalances the destruction unleashed on Arthur's reign. Utopia no longer has a social dimension *soz ciel.*

MANESSIER'S RESOLUTION

The role of individual salvation in the *Queste* is well known, but our understanding of the pervasive logic that connects that theme to some of the most basic, as well as the most radical, changes wrought by the rewriters of Chrétien's *Conte* can be deepened through triangulation, by looking at the relationship between Chrétien and the Vulgate Cycle from the perspective of the *Perceval* Continuations, and most particularly from that of the Third Continuation, Manessier's end to Chrétien's Grail campaign. If Manessier was writing between 1214 and 1227, as seems most probable, based on his reference to his patroness as 'Jehanne la contesse, | Qu'est de Flandres dame et mestresse' (42643–4: 'the Countess Jeanne who is lady and mistress of Flanders')—that is, during the time of her husband's imprisonment by Philip Augustus after the defeat at the battle of Bouvines, when she indeed governed Flanders under the watchful eye of the French king—then he is more or less contemporary with the anonymous romancers working on the *Lancelot-Grail*, whose approximate dates range between 1215 and 1220 for the earliest parts of the *Lancelot*, 1220–5 for the Agravain section that prepares the transition between *Lancelot* and the *Queste*, 1225–30 for the *Queste* itself, and shortly afterward, *c.*1230, for the *Mort.*[63]

Manessier has a number of characters and specific incidents in common with the *Lancelot* and the *Queste*, which has led to some debates about the order of influence and/or possible common sources.[64] Corin Corley argues convincingly

---

[62] Although the monasticism here is a secular one, it nevertheless eliminates sex and women in favor of male genealogies. Cf. McCracken (1999).

[63] On the dating of Manessier and a brief overview of the critical discussion of its relationship with the prose romances, see the introd. to Roach's edn., V, xiii–xv. From a historical point of view, it is not without interest that Chrétien at the beginning and Manessier at the end name patrons who place the *Perceval* romances in the late 12th and early 13th cents., within the geography and timeframe of intense rivalry between the French crown (in the person of Philip Augustus) and successive counts of Flanders, from Philip to his grand niece, Jeanne de Flandres. The problems of 'national' versus regional identity thus float in the margins of these literary displacements and invite speculation on possible interactions between the romances and their aristocratic publics. On the historical and political background, see Baldwin (1986), Nicholas (1992: esp. 56–161), Spiegel (1993), and Stiennon (1984). For a specific investigation of the patronage evoked here, see Stanger (1957) and Walters (1994: esp. 444–5, where she suggests a correspondence between the representation of Blancheflor and Manessier's patroness).

[64] Given the intertextual dialogue between these two cycles, it is useful to remember that, as Huot points out, '[t]he extant illuminated manuscripts of the *Conte du Graal* coincide with the growing popularity of the prose *Lancelot-Grail* cycle' (1996: 105): the parallels between them thus appear not only in the verbal text but in the iconographic programs as well as the use of rubrics. See also Hindman (1994: 194–7), Baumgartner (1993: 1, 490 n. 1, 496–8), and Busby (1993a: 1, 353–4, 360, 362; 1993c: 1, 371–2, 375).

that Manessier borrows from the romancers of the *Lancelot* and the *Queste* in a manner that indicates more artistry than he is generally given credit for (1986). This otherwise unidentified author shows himself in general to be a careful reader of his predecessors: Manessier clearly sets out in his own continuation to take his cues from the models before him.[65] He may not know Chrétien's original intentions for finishing the *Conte du Graal* any better than we do (and his talent may not be on a par with the first author's genius), but he has carefully read 'the old Perceval', along with the two earlier continuations which the manuscript tradition lines up in its wake. I have argued throughout this study that Chrétien remains the guiding spirit that oversees the continuators' work. But the appearance of characters like Bohort, Lionel, and Hector, all related to Lancelot in the enormous amplification of his biography constituted by the Prose *Lancelot*, and presented in the Third Continuation with no fanfare to a public expected to recognize them, suggests that Manessier includes among his models the oldest branches of the Vulgate Cycle. Indeed, Ferdinand Lot reads the epilogue's reference to Salisbury (where the written testimony of the knights has been recorded and preserved by King Arthur, V, 42662–8), as the author's way of specifically designating his borrowings from the *Lancelot-Grail* (1931: 123).

What then has Manessier been tempted to borrow from the prose romancers and what has he declined in order to complete 'Chrétien'?[66] Three areas are particularly relevant to the question of knightly violence and the Grail. First, Manessier has adopted the technique of multiple questers developed in the prose romances along with the interlace technique used to follow and combine multiple threads of plot. Of course, Chrétien's own romances offer examples of interlace, but the Prose *Lancelot* has clearly taken that embryonic technique to a more sophisticated level in its own intricate patterning. In Manessier, a number of Arthur's knights participate in two successive quests for Perceval, who thus remains at the center of the narrative, even though he is actually absent from a significant number of episodes. Or at least, he remains at the center as much as he typically does in the Grail romances, since they are characteristically decentered by the doubling of heroes from Chrétien on.[67]

---

[65] Lachat emphasizes how Manessier offers echoes, specular effects, and reversals to form a counterpoint with Chrétien's *Conte* and effectively close it down (1999: esp. 27–8). Whether or not Manessier knew Chrétien was not the author of what modern scholars designate as the First and Second Continuations remains open to debate. See the discussion in Ch. 1. The ambiguity of verses 42654–6—at least for modern readers—reminds us that our views and the views of medieval readers reflected in the manuscript tradition do not always show identical concerns or perceptions about authorship.

[66] See Ch. 1's discussion of how Manessier's treatment of Blancheflor is significantly influenced by the prose cycle.

[67] Roach's summary of Manessier's romance offers an excellent overview of the weaving process (V, xxii–lv). He divides thirty episodes into six parts, whose titles clearly map out the narrative movement: I. First Adventures of Perceval (2 episodes); II. Adventures of Sagremor (3 episodes); III. Adventures of Gauvain (6 episodes); IV. Second Adventures of Perceval (8 episodes); V. The Search for Perceval (5 episodes); and VI. Final Adventures of Perceval (6 episodes plus the epilogue). See the list of episodes in App. 1.

A second area of interest shared by Manessier and the *Lancelot-Grail* appears in episodes of temptation. In a well-known incident borrowed from the *Queste*, Manessier describes how Bohort must choose between helping his brother Lionel, who is being whipped by six knights, or saving a damsel, who is about to be raped. Praying for God's protection for his brother, Bohort decides to save the damsel, then goes to find Lionel, who in the meantime has been saved by Gauvain and now vows to kill his brother for abandoning him. Before finding his brother, Bohort succeeds in rejecting the temptation of despair set up by a false hermit who wants him to believe that Lionel is dead. When the two brothers meet, they are saved from killing each other only by the timely intervention of a heavenly voice, but not before Lionel has killed Calogrenant, another Arthurian knight who tried to prevent the bloodshed.

In the context of the Vulgate Cycle, where the *Queste*'s numerous hermits and priests explain the significance of such adventures in terms of salvation and damnation, this episode demonstrates the fratricidal character of Arthurian chivalry and justifies its destruction when measured by the standards of the Grail quest.[68] In the context of Manessier's continuation, Bohort and Lionel's confrontation makes clear that the Christianization of the Grail that has afflected all the French versions subsequent to Chrétien also plays an important role in Manessier and explains at least in part his interest in the religious discourse woven into the Vulgate Cycle. Many Christian elements used to frame the *Queste* appear in Manessier's romance, particularly in episodes of satanic temptation where prayers to God, celestial voices, devils in disguise, and religious interpretations abound, not to mention the personnel, rituals, and institutions of the Church, from chapels and hermitages to priests and confessions. But neither Bohort nor Lionel are engaged here in a quest for the Holy Grail. That is strictly the business of Perceval, who from the opening scene of Manessier's romance has, in fact, already achieved his objective at the castle of the Fisher King, though other quests will have to reach their conclusion before he can fully realize the fruits of that success.

Christian values abound in Manessier's continuation, but they have not been given the paramount and hierarchical role they play in the *Queste*, where all is subordinated to the pursuit of Christian salvation.[69] Manessier never loses sight of the social and political concerns of his first model text, Chrétien's *Perceval*. In so doing, he nevertheless shares a concern common to all three romances: the conditions and consequences of killing one's adversaries on the field of combat, which is as much at issue in the social as in the religious dimension.

---

[68] The same fratricidal theme appears in another episode, which Manessier borrows from the last section of the Prose *Lancelot*: without recognizing each other, Perceval and Hector fight until they are both on the point of death; they are healed only by the miraculous intervention of the Holy Grail. For a comparison of both episodes with their prose romance models, see Corley (1986: 581–5).

[69] While the explanatory Christian gloss controls meaning in the *Queste* (but not elsewhere in the branches of the *Lancelot-Grail*), other Grail romances like *Perlesvaus* as well as the verse continuations are more resistant to the replacement of narrative by allegorical interpretations.

The problem of mortal violence at the heart of knightly encounters thus constitutes a third point of connection between Manessier and the Vulgate Cycle and best explains the Third Continuation's interest in borrowing episodes of fratricidal slaughter. In another episode, which Manessier picks up from the Second Continuation (IV, 32071–129), Perceval ends the daily murder of knights at the Black Chapel: more than three thousand have been killed by a mysterious black hand, the devil's own, marking the site of matricide.[70] This adventure will introduce a whole series of episodes involving temptations by the devil. Perceval's triumph here results not from the power of his sword as a destructive weapon but rather his use of it to make the sign of the cross: 'le miracle | Que Diex i fist por lou saignacle' (V, 37403–4: 'the miracle God performed thanks to Perceval's cruciform signing'). Not exactly swords into plowshares but certainly a transformative view of how swords might operate without bloodshed. The episode ends with a discussion between Perceval and the ancient priest, who explains to him all about the Black Chapel and its cemetery. When the priest asks who he is and what he seeks, Perceval replies that he is a knight of the Round Table who travels the land to conquer honor and increase his worth (V, 37773–94).

> 'A maint chevalier me combat,
> Maint an ocis, maint abat
> Et maint an ai retenu pris;
> Einsins vois acroissant mon pris.'
>
> (37791–4)

('I fight against many knights, many I kill, many I unhorse and many I take prisoner. Thus I go increasing my worth.')

Not honor, but damnation is what he conquers, according to the hermit, who goes on to explain the horror of killing men: when they die on the field of battle without confession, they go right to hell, where they remain 'toz dis | Tant con Diex soit am paradis' (37831–2: 'forever as long as God is in Paradise'). Frightened, Perceval confesses his own sins and receives penance:

> Et li prodome sanz dotance
> Li encharja sa penitance,
> Que de ce s'alast bien gardant
> Que, se n'est sus lui desfandant,
> Que jamés home n'oceïst
> Ne grant pechié ne feïst.
>
> (37853–8)

---

[70] The devil's hand extinguishes the light on the altar where Queen Branguemore was murdered by her own son, as Perceval learned from the Fisher King in the opening scene of Manessier's romance (V, 33026–57): echoes of Perceval's own 'pechié de la mere' (*Le Conte du Graal*, 3593–4, 6393–402), the sin associated with his mother's death?

(And the worthy man without fear charged him with the penance that, unless it be in self-defense, he should never kill a man nor commit a great sin).

Thou shalt not kill: the prohibition clearly evokes the Ten Commandments, but the priest's conditional clause ('except in self-defense') still leaves the door open a crack to moral dilemmas.[71] The commandment against killing included in the Decalogue was generally understood as a prohibition of murder and did not foreclose the conduct of war or execution as capital punishment. But the accusations of treasonous murder brought against Gauvain in the *Conte* suggest that a fine (and often disputed) line may separate justifed and unjustified killing, whether in romance fictions or in the experience of contemporary readers. A knight's duty includes defense of widows and orphans and all those in need. So important is that knightly mission that it was repeated to Perceval three times in the *Conte du Graal*—by his mother, his chivalric mentor Gornemant, and his hermit uncle. If a knight is defined by the weapons he carries and the armor he wears, as suggested by Perceval's first encounter with the knights who rode into the forest on that fateful day at the beginning of Chrétien's romance, then how is he to defend the helpless without risking death, either his own or that of his adversaries?

Of course, Gornemant has instructed Perceval in the niceties of chivalric combat: if a defeated opponent requests mercy, he must give it—and Perceval does so numerous times.[72] But knightly combat does not always end in such good form. I have already commented on his mother's response to Perceval's admiration for creatures so beautiful they surpass God and his angels. She sees only the destructive force of their shining beauty, but the romance has demonstrated that, as true as her observation may seem, we cannot dismiss the issue so simply. When is knightly force justified? When is it sinful killing? This is an interrogation that Chrétien initiates in the *Conte du Graal* not only in the exchange between mother and son but in the very fabric of the romance, from the initial situation of Perceval's family, exiled and devastated by knightly aggression, to the sufflering of Perceval's cousin, and Blancheflor, and the Tent Maiden, the Fisher King, the Male Pucele, and so on. Twice accused of traitorous killing, Gauvain vigorously disclaims the charges and is ready to prove his innocence on the field of combat, but he is also ready to make amends in case he did somehow cross the line between acceptable and unacceptable killing. Practically every episode in the romance involves some kind of violence, which

---

[71] See e.g. Augustine's *City of God* I, 21 (1984). Cf. Sargent-Bauer's discussion of how voluntary and involuntary homicide is treated in medieval penitentials (2000: 155–6).

[72] Over and over again Manessier replays the *Conte*'s model negotiations for granting mercy, which took place at Biaurepaire, first with the seneschal Engygeron and then with his lord, Clamadeu des Illes: if the defeated knight fears death at Blancheflor's hands, then he should go to Gornemant; if Gornemant might seek revenge for his cousin, then the prisoner must go to King Arthur (2268–325; 2684–99). In a similar manner, Manessier's Perceval spares the life of the man who kidnapped Dodinel's *amie* (V, 38724–46) and sends him, as well as Blancheflor's new enemy, Aridés of Escavalon (V, 39214–55), to surrender to Arthur rather than risk death at the hands of the very people they have offended.

may or may not be corrected with further acts of violence. The images of Bresson's film come to mind again. Killing, justified and unjustified, is as much a social as a religious problem.

In Manessier's continuation, Perceval's penitence—his promise not to kill—lasts through several episodes until he encounters a cowardly knight (the Biau Chevalier), who wears his hauberk, shield, and helmet hanging down his back, in order to avoid combat (V, 39577–969). Afraid of being wounded or killed, this handsome knight thus hopes to go about his business by avoiding the business of being a knight. Perceval considers his conduct shameful, but the knight persists in it, even when Perceval goes to the rescue of two maidens about to be thrown in a fire by two men, guarded by ten knights. As Perceval attacks, the Biau Chevalier stands by under a tree. Even when one of the knights breaks his lance against him and begins to destroy his shield with great sword blows, the handsome knight disclaims any involvement in the affair. Wounded, he finally attacks and kills his knight, then a second. Now he is resolved to help Perceval, and between them they kill all twelve men persecuting the maidens. Later, for all his accomplishments, Perceval awards the knight a new name: 'le Biau Hardi' (41278). In the wake of Perceval's confession and repentance, the episode seems designed as a test case. Damsels in distress require protection; knights who shun their duty and expect not to fight not only appear foolish but find themselves involved and responsible even when they seek to avoid all responsibility. But if combat inevitably entails wounding and death, surely this incident fits into the priest's conditional clause. Does that solve the dilemma?

Whereas the *Queste* places univocal Christian values at the top of the hierarchy and discredits terrestrial chivalry that fails to live up to the standards of celestial knights like Galahad, Manessier's romance continues Chrétien's own more ambivalent meditation on the need for, as well as the abuse of, knightly prowess, the pursuit of chivalric valor, and the conquest of honor.[73] The discourse of hermit and priest accompanies and critiques that of warrior and king, but it does not monopolize value in the overall texture of the romance.[74] Indeed, Perceval's major task in Manessier's continuation, before he can accede to kingship at the Grail castle, is to avenge the Fisher King for the treacherous murder of his brother.[75] When Perceval defeats the murderer Partinal in combat, the vanquished

[73] In the *Queste*, killing is a sign of sin, associated with the knights like Gauvain who are unworthy of the Grail quest or with sinners punished by Galahad, e.g. at the Chastel Carcelois (1967: 230–3).

[74] The 'prodom' sent by God to comfort Perceval after the devil's repeated temptations offers him a choice of two white horses, a palfrey (i.e. a riding horse) or a *destrier* (a warhorse). Perceval chooses the warhorse and rides off with the worthy man's blessing (V, 38384–407). As Frappier points out, even in the *Queste* the heroes of celestial chivalry remain knights (1954: 197–8). See also Baumgartner (1981: 144–53).

[75] The Fisher King's wound, although self-inflicted, emblematizes his brother's unjust death, since the same sword struck them both. After a long journey, Perceval recognizes the murderer's castle by the Red Tower ('la Tor Vermoille', V, 41652), a distant echo of Perceval's first violent encounter with the Red Knight.

knight refuses to ask for mercy, even though Perceval twice urges him to request it. Finally Perceval cuts offl his head and takes it back to the Fisher King, who is healthy and happy as soon as he sees it (V, 41807–918).

This joyous tale of vengeance is presented as the necessary step toward resolution in the denouement. But Manessier offlered a more troubling episode earlier in the narrative to serve as an implicit comment on the problematic nature of revenge. In the First Continuation, when a knight under Gauvain's protection was mysteriously killed, suspicions fell on Keu (I, 12878–13002). In his continuation, Manessier picks up this suspended thread and develops it in a way that also echoes an important episode from Chrétien's *Chevalier au Lion*: the deadly combat between Yvain and Gauvain, both fighting incognito as the champions of two sisters, during which Arthur is repeatedly urged to intervene to save the knights from killing each other. In the Third Continuation, the murdered knight's sister, the Sore Pucelle, arrives seeking revenge for her brother's death. Gauvain agrees to carry out her request, despite his misgiving and the lack of proof inculpating the king's seneschal. Fighting incognito, Gauvain dips the pennant from Silimac's sister in Keu's blood, as promised. But when Keu refuses to ask for mercy, Gauvain sorely regrets his promise to undertake the task. As the sister urges him to kill and the Queen prays for the Virgin's help, an anguished Gauvain hesitates until Arthur's intervention saves Keu's life. The fratricidal killing is barely avoided.[76]

Both these episodes throw an interesting light on Cazelles's reading of the *Conte du Graal* as a story in which Perceval, as representative of the Grail lineage, should seek vengeance against Arthur. If Manessier seems to confirm that Chrétien's tale does indeed call for some kind of revenge, it demonstrates that the revenge sought does not necessarily involve Arthur (cf. Ménard 65–70). Far from suggesting any antagonism between Grail lineage and Arthurian kingship, the events of the Third Continuation show that Arthur and his court continue to honor Perceval's extraordinary heroism and serve as witness par excellence of his accomplishments (as in Chrétien's *Conte*). Grail quest and Grail kingship remain Perceval's own, without ill efflect on Arthur's kingdom. When Perceval has finally passed all the preliminary trials and is ready to be crowned king in the Fisher King's place, the appropriate heir to his maternal family line, Arthur and his court travel to Corbenic (as the Grail Castle is named in this final episode) to witness and celebrate his coronation, just as they went to Nantes at the end of Chrétien's first romance for Erec and Enide's coronation. Two bodies politic, two kingships remain in coexistence and mutual admiration.

[76] Cf. the combats between Lancelot and Meleagant, in which the Queen intervenes to save Meleagant at the behest of Bademagu: the killing twice avoided and then finally executed is not directly fratricidal in this case, but the father–son tie between Bademagu and Meleagant plays an important role (and Bademagu's death in the *Queste* furnishes another link here). These motifs, as well as the general issue of vengeance and violence, also play a significant role in Gerbert's continuation.

Once Perceval is crowned, Manessier's narrative accelerates to its conclusion. Perceval reigns for seven years, marries offl his cousins to continue the family line, then retires to the religious life, where the Grail accompanies him. After ten years of divine service, sustained only by the food and drink brought to him by the Grail, Perceval dies, and God claims him as his own. As Perceval is placed on the right hand of God, the Holy Grail, the lance, and the silver carver are lifted to heaven. Never again will they be seen on earth. We are back to the story of individual salvation obtained not through the instrumentation of the quest itself, as in the *Queste del Saint Graal*, but through the more traditional ending of a knight's life of service, first in arms, then in prayer.[77] Anyone who would like to verify Manessier's account is invited in the epilogue to check the written testimony at Salisbury, recorded by Arthur's scribes and sealed by the king. The Arthurian frame keeps sustaining Perceval's Grail story, just as his feats continue to enhance Arthur's kingship.

The *Perceval* Continuations and the Vulgate Cycle each respond in their own way to cues from Chrétien's text by reevaluating the relationship between individual salvation and the viability of the social contract. The other side of Galahad's final ecstatic vision at Sarraz is the dystopia played out to its disastrous end in *La Mort le roi Artu*. Writing more or less at the same time but without knowledge of each other, both Gerbert and Manessier must confront the *Queste's* popular rewriting of one particular strand singled out from the twisted fabric of the *Conte's* incongruous combinations. Under that common influence, the last two continuators reintegrate the Christian elements mysteriously woven into Chrétien's romance, whereas the first two continuators, writing at the end of the twelfth century or the very beginning of the thirteenth, tended to favor more traditional Celtic matter, especially love adventures, as demonstrated in preceding chapters. Interpreting Perceval's achievement of the Grail at the end of the Second Continuation as successful, Manessier's 'post-Grail' continuation returns to the problem of chivalric violence to encompass, in a satisfactorily happy ending, the contradictory strands of all his predecessors, now expanded from Chrétien and the first two continuations to include the Vulgate's *Queste*. If he has not avoided the pitfall of anticlimax (at least from a modern reader's point of view), he has nevertheless kept in view Chrétien's meditation on violence, the patterns of its rise and fall, the charitable hope that utopian idealism may restore the persistent failures of human nature. In the next chapter, we will see how Gerbert shares Manessier's tempered optimism for successful resolution and keeps open the momentum of the middle, powered by Chrétien's suspended beginning.

---

[77] A lexical analysis of the *Conte du Graal*'s two parts leads the 'Groupe de Linguistique Romane de Paris VII' to raise the question of individual versus collective salvation in the context of Chrétien's unfinished romance, associating the former with Perceval (given the failure of collective salvation at the Grail Castle) and the possibility for the latter with Gauvain (whose success at the Castle of Champguin still remains to be fully realized). See Cerquiglini *et al.* (1978).

5

Middles, Beginnings, and Ends

'Things must happen when it is time for them to happen. Quests may not simply be abandoned; prophecies may not be left to rot like unpicked fruit; unicorns may go unrescued for a long time, but not forever. The happy ending cannot come in the middle of the story'.

Peter S. Beagle, *The Last Unicorn*

A BEGINNING FOR MIDDLES AND ENDINGS

Basing his definition of the good plot on tragedy, Aristotle does not hesitate to point out the obvious: good plots are whole and complete; they have a beginning, a middle, and an end. As he goes on to explain:

The beginning, while not necessarily following something else, is, by definition, followed by something else. The end, on the contrary, follows something else by definition, either always or in most cases, but nothing else comes after it. The middle both itself follows something else and is followed by something else. To construct a good plot, one must neither begin nor end haphazardly but make a proper use of these three parts. (16)[1]

Upon closer scrutiny, the explanation may not be so obvious. Modifying phrases complicate what appeared at first glance utterly clear and simple. The end 'either always or in most cases' follows something—which leaves open the possibility that there are some cases, in stark contradiction with 'always', whose end does not follow something else: such an end precariously moves into the category of beginning. The middle emerges only once the beginning and end have been defined and seems the easiest to delimit with no qualifying exceptions, except insofar as we recall that the beginning, 'while not necessarily', may indeed be 'following something else'—at which point the definition seems to equate some ends with beginnings and some beginnings with middles. The complications are familiar to those who try to define the shape of a good plot in relation to medieval narrative.[2]

---

[1] Cf. Frye on the Bible and literature (1982: 108): 'Human life is a continuum that we join at birth and drop off at death. But, because *we* begin and end, we insist that beginnings and endings must be much more deeply built into the reality of things than the universe around us suggests, and we shape our myths accordingly' (emphasis in the original).

[2] Medieval textuality seems particularly inclined to find its place and pleasures in the middle (cf. Payen). See e.g. Zumthor's discussion in 'Le texte fragment' (1978: 81): since any given

The surreptitious movability of Aristotle's three parts—which seemed at first to be defined by their stable placement at beginning, middle, and end—may in fact prove to be precisely the starting point necessary for thinking about a set of romances that are usually seen by modern readers as contradicting what Aristotle had to say about good plots. As we have seen, the first Grail romance left unfinished constitutes the beginning of an extraordinarily rich and diverse stream of continuations and rewritings, which repeatedly seek to carry Chrétien's beginning through to an appropriate end (or at least move it farther in that direction). The seamless character of the manuscript tradition that hides the transitions from the *Conte* on through successive verse continuations compels us to recognize that medieval readers, writers, and editor-scribes did indeed consider them to form a good plot, however much the continuing installments resist, even as they tend toward, the siren call of the 'complete and whole'. Responding to the strange architecture of Chrétien's romance as a beginning, this 'Story of the Grail' (as opposed to rival versions from Robert de Boron's *Estoire* to the *Perlesvaus* and the *Queste*) appears to be a tale more interested in middles than ends, a story in which there is always something more to sandwich in before reaching the end. How do we understand this oddly decentered, overarching narrative structure? Can we glimpse how medieval writers and readers may have done so? I thus return to the question first articulated in Chapter 1 of how to make sense of what modern critical judgment often considers a miscellany, rather than a coherent set of continuations.[3] In order to respond anew to that question, I would like to examine here the issue of narrative framing, particularly in light of Gerbert's insertion between the Second and Third Continuations. The potential duplication of ending and the actual stretching of a narrative middle, as realized in manuscripts T and V, reveal important insights for understanding the malleability of this cycle's overall design as it spins out from Chrétien's beginning.

The sandwich as metaphor provides an apt model for conceptualizing the relationship between this Grail story's whole and its parts, the changing shape of the dialogue between Chrétien's opening movement and the shifting accumulation of middles and ends. Four continuations and two prequels provide a large variety of possible layers, but among the variations, one particular combination enjoys a kind of canonical status: the First, Second, and Third Continuations (P123) form an ensemble that appears in eight out of twelve extant manuscripts in Old French. Of course, 'canonical' in this context admits many different actualizations, given the three different redactions of the Gauvain Continuation

---

manifestation operates within the larger textual system of which it is a part (e.g. romance, courtly lyric, etc.), the notion of the whole necessarily shifts, as do the categories of finished and unfinished, conceived primarily as origin and end, and located outside any particular 'texte-fragment'.

[3] As Frappier remarks, 'On ne saurait prétendre en tout cas que les Continuations s'enchaînent clairement au *Perceval* inachevé' (1978: 133). In the same volume (*GRLMA*, IV/I), see also Payen (1978) on the continuations. Cf. Genette's definitions of *suite* and *continuation* (1982: 181–43) and the adjustments needed to apply them to medieval texts (Bruckner 1987–8: 224, 245–65).

(Short, Long, and Mixed), the addition of materials preceding Chrétien's romance, as well as the inclusion of the Fourth Continuation in TV.

The sense of closure implied by Aristotle's view of the good plot, balanced between beginning, middle, and end, does not disappear in this progressive series of realizations; rather it continues to shift in terms of placement and expectation. The perception and power of the incomplete middle may in fact be the motor force that drives the narrative structure as a whole. The First Continuation, like the *Conte* itself, makes no obvious claim to furnish an ending that would match Chrétien's beginning. Both Chrétien and the anonymous first continuator project the expectation that something else must follow and thus end each time somewhere in the middle. The Second Continuation is more ambiguous in this respect and may appear as either a middle or an end (just short of completion). In combination with the Gauvain Continuation, Wauchier de Denain's contribution completes the interlace of two heroes set up by Chrétien and brings Perceval to apparently successful achievement at the Grail Castle. He asks the appropriate questions and puts together the two parts of the broken sword (added in Gauvain's Grail Castle visits), though there is a visible notch left in the soldering. Three manuscripts, A, L, and K, offer this stage as an endpoint.[4] In most cases, however, the intermediate status of the Second Continuation is reinforced, perhaps in response to the curious ambiguity of the king's two-staged reaction. His first words of congratulations recognize that in arms Perceval is the best knight '[d]e trestoz ceus qui ore i sont' (IV, 32566: 'of all those currently alive'). But the king goes on to suggest that Perceval can rise to even greater heights in *amor, cortoisie, sens*, and *chevalerie* (32571–2) to become 'li miaudres... de toz | De toutes les hautes bontez' (32574–5: 'the best of all in all the highest qualities'). When Perceval heaves a great sigh at these words,

> Le rois lo voit, grant joie an a,
> Ses deus bras au col li gita
> Conme cortois et bien apris;
> Puis li a dist: 'Biaux doz amis,
> Sire soiez de ma meson.
> Je vos met tout an abandon
> Quanque je ai, sanz nul dongier;
> Et des or vos avrai plus chier
> Que nul autre qui jamés soit'.
> Atant revint cil a esploit
> Qui l'espee avoit aportee,
> Si l'a prise et anvelopee
> An un cendal, si l'am reporte;
> Et Percevaux se reconforte.

> (IV, 32581–94)

---

[4] A and L offer the same three-part ensemble, P 1 (Short Redaction) 2, although L also includes the prequel *Blancandrin* (Roach, ed. I, xvi–xvii, xx–xxii; Busby, ed. ix–xii, xix–xxi). K transcribes the Second Continuation by itself among various romances, *chansons de geste*, etc., and furnishes a quick ending by adding its own 34-line conclusion (Roach, I, xix).

(The king sees this and is filled with joy. He throws his arms around Perceval's neck, like a courteous and well-mannered man, and says to him: 'Fair, sweet friend, be the lord of my house. I leave to you all that I have, with no reservation. From now on I shall hold you dearer than anyone ever'. Then the one who had brought the sword promptly returned and took it and wrapped it in silk and carried it away. And Perceval is comforted.)

As we saw earlier, both Manessier and Gerbert read the last line as an incomplete sentence (cf. the last verse in Chrétien's initiating romance), but they do so in opposite ways. Reinforcing the change in Perceval's emotion, 'qui de l'aventure a tel joie' (V, 32595: 'who had such joy from the adventure'), Manessier offers a reading of the scene that proclaims the hero's success and gives him all the answers to his questions. The third continuator nevertheless extends his adventures some 10,000 verses, so that Perceval can avenge and cure the Fisher King before eventually taking his place (see the last chapter). Manessier's epilogue then furnishes the closing frame that corresponds to Chrétien's prologue (matching book ends, as it were). On the contrary, Gerbert's reading of the Second Continuation's last verse reverses the movement of Perceval's emotions once again: 'Et Perchevaus se reconforte | Qui parole au Roi Pescheor | Mais molt se tient a pecheor' (Williams, I, 1–2 [Potvin, V, 34934]: 'And Perceval who speaks to the Fisher King is comforted but considers himself a great sinner'). Perceval cannot yet hear the truth about the Grail, since Gerbert has picked up Wauchier's negative cue of the crack in the sword ('une creveüre | Petitet[e]', V, 32559–60) and now requires his hero to undergo a further series of purifying adventures, keyed to the themes of sin, repentance, and penitence inscribed in Chrétien's hermit episode.

The Fourth Continuation begins and ends with an exact repetition of the fourteen verses quoted above from the end of the Second Continuation, the same verses that introduce Manessier in the other manuscripts. It is this quirk of repetition that has invited scholarly speculation that Gerbert (*c.*1226–30) and Manessier (*c.*1214–27) worked independently to finish Perceval's story. Faced with two endings, an editor working near or after 1250 may have eliminated or rewritten the end of Gerbert (if it existed) in order to transform it into a middle passage on the way (back and forward) to Manessier's emphatically terminal continuation. If this scenario is reliable, Gerbert's insertion occurs late in the compilation, but it furnishes a key to understanding the nature of the verse continuations as a group.

Embedded in a culture in which every manuscript is to a greater or lesser extent an individual performance within the *mouvance* of a particular text,[5] a culture in which the notion of xerox copy could not be more foreign, this repetition stands out by contrast in its verbatim sameness. We may wonder why the redactor did not

---

[5] In 'Intertextualité', Zumthor (1981) summarizes his notion of *mouvance*, introduced and defined for literary usage in the *Essai* (1972: 70–5). Cf. its socio-political resonance in the realm of feudalism as 'the area within which a given lord has authority' (Haidu, private communication, 4 July 2006). Poirion's notion of 'l'écriture médiévale' as a 'manuscriture' (1981: 117), ties it to the physical movement of the writer's hand.

modify it to cover over the repeated transition between these continuations and thus remain in conformity with the manuscript tradition, where a strategy of smoothing over or disguising transitions, whether deceptive or involuntary, characterizes the transmission process as a whole. Unlike the *Rose* manuscript tradition, where rubrics clearly announce and distinguish the two parts by Guillaume de Lorris and Jean de Meun even before the god of Love's retrospective identification of the second author's intervention, the *Perceval* manuscripts contain no obvious signals to indicate when we pass from Chrétien to the First, Second, or Third Continuations—which explains why scholars spent so many years debating before finally agreeing on where Chrétien stopped and the continuators started.[6]

On the contrary, the telltale repetition of fourteen verses before and after the Fourth Continuation offers the attentive reader or listener a clear signal in the text for locating when and where it begins and ends. In fact, the public's attentiveness is prepared and reinforced by a whole series of recalls and exact repetitions as the narrator (redactor? author?) makes his way forward by going back to Wauchier's suspended ending, in order to write Perceval back to the moment when he (again) puts together the two halves of the sword. Two sets of reprises are marked by extended sequences that repeat the same rhyme words in the same order.[7] Other passages give less exact renderings of Wauchier's description or mix together references to earlier events from both the Second Continuation and the Fourth.[8] The variations suggest we are not dealing with a failure of technique or imagination: the author/narrator is fully capable of reengineering his predecessor(s). But in this case he seems to be pursuing a particular strategy to exploit and experiment with identity: how does repetition of the same produce something different?[9]

[6] The confusion in the continuations can be seen in manuscript M, which attributes its whole text (P 1 2 3) to a single author: 'Chrestien Manessier de Troyes' (A. Rieger 1993: 379). On the debate about Chrétien's authorship, see Ch. 1. On the *Rose* manuscript tradition, see Huot (1993). Cf. BN, fr. 1450 where, in order to announce the beginning of each work interpolated in the midst of Wace's *Brut*, the partial or complete titles of Chrétien's romances are written in brown ink on the top of the page, or occasionally somewhere else on the page, preceded by the end of the previous narrative. As Walters indicates, it cannot be determined if these have been added later or were part of the manuscript's original design (1985: 308).

[7] Gerbert, III, 16973–82 and 16986–90, repeat Second Continuation, IV, 32307–16 and 32318–22; and again, Gerbert, III, 17023–33 and 17036–8, repeat Second Continuation, IV, 32399–409 and 32412–14. Stephens (1996: 57) interprets these repetitions as a way to call attention to Perceval's opportunity (rare in romance adventure) to revisit the exact same test.

[8] See e.g. Gerbert, III, 17011–22, and Second Continuation, IV, 32387–98, for varied repetition; III, 16986–17009, for mixing events from the Second and Fourth Continuations. We may wonder if this is characteristic of Gerbert's or the editor's style. Although it may be impossible to disentangle, it is worth noticing a reprise of verses that connects two passages within the Fourth Continuation: 2913–31 and 15105–121 give the same combat description with some stylistic reworking (signaled by the notes to vol. III). There are other less extended repetitions of rhyme-word pairs (e.g. hache | hache, II, 10981–2, 11677–8, 11955–6). The editor scribe may simply repeat or elaborate Gerbert's own technique.

[9] In a similar experiment, Borges's Pierre Ménard aims to rewrite the *Quixote*, word for word, and yet the 19th-cent. French symbolist's recreation must necessarily differ profoundly, at the level of meaning, from the work of a one-armed Spanish ex-soldier writing after the Battle of Lepanto.

What then is the difference encoded in this verbatim repetition, as it plays out against the gradual accumulation of verbal echoes that call attention to the way the continuations are stitched together, continuous yet distinct? Within the general patterns of recurrence, the exact repetition of verses placed at the beginning and end of the Fourth Continuation subtly but distinctly stands out as an explicit act of framing, reinforced retrospectively by the dual claims of both Gerbert and Manessier that they began composing at the moment when Perceval resoldered the broken sword... resoldered the broken sword. Caught up in the expansions of narrative, Perceval is made to perform the same action twice, in order to elicit the permutations that lead twice toward and away from that critical gesture—hence the exact repetition of fourteen verses. But their contradictory sameness demands further attention. If, as Heraclitus maintains, you cannot step into the same river twice, what difference does this heretical identity reveal? A slight detour by way of the Bible may help elucidate possible answers.

VERBATIM REPETITION: A BIBLICAL EXAMPLE

The verbatim repetition encircling Gerbert resembles a similar tic of repetition in the editing of the Bible by early Jewish and Christian scholars, which appears in the shifting canonical order of Ezra, Nehemiah, and Chronicles.[10] Since the compilational strategies and effects within the two biblical traditions present useful parallels, mutatis mutandis, I offer here a brief description of the biblical example to help deepen our grasp of similar issues in the *Perceval* cycle.[11] In the Hebrew Bible, the history books appear last in the collection: the final words of 2 Chronicles (36: 22–3), at the very end, repeat the opening verses of Ezra (1: 1–3a), the first in the sequence of four. The ordering is not strictly chronological, since the events reported in Ezra and Nehemiah actually follow those narrated in Chronicles. In fact, the Septuagint and the Old Testament both order them according to the chronology of events (Chronicles, Ezra, Nehemiah), without eliminating the now back to back repetition of verses.[12]

---

[10] Miles's overview of biblical compilation (1996: 391–6) helped me formulate this comparison. For a detailed, scholarly discussion, see Barrera (1998: esp. 97, where he explains the use of 'catch-lines' to guide the copying of successive scrolls or codices). Particularly interesting for this study are Barrera's discussions of (1) the hypothesis of a *Hexateuch* ending with the Promise open (158), (2) the placement of Chronicles at the end of the Tanakh to connect 'the beginning and end of sacred history' (160), (3) the Bible as a group of collections always read in isolated fragments (168), and (4) the Hebrew Bible as a model for imitation (like the Greek and Latin classics) through recreating stories as 'the best and most faithful way to interpret it' (170).

[11] My analysis does not assume a cause and effect relationship between these two instances of verbatim repetition but is based rather on the idea that medieval readers' reception is informed (at least in part) by habits of reading and understanding the Bible. In a similar gesture, Maddox (1983: 44–7) relates the pattern of awakenings found in the crisis scenes in Chrétien's romances to an eschatological patterning derived from the Judeo-Christian tradition, which Ryding (1971) also recognizes generally in bipartite medieval narratives.

[12] Although medieval readers would frequently encounter the books of the Bible in separate groupings and manuscripts (and a lay public would know it primarily through the biblical selections

Two final editings thus produce two very different editions of the same collection. While the Old Testament arrangement leads from the history books to Prophets and fulfillment in the New Testament, a different strategy holds open the future history of restoration in the Hebrew Bible. The loop created by the verbatim repetition, like a coda, produces a round that may go on for ever, as the words repeated at the end loop back to the middle, that is, to the same words placed at the beginning of Ezra.[13] In fact, since Chronicles retell all of history beginning with Adam and continuing on down to David and Solomon, the end may be seen to recapitulate, or even move into the place of a much earlier beginning in Genesis. As a compilation of books, the Bible's compositional history, historiography, and organization illustrate the same kind of play in shifting middles and ends that we observe in the *Perceval* Continuations.

The Hebrew ordering is not unknown to the Christian community. In his program of education and Bible reading in the *Didascalicon*, Hugh of St Victor, one of the twelfth-century exegetes known for renewing interest in the literal or historical sense of Scripture, uses the Hebrew order of the Bible to recognize a symmetry between the Old and New Testaments, based on their corresponding three-part structure: the Law, Prophets, and Hagiographers, in the Old Testament; the Gospels, Apostles, and Fathers in the New (Hugh thus includes patristic writings in his biblical canon).[14] The *Didascalicon* emphasizes that reading the history books to ascertain the literal sense should precede and serve as a foundation to guide allegorical interpretation elsewhere.[15]

As Beryl Smalley points out, '[t]he Bible was the most studied book of the Middle Ages' (1952: xi). As the book of books, the Bible is perceived by the faithful to be both unitary and miscellaneous, diverse yet coherent, authorized

---

read out loud during the liturgy or preached in sermons), the single codex containing the whole Bible is also available in this period. More importantly, the notion of the Bible as a canon of books functions independently of its physical transmission in any given manuscript. For an overview of the Hebrew and Christian ordering, see App. 2.

[13] 'A round is typically composed to be sung by three or four voices simultaneously; and once the voices are all singing, it is impossible to say what is beginning, what middle, and what end. Just as a circle, unlike a line, has no beginning, middle, or end, so this circular form of song, at its exhilarating best, seems to defeat death' (Miles 1996: 392).

[14] Hugh's description of the canon is based on Jerome via Isidore of Seville, according to Signer (2005: 84).

[15] Hugh identifies Genesis, Exodus, Joshua, Kings, Chronicles, the four Gospels, and the Acts of the Apostles, as the books to be read for history; students reading for allegory then pass on to another set of books from the Old and New Testaments. While Hugh identified the literal sense primarily with its historical underpinnings, his disciple Andrew of St Victor gave it a more textual orientation in his exegesis focused on explicating the biblical text's plain or simple meaning (van Liere 2005: 74). Just as Champagne and the Ile de France have been connected as centers for the renewed interest in the *sensus literalis*, medievalists have pointed out similarities between the kinds of interpretation Chrétien's Grail story elicits and the Victorine focus on the literal sense (e.g. Sturges 1991: 42–7; Méla 1983: 220–1), but those suggestions remain to be explored in greater depth both in Chrétien's romance and through its effects on the *Perceval* cycle. Interestingly, Andrew of St Victor's work of the mid-12th cent. was even better known in the 13th (Smalley 1952: 182), when Gerbert was writing.

but multiple in authorship. Erich Auerbach suggests that, in comparison with the Homeric poems, the Bible is 'more obviously pieced together—but the various components all belong to one concept of universal history and its interpretation' (1968: 17). The combination of contradictory materials and unifying force field drives interpretation and invites elaboration of various kinds to cope with gaps or elements that do not immediately fit together (cf. Abelard's *Sic et Non*, in which contradictory passages from the Bible are juxtaposed for 'harmonization'). In medieval usage, whether for lay or clerical publics, the Bible remains subject to the controlling forces of canon formation, but it nevertheless encompasses a shifting set of apocryphal stories, explanatory glosses, liturgical settings, and vernacularizations.[16] The Bible so designed and received offers a valuable model for understanding not only how medieval writers and readers might comprehend the *Perceval* Continuations but also how the comprehensiveness of the cycle finds expression across its variety of components.

What difference does it make then to think about ms. T's particular assemblage of continuations with the analogy of the Bible as book compilation in mind? First, consider the overall effect of Gerbert's loop, which aligns the verse continuations with the coda-like arrangement of the Hebrew Bible, in contrast to the Vulgate Cycle's appropriation of the binary and typological pattern connecting the Old Testament to the New Testament. In biblical, as well as Arthurian materials, this choice of structure raises important issues about the way we read in and outside history, in and outside chronology, and the organizing categories of beginning, middle, and end. The relation between history and romance is crucial here. As noted, Chrétien himself introduces it explicitly, if enigmatically, in the *Conte du Graal*, the only romance in which he includes references to the historical frame constituted by the rise and fall of Arthur's kingship, begun in troubled civil war and ending in destruction.[17] If we generally associate romance with happy endings and history with the downfall of kings and kingdoms, then Chrétien's entangling of the two necessarily leads to questions about the contradictory

---

[16] In addition to Smalley, see *The Bible in the Medieval World* (1985), esp. the essay by David Lascombe on 'Peter Comestor' (109–29), and *The Bible in the Middle Ages* (1992), esp. John A. Alford, 'The Scriptural Self' (1–21), Robert G. Calkins, 'Pictorial Emphases in Early Bible Manuscripts' (77–102), and Madeline H. Caviness, 'Biblical Stories in Windows: Were They Bibles for the Poor?' (103–47). On the Bible, biblical exegesis, and medieval conceptions of authorship, see Minnis (1984). On translations of the Bible into Old French in the 12th and 13th cents., see Berger (1967).

[17] Cf. the Bible's U-shaped patterns of rise and fall, apostasy and restoration, that characterize Israel's history, as well as the sequence of heathen kingdoms that rise and fall (Frye 1982: 169–76). While Auerbach emphasizes about 'the confused, contradictory multiplicity of events, the psychological and factual cross-purposes' (1968: 20) give the biblical stories of Abraham, Jacob, and Moses, the characteristic density of true history, Frye highlights a kind of slippage in the Bible's treatment of historical materials: 'Whenever we move from the obviously legendary to the possibly historical, we never cross a clear boundary line. That is, the sense of historical fact as such is simply not delimited in the Bible, anywhere' (40). In the vernacular context of medieval French literature, the relation between history and romance is more complex than the simple opposition outlined in this section in order to bring out the contrasts between the two romance cycles. For an overview of romance and history linked in non-disjunctive opposition, see my discussion in *Shaping Romance* (1993b: 113–17).

impulses of optimism and pessimism, the potential for comedy and tragedy in human affairs.

In response to that dilemma, the Vulgate Cycle and the *Perceval* Continuations diverge from each other, as from their common model, each cycle taking a different tack to resolve the contradictory tension held in suspense by Chrétien's unfinished ending. In the prose romance cycle, the Grail quest is contained within one branch of the narrative, but its ramifications radiate back into the Prose *Lancelot* and forward into the *Mort le roi Artu*, while in the verse continuations the frame of the Grail quest stretches to include the whole scope of the narrative expansion.[18] While the *Lancelot-Grail* takes the path of romance as history with its two endings, the *Queste* messianic, the *Mort* apocalyptic, the *Perceval* Continuations remain on the path of *estoire* as romance: the messianic overtones of Perceval's redemptive role do not develop as they do for Galahad into salvation history.[19] As we saw in the last chapter, the Third Continuation's restoration of Grail kingship and kingdom still celebrates and is celebrated by the Arthurian ethical ideal, however many religious elements have been worked into the mosaic. From Manessier we do not move forward to Arthur's demise but back through the loop of Gerbert. History is kept at bay and Perceval has avoided or at least corrected the terrible destruction forecast by his cousin and the Hideous Damsel.[20]

Of course, the manuscripts do not place Gerbert after Manessier, as my reading through the chronology of compilation just did. But I would argue that the emblematic significance of that verbatim repetition of verses creating the loop through Gerbert on the way from the Second to the Third Continuation calls our attention to the power of middles over ends.[21] As long as you are not officially inscribed in the history books of Geoffrey or Wace—as Perceval, unlike Arthur, is not—you can keep going around the loop, learning and improving until you get it right. Hence the importance of marking not only the continuous linear advance inscribed in the manuscript tradition's erasure of boundaries but also the

[18] Once the Vulgate Cycle expands to include five branches, the *Estoire del saint Graal* gives Grail history first place, as in Robert de Boron's version. The story of the Grail appears as prequel or beginning, depending on the perspective taken, the chronology of events narrated or the chronology of composition. The Prose *Tristan*, on the other hand, will maintain a very different beginning and point of view when it integrates the Grail quest into Tristan's chivalric adventures, writing in the interstices of the *Queste* as well as rewriting and copying many of its passages as part of Tristan's story.

[19] The greater success of the prose version may reflect in part our human predilection for the pleasures of pathos over the joys of comedy: the great stories tend toward the tragic. See Pratt on Fortune in the *Mort*, as well as the definition of the tragic hero (1991: 81–109).

[20] Anticipating such optimistic strategies, Chrétien remodels Wace's *Brut* in *Cligès*, in order to avoid the potential disasters of the queen's kidnapping and Arthur's downfall through betrayal. Blumenfeld-Kosinski (1985) analyzes Chrétien's similar use of the *romans antiques* in *Cligès*, where references to the *Roman de Thèbes*, for example, allow the characters to avoid fratricidal destruction and the wasteland model.

[21] Cf. Gerbert's insertion in TV to BN, fr. 1450, where the scribe sandwiches all of Chrétien's romances into the *Roman de Brut* to fill out the *pax arthuriana* merely summarized by Wace: *Erec* is followed by *Perceval* and the Short Redaction of the First Continuation, then come *Cligès*, *Yvain*, and the *Charrette* (Micha 1966: 35–7, 297–315; Roach, ed. I, xxv–xxvi; Walters 1985).

discontinuous returns invited by the play of authorial naming and verbatim repetition. Gerbert's loop is emblematic precisely because it performs at the macrolevel of narrative organization exactly what characterizes the movement of each continuation at the microlevel of episodic construction.[22] Chrétien's romance itself initiates the pattern: Perceval the *nice* who mistakes a tent for a church and innocently wreaks havoc on the fortunes of the lady inside will have the opportunity to encounter that lady again and put an end to the deadly jealousy of her knight lover. Over and over again, we see Perceval grappling with the difficult slope of the learning curve from missing and misapplying the messages received from multiple counselors to finally grasping (or at least beginning to understand) what the message may be about. We may wonder if the repeated accusations of treasonous murder would play a similar function in Gauvain's story, had they been resolved before Chrétien stopped writing. Indeed, this particular repetition in the *Conte du Graal* offers a precedent for Gerbert's pattern of looping, since the second accusation by Guiromelant effectively brings the suspended end of Chrétien's romance back to the middle at Arthur's court when Gauvain was first accused by Guigambresil.

As amplified by the continuations, the underlying design anticipates the comic premise of a film whose emblematic title, *Ground Hog Day*, sets up the basic plot: the hero, played by Bill Murray, is forced to relive the mishaps of Ground Hog Day over and over again. First, he gets it wrong over and over again, but finally he learns how to learn, gradually mastering the task of self improvement and gift of self, so that he wins the girl in the happy ending. With Perceval, we may still be wondering about the girl and the Grail (unless we follow Manessier and Gerbert in accepting the *Queste*'s foreclosure), but the pedagogical imperative remains the same. In fact, the Ground Hog Day experience radiates out in the *Perceval* Continuations to envelop more than a single hero—another aspect prepared by Chrétien's authorizing text, where the elements and adventures of Perceval's story pass through the specular transformations of Gauvain's. In the verse continuations, each of the heroes will visit the Grail Castle not once but multiple times in their repeated efforts to get it right and achieve the test (see below). But the Grail Castle visits are only the most spectacular instance of a general pattern, in which visits to Biaurepaire and Blancheflor, to the Chastel as Puceles, and the blacksmith who repairs broken swords, recur from one continuation to another.

Highlighted in the *Conte*'s opening episodes, Perceval's foolishness makes us smile and even laugh along with the 'pucele qui rit'; in the continuations, the comic impulse finds new expression by inscribing the *nice*'s character into the narrative movement as a whole, which thereby carries an essentially comic and hopeful view.[23] Perceval himself no longer plays the simpleton, but he still needs

---

[22] It may be no coincidence that enjambment, which elides the verse end, by transforming it into a middle step on to the beginning of the next verse, constitutes one of the characteristic stylistic tics of Gerbert's narrator. See e.g. I, 5531–3; II, 10956–7; III, 15053–5; and passim.

[23] Cf. the analysis of Wauchier as *nice* in Ch. 1. In keeping with Gerbert's desire to renew direct connections with Chrétien's romance, his Perceval explicitly and self-accusingly recalls his characteristic *niceté* (II, 8890–9, and III, 14523–4).

repeated opportunities to return again to rescue Blancheflor or ask questions about the Grail and the lance—and the broken sword, and the silver carver, and the Black Hand at the chapel, and the child in the tree. Questions accumulate, as each retelling adds its own layers to the previous accounts. Each time, it is the same story and yet not quite. A similar rhythm characterizes the Bible's historical accounts, repeated from book to book in multiple versions marked as much by variation as concordance, as successive layers accumulate.[24] In this looping model, played out in biblical or romance mode, forward progress entails going back. Beginnings, middles, and ends perform a dance, shift places, as readers try to match narrative present and past in order to measure the differences. Hence again, the need for continuators to signal continuities as well as discontinuities.

But the process of recall may create confusions. The first time Gauvain arrives at the Grail Castle in the Short Redaction of the First Continuation, the scene is so changed, we may wonder if Gauvain has found a different place in which the lord of the castle is not infirm and the Grail travels mysteriously with no one holding it. As if to correct for possible misunderstandings, the Long and Mixed Redactions double the number of Gauvain's visits to better align them with Chrétien's original vision of the scene, but not without retaining new features from that earlier reimagining (the and/both logic of the *Conte* continues). If the characters are unfazed by such displacements in repetition, the readers may experience them differently, given our more comprehensive view of both heroes' experiences. The repeated elements guarantee continuity, without entirely masking certain discontinuities introduced by the invention of additional materials or different treatments of the same items from one visit to the next. Do we remember or misremember across the haze of accumulated variation?

Compare our experience as readers of the *Perceval* Continuations to the way memories are stored and triggered in the brain. According to contemporary research, we do not actually possess memories as ready-mades, pictures waiting on file; rather we recreate them at the return of certain clues that fire up our synapses in the same configuration we experienced in the past (Schacter 1996). Memory as reconstruction—subject to all the pressures and possibilities of forgetting and remodeling—looks very much like what continuators do as writers and what we are therefore required to decode as readers. Continuators, redactors, editors are rivals, as well as collaborators, in the production of the tale: using the powerful engine of reinvention, they bring back clues and fire up the recollections of their readers, putting into the place of memory successive visions of the Grail, covering over as much as they recall earlier versions. If we add the ancient and medieval metaphor of memory as a wax tablet, we can further

---

[24] For example, Chronicles begin with the generations from Adam and then recapitulate the events told in 1 and 2 Samuel and 1 and 2 Kings. Nehemiah repeats Ezra and includes another recall of Genesis with its summary of the creation, Abraham, the Exodus, etc. In the New Testament, the four Gospels work similarly, each telling the story of Jesus' life with additions and variations.

appreciate how layers of images overlap, efface previous ones in order to engrave a new and lasting impression on the public.[25]

GERBERT'S GRAIL-LIKE BARRELS

While the same process underlies the radical rewritings of authors from the anonymous *Queste* to Wolfram's *Parzival*, within the verse continuations it takes a particularly revealing spin in the Gerbert episode that most explicitly plays on the Ground Hog Day scenario: Perceval's return to Gornemant (I, 4869–6185). The hero arrives at the castle just as Gornemant and his four sons return from combat against the same forty knights they have killed over and over again. Each morning the knights reappear alive and ready to renew their attack. While the deathless knights have thus maintained their pitiless identity from day to day, Gornemant and his sons are on a downward curve, as first their men, then the father, and finally the sons find themselves unable to return to combat. They are spared annihilation only by the intervention of Perceval, who stays on the battlefield overnight in order to learn how the knights come back to life. What Perceval and the readers learn at this point reveals to what extent Gerbert is offering not only a close reading and commentary but a powerful reorientation of Chrétien's model text. Given that Gerbert systematically sends Perceval back to each of the major loci of his adventures in Chrétien's *Conte*, it is not surprising that he returns to Gornemant, the very figure in Chrétien's romance through whom the art of teaching and the process of learning was thematized. What is remarkable is the extent to which Gerbert reconstructs and clarifies connections operating implicitly in the originating text, while at the same time carrying forward through reinvention the threads and themes of Chrétien's masterplot. With the density of his reinventions, as well as his capacity for designing links and loops within the syntagm, Gerbert strives to rival Chrétien's own narrative gifts: the continuator thus implicitly claims to be an *auctor* in his own right.[26]

Gerbert introduces Perceval's new adventure with Gornemant after an elaborate Tristan episode, in which he opens a space for amorous adventure otherwise expunged from his chaste treatment of Perceval and Blancheflor. In the transition, the narrator promises to tell us first of Perceval 'une partie' before returning to follow Gauvain (I, 4866–8). By thus explicitly bracketing the two, the narrator recalls the way Chrétien introduced and configured his two heroes in one of the most characteristic traits of his enigmatic romance. What was startling in Chrétien has by now become routine for the continuators, who must find new routes to recreate the surprise of *aventure* within the customary byways of the

---

[25] See Carruthers's first chapter on 'Models for the Memory' (1990).

[26] Manessier's more linear and summary approach aims rather to close down the narrative impetus in the pursuit of an ending.

decentered Grail romance. Gerbert now follows the order of episodes in the *Conte*, leading Perceval first to Gornemant's, then to Blancheflor's castle. But what appeared as chance juxtaposition in Chrétien's romance is now acknowledged by Gerbert's rewriting as a significant and purposeful concatenation.

When Gornemant notes Perceval's resemblance to the *valet* he knighted some time ago (4989–91), the recognition that follows leads into Perceval's detailed retelling of his failures during two Grail Castle visits, along with some musing on what might constitute the sin still blocking his success in completely resoldering the broken sword. Gornemant supports Perceval's insight that it must be his failure to fulfill the promise to marry Blancheflor. Returning to his earlier role as advisor and teacher, Gornemant now urges Perceval to marry, eliminate the crack in the sword, and thus learn the secrets of the Grail and the lance.[27] When Perceval carries out this plan in the next episode, Gerbert fulfills and then departs from the other continuators' pattern of retelling the Biau Repaire returns on the same model as Chrétien's first visit—that is, as a rescue mission to save Blancheflor from attack by an unwanted suitor. Alone of the continuators, Gerbert advances Perceval's relationship with Blancheflor and allows Gornemant to recognize his obligation to his niece (inexplicably neglected in the *Conte*). Of course, as already noted, the marriage will be left unconsummated and overdetermined, corresponding not only to the unfinished business left by the first romancer, but also to the Vulgate Cycle's demands for virginal Grail heroes.

This elaboration of the Gornemant episode reinforces and foregrounds the ties linking it to Biau Repaire and the Grail Castle. The connections with the Grail quest are further enhanced through another set of recalls that echo through the newest elements in Gerbert's recasting. When Perceval spends the night on the battlefield, he witnesses a singular scene. A bright light and loud noise announce the entrance of a hideous old woman holding two small but precious ivory barrels. She places the severed head of a knight next to his body, puts a drop of balm from one of the barrels on his mouth and brings him back to life, whole and cured of all wounds. She proceeds likewise with other knights until Perceval intervenes. He now learns that she has been sent by the Roi de la Gaste Chité, an unbeliever and ally of the devil, to punish Gornemant for giving Perceval the order of chivalry and enabling him to undo the work of the *anemis* (5710). As she proceeds with her task of reviving the dead, Perceval further learns that he will never achieve the Grail quest unless he kills her. The adventure at Gornemant's castle thus not only prepares Perceval's marriage as a step toward achieving the

---

[27] A recurrent thread in Gerbert's narrative, the proper fulfillment of marriage promises appears to be one of the important homiletic messages inscribed in the Fourth Continuation: cf. episodes in which Perceval helps his cousin marry the knight who has falsely promised marriage (1757–2424) and saves a damsel forced into marriage by Dragoniau le Cruel (7140–379). Earlier in the narrative, when he sits on the Empty Chair at Arthur's court, Perceval hears a message against sodomy and in favor of heterosexual bonds with wives and lovers (1554–1601). See Burgwinkle's chapter on Gerbert (2004: 89–137).

Grail, it has itself become another of the many qualifying tests that measure Perceval's readiness to be the best of all in all the highest virtues, as specified by the Fisher King at the end of the Second Continuation (and thus in the opening passage of Gerbert's continuation).

Two sets of descriptions play a key role here. The first is the detailed portrait of the old woman (5528–77), clearly modeled on Chrétien's rhetorical flourishes in depicting the Hideous Damsel (4611–41). Both are women of unsurpassed ugliness:

> Onques rien si laide a devise
> Ne fu neïs dedens enfer
>
> (Chrétien, 4618–19)

(never was there so totally ugly a woman even in Hell)

> onques si laide creature
> ne fu veüe en escripture.
>
> (Gerbert, 5529–30)

(never was such an ugly woman seen in Scripture.)

They are black of skin, twisted and humpback in body, with yellow teeth and hair in braids, the Hideous Damsel's twisted and black, the old woman's '[d]eus queues de rates pelees' (5549: two skinned rat tails). In both cases, animal comparisons turn their features into caricatured visual amalgams, verbal fantasies lively and repugnant. Gerbert's imitation pointedly recalls his model while at the same time establishing his independence. If the Hideous Damsel was the one who announced for all to hear at Arthur's court that Perceval failed the adventure at the Grail Castle without the possibility of a second chance, the old woman announces to Perceval that no battle or assault can prevent him from completing his quest: he will learn the answers to his questions about the Grail and the lance, but not as long as she remains alive. By validating Perceval's spontaneous impulse to redress his initial error, her words contradict—or correct—those of the Hideous Damsel. That correction operates not only in the realm of the characters' discourse; it is written into the episode's action as well, with description once again highlighting the way.

In describing the two ivory barrels carried by the old woman (and appropriated by Perceval once he kills her), Gerbert borrows the most salient characteristics of the Grail featured in Chrétien's narrative. Both Grail and barrel hoops are made of the most precious materials: gold encrusted with gems (Chrétien, 3232–9; Gerbert, 5515–24, 5771–81, 5895–911). Even more striking is the light that emanates from both objects.

CHRÉTIEN:	GERBERT:
Atot le graal qu'ele tint,	. . . li doi barisel d'yvoire
Une *si grans clartez* i vint	Que Perchevaus ot conquesté
Qu'ausi perdirent les chandoiles	Font par laiens *si grant clarté*

Lor clarté comme les estoiles
Quant li solaus lieve ou la lune.

(3225–9; emphasis added)

Qu'*ausi cler* i fait, ce vos di,
Con s'il fust a plain mie di.
Perchevaus, quant s'esveilla,
De la clarté se merveilla,
Mais bien set ce n'est nus perius,
Que *la clarté* vient des barieus:
Bien set que ce est *sainte chose*.

(6128–37; emphasis added)

(Chrétien: Along with the Grail she carried came a great light so that the candles lost their brightness just as the stars do when the sun or moon rises.)
(Gerbert: the two ivory barrels that Perceval conquered give off around them such a great light that, I'm telling you, it was as bright as noon time. When he awoke, Perceval was amazed by the light, but he knows well that it is not perilous for the brightness comes from the barrels: he knows well it is a holy thing.)

The pattern of verbal recalls moves from description to function. Perceval's hermit uncle referred to the Grail as '[t]ant sainte chose' (6425) precisely when he described how the single host it contains supports the life of the Fisher King's father. It is in this life-giving function that Gerbert's rapprochement and redesign are most apparent, as his displaced and indirect gloss of the Grail takes shape through the narrative development. According to the narrator, the balm contained in the two barrels has the capacity to restore life because it is the very ointment placed on Christ's body in the tomb (5628–33).[28] Both Grail and ivory barrels are 'si riche saintuaire' (5678) because they are tied to Christianity's most sacred moments—the Passion and the Resurrection. Since Gerbert is writing his continuation after the equation of the Holy Grail with the cup in which Joseph of Arimathea collected Christ's blood, such Christian symbolism is not unexpected here.

But what stands out in Gerbert's free reimagining of a Grail-like object is his return to the mix of Arthurian and Christian marvelous that characterizes Chrétien's overall treatment of that wide and deep dish unexpectedly serving a host instead of a large fish in the castle of an invalid lord whose fate is tied to the asking of questions. The balm has been given a Christian history, but the deathless knights who fight against Gornemant are still popular fare in modern storytelling inspired by the *matière de Bretagne*. Their most recent forms appear in 'children''s fantasy literature caught up in recurrent battles between the forces of good and evil, from Lloyd Alexander's chronicles of Prydain to Susan Cooper's *The Dark is Rising* sequence, from Tolkien's *Lord of the Rings* cycle to Philip Pullman's *His Dark Materials*, a trilogy combining the physics of quantum theory with Milton's *Paradise Lost*. In Chrétien's romance, it is precisely the incongruous interaction of Celtic and Christian elements that resists easy allegorization of the

---

[28] Gerbert may also be alluding to incidents in the *Queste* where the Grail appears to give miraculous healing, e.g. after the combat between Hector and Bohort. Cf. Baumgartner (1984) on the Grail and the drinking horn (from the First Continuation and the *Lai du cor*) associated by their common feature as life-producing objects.

Grail (witness the proliferation of theories of origin). Multiple facets, combined at the pleasure of an author who uses the and/both logic of his complex vision to resist the black and white oppositions of good and evil, shape an elusive yet compelling story that will not easily fit into any single interpretive grid. The narrative continually escapes the bounds of any efforts to pin it down, make it signify through simple theories of meaning. Successive continuations add to the multiplicity through their own narrative rewriting.

Gerbert's clever reimagining of the Grail, through the invention of a Grail-like object, allows him to foreground at the episodic level the very issues that animate this discussion, that is, the strategies of middle-building and compilation that characterize this story in search of—or in fear of?—an ending. The narrator's first description of the ivory barrels culminates with a comment on their value exceeding all of Arthur's treasure (5522–4):

> Bien en orrez la prove fine
> Ainchois que li contes define
> Qui onques ne fu trais a fin.
>
> (5525–7)

(You will hear the perfect proof before the story finishes that has never before been brought to a finish.)

The word play in the rhyme words insists both on the existence of an ending and a history of failure or suspension in the efforts to reach it. The formulation echoes all those places from which no one has ever returned (cf. the leitmotif of Gorre in the *Charrette*), the boundaries no one has passed and the fords no one has jumped (e.g. Gauvain's adventures in the *Conte*). From Gerbert's perspective (presumably writing without knowledge of Manessier's ending), this is the narrative from which no one has yet returned or emerged.

For many modern readers, as for Gerbert, this narrative is as deathless as those forty knights brought back to life by the ministrations of the old woman. Is she a figure for the authors who have continued the tale, a figure for the tale itself as lively amalgam with parts that appear to be going in different directions and yet hang together like the old woman's body parts? At the end of the next episode, when Gerbert names himself as continuator and identifies Chrétien de Troyes as the author of the beginning ('Qui de Percheval comencha', 6983: 'he who began Perceval's story'), he explicitly poses the problem of death and the narrative. Chrétien was unable to finish the romance because 'la mors qui l'adevancha | Ne li laissa pas traire affin' (6986–87: 'death went before him and didn't allow him to finish it'). The rhyme word again underlines the issue of ending, and Gerbert will sound that note once again when he prays to be the one who can reach the ending (7004: 'que il puist la fin ataindre').[29] Gerbert wants to stand at the end as

---

[29] See the discussion of authorial naming in Ch. 1. The variations on *fin* abound in this episode and continue to associate death and ending. When Perceval kills the last of the forty knights, the

counterpart to Chrétien, thus surpassing those unnamed middlemen in between: 'Gerbers, qui a reprise l'oevre, | Quant chascuns trovere le laisse' (6998–9: 'Gerbert who has taken up the work again when every [other] poet abandons it'). The four repetitions of his name (6998, 7001, 7008, 7016) suggest an author cognizant of the value of proper names to fix and hold a place in narrative transmission. Knowing the uncertainties of ending, he has wisely not waited for an epilogue in order to claim his place.

Just as Gerbert is the continuator who guarantees his legitimacy by naming and announcing Chrétien's death, so is he the one who anticipates the delight modern scholars take in playing on the hero's name. Using as his mouthpiece the same old woman who guarantees Perceval's future success in the Grail quest, Gerbert offers a close reading of the hero's name by breaking it down into its constituent parts:

'A drois avez non Perchevaus,
Car par vous est li vaus perchiez
Et li lius frais et depechiez
Ou li basmes est enserrez,
Que vous tot cuitement arez,
Se vers ciaus le poez conquerre.'

(5668–73)

('You are rightfully named Perceval for by you is the valley pierced and the place broken into pieces where the balm is enclosed, which you will have uncontested if you can conquer it from them.')

While her interpretation is localized to the current episode, the episode itself emblematically reenacts the essentials of Perceval's characterization and the momentum that drives the narrative forward, although rarely in a straight, linear fashion. The old woman is herself both opponent and adjuvant in Perceval's quest, blocking his path but supplying the information and the two barrels that make it possible for him to succeed. Once he has defeated the revived knights a second time, Perceval returns to heal Gornemant and his four sons (as he will ultimately heal the Fisher King), before proceeding to Biau Repaire with the precious barrels safely in his possession.

But after he marries Blancheflor, Perceval's haste to depart is so great that he forgets the barrels. They have done their job and must now make way for a return to the Grail and narrative suspense (who could worry about a hero with a life-guaranteeing balm?). We ultimately want neither deathless heroes nor deathless narratives. Although the narrator projects future moments when Perceval will

narrator specifies: 'Tout sont affiné et ocis' (5375: 'they are all finished off and killed'). Perceval later announces his victory at the castle: 'Affiné ai les grans travaus | Que vostre gent soelent sosfrir' (5960–1: 'I have put an end to the great troubles your people have gotten used to suffering'). Cf. also the use of the verb *assomer* to announce Perceval's completion of the Grail quest guaranteed once he has married Blancheflor (I, 6675–8; II, 13988–9). Gerbert sounds a polemical tone as he affirms that Perceval alone ended the adventures and learned the Grail secrets, which may be an implicit acknowledgment and put down of Galahad.

have great need of the barrels and will go back to retrieve them after great travail (II, 7040–57), that loose end is characteristically left hanging when the narrative loops back to the end of the Second Continuation to be sutured to the beginning of Manessier's final act. Through whatever ironies of fate and editing, Gerbert's narrative does not take its place at the end but rather fulfills its destiny in TV by retracing the continuations' typical strategy of extending the middle, now enriched with the Fourth Continuation's own extensive loop.[30]

GRAIL CASTLE VISITS MULTIPLIED

However much the description and function of the ivory barrels recall the Grail, there is no mistaking a Grail-like object for the Grail itself. The 'coda' takes us away from and then back to the Grail, clarifying its identity through doubling and difference. But the same layering, backward and forward across the cycle, can be observed in the various repetitions of the Grail episode as well, as they set up what have become the key signposts of the entire cycle. Consider the interplay between Perceval's visit to the Fisher King as told in the *Conte* and Gauvain's Grail Castle visits as narrated in the different redactions of the First Continuation. In addition to the major switch from one hero to the other, these episodes show considerable disagreement about where the castle is located, who lives there, how the Grail moves, whom it serves, and so on. Accumulation as a form of amplification especially favored by the continuators plays an important role here. As Gauvain's visits multiply from one in the Short Redaction to two in the Long and Mixed Redactions (composed after the Second Continuation), they trace a trajectory that moves in an elliptical orbit around Chrétien's model, now farther away, now closer, depending on the play of difference and repetition. How should we make sense of this contradictory—or is it complementary?—proliferation of episodes that explore the multifaceted mysteries of the Grail?

From a philological point of view, the chronology of composition suggests the maximal movement away from Chrétien occurs first.[31] The Short Redaction invents a single Grail scene that has little or nothing to do with the *Conte*. Funeral services take place around a body placed on a bier with a broken sword lying on top. At dinner, the Grail makes its entrance with no procession, flies through the air, and provides each person with food and drink, while the lance stands on a rack and bleeds into a silver vessel.[32] In ms. T's Mixed Redaction, the desire to

[30] With no evidence outside the edited text of TV, it cannot be determined with certainty whether Gerbert actually finished the story or not. For further discussion, see Ch. 1.

[31] My summary here cannot do justice to the complexities of the multiple versions of each redaction and the possible relationships among them. For a more comprehensive discussion, see Roach's introductions to the three volumes of the Gauvain Continuation, Vial (1987: 118–36), Gallais (1988–9: 1, 115–433; 4, 2259–83), and Van Coolput (1986: 19–23).

[32] For a more detailed analysis of all the differences, see Roach (1966: 162–3), Thompson (1959: 213–15), Séguy (2001a: 19–121).

Fig. 6. BN, fr. 12577, f. 74v. At the Grail Castle, while seated at a table with the Fisher King, Gauvain witnesses the Grail procession.

return to Chrétien has clearly reasserted itself, though the realignment is double, since the new version not only retains key elements from Perceval's Grail experience, it also includes significant innovations found in the Short Redaction, whose version will be repeated *grosso modo* later in the narrative sequence. According to T's revised ordering of events, Gauvain's first visit to the Fisher King's castle thus introduces the body on the bier and the broken sword as a test for receiving the secrets of the Grail.

The textual developments can be seen visually in BN, fr. 12577 (U), which contains the Long Redaction of the First Continuation: there are three miniatures that illustrate scenes at the Grail Castle, first Perceval's (f. 18v), then Gauvain's first of two visits (f. 74v, seen above in Fig. 6), and finally Perceval's return in the Second Continuation (f. 209).[33] The last one is a single square miniature that shows Perceval arriving on horseback on the left and then seated at a table with the Fisher King on the right. They converse with animated gestures, while two youths kneel before them: one holds up the Grail (always represented in this manuscript in the form of a ciborium topped by a cross), the other a very vertical bleeding lance (a sword mentioned in the rubric is not visible). The first two miniatures, beautifully extended across two columns, are strikingly similar in layout. They call attention to the damsel carrying the Grail followed by the youth holding the lance, by placing them near or at the center, the transition between

[33] See the second volume of *Manuscripts* for all three illustrations (1993: 509, 512, 519), two also shown in color (348), and the rubrics (288, 290, 294).

the right- and left-hand scenes, which are set off by their frames and alternating red and blue diapered backgrounds. The two figures lead the procession and clearly show the forward movement that will take them before the table where the Fisher King gestures in their direction. Curiously, Perceval is absent in the first miniature (though the blazing fire mentioned by Chrétien is clearly shown at the right side under its mantelpiece); the king is seated beside an unidentified queen who will reappear next to Gauvain in the second miniature (a reflex gesture of the illuminator used to representing other courtly scenes?). On the left-hand side, corresponding images visually connect the sword that Perceval receives as he arrives at the Grail Castle (f. 18v) and the sword laid across the body on the bier carried by four men, added in Gauvain's visit (Fig. 6, f. 74v). The body is vividly covered by red drapery and the sword (clearly viewed from above) appears to be whole, although Gauvain will have to put together its broken pieces. In BN, fr. 12576, our most cyclical T, the only representation of the Grail appears at the end of Manessier. Partially covered, it is held by a large and imposing female figure before a kneeling Perceval (Fig. 7): the perplexing ambiguity of the scene will require study in the Conclusion.

In the First Continuation, Gauvain will once again fail to join the sword's two pieces when he returns to the Grail Castle, but the return itself is favorably interpreted. The limited success achieved during his second visit, reflected in the partial restoration of the landscape around the Fisher King's castle, becomes a measure of Gauvain's progress in chivalry. He is permitted to ask questions and begins by asking about the lance; he learns it belonged to Longinus and will cause the destruction of Logres, but falls asleep before learning about the corpse and the sword (13442–521). Of course, Gauvain's partial success must still be restricted by partial failure, in order to reserve the achievement of the Grail for Perceval, who ultimately remains the designated hero. Faced with a multiplicity of views that place before both heroes, as before readers and successive rewriters, an image of the Grail that evokes the changing and untotalizable perspectives of a cubist painting, what stands out in a continuous reading of ms. T from Chrétien's Grail episode through the two versions of the Gauvain Continuation, whatever the original order of composition, is the process of accumulation as guiding spirit: nothing is ever lost but more can always be added, as new threads are interwoven with old ones in a pattern of repetition and contrast, according to the logic of and/both.

Keeping in mind the complexities of this overall design, I would like to focus briefly but more specifically on the textual recalls written into the fabric of Gauvain's first pivotal Grail visit, in order to follow more closely how the microlevel of verbal inventions supports the macrolevel of narrative structure with its shifting beginnings, middles, and ends. As indicated, the reader of ms. T may be unaware of the passage between Chrétien's unfinished romance and the First Continuation, although the invocation of *Crestïen* (I, 1234) at the beginning of the Grail Castle visit signals the possibility of intertextual play (see the Introduction for discussion of this passage). While Gauvain's approach on a dead man's horse across a causeway near the sea differs considerably from Perceval's initial meeting with the Fisher King and his descent into a valley, some geographical and architectural details link them: *riviere* (P 2986; GC 1198), *roche* (P 2995; GC 1223), drawbridge (P 3067–8; GC 1239–40). Once in the castle, four valets emerge to disarm Perceval, more than a hundred converge on Gauvain. This anonymous continuator has a penchant for big numbers, but he also likes to repeat Chrétien's text, as when he simply reverses the rhyme words *loges/Limoges* (P 3086; GC 1264) or presents the Fisher King as *un bel preudome* (P 3086; GC 1264), wearing a hat of *sebelin* (P 3089; GC 1271).

Changes introduced play more prominently against this common background. The introduction and order of the Grail procession are first slightly modified: 'Un graal' (P 3220) becomes 'le saint Graal' carried by a *pucele* who is crying, to Gauvain's amazement (GC 1364–70). But the most striking new elements appear once the procession enters the room with a body carried on a bier and a sword placed on top of the silk cover.

> ...une espee...
> Que par miliu ert pechoïe,
> Mais a malaise ert percheüe,
> Se ce ne fust chose seüe,
> Qu'ele samblast tote entiere.

> (1379–83)

(a sword that was broken in the middle but this was not easily seen unless already known, for it appeared to be whole)

The sword does not appear in Chrétien's Grail procession, but this description recalls the sword given to Perceval by the Fisher King and seen through his eyes, just before the bleeding lance enters:

> si vit bien ou ele fu faite,
> Car en l'espee estoit escrit.
> Et avec che encore i vit
> Qu'ele estoit de si bon achier
> Que ja ne porroit depechier,
> Fors que par un tot seul peril
> Que nus ne savoit fors cil
> Qui l'avoit forgie et tempree.

> (3136–43)

([The Fisher King] saw where [the sword] was made for it was written on the sword. And with this he saw that it was made of such good steel that it couldn't break except in a single peril that no one knew but the one who had forged and tempered it.)

This enigmatic description anticipates a moment when the sword will break in two, an event which three manuscripts (including T) interpolate into Perceval's duel with the Orgueilleux de la Lande.[34] Here, given the elliptical syntax and the uncertain passage between what is visible and what is known, we may be puzzled by just what it is that the Fisher King actually sees when he looks at the sword. In any case, both swords are sent by the Fisher King's niece (P 3145–7; GC 1440–2) and designate the Grail hero, Chrétien's by destination (3168), the First Continuation's by testing: Gauvain must reunite the two pieces before his questions about the Grail can be answered (the new reason found for delaying the answers, despite Gauvain's more prompt inquiries). Though initially it appears that Gauvain has successfully made the sword whole again, it easily comes apart when the Fisher King orders Gauvain to test the juncture by pulling.

> Et trestot cil qui le veoient
> Cuidoient qu'ele fust rejointe. . . .
> Et Gavains prent l'espee et sache,
> Mais l'un achier de l'autre errache
> Et desjoint al premerain trait.
>
> (1458–9, 1467–9)

(And all those who saw it think that [the sword] was rejoined. And Gauvain takes the sword and pulls, but one piece of steel comes apart from the other and separates at the first pull.)

The play with a deceptive appearance of wholeness echoes Chrétien's description, although without the enigma of secret knowledge and delayed discovery.

Through repeated textual reverberations, the continuator thus works together the details of Perceval's visit in the *Conte* with those from Gauvain's visit in the Short Redaction: both models are fused in the accumulation of materials. In the Fisher King's comment on Gauvain's failure, the process continues, as the narrator anticipates his repetition of the episode:

> . . . 'N'avez tant fait
> D'armes encore que le voir
> Puissiez de ceste oeuvre savoir,
> Car cil que le voir en sara
> Le pris de tot le monde ara
> Et le los, je vos affi.
> Mais encor puet bien estre ensi
> Que vos le voir en sariies
> Et que vos conquis arriiez
> Du monde par chevalerie
> Tot le los et la seignorie.'
>
> (1470–80)

('You haven't yet achieved enough in arms to be able to know the truth of this feat, for the one who will know the truth will have the esteem and praise of everyone, I assure you. But it may still be that you will know the truth and you will have conquered through chivalry all the praise and lordship of the world.')

---

[34] See the notes in Poirion's edn. (1994a: 1355 n. 2).

These verses not only echo the laughing maiden's prophecy for Perceval, they duplicate in advance the invitation to try harder (13411–16) that will reappear in the reprise of Gauvain's Grail Castle visit borrowed from the Short Redaction. The *remanieurs* of the Long and Mixed Redactions have themselves taken and multiplied that invitation not only by doubling Gauvain's Grail adventure but by including his report of the (second) visit before Arthur's court (14088–98).[35] Indeed, the possibility of another return remains open, since at the end of the second visit, when Gauvain awakens outside the castle, as he did the first time, he vows to come back again and ask about the Grail service (13537–57), although this time the potential reprise remains unrealized.

This pattern of repeated returns has already been anticipated in Chrétien's *Conte du Graal* by the multiple renarrations of Perceval's Grail Castle visit, as well as his decision to take up the Grail quest after the Hideous Damsel's public rebuke (4727–40), even though he is not invited to do so by the three interpreters of his failure. Despite her detailed interrogation about all the particulars of his visit, his cousin does not tell Perceval to go back to the Fisher King; her information, on the contrary, leads him away to combat with the Orgueilleux, after which the narrator describes Perceval as seeking 'aventure et chevalerie' (4167). But with the second reproach, his reaction is translated into a desire to return and correct his failure, as if he could not understand the implications of his cousin's words until they were reiterated by the Hideous Damsel before Arthur's court. This is Perceval's typically delayed learning curve, but the five years of fruitless adventures that precede the hermit episode suggest that the *nice* has regressed rather than progressed in the interim. The limits of his understanding are further emphasized by the hermit's censure, but again the advice given includes no command to seek the Grail, and there is no indication how Perceval will put into effect his uncle's instructions beyond remembering to go to church every day. The last episode in which we see the presumed Grail hero in Chrétien's romance thus ends with no specific mention of his future plans, though his quest vow still holds the promise of a return to the Fisher King, just as the promise to Blancheflor still holds open the return to Biaurepaire—promises that the continuators repeatedly seek to fulfill and defer.[36]

---

[35] In the Second Continuation, Gauvain twice retells his Grail Castle visit, first to Arthur, then to his son. The first account (IV, 29115–47) seems to refer to the second visit (i.e., the one borrowed from the Short Redaction): when volunteering to quest for the Fisher King, he mentions the questions that he failed to ask earlier, since he fell asleep. The second account (IV, 31108–253) is much longer and includes details from both visits: the mysterious quester whose place he took, the events at the chapel, the body, lance, and broken sword, the Grail carried by a maiden, the question he asked about the lance and then his involuntary fall into slumber.

[36] From the point of view of the hermit, Perceval's adventures in the Second Continuation might appear as another regression, this time from his Easter conversion, before renewed progress toward a more pious chivalry in Gerbert's continuation. Wauchier's Perceval seems poised to advance in an amorous vein, but Gerbert and Manessier cut off erotic advancement in his progress toward achieving the Grail. Together the continuations retain the backward and forward movement typical of Perceval's and Gauvain's trajectories in the *Conte du Graal*.

From the *Conte* to successive continuations, the accumulation of Grail Castle adventures, retold or directly experienced by Perceval and Gauvain, appears to make abundantly explicit (whatever we think of the additions and interpretations provided) what was initially elliptical and mysterious in Chrétien's first account, offered through the eyes of a naïf who remains silent when he should speak out. Despite this move toward greater expression, the redactors of ms. T are themselves content to remain silent about their juxtaposition—across the space of some 12,000 verses—of two remarkably different accounts of the Grail's action and location. While they take care to add the lengthy first visit for Gauvain and make sure the readers can connect it to Perceval's (told about 7,000 verses earlier), they make no explicit reference to Gauvain's first visit when they narrate the second, just as the scribe editor who splices Gerbert into the slot created by the verbatim repetition at the end of the Second and Fourth Continuations finesses without comment the 17,000 verse interpolation. Since discontinuities can be as easily smoothed over as unexpected repetitions, we may interpret their silence as an invitation to explore the gap of difference across the network of implicit references. In ms. T's Mixed Redaction, Gauvain's first Grail visit thus becomes the axis around which Chrétien's version swings in order to converge with the Short Redaction's reinventions, before the process of renovation revolves again on an ever-widening path of divergence—until the next continuator or redactor heads back for a fresh encounter with their common textual model. Reprise and reinvention set up multiple cycles of movement back to and out from Chrétien's generating romance.

The retellings of the Grail episode through the first two continuations reflect the general process of assimilation between the two heroes, and more specifically here, between Perceval's quest and Gauvain's as initially represented in *Le Conte du Graal*. Gauvain's obligation to bring the bleeding lance back to Escavalon is displaced by his desire to ask questions about the Grail, the lance, the broken sword, and the body on the bier. Like Perceval, Gauvain has become involved in a test of merit, not merely an escape strategy from the ethical dilemma posed at Escavalon. Now it is not enough to ask questions, one must be worthy to receive the answers. Gauvain's failure to get all the answers desired is linked to his insufficient achievement as knight, but that insufficiency is presented as relative rather than definitive, as demonstrated by his partial success on the second try. If the verse continuators cannot imagine Gauvain actually replacing Perceval as Grail champion (as Galahad does in the *Queste del Saint Graal*), they do give the second hero a considerable role to play in Perceval's own scenario of cure through questions. And the same testing device can subsequently be used for Perceval as well: resoldering the sword will function henceforth as the gateway to answers, even when Perceval has successfully articulated the questions. If we read across the interlace, it is as if each of these heroes generated his own possible world of fiction but then found that the other one entered it as well.[37] Or, more importantly in the context of Chrétien's two-hero model as it continues to exert its influence throughout the cycle, we can recognize here once again Gauvain's and Perceval's strange need for each other in a decentered romance anchored *in medias res*.[38]

Once we have so frequently followed both Perceval and Gauvain back to the castle of the Fisher King across the accumulated layers of four continuations, the workings of memory and reconstruction become confused. I mentioned earlier the possible bewilderment created by radically different imaginings of the Grail but, paradoxically, it is also true that the closer the recall between Grail scenes, the more interference with remembering, as the imaginative recreation claims to duplicate and replace the past, the way photographs tend to replace memories. I have no trouble distinguishing the Short Redaction's version of the Grail Castle visit; I have to work much harder to disentangle the Second Continuation's version from Gauvain's second visit in the Long and Mixed Redactions, or to fine tune my appreciation of Manessier's and Gerbert's subsequent permutations. Where are the damsels going with which objects? Is this broken sword related to the one Perceval received in Chrétien's version from the Fisher King's niece? How and why has the Grail adventure come to be defined as one that defies completion and resists ending?

Our questions at this point are not the same as Perceval's. In fact, if we were paying attention, we have known the answers to his questions about the Grail since Chrétien's hermit episode, and those concerning the lance since Gauvain's Escavalon visit in the *Conte* plus his first or second Grail visit (depending on the redaction). Admittedly, Perceval himself will not be permitted to put it all together until he reaches Manessier's continuation, but we are certainly not reading for the unsuspenseful resolution of these questions. By this point in the continuations, we know what the end of the Grail adventure will be (even if we are still uncertain that the ending is Chrétien's).[39] But that does not lessen our appetite for intermediate adventures that move toward, even as they continue to defer, the culmination. Our attention is riveted on the process, how we and the characters get to where we know they are going through *errances* and *aventures*. We loop backward and forward across thousands of verses, flipping pages or searching memories, remembering and forgetting the exact details from one

---

[37] Cf. how Doležel explores the concept of other worlds in literary fiction.

[38] The invention of a hierarchical trio of Grail heroes in the *Queste* recognizes the impossibility of eliminating Perceval from the field (given the influence of Chrétien's version), while at the same time it takes advantage of and redirects the First Continuation's addition of Gauvain as a runner-up in the Grail stakes.

[39] Cf. Wood's first two propositions for defining the unfinishable work, discussed in the last chapter: '1. A work devoted to its own unfinishability can end only when we are no longer interested in its ending. 2. Such a work can end only some time after it has already ended' (2007: 1401).

version to the next, deepening the potential for pleasure as well as meaning in the play of romance.[40]

Once engaged in the process, we readers experience along with Perceval the travails of the learning curve. We loop even more extensively than he does in the course of reading Chrétien's romance and its four continuations. The powerful combination of continuity and discontinuity, signaled by recalls and returns, require us to measure, sift, and reevaluate the successive loops. The greater the looping, the greater the learning potential, as we look for a happier ending that can be achieved only through replays that loop back to the middle and give us another chance to find our way to the anticipated end. If the *Perceval* Continuations, like the collection of books in the biblical canon, do reach an endpoint, the loops built into the narrative bring us back into the flow, urge us to seek more answers to puzzles embedded in the byways of adventure. The audacity inscribed in the *Conte du Graal*'s beginning can be measured by the extent to which our romance looping now entails religious and historical questions left out of the loop in his earlier romances.[41] And there, for better and worse, Chrétien has left us all *in medias res*.[42]

---

[40] A good example of the kind of confusions generated occurs when Gerbert's Perceval asks again for an explanation about the child in the tree, a question that the Fisher King already answered in the Second Continuation, when it was first posed (and when the incident occurred without being recycled in the Fourth Continuation). Does it suggest that answers given never completely satisfy or exhaust the play of possible meanings? In any case, we may wonder if Gerbert has forgotten or simply overlooked the answer, as he follows the rhythm of repetition already built up by other repeated questions about the Grail and the lance and the sword. His repetition of the question, whether voluntary or not, dramatizes the issue of memory and forgetfulness, calls into play the readers' share in the process. While a medieval public listening to a manuscript read out loud may be less inclined to go back and verify those earlier passages than the modern reader whose printed edition facilitates retrieval, the romance nevertheless demands a process of reflection from its reader/listeners who are aided by the multiple techniques of repetition and variation which establish a network of allusions and recalls that criss-cross the patterns of narrative. Cf. Regalado on the art of misquotation in Villon's *Testament* as a trigger for the reader to recall, compare, and interpret texts put into play by apparent mistakes (1999).

[41] In *A Preface to Chaucer*, Robertson quotes from a sermon addressed to listeners who would rather stay up late to hear about Perceval than follow the priest's, i.e., God's words (1962: 89–90). The competition for audience attention between sermonizers and romancers that Robertson describes may have been more keenly felt once romance intruded into the domain of religion through the appeal of the Grail stories. Gerbert certainly uses his continuation as a vehicle for sermonizing through the narrator, as well as the characters (including Perceval himself who on repeated occasions assumes a clerical perspective). On churchmen's critiques of Arthurian literature, see also Bäuml (1980: 255) and Haidu (1977: 882–3). Cf. the author/narrator of the Prose *Tristan*, Luce de Gat, who presents himself as a knight and claims that the archbishop of Canterbury has forbidden him to tell about things pertaining to divinity ('qui a la devinité apartiegne'): he will, therefore, have to leave out St Augustine's 'biaus essamples' (1986: I, 106: ¶ 171, ll. 10–14).

[42] Cf. Jeffrey's overview of medieval thought on the Christian notion of 'man's place in the middle' (1979: 1), based on the biblical model of history and the limited understanding of 'in the beginning' available to human beings of finite existence, which results in our 'lostness in the middle' (3). I would like to thank Kinsley Hyland Alexander for bringing Jeffrey's work to my attention.

Conclusion

> The anthropologist agreed when I suggested that the tent, the woman's skirt, and the sanctuary were symbols of the good and protective mother... and that the ban on killing within one's own tent linked with the rules of hospitality. My conclusion about the last point is that fundamentally hospitality links with family life, with the relation of children to one another, and in particular to the mother. For, as I suggested earlier, the tent represents the mother who protects the family.
>
> Melanie Klein, 'Our Adult World and its Roots in Infancy'[1]

Throughout this book I have traced the dialogue between Chrétien de Troyes's *Conte du Graal* and his verse continuators, as it emerges from the patterns of reading and rewriting inscribed in the changing shape of a dynamic manuscript tradition. As I said in the Introduction, this is not a book about the Grail per se but rather a study of how the 'Story of the Grail' initiates and sustains the process of continuation generated by its powerful resistance to ending, an examination of the way successive continuators map out through their own inventions what the master text, always present back at the beginning, has taught them with its implicit and explicit questions, its puzzles and problems. Not a book about the Grail then, but as the last chapter demonstrated, those who adventure into the byways of this romance prolonged through multiple continuations, whatever their intentions, inevitably find themselves on a path back to the Grail Castle and its mysteries. And so, in an effort to push further in this final space of conclusion what the continuations have taught us about reading Chrétien, I find myself going back to the mother text, to the mother and the text, to the mother and the Grail.

---

[1] (1975: 263). This passage appears in a postscript that records Klein's conversation with an anthropologist whose field experience confirmed her view of character development only when he described how a man could claim mercy from his adversary if he made it to a man's tent or if he placed himself behind a woman so that he was covered by her skirt. Klein's conclusion encourages my efforts to pursue connections: 'I am quoting this instance to suggest possible links between cultures that appear to be entirely different, and to indicate that these links are found in the relation to the primal good object, the mother, whatever may be the forms in which distortions of character are accepted and even admired' (263). I would like to thank Joseph Youngerman, MD, for bringing this essay to my attention. On the role of mothers and covering seen in Lacanian terms, cf. Kay's discussion of *Lanval* as a 'Marian' lay, in particular 'the "fixation" of the veil ... materialized through lingering attention to forms of covering—clothing, the *fée*'s tent—which also serve as figures of representation'. She pursues the 'logic of the veil' in *Fresne* as well: 'a cover which conjures a fullness of meaning behind it' (2001: 203).

A myriad of threads woven across Chrétien's romance establish the Grail in a web of connections. Perceval's itinerary, echoed by Gauvain's, sets the Grail into a triangular relationship with mother and *pucele*, the Veuve Dame and Blancheflor. Chrétien's Grail thus operates within links that criss-cross family, society, and sexuality, in addition to the religious values introduced by his mother and uncle. What light do the continuators' rewritings shine back to help illuminate these issues embedded within the originating text? Is there a necessary relation between gender and the Grail, as initially set up in the *Conte du Graal*? What follows represents a response to that question framed not as a feminist critique of the romance from the point of view of contemporary debate on what constitutes masculine and feminine or the tension between essentialist and constructionist definitions of gender, but offered rather as an analysis of how the text itself phrases an understanding of those categories. From such an angle, the distinctly medieval character of a gendered Grail may continue to reverberate in the space that both separates and connects Chrétien's Grail story to our contemporary concerns.

As noted in Chapter 1, among the surprising moves of Chrétien's prologue is the proffered model of exegetical reading. Although it has elicited for the Grail the kind of glosses offered by priests and hermits in the *Queste del Saint Graal*, I have argued here that the example, as manipulated by Chrétien's rhetorical ploys and referential games, should serve to make readers pay closer attention to the letter of his text, including its possible deeper senses, to be sure, levels of meaning I would qualify as figurative but not necessarily allegorical. Have we read the *Conte du Graal* in the full potential of its *sensus litteralis*? Chrétien's aesthetic, as articulated in *Erec et Enide* and demonstrated throughout his corpus, emphasizes the art of the *bele conjointure*. Beauty is found in the joining, and, if we consent to the poetic maxim that beauty is truth and truth beauty, then we need to locate the search for answers to the Grail's puzzles in the narrative concatenation of the romance. Whatever meanings we are led to discover in Chrétien's works, since his prologues explicitly invite us to look for *sen(s)*—which in Old French includes sense, wisdom, direction, and signification—our interpretations should emerge from the particular patterns he gives to his narrative, as well as the common storymatter and forms shared with oral and written traditions. In his last, unfinished romance, the Grail makes its first verbal appearance in the unusual title announced in the prologue, 'li Contes del graal' (66), then makes its actual entrance into narrative as 'un graal' (3220) whose dazzling appearance, as part of an elaborate procession that passes repeatedly before the amazed but silent Perceval, is designed to elicit questions the hero fails to ask. Our questions, unlike Perceval's, continue to multiply, as the Grail reveals new facets, elusively hints of something more.

This seems especially true when we notice that the Grail and the bleeding lance, placed in tandem at the Grail Castle along with their associated questions, constitute a gendered set, insofar as they steer us along a path peopled respectively by the male and female characters who gravitate around Perceval. You need not be a Freudian to notice that as a receptacle the Grail is a feminine object suitably, though mysteriously, carried by a young girl, the lance a masculine object unsurprisingly but enigmatically held by a young man. The Grail, let us not forget, is here represented as a deep, wide serving dish whose initial description emphasizes without explaining its inestimable value. We see through Perceval's eyes gold and precious gems, intense light, as it passes repeatedly into another room. Later at the hermit's, Perceval learns that the Grail, 'tant sainte chose' (6425), does not contain the large fish its size implies, but a single host that feeds the Fisher King's father, his only nourishment for twelve years.[2] The Grail as container is located at the intersection of spiritual and physical senses: food, sustenance, nourishment, life—all linked to Perceval's maternal family and holy things. The lance, from whose tip blood drips down the shaft to the young man's hand, just as inevitably symbolizes, as it enacts (from the past and into the future) male aggression and violence. The lance no less than the Grail puts into relief what can sustain life, protect, or end it. Is the bleeding lance part of the Grail procession or a separate act? In any case, the two questions Perceval must ask associate them, even as the lance moves from his orbit into the separate (but not entirely separate) trajectory of Gauvain's adventures.

The sense of opposition or complementarity between masculine and feminine objects can be strongly sensed from all the visual elements described, and Chrétien's medieval public was probably just as attuned to that potential as modern readers. Consider again Gerbert's rewriting of the luminous Grail as two ivory, gem-encrusted barrels, emanating enough light to make the night as bright as midday and carried by an old woman whose description echoes that of the Hideous Damsel. The balm they contain repeatedly brings back to life the knights killed in combat at Gornemant's castle, where Perceval's adventures in the Fourth Continuation have returned him. The vicious cycle of undeath and rebirth that has nearly destroyed Gornemant's family finally ends when Perceval kills the old woman and becomes master of the ivory barrels. Gerbert's descriptions and narrative reinvention reinforce our view of Chrétien's Grail as somehow connected with the restoration of life threatened by violence.[3] In this new episode, Perceval's appropriation of the Grail-like objects takes a correspondingly violent form, presented as an action necessary to qualify for success in the quest for the Grail itself.

---

[2] Eleven, fifteen, and twenty years are given in various manuscripts. See Busby's edn. (1993: 272) for the variants on v. 6429.

[3] Is that 'somehow' in the realm of myth, magic or miracle, the Breton marvelous or the Christian miraculous? Walter discusses the Grail as serving dish as the possible intersection of a Christian symbol represented by the host and the salmon as the mythical fish of the Celts (2004: see esp. 233). Cf. the disagreements as to whether the single host is placed in the Grail or actually produced by it, which I take to be a debate on where the holiness of the dish, asserted by the hermit, actually resides: in the dish itself or in its association with the host as the body of Christ. Metaphor or metonymy?

Of course, the qualifying test in Chrétien's romance is not an aggressive action but a speech act, which Perceval has failed. Lance and Grail are supposed to elicit questions, reiterated in their appropriate formulation numerous times (3204–5, 3244–5, 3292–3, 3398–401, 3552–3, 3568–70): whom does it serve, why does it bleed? If the questions are asked, the Fisher King will be cured; unasked questions prelude the devastation of his land, the killing of his knights, the suffering of widows and orphans. Life and healing, on the one hand; violence, death, and destruction, on the other. Apparent oppositions that will be revealed as interlaced, imbricated. Chrétien's questions for Perceval (and for the readers) do not focus on the objects per se.[4] They are not aimed to furnish a definition or equivalence, as in the *Queste* (and later continuations influenced by it), where the dish has been replaced by Robert de Boron's cup, the chalice of the Last Supper, the vessel given to Joseph of Arimathea and used to catch the blood of the crucified Christ, interpreted as the symbol of the Eucharist or God's grace; where the lance is identified, as in the First Continuation, with the instrument of the Passion, the lance of Longinus. Francis Dubost suggests that the *Conte*'s particular questions point to origins and ends (1998: esp. 169–85). They remain on the horizontal syntagm of narrative meaning, connecting us to Arthurian history and Perceval's family history: a family dispersed, fragmented, in need of repair, a reign suspended between civil wars and calamitous destruction. These narrative links appear gradually across what seems at first to be a series of disconnected adventures, episodes merely juxtaposed in the narrative but which uncover siblings and cousins, uncles and mothers, filiations of kinship and history.

Will Perceval be able to integrate the multiple demands and desires either chosen or imposed upon him?[5] Can he coordinate mother and girl, Grail and sexuality, lance and Grail? Chrétien's romance multiplies the possibilities and contradictions. In its unfinished state, it allows for both the success and failure of the hero, or rather heroes, as Perceval's story is extended through the echoes created by Gauvain's adventures, the second hero both separate from and strangely connected to the first across the interlace of their itineraries. We need both of their stories to follow the play of gender and the Grail.

The story starts with a boy and his mother, who raises Perceval in isolation in order to protect him from the destructions of chivalry. Forced by his insistent desire, she sends him out into the world with a set of new clothes and lots of good advice, and then dies (as do so many mothers whose deaths give birth to the hero's narrative). Nevertheless, the Veuve Dame continues to play a role in

---

[4] Haidu's reading underlines that the Grail signifies only insofar as it remains mysterious (1968: 172). Burgwinkle compares the Grail to Lacan's *objet a* 'whose ultimate significance is, and can only ever be, veiled' (2004: 94): as the screen onto which desires are projected, the Grail's power is a function of the value others attribute to it.

[5] Cazelles (1996) interprets the romance action as the imposition of a vendetta unfairly placed on Perceval by his maternal family.

Perceval's story and throughout Chrétien's romance, as the figure of the mother goes through a variety of shapes and episodes.[6]

Chrétien's text thus calls for evaluating positive as well as negative aspects connected to the mother as obstacle to and path toward the Grail, knighthood, and amorous connection. Her parting advice sets a model for Perceval's other mentors whose subsequent counsel will reprise the categories she first introduces, the very ones that map out the areas for contradiction followed throughout this study: relations with women, conduct in chivalry, religious practice. But the mother's advice, which she describes as 'un sens [que] vos weil aprendre' (527: 'a lesson/good sense/meaning/direction that I want to teach you'), is the most comprehensive in the realm of interaction with the fair sex. She recommends multiple connections with maidens and ladies, ranging from aid to those in need of help to delicate matters of love. As we have seen, her request to her son blocks any 'surplus'—'Se laissier le volez por moi' (549: 'if you will leave it for my sake')—and thus puts into question not only the enjoyment of sexual pleasure but the eventual role of Blancheflor and marriage.

Perceval fails to ask the questions because of a sin against his mother, yet even in death, her parting commendation to God keeps him alive and safe (617–19, 6396–408). Though she has kept it a secret, the Veuve Dame is Perceval's link to both the tradition of knighthood and the Grail family. A severe critic of knights, those killing angels, she teaches the basics of religion but limits Perceval's knowledge and experience to produce a naïve boy who throws javelins with deadly accuracy and asks questions with comic, but endearing enthusiasm—until Gornemant's advice and her death interrupt the flow of words. Is she more of an obstacle dead than alive?

In some sense, her death is required so that a series of substitutions may begin and allow for displacement and reflection, as Perceval first separates from and then, after a process of reflection, must rediscover his mother and her continuing role. The unexpected and atypical highlighting of Perceval's, Gauvain's, and Arthur's mothers in the *Conte du Graal* constitutes an invitation to explore how, as both subject and object, mothers model all types of love in the different phases of human development, from sexual love to the sublime charity of Chrétien's prologue.[7] The romance delineates the importance of differentiating and following appropriate stages. Perceval's first departure was not meant as an abandonment; he tried repeatedly to return to his mother's manor until learning

---

[6] In this respect, we might compare her role in the text with Melanie Klein's view of the mother as primal object, introjected and projected, reconstructed in the child's inner psyche and outside world as good and bad. The patterns established in infancy and early childhood continue to operate in adulthood and become visible through transference, since 'nothing that ever existed in the unconscious completely loses its influence on the personality' (1975: 262). Klein's work adds another perspective to the many psychoanalytic readings of Perceval.

[7] In analyzing the 'maternal influence' in the *Conte*, Schwartz sees the role played by Perceval's memories of his mother and his love for Blancheflor as stages in his development of *carité* as caring for others (1996).

of her death. Toward the end of his stay at Biaurepaire, Perceval's desire to return to his mother is even stronger than his desire to stay with Blancheflor. As a result, many modern readers intrepret it as regressive, a negative aspect of his maternal attachment:

> Delez li [Blancheflor] se jue et delite.
> Et si fust soie toute quite
> La terre, se il li pleüst
> Que son corage aillors n'eüst;
> Mais d'autre ore plus li sovient,
> Que de sa mere au cuer li tient
> Que il vit pasmee cheoir
> S'a talent qu'il l'aille veoir
> Plus grant que de nule autre chose.
>
> (2913–21)

(He plays and delights by [Blancheflor's] side. And her land would be entirely his, if it would please him not to have his heart in any other place. But at other times he remembers more that his heart is drawn to his mother, whom he saw fall in a faint, and he wants to go to see her more than anything else.)

One might argue, on the other hand, that Perceval's promise to Blancheflor to bring his mother back to Biaurepaire, willy nilly, dead or alive, sets up an expectation for successful integration and resolution, despite his momentarily conflicting desires. His promise of return suggests progress along the *gradus amoris*, the stages of love ostensibly stalled at the initial phase of courtship, despite the desire of everyone at Biaurepaire—including Blancheflor and Perceval—to move on to the logical conclusion, the reward for his conquest of the lady and her land. His plan to hold on to the land and, therefore, implicitly to his beloved Blancheflor, is specifically expressed and framed by his promise to return with his mother. As the narrator reports in indirect discourse:

> . . . il met en covenant,
> S'il trove sa mere vivant,
> Qu'avec lui l'en amera la
> Et d'enqui en avant tendra
> La terre, ce sachent de fi,
> Et se ele est morte, autresi.
>
> (2930–5)

(he makes a covenant that if he finds his mother alive he'll bring her there with him and from then on hold the land, they should know this by faith, and if she is dead, likewise.)

Of course, it is this desire to go back to the mother that paradoxically leads Perceval elsewhere, on to the ambiguous location of the Grail Castle, where his failure to ask the questions, according to his uncle's later explanation, is also paradoxically tied to the departure from his mother. The initial departure is both a plus and a minus, the promised return negative and positive. And then, despite Perceval's promise to return with his mother to Biaurepaire and place her with the nuns in a convent, if she is alive, or have her yearly memorial service chanted there, if dead, a second, more definitive abandonment occurs. A surprising volteface—the dead with the dead and the living with the living—that leads Perceval in a new direction with dire consequences for the future of his narrative. Forgetting his mother leads in turn to forgetting God and his failure to return not only to the Grail but to Blancheflor, despite his newly developed ability to remember her *semblance* in her absence.

The orderly passage from mother to beloved to the stage of the surplus and beyond is disrupted, suspended until the connection can be re-established. Is it played out in anticipation in Gauvain's plot line with its own twists and turns? The expectation of love leading to marriage, not uncommon in Chrétien's romances, is reinforced by Perceval's promises at Biaurepaire and then again by Gauvain's experience at the Roche de Champguin, where two mothers mistakenly plot marriage for him and his sister, substitute mothers who approve marriage for a substitute sibling (Perceval's brother in arms) with a substitute *pucele*. Marriage in Chrétien's romances, when it occurs, generally involves love between the couple, linked to crisis and problematized to be sure, but ideally integrated into family, lineage, and social structure. In the *Conte*, however, the threads are left hanging; they remain tantalizingly untied.[8]

Following Chrétien's authorization to use biblical comparisons, we might match the pattern sketched here *in potentia* with the description in Genesis 24: 67, when Abraham has arranged for his son's marriage and Rebecca replaces Sarah, the dead mother, and thus restores comfort to the tent. In the Vulgate version: 'Qui introduxit eam in tabernaculum Sarae matris suae, et accepit eam uxorem: et in tantum dilexit eam, ut dolorem, qui ex morte matris eius acciderat, temperaret' ('[Isaac] brought her into his mother Sarah's tent and accepted her as his wife and loved her so much that the sorrow, which befell him as a result of his mother's death, was tempered').[9] The description is brief, but the connections between mother and wife, death and life, grief and comfort, are clearly outlined. Just as the dual objects of Isaac's love are linked to each through him, they in turn link him to the renewal of generations, as past, present, and future are physically and spiritually joined. By contrast, with neither mother nor father, without some

---

[8] Baumgartner observes that the similarities between Gauvain's experience at the Château des Reines and Perceval's isolated youth at his mother's manor might lead to speculation on Perceval's future: 'Le destin programmé de Perceval le chétif, l'infortuné, n'était-il pas, au long cours de son errance arthurienne, de retrouver son être au monde, son vrai nom, "Perceval le Gallois," et de revenir, dans la joie retrouvée, au royaume rêvé de l'enfance?' (1999: 113). Similarly, Pickens analyzes links between Perceval's mother and his hermit uncle to suggest that the sojourn at the hermitage functions as a symbolic return to the mother, whose value system is epitomized in the Welshness inscribed in Perceval's name, 'Perceval le Gallois' (1977: 48–53, 108–33).

[9] This is my translation from the Vulgate. Cf. the Jerusalem Bible: 'And Isaac led Rebekah to his tent and made her his wife; and he loved her. And so Isaac was consoled for the loss of his mother' (1971).

parental authorization, the young Perceval seems frozen, unable to move on to the next stage, as he promised when leaving Blancheflor. That promise has been (temporarily?) forgotten by the narrative, as Perceval himself seems to have forgotten, but Gauvain's experience seems to anticipate and move forward the stages of Perceval's progress in love across the interlace. If Gauvain's achievement at the Roche de Champguin unfreezes the lives of grandmother, mother, and sister, their future marriage plans, properly displaced according to the narrator's reassurance, anticipate redirection and continued development for mothers and lovers and sons, left unrealized in an unfinished story.

Read through the lens of Genesis, the *Conte du Graal*'s combination of mother, tent, and beloved appears as the very figure of continuation, both in the plot and in the narrative cycle. The difficulty of assigning a place to the lady in the tent is itself suggestive of the difficulty, for both heroes and romancers, of making the connection between Blancheflor and the mother, the girl and the Grail. Contrasting poles gather together in the image of the tent: mobility linked to impermanence and changeability, on the one hand; continuity connected with love in emotional and spiritual realms across generation and generations, on the other. The tent that first appears in Perceval's storyline and then resurfaces periodically in Gauvain's adventures in the continuations may thus be read as a metaphor for the narrative architecture of the cycle as a whole, its continual displacements as well as its inevitable convergences.[10]

Perceval's first stop after leaving home is a tent, which he believes to be a church. Reflected through his mother's advice and her vivid descriptions, gold, bright colors, and especially light are the common threads linking churches, tents, Blancheflor, and the Grail. Perceval hastens to enter the place of prayer, which turns out to be a place of love and violence, extending from Perceval's caricature of rape when he climbs on top of the *pucele* to the murderous jealousy of her *ami*, the Orgueilleux de la Lande. The figure of the mother thus initiates a series of links working, in Perceval's plot line, through the tent episode, Biaurepaire, the Fisher King, Perceval's cousin, the reprise with the Tent Maiden, and finally the hermit episode. They complement the Arthurian links (cf. Pickens 1977, Maddox 1991a) that lead Perceval twice to Arthur's court and then spin off further along the Arthurian line to follow Gauvain on his adventures. These ultimately intersect with Perceval's problems and tasks, from the quest for the bleeding lance and the discovery of mothers thought to be dead, to the flirtations of the ladies' man with the little sister at the tournament, the big sister at Escavalon, and the Male Pucele (see Chapter 2).

The lines of opposition between mothers, lovers, and sons, protection and destruction, continually cross over and remind us again that the question linked

---

[10] I would like to thank Kathy Lavezzo who suggested reading the tent as a metaphor of the narrative during a discussion of an earlier version of Ch. 2 presented at the University of Michigan Medieval Seminar, 30 Oct. 2005.

to the Grail—whom does it serve?—focuses precisely on connection. It is a question that interrogates certain exclusions that need to be healed, inclusions denied that call for re-instatement within the Arthurian body politic. The two questions associating Grail and lance woven together in the complexities of the romance generate a series of analogies: the Grail is to the lance as feminine is to masculine as connection is to exclusion.[11] Does this seem too simple? These analogies cannot simply be read as two terms repeatedly opposed, the right hand and the left. They provide, on the contrary, another set of non-disjunctive oppositions to add to those already put into motion in Chrétien's previous romances (see Bruckner 1993b), another example of the romancer's and/both logic. What is at stake in the interplay suggests that we, like the characters, cannot forget that women's roles include mother as well as lover. And, perhaps just as disconcerting for our romance habits, the mother's link to the Grail forces us to consider a feminine connection to the puzzle of religious discourse unexpectedly present in Chrétien's last romance (and usually connected to the masculine voices of hermits).[12]

As we saw in Chapter 3, the interplay of exclusion and inclusion, violence and love, contained in the combustive mix of mothers, sons, and sex, reappears in the anonymous First Continuation's *Livre de Caradoc*. Once Caradoc, like Perceval, has done penance for the sin against his mother (I, 6889–99) and been reconciled with her, he still requires a good mother to remove the life-sapping snake that the bad mother Ysave (the mother as lover) had twisted around her son's arm. Guignier, Caradoc's beloved, consents to stand in a barrel of milk with naked breasts exposed (the lover as mother) and thus tempt away the snake, who will be killed by her brother as it leaps for her breast, just the tip of which will be sacrificed and replaced by a golden nipple, a secret later used as a symbol of her chastity. Sexuality that seeks to destroy the son is thus corrected by a sexuality as pure as a virginal mother's milk.[13] Given the power of the interlace, we might

[11] Cf. Burgwinkle's discussion of the broken swords from the *Conte* through the continuations: 'As with so many signs of the markers of elite masculinity, the sword serves to eliminate and discriminate rather than to bring together' (2004: 119).

[12] Dan Brown's *Da Vinci Code* and its presentation of Mary Magdalene's motherhood as wife of Jesus (cf. Goodwin 1994) certainly goes beyond any medieval understanding of the Holy Grail, as Lacy's review amply demonstrates (2004). But Brown's book is curiously sensitive to the basic connections initially set up in the *Conte du Graal*, insofar as Chrétien's romance shapes a narrative concatenation that locates the Grail in the triangle of relationships linking a mother, a young man, and a girl, that is, in the tensions generated between motherhood and sexuality. In the *Conte*, the story of Jesus in the credo recited by Perceval's mother and the penitent knight is the place for unexpected anti-Jewish invective, a reminder that although this romance is not an allegory of Christian truths, it does require us to deal with a religious dimension uncharacteristically inter-twined with the *matière de Bretagne*, a religious dimension that is not infrequently connected with violence, persecution, and aggression.

[13] See Sinclair's overview of medieval views on milk and menstrual blood, as well as their role in nurturing and inheritance. Both were believed to come from the same matter, but milk, made from blood that has been heated, has been refined of impurities (2003: 22, 32, 36–40). Cf. the two barrels in Caradoc's story, filled with vinegar and milk respectively, with the two ivory barrels filled with life-giving balm in Gerbert.

read elements of Caradoc's story as a prelude to Perceval's encounter with the Chessboard Lady in the Second Continuation: each version presents a possible model for reconciliation between love and heroic quests, sets up a range of variations for discovering possible resolutions involving love and the Grail.

This interplay of permissible and impermissible sexuality may remind us that in Chrétien's *Conte*, where the mother is both bridge and impediment to amorous experience, Perceval's encounters with women develop through comic play and then serious relationship only to reach a point of unresolved ambiguity. How far does he go with Blancheflor? And, equally important, what ultimately is the relationship between Perceval's love for Blancheflor and his quest for the Grail? In the hermit episode, the spiritual link connecting mother and Grail, sustenance and life, has been made, but the link adding Blancheflor (love with a potential for new life) has been left out, though it is clear that the figure of the mother stands at the nexus and potentially gathers all the strands that await a final weaving together.

The echoes between Perceval's and Gauvain's trajectories explore by displacement how and if the links between mothers, maidens, and the Grail may be achieved. In the *Conte* itself, the two heroes' relation to love appears initially to distinguish them but ends up bringing them surprisingly close together, a trend that increases in the First and Second Continuations, as Perceval's Tent Maiden adventures, along with the Grail quest, cross over into Gauvain's story, while Gauvain's dalliance with the fair sex appears in Perceval's quest for the Chessboard Lady's favors. Gauvain's potency is played out in the First Continuation, but the seeds for such amplification are to be found earlier in the *Conte* in his heroic accomplishments at the 'Lit de la Merveille' (7805) and the Perilous Ford. His success with women and at least partial success in the Grail test open the possibility, intimated in Chrétien's romance as well, that Perceval will eventually succeed in the Grail quest and reunite with Blancheflor.

The triangular configuration of mother, maiden, and Grail intersecting around the hero is thus reinforced by the continuations, but with a significant difference between those written before or after *La Queste del Saint Graal*. The ambiguity characteristic of Chrétien's unfinished romance is sustained by the first two continuations, throughout which the combination of love, sex, and the Grail remains plausible, continually kept in play with substitutes for either Perceval or Blancheflor. By diverting Perceval to the Chessboard Lady and the White Stag quest as a parallel to and substitute for Blancheflor and the Grail quest, the Second Continuation keeps open the question of how to bring together the beloved and the Grail, while nevertheless implying that love consummated with one lady creates a promising perspective for the fulfillment of Perceval's more longstanding promise to the other (as we saw in Chapter 1). That potential is closed off, once the *Queste*'s male priesthood of the Grail excludes all sexuality and sacrifices Perceval's sister. As a result, the last two continuations abandon the earlier convergence between Perceval and Gauvain, the latter reduced to his traditional role as secondary hero appearing in significant, but isolated episodes.

Certain negative potentials set into motion by the *Conte*, selected and magnified by the *Queste*'s rewriting in order to establish claims of exclusivity between sex and salvation, Arthurian chivalry and Grail chivalry, end up eliminating, across the closing stages of the prose cycle, other positive outcomes and possibilities equally contained in Chrétien's suspended narrative. The Fourth Continuation's reinsertion of religious discourse, muted in the earlier continuations, manages to combine marriage and virginity and thus fulfills the forgotten promise to Blancheflor, now interpreted as necessary for removing the last sinful obstacle to Perceval's success, but does so by sacrificing sexuality and mothers. Although Manessier's more affirmative conclusion avoids the catastrophic consequences of the Grail quest within the Vulgate Cycle, even in the verse continuations, exclusion finally trumps inclusion and measures how far we have wandered from the originating spirit of Chrétien's *Conte*.

The last image in ms. T (f. 129, Fig. 7), the only image of the Grail that appears in what has served as the base manuscript for this study, provides a visual commentary on this final state of the Grail viewed across the cycle, a commentary that remains almost as enigmatic as Chrétien's original description. Sylvia Huot's review of *The Manuscripts of Chrétien de Troyes* and Sandra Hindman's *Sealed in Parchment* points out how many different interpretations it has elicited (1996: 104–5). First and foremost, the object everyone identifies unhesitatingly as the Grail is rising or descending, given or received between the angel and the female figure, which Hindman interprets as Ecclesia (37). All agree that Perceval is the kneeling figure dressed in clerical garb—a monk's habit, according to Baumgartner (1993: 1, 497)—but disagree on the standing figure: Perceval, according to Hindman (1994: 37); not Perceval, according to Stones (1993: 1, 242). Baumgartner suggests he is a knight carrying away Perceval's sword, signifying the turn away from earthly chivalry and toward heavenly things (as in the *Queste*);[14] the kneeling Perceval's head tilts appropriately upward, his gaze aligned with the Grail and the angel wielding a censer. But that pointy object held vertically in two hands by the young man who seems to be heading out of the scene to the right appears as a burning lance to Hindman (37), or to Stones as a lighted candle whose visible flames mount from the tip, as in another miniature found in BN, fr. 17229, which represents the miracle of the candle given by the Virgin to two jongleurs and widely celebrated in Arras.[15] Huot extrapolates the implicit argument underlying Stones's comparison by suggesting that the final image in T

[14] Baumgartner analyzes the contrast and counterpoint between the opening and final images of BN, fr. 12576, as well as the progress in Perceval's development represented in the sequence of intervening miniatures (1993: 1, 496–8).

[15] Two of the manuscripts Stones analyzes to provide an artistic context for T are connected with Arras, which accords with the dominant north-eastern location in the manuscript tradition (1993: 1, 240–2).

Fig. 7. BN, fr. 12576, f. 261. Perceval kneels before a maiden who holds the partially covered Grail, while an angel reaches toward it from heaven.

would thus create a parallel between the salvific powers of the Grail and the healing power of the candle (cf. Gerbert's two barrels of balm). In any case, this final image emphasizes 'the sanctity of the Grail and the spiritual message of the romance', though it may seem strange that no illustrations elaborate the spiritual themes by showing the Grail Castle or the events that take place there (1996: 104).

Indeed, one of the striking characteristics of this miniature is its lack of specific narrative connection. It appears on the folio about half way down the second column after the explicit marking the end of Manessier's continuation, almost centered on the page. Its gold foil background illumines the three human figures, while the angels occupy white clouds above; only a red column along the left border supplies a vague architectural suggestion. Are we in a church, with Perceval praying before the Grail in a kind of replica of the mass (cf. Galahad in the *Queste*)? Is this another Grail procession like those seen repeatedly by Perceval and Gauvain at the Fisher King's castle? Does the image refer to the romance's final moments when Perceval dies and the Grail, lance, and trencher are ravished to heaven, never to reappear? The alternating reds and blues of the frame and clothing create a visual swirl: Perceval's blue robe in the center (echoed by the angel above his head) plays off against the red robes of the two figures on either side, who form a procession like the maiden and youth holding Grail and lance in the miniatures of BN, fr. 12577 (see Fig. 6). Both gaze forward over and beyond the kneeling Perceval. Their three heads form a triangle (or, with the angel haloed in red, a diamond) around a very red Grail. The chalice-like Grail is partially covered by a white veil, suggesting the mystery that surrounds it still, no matter how many questions and answers have accumulated around it. The multiplicity of responses offered to decipher the Grail and this final image in T corresponds perfectly to the evasive character of the initiating romance. The enigmas remain but the yin and yang of male and female figures, female-shaped and male-shaped objects are clearly represented: the connecting Grail held up between two sets of hands, linking the elegantly swayed, large female figure and the angel in blue like Perceval; the thrust of the vertical sword/candle going before, separated by the kneeling figure (who turns his back to the youth), yet remaining imbricated in the scene. In T's opening image, Perceval kneeled before a knight, his three javelins pointedly filling the entire frame from top to bottom; here he kneels in prayer without arms, while a Grail-carrying woman (a maiden with hair uncovered? mother church with incense?) has replaced the armored knight on horseback, even as chivalric echoes reverberate in the youth's smaller but still lance-like object.

So what may we conclude about gender and the Grail? In Chrétien's *Conte* two questions take shape at the Grail Castle: why does the lance bleed and whom does the Grail serve? Both questions direct our attention to a function. And both questions are answered in the unfinished text as we have it.[16] The Grail serves the

---

[16] Though we have possible answers, they are divided among the two heroes, another perplexing ramification of their doubling. As scholars have pointed out, there is simultaneously and paradoxically so little and so much left undone at the suspended end of Chrétien's romance, depending on

Fisher King's father, as Perceval learns from his hermit uncle, and the lance
bleeds because it is associated with the destruction of Arthur's kingdom, as we
learn at Escavalon with Gauvain. It is not the answers that remain unclarified
(although continuators and rewriters will invent others to suit their own pur-
poses). What remains to be determined is rather the role and nature of the
questions, or the multiple routes between question and answer for the heroes as
well as the readers of romance. In this respect my new question—what is gender
to the Grail?—suggests a certain route along which to look for answers that take
into account Chrétien's narrative and the way it frames the questions, calls for
question and answer as integral to the unfinishable process of questing for the
Grail as a web of connections, looks for life-sustaining feminine lines of inclusion
that intersect and engage the masculine violence of exclusions, as defined within
the *Conte*'s narrative.

We might follow that line of inclusion from the Grail back to the prologue's
praise of charity, connecting it as well to Isaiah's prophecy of swords beaten into
plowshares, the utopian vision glimpsed in the outline of disconcerting details
and hints scattered throughout Chrétien's romance. If scriptural precedent as
given in the prologue defines God as charity that is love, gifts, donations,
offerings, whether in St Paul or St John ('Diex est caritez', 47), the body of the
romance weaves a network around love and violence, connecting courtly, chivalric, and religious values that call for a vision of compassion necessary for
continued life and restoration in the face of our contradictory and violent
human condition.[17] The Grail as a symbol of sustenance and inclusion, connection and caring for others, whose power is released only by the appropriate
questions, operates at the Fisher King's castle in obscure relationship with forces
of exclusion, fatal separations represented by a lance already bleeding before
carrying out its prophesized destruction. In the Vulgate Cycle's Grail quest, the
hope of life has shifted to the spiritual realm, leaving only destruction for the
terrestrial sphere, but the verse continuations, even as they register the influence
of that powerful negative vision of Arthurian society, also retain the potentially
positive vision, equally inscribed in *Le Conte du Graal*, of a life-giving Grail that
encompasses and ultimately promises to overcome, within the scope of human
societies, the negative entropy of the lance—if only the story can be continued in
all its complexities. This is the work of a lifetime, or rather many lifetimes, across
the unscrolling future of history and the writing and rewriting of romance in the
space between the last day and the last day of all.

---

what level we consider: plot or meaning. See e.g. Roach's list of unfinished episodes: two for Perceval
(the Grail Castle and Blancheflor), two for Gauvain (the bleeding lance and Montesclaire) (1956:
111–13).

[17] Wolfram (1980) may be the best medieval reader/rewriter of Chrétien's *Perceval* in retaining
the positive, inclusive gestures associated with the Grail, which include in his version the son who is
part white, part black, as well as the compatibility of Grail and marriage, if not simultaneously, at
least successively in the stages of human life.

The notion of continuation is thus built into the role of mothers and their links with lovers and sons, just as the opening parable of the sower links the fertility of the word to the fruitfulness of mother earth. Continuation appears not only as an essential aspect of the Grail theme but finds embodiment as the formal element constitutive of the *Perceval* cycle as a whole. Indeed, continuation as a principle and technique is already embedded in the originating romance in a variety of ways. If we understand that continuation is another way of defining inclusion (and vice versa), then the underlying logic of and/both built into the *Conte* and played out across the continuations expresses, however non-mimetically, the human condition caught in paradox: contradictions and oppositions are repeatedly staged at different levels of the text, to be absorbed, exploited, and accepted together in the ongoing narrative syntagm. Continuation is as strongly written into the *Conte du Graal* as suspension, exclusion, (un)finishedness, (un)closure.[18] Though they might be seen as contradictory narrative impulses, they are here complementary, necessarily matched across the interplay between the two parts of Chrétien's romance, as between the 'old Perceval' and its four verse continuations, written individually and yet collectively under the guiding hand of the master text. The decentered Story of the Grail demonstrates how the mother text blocks certain ends, however temporarily, invites continuation along numerous paths, allows for gaps and contradictions in the interplay of narrative and interpretation, rewrites across the interlace to explore continuities and discontinuities between heroes as between successive segments of a narrative that claims a certain wholeness even as it asserts the intervention of multiple writers, named and nameless, authorized and authorizing. And so the dialogue between Chrétien de Troyes and his successors has continued into the present day and may be expected to continue recycling as long as modern readers join their discordant and harmonious voices to those inscribed on parchment.

[18] Cf. Dragonetti's last chapter on 'L'œuvre "assomee"' (1980) where he links Chrétien's unfinished romance to the continual renewal of language.

APPENDIX 1

Episodes and Segments in the First, Second, Third, and Fourth Continuations

In the introductory material to his editions of the first three continuations, William Roach supplies the list of episodes and segments identified below. I have made a list with brief titles to identify the episodes in the three volumes of Gerbert's Fourth Continuation.

THE FIRST CONTINUATION

Roach divides the First Continuation into six sections with sixty-six episodes; some of them are alternates that appear in the Short, Mixed, and Long Redactions, and not all episodes appear in all three redactions (I, xlvi–lxii). He names the sections and summarizes the numbered episodes. I have listed below and supplied short titles only for the episodes that appear in ms. T.

I. Guiromelant (10 episodes)
  1. Gauvain's messenger at Arthur's court
  2. Arthur at Ygerne's castle
  3. Preparations for combat with Guiromelant
  4. Gauvain fights Guiromelant
  5. Learning about Clarissant's marriage to Guiromelant, Gauvain leaves in anger
  6. Gauvain encounters a maiden carrying a horn and a maiden who set a trap for Greoreas
  7. Gauvain's first visit to the Grail Castle
  8. Gauvain at Montesclaire
  9. Gauvain fights Dinasdarés
  10. Gauvain returns to Escavalon

II. Brun de Branlant (8 episodes)
  1. Arthur lays siege to Brun's castle
  2. Two damsels appeal for relief then the seige continues
  3. Gauvain wounded by Brun
  4. Gauvain rides out after a long convalescence
  5. Gauvain seduced by the Tent Maiden
  6. Gauvain kills her father
  7. Her brother Bran de Lis pursues Gauvain
  8. Gauvain returns to the siege

III. Carados[1] (16 episodes)
  1. Ysave's marriage to King Carados of Nantes

---

[1] Rouch uses the nominative form 'Carados', as given in the manuscripts, rather than 'Caradoc', the oblique form generally retained in modern usage.

2. Her son Carados sent to Arthur's court
3. Carados and 50 others knighted
4. The Beheading contest: first blow
5. The Beheading contest: a year later, Carados learns who is his real father
6. Carados reveals his mother's adultery
7. Carados rescues Guignier from Alardin
8. Her brother Cador cured of wounds at tent
9. A great tournament
10. Carados punishes Eliavrés for continued adultery with his mother
11. Revenge against Carados
12. Carados flees and does penance for sin against his mother and father
13. Cador finds him after two year search
14. Carados saved from the serpent entwined round his arm, marries Guignier
15. Carados gets magic shield from Alardin to restore tip of Guignier's breast
16. The drinking horn test at Arthur's court

IV. Chastel Orguelleus (16 episodes)
1. Arthur decides to hold great feast on Pentecost
2. An empty seat prompts Arthur to send knights to rescue Girflet
3. Keu runs afoul a dwarf and a roasted bird
4. Gauvain arrives at a castle and sees a shield that causes him to arm immediately
5. Gauvain forced to tell story of Tent Maiden's rape
6. Bran discovers Gauvain
7. Their combat finally stops when Gauvain's son is placed by his mother in their midst
8. Before the Chastel Orguelleus
9. Lucan fails against the champion
10. Lucan meets Girflet in prison
11. Bran de Lis and Keu against the champion
12. During a hunting interlude Gauvain meets the Riche Soudoier
13. Yvain against the champion
14. Gauvain against the champion who is the Riche Soudoier this time
15. After Gauvain helps him with his amie, the Riche Soudoier surrenders the castle
16. A stop at the Chastel de Lis

V. Gauvain's Grail Visit (8 episodes)
1. Keu mistreats a stranger, Gauvain brings him back to court
2. Keu accused of killing the stranger whose mission is taken on by Gauvain
3. The horse leads Gauvain through a stormy night to the Chapel of the Black Hand
4. Gauvain's second visit at the Grail Castle
5. Gauvain's host relates the story of Joseph of Arimathea and the Grail's arrival in England.
6. Gauvain falls asleep and awakens far away the next morning
7. A young man and damsel riding through the forest
8. Gauvain fights with a man who turns out to be his son

VI. Guerrehés (8 episodes)
1. A boat drawn by a swan arrives at Arthur's court
2. A body in the hall and a note that promises the same shame suffered by Guerrehés to the knight who fails to avenge him
3. Guerrehés at a deserted castle finds a damsel in a tent
4. Guerrehés defeated by a small knight
5. Guerrehés forced to leave garden through the window shamed by all who know of his defeat
6. Guerrehés inadvertently becomes the one who must avenge the dead knight; he recounts the incident in the garden
7. Guerrehés avenges the knight by killing the Petit Chevalier and his master
8. Guerrehés arrives at Arthur's court on the swan boat

THE SECOND CONTINUATION

Roach identifies thirty-five episodes after an introductory passage making the transition from Perceval's departure from the hermitage at the end of Chrétien's *Conte* (IV, xix–xxxviii).

Introductory Passage
1. The Castle of the Ivory Horn
2. The Knight of the Horn at King Arthur's Court
3. A damsel attempts to drown Perceval
4. The Castle of the Magic Chessboard
5. Perceval hunts the white stag and fights with the Black Knight
6. A hunter gives Perceval lodging for the night
7. A murdered varlet is avenged by Perceval
8. An old knight gives Perceval directions
9. Perceval at the castle of Abrioris
10. Abrioris at King Arthur's court
11. Perceval finds a dead knight and later his 'amie'
12. Perceval kills a giant and frees a captive
13. Perceval at the Gué Amorous
14. Perceval meets the Biau Desconneü and his 'amie'
15. Perceval returns to Blancheflor at Biau Repaire
16. Perceval meets the Biau Mauvais and his ugly damsel
17. The Biau Mauvais at King Arthur's court
18. Perceval returns to his mother's home
19. Perceval visits his Hermit Uncle
20. Perceval at the Castle of Maidens
21. Perceval recovers the hounds and the head of the white stag; he hears the story of the knight painted on the tomb
22. Perceval meets the damsel who lends him the magic ring and the white mule; he crosses the Glass Bridge
23. Perceval meets Briol; he crosses the unfinished bridge
24. The tournament at Chastel Orguellous

25. Perceval frees the knight imprisoned in the tomb; he returns the ring and the mule to the damsel
26. Perceval returns to the Castle of the Magic Chessboard
27. Perceval meets Bagomedés
28. Bagomedés at King Arthur's court
29. Gauvain with the Petit Chevalier and his sister
30. The tournament in the Blanche Lande
31. Gauvain meets the Pensive Knight and rescues his 'amie'
32. Gauvain meets his son Guinglain and returns with him to King Arthur
33. Perceval goes to the Mont Dolerous
34. Perceval on the road to the Grail Castle
35. Perceval at the Grail Castle

THE THIRD CONTINUATION

Roach divides thirty episodes into six parts, whose titles clearly map out the narrative movement (V, xxii–lv).

I. First Adventures of Perceval (2 episodes)
   1. Perceval at the Grail Castle
   2. Perceval and Sagremor

II. Adventures of Sagremor (3 episodes)
   3. Sagremor and the Robber Knight
   4. Sagremor at the Castle of Maidens
   5. Sagremor rescues a damsel

III. Adventures of Gauvain (6 episodes)
   6. Gauvain and the sister of Silimac
   7. Gauvain rescues Dodinel
   8. Gauvain defeats King Margon
   9. Gauvain and the Sore Pucelle
   10. Gauvain's duel with Keu
   11. Gauvain and Agravain

IV. Second Adventures of Perceval (8 episodes)
   12. Perceval in the Chapel of the Black Hand
   13. Perceval is tempted by the Devil
   14. Perceval defeats the Knight of Lindesores
   15. Perceval rescues Dodinel's amie
   16. Perceval's visit to Tribüet
   17. Perceval returns to Biau Repaire
   18. Perceval's prisoners at Arthur's court
   19. Perceval meets the Coward Knight

V. The Search for Perceval (5 episodes)
   20. Arthur's court: Pentecost at Camelot

21. Boort abandons Lionel to save a maiden
22. Gauvain rescues Lionel
23. Boort is tempted by the Devil
24. Boort and Lionel fight and are reconciled

VI. Final Adventures of Perceval (6 episodes plus the epilogue)
    25. The Biau Mauvais becomes the Biau Hardi
    26. Perceval fights with Hestor
    27. Perceval defeats and kills Partinal
    28. Perceval's final visit to the Fisher King
    29. Perceval's last visit to Arthur's court
    30. Perceval's coronation, reign, and death

Epilogue

THE FOURTH CONTINUATION

I have identified thirty-one episodes in Gerbert's continuation, which begins and ends at the Grail Castle. The division into three volumes, based on the CFMA editions, represents the succession of publication dates rather than a logical division of the narrative. The first two volumes include approximately 7,000 verses each, the third some 3,000 verses.

Volume I
    1. At the Grail Castle
    2. At the door of the Paradis Terrestre where Perceval breaks his sword
    3. A castle leading to the blacksmith who repairs his sword
    4. Merlin's Pillars at Mont Dolerous
    5. The Empty Chair at Arthur's court
    6. False Marriage Promise
    7. Temptation by a *pucele* (Devil in disguise)
    8. Return home to visit sister, hermit, and mother's grave
    9. Perceval escorts sister to the Chastel as Puceles
    10. 'Tristan le menestrel' (two parts: at Arthur's court and the tournament at Mark's court)
    11. Perceval at Gornemant's castle
    12. Perceval at Biaurepaire: marriage with Blancheflor

Volume II
    13. Hospitality with hermit and then defense of maiden beaten by her abductor
    14. Parsamant's castle with bad custom of humiliating knights
    15. Perceval on the Voie Aventureuse to Hermit King's castle
    16. Encounter with Claire la Pucele as Draps Envers
    17. Mordrain episode
    18. At the Red Knight's castle
    19. Gauvain's Tent Maiden adventure

Volume III
    20. Perceval on the road from which no one has returned
    21. The Devil under a stone
    22. Lugarel avenging his beloved's death at a tomb at the crossroads
    23. A damsel at the fountain: defense and treachery
    24. Food from a pilgrim
    25. Felisse de la Blanclose and the five thieves
    26. A hermit gives advice on knighthood
    27. Encounter with Madiex a le Cote Maltaillie
    28. Giant seeks vengeance for brother's death
    29. News of Perceval arrives at Arthur's court
    30. Combat with Keu and Goullain
    31. Return to the Grail Castle

APPENDIX 2

Comparative Tables: Ordering the Books of the Bible

Hebrew Bible: Pentateuch, Prophets, Writings

Genesis	Ezekiel	Psalms
Exodus	Hosea	Proverbs
Leviticus	Joel	Job
Numbers	Amos	Song of Songs
Deuteronomy	Obadiah	Ruth
Joshua	Jonah	Lamentations
Judges	Micah	Ecclesiastes
1 Samuel	Nahum	Esther
2 Samuel	Habakkuk	Daniel
1 Kings	Zephaniah	**Ezra**
2 Kings	Haggai	**Nehemiah**
Isaiah	Zachariah	**1 Chronicles**
Jeremiah	Malachi	**2 Chronicles**

Old Testament in Christian Bible

Genesis	**2 Chronicles**	Daniel
Exodus	**Ezra**	Hosea
Leviticus	**Nehemiah**	Joel
Numbers	Esther	Amos
Deuteronomy	Job	Obadiah
Joshua	Psalms	Jonah
Judges	Proverbs	Micah
Ruth	Ecclesiastes	Nahum
1 Samuel	Song of Songs	Habakkuk
2 Samuel	Isaiah	Zephaniah
1 Kings	Jeremiah	Haggai
2 Kings	Lamentations	Zachariah
1 Chronicles	Ezekiel	Malachi

Bibliography

PRIMARY TEXTS

Alexis (1968). *La Vie de Saint Alexis*, ed. Christopher Storey. Geneva: Droz.

Augustine (1984). *City of God*, trans. Henry Bettenson. London: Penguin Books.

Benoît de Sainte-Maure (1998). *Le Roman de Troie: Extraits du manuscrit Milan*, ed. and trans. Emmanuèle Baumgartner and Françoise Vielliard. Lettres Gothiques. Paris: Livre de poche.

Bible (1965). *Biblia Sacra iuxta Vulgatam Clementinam*, ed. Alberto Colunga, OP and Laurentio Turrado. Madrid: Biblioteca de Autores Cristianos.

—— (1971). *The Jerusalem Bible: Reader's Edition*. Garden City, NY: Doubleday.

Bliocadran (1976). *Bliocadran: A Prologue to the Perceval of Chrétien de Troyes: Edition and Critical Study*, ed. Lenora D. Wolfgang. Tübingen: Niemeyer.

Chrétien de Troyes (1994a). *Œuvres complètes*, gen. ed. Daniel Poirion. Bibliothèque de la Pléiade. Paris: Gallimard.

—— (1994b). *Romans*. La Pochothèque. Paris: Librairie Générale Française.

—— (1959). *Le Roman de Perceval ou le Conte du Graal*, ed. William Roach. Geneva: Droz.

—— (1993). *Le Roman de Perceval ou le Conte du Graal*, ed. Keith Busby. Tübingen: Max Niemeyer.

—— (1990). *The Story of the Grail (Li Contes del Graal), or Perceval*, ed. Rupert T. Pickens. New York: Garland.

Elucidation (1931). *L'Elucidation*, ed. Albert Wilder Thompson. New York: Publications of the Institute of French Studies.

Eneas (1964). *Eneas: Roman du XIIe siècle*, ed. J.-J. Salverda de Grave, 2 vols. Paris: CFMA.

Flamenca (1960). In *Les Troubadours (Jaufre, Flamenca, Barlaam et Josaphat)*, trans. René Lavaud and René Nelli. Bourges: Bibliothèque Européenne. Desclée De Brouwer.

Gerbert de Montreuil (1922, 1925, 1975). *La Continuation du Perceval*, ed. Mary Williams (vol. I and II) and Marguerite Oswald (vol. III). Paris: CFMA.

—— (1928). *Roman de la Violette ou de Gerart de Nevers*, ed. Douglas Labaree Buffum. Paris: SATF.

Guillaume de Lorris and Jean de Meun (1966, 1968, 1970). *Le Roman de la Rose*, ed. Félix Lecoy, 3 vols. Paris: CFMA.

Hugh of St Victor (1961). *The Didascalicon of Hugh of St Victor: A Medieval Guide to the Arts*, trans. Jerome Taylor. New York: Columbia University Press.

Lais anonymes (1976). *Lais anonymes bretons*, ed. Prudence Mary O'Hara Tobin. Geneva: Droz.

Lancelot (1978–83). *Lancelot: Roman en prose du XIIIe siècle*, ed. Alexandre Micha, 9 vols. Paris-Geneva: Droz.

—— (1980). *Lancelot do Lac: The Non-Cyclic Old French Prose Romance*, ed. Elspeth Kennedy, 2 vols. Oxford: Clarendon Press.

Mabinogion (1981). *The Mabinogion*, trans. Jeffrey Gantz. Hammondsworth, Middlesex: Penguin Books, orig. 1976.

Marie de France (1969). *Les Lais de Marie de France*, ed. Jean Rychner. Paris: CFMA.

Mort le roi Artu (1964). *La Mort le roi Artu: Roman de XIIIe siècle*, ed. Jean Frappier. Geneva: Droz.

Perceval Continuations (1965–83). *The Continuations of the Old French Perceval of Chrétien de Troyes*, ed. William Roach. Vols. I–V. Philadephia: American Philosophical Society.

Première Continuation (1993). *Première Continuation de Perceval (Continuation-Gauvain)*, ed. W. Roach; trans. Colette-Anne Van Coolput-Storms. Paris: Livre de Poche.

Queste del Saint Graal (1967). *La Queste del Saint Graal: Roman du XIIIe siècle*, ed. Albert Pauphilet. Paris: Champion.

Robert de Boron (1927). *Roman de l'estoire dou Graal*, ed. William A. Nitze. Paris: Champion.

Thèbes (1969). *Le Roman de Thèbes*, ed. Guy Raynaud de Lage, 2 vols. Paris: CFMA.

Tristan en prose (1986). *Le Roman de Tristan en prose*, ed. Renée L. Curtis, 3 vols. Cambridge: D. S. Brewer (rpt. from Max Hueber, 1963).

—— (1987–97). *Le Roman de Tristan en prose*, ed. Philippe Ménard *et al.*, 9 vols. Geneva: Droz.

Virgil (1916). *Aeneid*, trans. H. Rushton Fairclough. New York: G. P. Putnam's Sons.

Wace (1962). *La Partie arthurienne du Roman de Brut*, ed. I. D. O. Arnold and M. M. Pelan. Paris: Klincksieck.

Wolfram von Eschenbach (1980). *Parzival*, trans. A. T. Hatto. London and New York: Penguin Books.

SECONDARY LITERATURE

Adams, Tracy (2005). *Violent Passions in the Old French Verse Romance*. New York: Palgrave Macmillan.

Amazawa, Taijiro (1998). 'La *Devineuse* du nom de Perceval', in J. Claude Faucon, Alain Labbé, and Danielle Quéruel (eds.), *Miscellanea Mediaevalia: Mélanges offerts à Philippe Ménard*, 2 vols. Paris: Champion, 1: 33–6.

Aristotle (1958). *On Poetry and Style*, trans. G. M. A. Grube. Indianapolis: Bobs-Merrill.

Arthur of the English (2001). *The Arthur of the English: The Arthurian Legend in Medieval English Life and Literature*, ed. W. R. J. Barron. Cardiff: University of Wales Press.

Arthur of the Welsh (1991). *The Arthur of the Welsh: The Arthurian Legend in Medieval Welsh Literature*, ed. Rachel Bromwich, A. O. H. Jarman, and Brynley F. Roberts. Cardiff: University of Wales Press.

Auctor et auctoritas (2001). *Auctor et auctoritas: Invention et conformisme dans l'écriture médiévale. Actes du colloque tenu à l'Université de Versailles-Saint-Quentin-en-Yvelines (14–16 juin 1999)*, ed. Michel Zimmerman. Paris: École des Chartes.

Auerbach, Erich (1968). *Mimesis: The Representation of Reality in Western Literature*, trans. Willard R. Trask. Princeton: Princeton University Press.

Backman, Clifford R. (1995). 'Crusades', in William W. Kibler and Grover A. Zinn (eds.), *Medieval France: An Encyclopedia*. New York: Garland, 277–80.

Baldwin, John (1986). *The Government of Philip Augustus: Foundations of French Royal Power in the Middle Ages*. Berkeley and Los Angeles: University of California Press.

Balsamo, Gian (1993). 'Son, Knight, and Lover: Perceval's Dilemma at the Castle of Beaurepaire'. *Exemplaria*, 5: 263–81.

Barrera, Julio Trebolle (1998). *The Jewish Bible and the Christian Bible: An Introduction to the History of the Bible*, trans. Wilfred G. E. Watson. Leiden: Brill.

Baudry, Robert (1998). 'Pourquoi tant de veuves, tant de fils de veuves?' *Bien dire et bien aprandre: Revue de médiévistique*, 16: 19–28.

Baumgartner, Emmanuèle (1977). 'Le Défi du *chevalier rouge* dans *Perceval* et dans *Jaufré*'. *Le Moyen Âge*, 83: 239–54.

—— (1981). *L'Arbre et le Pain: Essai sur 'La Queste del Saint Graal'*. Paris: SEDES.

—— (1984). 'Caradoc ou de la séduction', in *Mélanges de langue et de littérature médiévales offertes à Alice Planche*. Paris: Belles Lettres, 1: 61–9.

—— (1985a). 'L'Écriture romanesque et son modèle scripturaire: Écriture et réécriture du Graal', in *L'Imitation, aliénation ou source de liberté*. Paris: La Documentation française, 129–43.

—— (1985b). 'Géants et chevaliers', in Glyn Burgess and Robert Taylor (eds.), *The Spirit of the Court*. Cambridge: D. S. Brewer, 9–22.

—— (1987–8). 'Les Techniques narratives dans le roman en prose', in *Legacy* (1987–8: 1, 167–90).

—— (1988). 'Peinture et écriture: La Description de la tente dans les romans antiques au XIIᵉ siècle', in *Sammlung, Deutung, Wertung: Erlebnis, Probleme, Tendenzen und Perspektiven philologischer Arbeit: mélanges de littérature médiévale et de linguistique allemande offerts à Wolfgang Spiewok à l'occasion de son soixantième anniversaire par ses collègues et amis*. Amiens: Université de Picardie, 3–11.

—— (1990). *La Harpe et l'Épée: Tradition et renouvellement dans le* Tristan *en prose*. Paris: SEDES.

—— (1993). 'Les Scènes du Graal et leur illustration dans les manuscrits du *Conte du Graal* et des *Continuations*', in *Manuscripts* (1993: 1, 489–503).

—— (1999). *Chrétien de Troyes: Le Conte du Graal*. Paris: PUF.

—— (2003). 'The *Queste del saint Graal:* From semblance to veraie semblance', in Carol Dover (ed.), *A Companion to the Lancelot-Grail Cycle*. Cambridge: D. S. Brewer, 107–14.

Bäuml, Franz H. (1980). 'Varieties and Consequences of Medieval Literacy and Illiteracy'. *Speculum*, 55: 237–65.

Bennett, Matthew (1998). 'Violence in Eleventh-Century Normandy: Feud, Warfare and Politics', in Guy Halsall (ed.), *Violence and Society in the Early Medieval West*. Woodbridge: Boydell Press.

Benton, John F. (1961). 'The Court of Champagne as a Literary Center'. *Speculum*, 36: 551–91.

Berger, Samuel (1967). *La Bible française au Moyen Âge: Étude sur les plus anciennes versions de la Bible écrites en prose de langue d'oïl*. Geneva: Slatkine Reprints.

Berthelot, Anne (1991). *Figures et fonction de l'écrivain au XIIIᵉ siècle*. Montreal: Institut d'études médiévales/Paris: Vrin.

—— (2006). 'From One Mask to Another: The Trials and Tribulations of an Author of Romance at the Time of *Perceforest*', in Virginie Greene (ed.), *The Medieval Author in Medieval French Literature*. New York: Houndsmills/Basingstoke: Palgrave Macmillan, 103–15.

Bible in the Medieval World (1985). *The Bible in the Medieval World: Essays in Honor of Beryl Smalley*, eds. Katharine Walsh and Diana Wood. Oxford: Basil Blackwell.

Bible in the Middle Ages (1992). *The Bible in the Middle Ages: Its Influence on Literature and Art*, ed. Bernard S. Levy. Binghamton, NY: Medieval and Renaissance Texts and Studies.

Bisson, Thomas N. (*c*.1982–9). 'Peace of God, Truce of God', in Joseph Strayer (ed.), *Dictionary of the Middle Ages*. New York: Scribner, 473–5.

Blaess, Madeleine (1978). 'Perceval et les "Illes de mer"', in *Mélanges de littérature du Moyen Âge offerts à Mlle Jeanne Lods*. Paris: Collection de l'École normale supérieure de jeunes filles.

Bloch, R. Howard (1983). *Etymologies and Genealogies: A Literary Anthology of the Middle Ages*. Chicago: University of Chicago Press.

Bloom, Harold (1975). *The Anxiety of Influence*. Oxford: Oxford University Press.

Blumenfeld-Kosinski, Renate (1985). 'Chrétien de Troyes as a Reader of the *Romans Antiques*'. *Philological Quarterly*, 64: 398–405.

Bolduc, Michelle (2007). 'The Dialectic of Naming Names: Matfre Ermengaud's Use of Troubadour Quotations'. *Tenso*, 22: 41–74.

Bouchard, Constance B. (2003). *'Every Valley Shall Be Exalted': The Discourse of Opposites in Twelfth-Century Thought*. Ithaca, NY: Cornell University Press.

—— (2002). Review of Sarah Kay's *Courtly Contradictions*. *H-France Review*, 2/43: www. h-france.net/vol2reviews/bouchard.html.

Braet, Herman (1981). 'Tyolet/Perceval: The Father Quest', in Kenneth Varty (ed.), *An Arthurian Tapestry: Essays in Memory of Lewis Thorpe*. University of Glasgow: French Department, 299–307.

Brodman, Marian Masiuk (1991a). 'The *Livre de Caradoc*'s Chastity Test'. *Neuphilologische Mitteilungen*, 9: 417–84.

—— (1991b). 'Terra Mater-Luxuria Iconography and the *Caradoc* Serpent Episode'. *Quondam et Futurus: A Journal of Arthurian Interpretations*, 2: 38–44.

Brown, Catherine (1998). *Contrary Things: Exegesis, Dialectic and the Poetics of Didacticism*. Stanford: Stanford University Press.

Brownlee, Kevin (1990). 'Transformations of the *Charrete*: Godefroi de Leigni Rewrites Chrétien de Troyes'. *Stanford French Review*, 14: 161–78.

Bruckner, Matilda Tomaryn (1987–8). 'Intertextuality', in *Legacy* (1987–8: 1, 223–65).

—— (1993a). 'The Poetics of Continuation in Medieval French Romance: From Chrétien's *Conte du Graal* to the *Perceval* Continuations'. *French Forum* 18: 133–49.

—— (1993b). *Shaping Romance: Interpretation, Truth and Closure in Twelfth-Century French Fictions*. Philadelphia: University of Pennsylvania Press.

—— (1996). 'Rewriting Chrétien's *Conte du Graal*. Mothers and Sons: Questions, Contradictions, and Connections', in Douglas Kelly (ed.), *The Medieval Opus: Imitation, Rewriting, and Transmission in the French Tradition*. Amsterdam: Rodopi, 213–44.

—— (1999). 'Knightly Violence and Grail Quest Endings: Conflicting Views from the Vulgate Cycle to the *Perceval* Continuations'. *Medievalia et Humanistica*, NS 26: 17–32.

—— (2000a). 'Looping the Loop Through a Tale of Beginnings, Middles and Ends: From Chrétien to Gerbert in the *Perceval* Continuations', in Keith Busby and Catherine M. Jones (eds.), *'Por le soie amisté': Essays in Honor of Norris Lacy*. Amsterdam: Rodopi, 33–51.

—— (2000b). 'The Shape of Romance', in Roberta L. Krueger (ed.), *The Cambridge Companion to Medieval Romance*. Cambridge: Cambridge University Press, 13–28.

—— (2003a). 'L'Imaginaire du progrès dans les cycles romanesques du graal', in *Progrès, Réaction, Décadence dans L'Occident médiéval*. Études recueillies par Emmanuèle Baumgartner et Laurence Harf-Lancner. Geneva: Droz, 111–21.

—— (2003b). 'Of Swords and Plowshares: Dislocations and Transformations in Chrétien's Grail Story', in Rosemarie Deist in collaboration with Harald Kleinschmidt (eds.), *Knight and Samurai: Actions and Images of Elite Warriors in Europe and East Asia*. Göppingen, Germany: Kümmerle, 31–45.

—— (2003c). 'Refining the Center: Verse and Prose Charrette', in Carol Dover (ed.), *A Companion to the Lancelot-Grail Cycle*. Cambridge: D. S. Brewer, 96–105.

—— (2005). '*Le Chevalier de la Charrette:* That Obscure Object of Desire, Lancelot', in Norris Lacy and Joan Tasker Grimbert (eds.), *A Companion to Chrétien de Troyes*. Cambridge: D. S. Brewer, 137–55.

—— (2006a). 'Authorial Relays: Continuing Chrétien's *Conte du Graal*', in Virginie Greene (ed.), *Toward the Medieval Author: Essays in French Medieval Literature*. Basingstoke: Palgrave Macmillan, 13–28.

—— (2006b). 'Clever Foxes, Fierce Lions, Diabolical Dragons: Animals Tell Tales in Medieval Arts and Letters', in Nancy Netzer (ed.), *Secular Sacred, 11th–16th Century: Works from the Boston Public Library and the Museum of Fine Arts*. McMullen Museum of Art, Boston College, 19–42.

—— (2008). 'Chrétien de Troyes', in *Companion to Medieval French Literature*, (2008).

Burgwinkle, William E. (2004). *Sodomy, Masculinity, and Law in Medieval Literature: France and England, 1050–1230*. Cambridge: Cambridge University Press.

Burns, E. Jane (1985). *Arthurian Fictions: Rereading the Vulgate Cycle*. Columbus: Ohio State University Press (for Miami University).

—— (1993). *Bodytalk: When Women Speak in Old French Literature*. Philadelphia, PA: University of Pennsylvania Press.

Busby, Keith (1980). *Gauvain in Old French Literature*. Amsterdam: Rodopi.

—— (1993a). 'The Illustrated Manuscripts of Chrétien's *Perceval*', in *Manuscripts* (1993: 1, 351–64) (rpt. from *Zeitschrift für Französische Sprache und Literatur* 98 [1988]: 41–52).

—— (1993b). 'The Scribe of MSS *T* and *V* of Chrétien's *Perceval* and its *Continuations*', in *Manuscripts* (1993: 1, 49–65).

—— (1993c). 'Text, Miniature, and Rubric in the Continuations of Chrétien's *Perceval*', in *Manuscripts* (1993: 1, 365–76).

—— (1998a). ' "Estrangement se merveilla": L'Autre dans les *Continuations* de *Perceval*', in J. Claude Faucon, Alain Labbé, and Danielle Quéruel (eds.), *Miscellanea Mediaevalia: Mélanges offerts à Philippe Ménard*, 2 vols. Paris: Champion, 1: 279–97.

—— (1998b). 'Medieval French Arthurian Literature: Recent Progress and Critical Trends', in Mette Pors (ed.), *The Vitality of the Arthurian Legend: A Symposium*. Odense: Odense University Press, 45–70.

—— (2005). 'The Manuscripts of Chrétien's Romances', in Norris J. Lacy and Joan Tasker Grimbert (eds.), *A Companion to Chrétien de Troyes*. Woodbridge: D. S. Brewer, 64–75.

—— (2006). 'Perceval and the Grail: The Continuations', in Glyn Burgess and Karen Pratt (eds.), *Arthurian Literature in the Middle Ages, IV The Arthur of the French*. Cardiff: University of Wales Press, 222–47.

Carruthers, Mary (1990). *The Book of Memory: A Study of Memory in Medieval Culture*. Cambridge: Cambridge University Press.

Castellani, Marie-Madeleine (1993). 'La Description de la tente du roi Bilas dans le roman d'*Athis et Prophilias*', in Jean-Claude Aubailly *et al.* (eds.), *'Et c'est la fin pour quoy sommes ensemble': Hommage à Jean Dufournet*, 2 vols. Paris: Champion, 1: 327–39.

Cazelles, Brigitte (1996). *The Unholy Grail: A Social Reading of Chrétien de Troyes's Conte du Graal*. Stanford: Stanford University Press.

Cerquiglini, Jacqueline *et al.* (1978). 'D'une quête l'autre: De Perceval à Gauvain, ou la forme d'une différence', in *Mélanges de littérature du Moyen Âge au XXe siècle offerts à Mlle Jeanne Lods*. Paris: Collection de l'École normale supérieure de jeunes filles, 1: 269–96.

Chenu, Marie-Dominique (1927). 'Auctor, Actor, Autor.' *Bulletin du Cange: Archivum Latinitatis Medii Aevi*, 3: 81–6.

—— (1976). *La Théologie au douzième siècle*. Paris: Vrin.

Cheyette, Frederic L., and Chickering, Howell (2005). 'Love, Anger, and Peace: Social Practice and Poetic Play in the Ending of *Yvain*'. *Speculum*, 80: 75–117.

Companion to Medieval French Literature (2008). *The Cambridge Companion to Medieval French Literature*, ed. Simon Gaunt and Sarah Kay. Cambridge: Cambridge University Press.

Corley, Corin (1982). 'Réflexions sur les deux premières continuations de *Perceval*'. *Romania*, 103: 235–58.

—— (1984). 'Wauchier de Denain et la Deuxième Continuation de *Perceval*'. *Romania*, 105: 352–9.

—— (1986). 'Manessier's Continuation of *Perceval* and the Prose *Lancelot* Cycle'. *Modern Language Review*, 81: 574–91.

—— (1987). *The Second Continuation of the Old French Perceval: A Critical and Lexicographical Study*. London: Modern Humanities Research Association.

Davis, Natalie Zemon (1983). Introduction to Duby (1983: vii–xv).

de Combarieu, Micheline (1984). 'Le *Lancelot* comme roman d'apprentissage: Enfance, démesure et chevalerie', in Jean Dufournet (ed.), *Approches du Lancelot en prose*. Geneva: Slatkine, 101–36.

de Riquer, Martin (1957). 'Perceval y Gauvain en "Li Contes del Graal"'. *Filologia Romanza*, 4: 119–47.

—— (1957–8). 'La composición de "Li Contes del Graal" y el "Guiromelant"'. *Boletín de la Real Academia de Buenas Letras de Barcelona*, 27: 279–320.

Deist, Rosemarie (1995). 'Mother and Child in Chrétien's *Perceval* and Wolfram's *Parzival*'. Paper delivered at the 30th International Congress on Medieval Studies, Western Michigan University.

—— (2003). *Gender and Power: Counsellors and their Masters in Antiquity and Medieval Courtly Romance*. Heidelberg: Universitätsverlag Winter.

Delcourt, Denyse (1990). *L'Éthique du changement dans le roman français du XIIe siècle*. Geneva: Droz.

Desclais-Berkvam, Doris (1981). *Enfances et maternité dans la littérature française des XIIe et XIIIe siècles*. Paris: Champion.

Diamond, Jared (1999). *Guns, Germs, and Steel: The Fates of Human Societies*. New York: Norton.

Doležel, Lubomír (1998). *Heterocosmica: Fiction and Possible Worlds*. Baltimore: The Johns Hopkins University Press.

Dragonetti, Roger (1978a). 'Pygmalion ou les pièges de la fiction dans le "Roman de la Rose"', in Georges Guntert *et al.* (eds.), *Orbis Mediaevalis: Mélanges de langue et de littérature médiévales offerts à Reto Raduolf Bezzola à l'occasion de son quatre-vingtième anniversaire*. Berne: Francke, 89–111.

—— (1978b). 'Le Singe de la Nature dans le "Roman de la Rose"'. *Travaux de linguistique et de littérature*, 16: 149–60.

—— (1980). *La Vie de la lettre au Moyen Âge: Le Conte du graal*. Paris: Seuil.

—— (1987). *Le Mirage des sources, l'art du faux dans le roman médiéval*. Paris: Seuil.

Dubost, Francis (1998). *Le Conte du Graal ou l'art de faire signe*. Paris: Champion.

Duby, Georges (1973). *Le Dimanche de Bouvines, 27 juillet 1214*. Paris: Gallimard.

—— (1981). *Le Chevalier, la Femme et le Prêtre*. Paris: Hachette.

—— (1983). *The Knight, the Lady and the Priest: The Making of Modern Marriage in Medieval France*, trans. Barbara Bray. New York: Pantheon Books.

Eskénazi, André (1993). '*Tref, Pavellon, Tante* dans les romans de Chrétien de Troyes', in Jean-Claude Aubailly *et al.* (eds.), *'Et c'est la fin pour quoy sommes ensemble': Hommage à Jean Dufournet*, 2 vols. Paris: Champion, 2: 549–62.

Fleishman, Suzanne (1996). 'Medieval Vernaculars and the Myth of Monoglossia: A Conspiracy of Linguistics and Philology', in Seth Lerer (ed.), *Literary History and the Challenge of Philology*. Stanford, CA: Stanford University Press, 92–104.

Flori, Jean (1998). *Chevaliers et chevalerie au Moyen Âge*. Paris: Hachette.

Fraenkel, Béatrice (1992). *La Signature: Genèse d'un signe*. Paris: Gallimard.

Frappier, Jean (1954). 'Le Graal et la chevalerie.' *Romania*, 75: 165–210.

—— (1958). 'Le Personnage de Gauvain dans la *Première Continuation de Perceval (Conte du Graal)*'. *Romance Philology*, 11: 331–44.

—— (1972a). *Chrétien de Troyes et le mythe du Graal*. Paris: SEDES.

—— (1972b). 'Le Prologue du *Chevalier de la Charrete* et son interprétation'. *Romania*, 93: 337–77.

—— (1977a). 'Note complémentaire sur la composition du *Conte du Graal*', in *Autour du Graal*. Geneva: Droz, 185–210.

—— (1977b). 'Sur la composition du *Conte du Graal*', in *Autour du Graal*. Geneva: Droz, 155–83.

—— (1978). '*Le Conte du Graal (Perceval)* de Chrétien de Troyes', in Jean Frappier and Reinhold R. Grimm (eds.), *Grundriss der romanischen Literaturen des Mittelalters*. Heidelberg: Carl Winter, IV/I: 332–54.

Friedman, Richard Elliot (1989). *Who Wrote the Bible?* New York: HarperCollins.

Frye, Northrop (1982). *The Great Code: The Bible and Literature*. New York: Harcourt Brace Jovanovich.

Gallais, Pierre (1964a). 'Formules de conteur'. *Romania*, 85: 181–229.

—— (1964b). 'Gauvain et la Pucelle de Lis', in *Mélanges de linguistique romane et de philologie médiévale offerts à M. Maurice Delbouille*, 2 vols. Gembloux: J. Duculot, 2: 207–29.

—— (1988–9). *L'Imaginaire d'un romancier français de la fin du XIIe siècle: Description raisonnée, comparée et commentée de la Continuation-Gauvain (Première suite du Conte du Graal de Chrétien de Troyes)*, 4 vols. Amsterdam: Rodopi.

Gallais, Pierre (1992). *La Fée à la fontaine et à l'arbre: Un archetype du conte merveilleux et du récit courtois*. Amsterdam and Atlanta: Rodopi.

Geary, Patrick J. (1985). 'Liturgical Perspective in *La Queste del Saint Graal*'. *Historical Reflections/Réflexions historiques*, 12: 205–17.

Genette, Gérard (1982). *Palimpsestes: La Littérature au second degré*. Paris: Seuil.

Goodwin, Malcolm (1994). *The Holy Grail: Its Origins, Secrets & Meaning Revealed*. Harmondsworth, England: Viking Studio Books.

Gouttebroze, Jean Guy (1976). 'L'Arrière-plan psychique et mythique de l'itinéraire de Perceval dans le *Conte du Graal* de Chrétien de Troyes'. *Senefiance*, 2: 339–52.

—— (1983). *Qui perd gagne: Le Perceval de Chrétien de Troyes comme représentation de l'Œdipe inversé*. Nice: Centre d'Études médiévales de Nice.

—— (1995). 'Un phénomène d'intertextualité biblique dans le *Conte du Graal:* "Qu'il soient une char andui" (éd. W. Roach, v. 9064)', in Friedrich Wolfzettel (ed.), *Arthurian Romance and Gender: Selected Proceedings of the XVIIth International Arthurian Congress*. Amsterdam: Rodopi, 165–75.

—— (1996). ' "Sainz Pos lo dit, et je le lui": Chrétien de Troyes lecteur'. *Romania*, 114: 524–35.

Gowans, Linda (2004). 'What Did Robert de Boron Really Write?', in Bonnie Wheeler (ed.), *Arthurian Studies in Honour of P. J. C. Field*. Cambridge: D. S. Brewer, 15–28.

Gravdal, Kathryn (1991). *Ravishing Maidens: Writing Rape in French Literature and Law*. Philadelphia: University of Pennsylvania Press.

Guézennec, Sophie (2000). 'Violences dans le *Conte du graal:* La Mise en question d'une notion ambivalente'. Brest: Centre de recherche bretonne, 69–104.

Hahn, Thomas, ed. (1995). 'Introduction', *The Jeaste of Sir Gawain*. TEAMS Middle English Texts. http://www.lib.rochester.edu/camelot/teams/jeastint.htm.

Haidu, Peter (1968). *Aesthetic Distance in Chrétien de Troyes: Irony and Comedy in Cligès and Perceval*. Geneva: Droz.

—— (1977). 'Repetition: Modern Reflections on Medieval Aesthetics'. *Modern Language Notes*, 92: 875–87.

—— (1983). 'The Hermit's Pottage', in Rupert T. Pickens (ed.), *The Sower and His Seed: Essays on Chrétien de Troyes*. Lexington, KY: French Forum, 127–45.

—— (1986). 'Idealism *vs.* Dialectics in Some Contemporary Theory'. *Canadian Review of Comparative Literature/Revue canadienne de littérature comparée*, 13: 421–49.

—— (1993). *The Subject of Violence: The* Song of Roland *and the Birth of the State*. Bloomington: Indiana University Press.

—— (spring 1998–fall 2003). 'Violence, Perspective, and Postmodern Historiography in *Raoul de Cambrai*'. *Olifant* 22/1–4: 41–72.

—— (2004). *The Subject Medieval/Modern: Text and Governance in the Middle Ages*. Stanford, CA: Stanford University Press.

Harf-Lancner, Laurence (1984). *Les Fées au Moyen Âge: Morgane et Mélusine, La naissance des fées*. Paris: Champion.

—— (1993). 'L'Image et le fantastique dans les manuscrits des romans de Chrétien de Troyes', in *Manuscrits* (1993: 1, 457–88).

Heng, Geraldine (2003). *Empire of Magic: Medieval Romance and the Poetics of Cultural Fantasy*. New York: Columbia University Press.

Heyworth, G. G. (2000). 'Perceval and the Seeds of Culture: Work, Profit and Leisure in the Prologue of *Perceval*'. *Neophilologus*, 84: 19–35.

Hindman, Sandra (1994). *Sealed in Parchment: Rereadings of Knighthood in the Illuminated Manuscripts of Chrétien de Troyes*. Chicago: University of Chicago Press.

Hofer, Stefan (1956). 'La Structure du *Conte du Graal* examinée à la lumière de l'œuvre de Chrétien de Troyes', in *Les Romans du Graal aux XIIe et XIIIe siècles*. Paris: CNRS, 15–26.

Holmes, Urban Tigner, Jr. (1948). A *New Interpretation of Chrétien's 'Conte del Graal'*. Chapel Hill: University of North Carolina Press.

——and Sister M. Amelia Klenke, OP (1959). *Chrétien, Troyes, and the Grail*. Chapel Hill: University of North Carolina Press.

Holzbacher, Ana María (1998). 'La Mère dans les romans de Chrétien de Troyes'. *Bien dire et bien aprandre: Revue de médiévistique*, 16: 159–69.

Huchet, Jean (1980). 'Mereceval'. *Littérature*, 40: 69–94.

——(1987–8). 'Le Nom et l'Image', in *Legacy* (1987–8: 2, 1–16).

Hult, David F. (1986). *Self-fulfilling Prophecies: Readership and Authority in the First Roman de la Rose*. Cambridge: Cambridge University Press.

——(1989). 'Author/Narrator/Speaker: the Voice of Authority in Chrétien's *Charrete*', in Kevin Brownlee and Walter Stephens (eds.), *Discourses of Authority in Medieval and Renaissance Literature*. Hanover, NH: University Press of New England, 76–96.

Hunt, Tony (1971). 'The Prologue to Chrestien's *Li Contes del graal*'. *Romania*, 92: 357–79.

——(1979). 'Aristotle, Dialectic, and Courtly Literature'. *Viator*, 10: 95–129.

——(1994). 'Chrétien's Prologues Reconsidered', in Keith Busby and Norris Lacy (eds.), *Conjunctures: Medieval Studies in Honor of Douglas Kelly*. Amsterdam: Rodopi, 153–68.

Huot, Sylvia (1993). *The* Romance of the Rose *and its Medieval Readers: Reception, Interpretation, Manuscript Transmission*. Cambridge: Cambridge University Press.

——(1996). 'Reading the Manuscripts of Chrétien de Troyes'. *Medievalia et Humanistica* 23: 99–109.

Jameson, Frederic (1975–6). 'Magical Narratives: Romance as Genre'. *New Literary History*, 7: 135–63.

Jauss, Hans Erich (1982). 'Theory of Genres and Medieval Literature', in *Toward an Aesthetic of Reception*, trans. Timothy Bahti. Minneapolis: University of Minnesota Press.

Jeffrey, David. L. (1979). 'Introduction: The Self and the Book: Reference and Recognition in Medieval Thought', in David L. Jeffrey (ed.), *By Things Seen: Reference and Recognition in Medieval Thought*. Ottawa: University of Ottawa Press, 1–17.

Kay, Sarah (1995). *The* Chanson de geste *in the Age of Romance: Political Fictions*. Oxford: Clarendon Press.

——(1997). 'Who Was Chrétien de Troyes?' *Arthurian Literature*, 15: 1–35.

——(2000). 'Courts, Clerks, and Courtly Love', in Roberta M. Krueger (ed.), *The Cambridge Companion to Medieval Romance*. Cambridge: Cambridge University Press, 81–96.

——(2001). *Courtly Contradictions: The Emergence of the Literary Object in the Twelfth Century*. Stanford: Stanford University Press.

——and Rubin, Miri, eds. (1994). *Framing Medieval Bodies*. Manchester: Manchester University Press.

Keller, Hans-Erich (1990). 'L'Esprit courtois et le *Roman de la Violette*', in Keith Busby and Erik Kooper (eds.), *Courtly Literature: Culture and Context*. Amsterdam: John Benjamins, 323–35.

Kellermann, Wilhelm (1956). 'Le Problème de Breri', in *Les Romans du Graal aux XIIe et XIIIe siècles. Strasbourg, 29 mars–1 avril 1954*. Paris: CNRS, 137–48.

Kelly, Douglas (1974). '*Matiere* and *Genera dicendi* in Medieval Romance'. *Yale French Studies*, 51: 147–59.

—— (1993). *Medieval French Romance*. New York: Twayne Publishers.

—— (1994). 'Le Nom de Perceval', in *Perceval-Parzival: Hier et Aujourd'hui et autres essais sur la littérature allemande du Moyen Âge et de la Renaissance. Recueil d'études assemblées par Danielle Buschinger et Woflgang Spiewok pour fêter les 95 ans de Jean Fourquet*. Griefswald: Reinecke, 123–9.

Kennedy, Elspeth (1986). 'The Re-writing and Re-reading of a Text: The Evolution of the Prose *Lancelot*', in A. Adams *et al.* (eds.), *The Changing Face of Arthurian Romance: Essays on Arthurian Prose Romance in Memory of Cedric E. Pickford*. Cambridge: Cambridge University Press, 1–9.

Kjaer, Jonna (1990). 'L'Épisode de "Tristan menestrel" dans la "Continuation de Perceval" par Gerbert de Montreuil (XIIIe siècle): Essai d'interprétation'. *Revue romane*, 25: 356–66.

Klein, Melanie (1975). 'Our Adult World and its Roots in Infancy', in *Envy and Gratitude, and Other Works (1946–1963)*. New York: Free Press, 247–63.

Köhler, Erich (1960). 'Le Rôle de la coutume dans les romans de Chrétien de Troyes'. *Romania* 81: 386–97.

Koziol, Geoffrey (1995). 'England, France, and the Problem of Sacrality in Twelfth-Century Ritual', in Thomas N. Bisson (ed.), *Cultures of Power: Lordship, Status and Process in Twelfth-Century Europe*. Philadelphia: University of Pennsylvania Press, 124–48.

Krause, Kathy (2003). 'Courtly Morality in the Romances of Gerbert de Montreuil'. Paper at the MLA Convention.

Kristeva, Julia (1969). *Semeiotikè: Recherches pour une sémanalyse (extraits)*. Paris: Seuil.

Krueger, Roberta L. (1993). *Women Readers and the Ideology of Gender in Old French Verse Romance*. Cambridge: Cambridge University Press.

Lachat, Claude (1999). '*Les Continuations de Perceval* ou l'art de donner le coup de "grâce" au récit du Graal', in *L'Œuvre inachevé, Actes du Colloque International (11 et 12 décembre 1998)*. Textes rassemblés par Annie Rivara et Guy Lavorel. Lyons: CEDIC, 21–9.

Lacy, Norris (2004). 'The Da Vinci Code: Dan Brown and the Grail That Never Was'. *Arthuriana* 14: 81–93.

Laranjinha, Ana Sofia (1998). 'L'Ironie comme principe structurant chez Chrétien de Troyes'. *Cahiers de civilisation médiévale*, 41: 175–82.

Larmat, Jean (1974). 'Le Péché de Perceval dans la *Continuation* de Gerbert', in Jacques de Caluwé, Jean-Marie d'Heur, and René Dumas (eds.), *Mélanges d'histoire littéraire, de linguistique et de philologie romanes offerts à Charles Rostaing*. Liège: L'Association des Romanistes de l'Université de Liège, 541–57.

Laurie, Helen C. R. (1971). 'Towards an Interpretation of the "Conte du Graal"'. *Modern Language Review*, 66: 775–85.

Lefay-Toury, Marie-Noëlle (1972). 'Roman breton et mythes courtois: L'Évolution du personnage féminin dans les romans de Chrétien de Troyes'. *Cahiers de civilisation médiévale*, 15: 193–204 and 283–93.

Legacy (1987–8). *The Legacy of Chrétien de Troyes*, ed. Norris J. Lacy, Douglas Kelly, and Keith Busby, 2 vols. Amsterdam: Rodopi.

Le Goff, Jacques, and Vidal-Naquet, Pierre (1979). 'Lévi-Strauss en Brocéliande: Esquisse pour une analyse d'un roman courtois', in *Claude Lévi-Strauss*. Paris: Gallimard, Collection Idées.

Le Menn, Gwennolé (1985). *La Femme au sein d'or: Des chants populaires bretons aux légendes celtiques*. St Brieuc: Skol, 86–88.

Le Rider, Paule (1978). *Le Chevalier dans le Conte du Graal*. Paris: SEDES.

Leupin, Alexandre (1979). 'Les Enfants de la Mimésis: Différence et répétition dans la "Première Continuation du Perceval"'. *Vox Romanica*, 38: 110–26.

——(1982). 'La Faille et l'écriture dans les continuations du *Perceval*'. *Moyen Âge*, 88: 237–69.

Lévi-Strauss, Claude (1973). *Anthropologie structurale*, vol. 2. Paris: Plon.

Levy, Raphael (1931). 'Old French *Goz* and *Crestiiens Li Gois*'. *PMLA*, 46: 312–20.

Lods, Jeanne (1978). 'La Pucelle as manches petites', in Jacques de Caluwé (ed.), *Mélanges de philologie et de littérature romanes offerts à Jeanne Wathelet-Willem*. Liège: Cahiers de l'ARULg, 357–79.

Loomis, Roger Sherman (1965). 'The Strange History of Caradoc of Vannes', in Jess B. Bessinger, Jr. and Robert P. Creed (eds.), *Franciplegius: Medieval and Linguistic Studies in Honor of Francis Peabody Magoun, Jr*. New York: New York University Press, 231–9.

Lot, Ferdinand (1931). 'Les Auteurs du Conte du Graal'. *Romania*, 57: 117–36.

Luttrell, Claude (1983). 'The Prologue of Crestien's *Li Contes du Graal*'. *Arthurian Literature*, 3: 1–25.

McCracken, Peggy (1998a). 'Mothers in the Grail Quest: Desire, Pleasure, and Conception'. *Arthuriana*, 8: 35–48.

——(1998b). *The Romance of Adultery: Queenship and Sexual Transgression in Old French Literature*. Philadelphia: University of Pennsylvania Press.

——(1999). 'The Poetics of Sacrifice: Allegory and Myth in the Grail Quest'. *Yale French Studies*, 95: 152–68.

Maddox, Donald (1983). 'The Awakening: A Key Motif in Chrétien's Romances', in Rupert T. Pickens (ed.), *The Sower and his Seed: Essays on Chrétien de Troyes*. Lexington, KY: French Forum, 31–51.

——(1991a). *The Arthurian Romances of Chrétien de Troyes: Once and Future Fictions*. Cambridge: Cambridge University Press.

——(1991b). 'Specular Stories, Family Romance, and the Fictions of Courtly Culture'. *Exemplaria*, 3: 299–326.

——(1994). 'Lévi-Strauss in Camelot: Interrupted Communication in Arthurian Feudal Fictions', in Martin B. Shichtman and James P. Carley (eds.), *Culture and King: The Social Implications of the Arthurian Legend*. Albany: State University of New York Press, 35–53.

Manuscripts (1993). *The Manuscripts of Chrétien de Troyes*, ed. Keith Busby, Terry Nixon, Alison Stones, and Lori Walters, 2 vols. Amsterdam: Rodopi.

Marnette, Sophie (1998). *Narrateur et points de vue dans la littérature française médiévale: Une approche linguistique.* Berne: Peter Lang.

Marx, Jean (1965). 'Manessier et la *Queste del saint Graal*', in *Nouvelles recherches sur la littérature arthurienne.* Paris: Klincksieck, 239–59.

Matarasso, Pauline M. (1979). *The Redemption of Chivalry.* Geneva: Droz.

Méla, Charles (1977). 'Perceval'. *Yale French Studies*, 55/6: 253–79.

—— (1979). *Blanchefleur et le saint homme ou la semblance des reliques.* Paris: Seuil.

—— (1983). '"La Lettre tue": Cryptographie du Graal (A propos de Roger Dragonetti, *La Vie de la lettre*)'. *Cahiers de civilisation médiévale*, 26: 209–21.

—— (1984). *La Reine et le Graal: La Conjointure dans les romans du Graal, de Chrétien de Troyes au Livre de Lancelot.* Paris: Seuil.

Ménard, Philippe (1984). 'Problèmes et mystères du *"Conte du Graal"*: Essai d'interprétation', in *Chrétien de Troyes et le Graal (Colloque arthurien belge de Bruges).* Paris: Nizet, 61–76.

—— (1995). 'La Révélation du nom pour le héros du *Conte du Graal*', in *Amour et chevalerie dans les romans de Chrétien de Troyes.* Paris: Les Belles Lettres, 47–59.

Micha, Alexandre (1966). *La Tradition manuscrite des romans de Chrétien de Troyes.* Geneva: Droz.

Mickel, Emmanuel J. (1972). 'A Reconsideration of Chrétien's *Erec*'. *Romanische Forschungen*, 84: 18–44.

Miles, Jack (1996). *God: A Biography.* New York: Vintage Books.

Minnis, Alastair J. (1979). 'Late-Medieval Discussions of *Compilatio* and the Role of the *Compilator*'. *Beiträge zur Geschichte des Deutschen Sprache und Literatur*, 101: 385–421.

—— (1984). *Medieval Theory of Authorship. Scholastic Literary Attitudes in the Later Middle Ages.* London: Scolar Press.

Motte, Warren F., Jr. (1984). 'Le Puzzle de/dans *La Vie mode d'emploi* de Perec'. *Romance Notes*, 24: 207–13.

Nicholas, David (1992). *Medieval Flanders.* London: Longman.

Nixon, Terry (1993). 'Romance Collections and the Manuscripts of Chrétien de Troyes', in *Manuscripts* (1993: 1, 17–26).

Nykrog, Per (1973). 'Two Creators of Narrative Form in Twelfth-Century France: Gautier d'Arras and Chrétien de Troyes'. *Speculum*, 48: 258–76.

Paradis, Françoise (1984). 'La Triple mise au monde d'un héros, ou trois images d'une féminité maîtrisée dans le début du Lancelot en prose', in Jean Dufournet (ed.), *Approches du Lancelot en prose.* Geneva and Paris: Slatkine, 157–76.

Payen, Jean-Charles (1978). 'Les Continuations de Perceval', in Jean Frappier and Reinhold R. Grimm (eds.), *Grundriss der romanischen Literaturen des Mittelalters.* Heidelberg: Carl Winter Universitäts-verlag, 4/1: 354–61.

Pickens, Rupert T. (1977). *The Welsh Knight: Paradoxicality in Chrétien's* Conte del Graal. Lexington, KY: French Forum, Pub.

—— (1988). 'Histoire et commentaire chez Chrétien de Troyes et Robert de Boron et le livre de Philippe de Flandre', in *Legacy* (1987–8: 2, 17–39).

—— (2006a). 'Perceval and the Grail: The Prologues: The *Elucidation* and *Bliocadran*', in Glyn Burgess and Karen Pratt (eds.), *Arthurian Literature in the Middle Ages, IV The Arthur of the French.* Cardiff: University of Wales Press, 215–21.

—— (2006b). 'Perceval and the Grail: Robert de Boron (the *Estoire dou Graal*, *Merlin*, and the *Didot-Perceval*)', in Glyn Burgess and Karen Pratt (eds.), *Arthurian Literature in the Middle Ages, IV The Arthur of the French*. Cardiff: University of Wales Press, 247–59.

Pinker, Stephen (1997). *How the Mind Works*. New York: Norton.

Poirion, Daniel (1973). 'L'Ombre mythique de Perceval dans le *Conte du Graal*'. *Cahiers de civilisation médiévale*, 16: 191–8.

—— (1977). 'Du sang sur la neige: Nature et fonction de l'image dans le *Conte du Graal*', in Raymond J. Cormier (ed.), *Voices of Conscience: Essays on Medieval and Modern French Literature in Memory of James D. Powell and Rosemary Hodgins*. Philadelphia, PA: Temple University Press, 162–3.

—— (1981). 'Écriture et ré-écriture au Moyen Âge'. *Littérature*, 41: 109–18.

—— (1986). *Résurgences, mythes et littérature à l'âge du symbole (XIIᵉ siècle)*. Paris: PUF.

Pratt, Karen (1991). 'Aristotle, Augustine or Boethius? *La Mort le roi Artu* as Tragedy'. *Nottingham French Studies*, 30: 81–109.

Progrès (2003). *Progrès, Réaction, Décadence dans L'Occident médiéval*. Études recueillies par Emmanuèle Baumgartner et Laurence Harf-Lancner. Geneva: Droz.

Putter, Ad (1995). 'Knights and Clerics at the Court of Champagne: Chrétien de Troyes's Romances in Context', in Christopher Harper-Bill and Ruth Harvey (eds.), *Ideals and Practices of Medieval Knighthood*, V. Woodbridge: Boydell, 243–66.

—— (2004). 'Story line and Story Shape in *Sir Percyvell of Gales* and Chrétien de Troyes's *Conte du Graal*', in Nicola McDonald (ed.), *Pulp Fictions of Medieval England: Essays in Popular Romance*. Manchester: Manchester University Press, 171–96.

Raugei, Anna Maria (1993). 'La Bibbia nell'opera di Chrétien de Troyes'. *Acme: annali della Facoltà di lettere e filosofia dell'Università degli statale di Milano*. Milan: Industrie Grafiche, 204–45.

Regalado, Nancy Freeman (1981). ' "Des contraires choses": La Fonction poétique de la citation et des exempla dans le "Roman de la Rose" de Jean de Meun'. *Littérature*, 41: 62–81.

—— (1985). 'La Chevalerie celestiel: Spiritual Transformations of Secular Romance in *La Queste del Saint Graal*', in Kevin Brownlee and Marina S. Brownlee (eds.), *Romance: Generic Transformation from Chrétien de Troyes to Cervantes*. Hanover, NH and London: University Press of New England, 91–113.

—— (1999). 'Villon's Legacy from "Le Testament of Jean de Meun": Misquotation, Memory, and the Wisdom of Fools', in Jane Taylor and Michael Freeman (eds.), *Villon at Oxford: The Drama of the Text*. Amsterdam: Rodopi.

Régnier-Bohler, Danielle (1980). 'Figures féminines et imaginaire généalogique: Étude comparée de quelques récits brefs', in Danielle Buschinger (ed.), *Le Récit bref au Moyen Âge. Actes du Colloque des 27, 28 et 29 avril 1979*. Paris: Champion, 73–95.

—— (1995). 'La Fonction symbolique du féminin: Le Savoir des mères, le secret des sœurs et le devenir des héros', in Friedrich Wolfzettel (ed.), *Arthurian Romance and Gender: Selected Proceedings of the XVIIth International Arthurian Congress*. Amsterdam: Rodopi, 4–25.

Reichert, Michelle (2006). *Between Courtly Literature and Al-Andalus: 'Matière d'Orient' and the Importance of Spain in the Romances of the Twelfth-Century Writer Chrétien de Troyes*. New York and London: Routledge.

Rey-Flaud, Henri (1980). 'Le Sang sur la neige: Analyse d'une image-écran de Chrétien de Troyes'. *Littérature*, 37: 15–24.

—— (1998). *Le Sphinx et le Graal: Le Secret et l'énigme*. Paris: Payot.

—— (1999). *Le Chevalier, l'Autre et la Mort: Les Aventures de Gauvain dans 'le Conte du Graal'*. Paris: Payot et Rivages.

Ribard, Jacques (1976). 'De Chrétien de Troyes à Guillaume de Lorris: Ces quêtes qu'on dit inachevées', in *Voyages, quête et pèlerinage dans la littérature et la civilisation médiévales*. Aix-en-Provence: CUERMA, 315–21.

—— (1980–1). 'Ecriture symbolique et visée allégorique dans *Le Conte du Graal*'. *Œuvres et critiques*, 5: 103–9.

—— (1984). *Le Moyen Âge: Littérature et symbolisme*. Paris: Champion.

Rider, Jeff (1985). 'Courtly Marriage in Robert Biket's *Lai du cor*'. *Romania*, 106: 173–97.

—— (1998). 'The Perpetual Enigma of Chrétien's Grail Episode.' *Arthuriana*, 8: 6–21.

—— (2001). '"Wild Oats": The Parable of the Sower in the Prologue to Chrétien de Troyes' *Conte du Graal*', in Joan Tasker Grimbert and Carol J. Chase (eds.), *Philologies Old and New: Essays in Honor of Peter Florian Dembowski*. Princeton: Princeton University Press, 251–66.

Rieger, Angelica (1993). 'Le Programme iconographique du *Perceval* montpelliérain', in *Manuscripts* (1993: 2, 377–435).

Rieger, Dietmar (1988). 'Le Motif du viol dans la littérature de la France médiévale entre norme courtoise et réalité courtoise'. *Cahiers de civilisation médiévale*, 31: 241–67.

Roach, William (1956). 'Les Continuations du *Conte du Graal*', in *Les Romans du Graal aux XIIe et XIIIe siècles*. Paris: CNRS, 106–18.

—— (1966). 'Transformations of the Grail Theme in the First Two Continuations of the Old French *Perceval*'. *Proceedings of the American Philosophical Society*, 110: 160–4.

Robertson, D. W., Jr. (1962). *A Preface to Chaucer*. Princeton: Princeton University Press.

Rollo, David (1998). *Historical Fabrication, Ethnic Fable and French Romance in Twelfth-Century England*. Lexington, KY: French Forum.

—— (2000). *Glamorous Sorcery: Magic and Literacy in the High Middle Ages*. Medieval Cultures 25. Minneapolis and London: University of Minnesota Press.

Rossi, Marguerite (1980). 'Sur l'épisode de Caradoc de la *Continuation Gauvain*', in *Mélanges de langue et de littérature françaises du Moyen Âge et de la Renaissance offerts à Monsieur Charles Foulon (Marche Romane* 30). Rennes: Institut de français, Université de Haut-Bretagne, 2 vols. 2: 247–54.

Ryding, William W. (1971). *Structure in Medieval Narrative*. The Hague and Paris: Mouton.

Saly, Antoinette (1976). 'L'Itinéraire intérieur dans le *Perceval* de Chrétien de Troyes et la structure de la quête de Gauvain', in *Voyage, quête, pèlerinage dans la littérature et la civilisation médiévales*. Aix-en-Provence: CUERMA, 353–61.

—— (1984). *Images, Structure et Sens: Etudes Arthuriennes*. Aix-en-Provence: CUERMA.

—— (1994a). 'La Demoiselle Hideuse dans le roman arthurien'. *Travaux de littérature*, 7: 27–51.

—— (1994b). 'Sur quelques vers du *Perceval*: La Biche manquée (vv. 5656–5702)', in *Perceval-Parzival: Hier et Aujourd'hui et autres essais sur la littérature allemande du Moyen Âge et de la Renaissance. Recueil d'études assemblées par Danielle Buschinger et Woflgang Spiewok pour fêter les 95 ans de Jean Fourquet*. Griefswald: Reinecke, 259–69.

Sargent-Baur, Barbara N. (1992). 'Love in Theory and Practice in the *Conte du Graal*'. *Arthurian Yearbook*, 2: 179–89.

—— (2000). *La Destre et la Senestre: Étude sur le* Conte du Graal *de Chrétien de Troyes*. Amsterdam: Rodopi.

—— (2001). 'Le Jeu des noms de personnes dans le *Conte du Graal*.' *Neophilologus*, 85: 485–99.

Sasaki, Shigemi (1984). 'Le Mystère de la lance et la chapelle à la main noire dans trois *Continuations* de *Perceval*', in *Actes du 14ᵉ Congrès International Arthurien*, 2 vols. Rennes: Presses universitaires, 2, 536–57.

Savage, Grace Armstrong (1977). 'Father and Son in the *Queste del Saint Graal*'. *Romance Philology*, 31: 1–16.

Schacter, Daniel L. (1996). *Searching for Memory: The Brain, the Mind, the Past*. New York: Basic Books.

Schmid, Elisabeth (1986). *Familiengeschichte und Heilsmythologie: Die Verwandschafts-strukturen in den französischen und deutschen Gralromanen des 12. und 13. Jahrhunderts*. Tübingen: Niemeyer.

Schmolke-Hasselmann, Beate (1980a). *Der arturische Versroman von Chrestien bis Frois-sart*. Tübingen: Max Niemeyer.

—— (1980b). 'L'Intégration de quelques récits brefs arthuriens (*Cor, Mantel, Espee*) dans les romans arthuriens du XIIIᵉ siècle', in Danielle Buschinger (ed.), *Le Récit bref au Moyen Âge: Actes du Colloque des 27, 28 et 29 avril 1979*. Paris: Champion, 107–28.

—— (1981). 'Henry II Plantagenêt, roi d'Angleterre, et la genèse d'*Erec et Enidè*. *Cahiers de civilisation médiévale*, 24: 241–6.

Schwartz, Debora B. (1996) ' "A la guise de Gales l'atorna": Maternal Influence in Chrétien's *Conte du Graal*'. *Essays in Medieval Studies*, 12. <http://www.illinoismedieval. org/ems/Vol12/schwartz.html>.

Segal, Hanna (1973). *Introduction to the Work of Melanie Klein*. New York: Basic Books, orig. 1964.

Séguy, Mireille (2001a). *Les Romans du graal ou le signe imaginé*. Paris: Champion.

—— (2001b). 'Le Sceau brisé: L'Impossible fin de la *Troisième continuation* du *Conte du Graal*'. *Bien dire et bien aprandre*, 19: 213–24.

Signer, Michael A. (2005). 'Consolation and Confrontation: Jewish and Christian Inter-pretation of the Prophetic Books', in Thomas J. Heffernan and Thomas E. Burman (eds.), *Scripture and Pluralism: Reading the Bible in the Religiously Plural Worlds of the Middle Ages and Renaissance*. Leiden: Brill, 76–93.

Sinclair, Finn E. (2003). *Milk & Blood: Gender and Genealogy in the 'Chanson de geste'*. Oxford and Berne: Peter Lang.

Smalley, Beryl (1952). *The Study of the Bible in the Middle Ages*. Oxford: Basil Blackwell.

Smith, Gregory A. (2002). '*Sine rege, sine principe*: Peter the Venerable on Violence in 12th c. Burgundy'. *Speculum*, 77: 1–33.

Spiegel, Gabrielle M. (1983). 'Genealogy: Form and Function in Medieval Historical Narrative'. *History and Theory*, 22: 43–53.

—— (1993). *Romancing the Past: The Rise of Vernacular Prose Historiography in Thirteenth-Century France*. Berkeley and Los Angeles: University of California Press.

Stanesco, Michel (1981). 'Le Chemin le plus long: De la parole intempestive à l'économie du dire dans *Le Conte du Graal*', in Kenneth Varty (ed.), *An Arthurian Tapestry: Essays in Memory of Lewis Thorpe*. University of Glasgow: French Department, 287–97.

Stanesco, Michel (1993). 'Le Texte primitif et la parole poétique médiévale', in *Écriture et modes de pensée au Moyen Âge (VIIIᵉ-XVᵉ siècle): Études rassemblées par D. Boutet et L. Harf-Lancner*. Paris: Presses de l'ENS, 15–55.

—— (1998). 'Parole autoritaire et "accord des semblances" dans *La Queste del saint Graal*', in *Miscellanea Mediaevalia: Mélanges offerts à Philippe Ménard. Études réunies par J. Claude Faucon, Alain Labbé et Danielle Quéruel*, 2 vols. Paris: Champion, 2: 1267–79.

—— (2002). 'Le Secret du Graal et la voie interrogative', in *'D'armes et d'amours': Études de littérature arthurienne*. Orléans: Paradigme, 163–79.

Stanger, Mary D. (1957). 'Literary Patronage at the Medieval Court of Flanders'. *French Studies*, 11: 214–29.

Stanton, Amida (1942). *Gerbert de Montreuil as a Writer of Grail Romance: An Investigation of the Date and the more Immediate Sources of the Continuation of* Perceval. Chicago: University of Chicago Libraries.

Steele, Stephen (1993). 'Qu'est-ce qu'un Chrétien de Troyes?' *Florilegium*, 12: 99–106.

Steiner, George (1971). *In Bluebeard's Castle: Some Notes Towards the Redefinition of Culture*. New Haven: Yale University Press.

Stiennon, Jacques (1984). 'Bruges, Philippe d'Alsace, Chrétien de Troyes et le Graal', in *Chrétien de Troyes et le Graal (Colloque arthurien belge de Bruges)*. Paris: Nizet, 5–15.

Stephens, Leslie (1996). 'Gerbert and Manessier: The Case for a Connection'. *Arthurian Literature*, 14: 53–68.

Stones, Alison (1993). 'The Illustrated Chrétien Manuscripts and their Artistic Context', in *Manuscripts* (1993: 1, 277–322).

Sturges, Robert (1991). *Medieval Interpretation: Models of Reading in Literary Narrative, 1100–1500*. Carbondale and Edwardsville: Southern Illinois Press.

Sturm-Maddox, Sara (1984). '"Tenir sa terre en pais": Social Order in the *Brut* and the *Conte du Graal*'. *Studies in Philology*, 81: 28–41.

—— (1992). '"Tout est par senefiance": Gerbert's *Perceval*'. *Arthurian Yearbook*, 2: 191–207.

Szkilnik, Michelle (1986). 'Écrire en vers, écrire en prose: Le Choix de Wauchier de Denain'. *Romania*, 107: 208–30.

—— (1989). 'Les Deux Pères de Caradoc'. *Bibliographical Bulletin of the International Arthurian Society*, 40: 268–86.

Thompson, Albert W. (1959). 'Additions to Chrétien's *Perceval*—Prologues and Continuations', in Roger Sherman Loomis (ed.), *Arthurian Literature in the Middle Ages*. Oxford: Clarendon Press, 207–12.

Todorov (1965). *Théorie de la littérature: Textes des Formalistes russes réunis, présentés et traduits par Tzvetan Todorov*. Paris: Seuil.

Van Caenegem, R. C. (1995). 'Law and Power in Twelfth-Century Flanders', in Thomas N. Bisson (ed.), *Cultures of Power: Lordship, Status and Process in Twelfth-Century Europe*. Philadelphia: University of Pennsylvania Press, 149–68.

Van Coolput, Colette-Anne (1986). *Aventures querant et le sens du monde: Aspects de la réception productive des premiers romans du Graal cycliques dans le* Tristan en prose. Leuven: Leuven University Press.

Van Creveld, Martin (1991). *The Transformation of War*. New York: Free Press.

Van Liere, Frans (2005). 'Andrew of St Victor, Jerome, and the Jews', in Thomas J. Heffernan and Thomas E. Burman (eds.), *Scripture and Pluralism: Reading the*

Bible in the Religiously Plural Worlds of the Middle Ages and Renaissance. Leiden and Boston: Brill, 59–75.

Van Mulken, Margot (1993). '*Perceval* and Stemmata', in *Manuscripts* (1993: 2, 41–8).

Vance, Eugene (1973). 'Signs of the City: Medieval Poetry as Detour'. *New Literary History*, 4: 557–74.

—— (1987). *From Topic to Tale: Logic and Narrativity in the Middle Ages*. Theory and History of Literature, 47. Minneapolis: University of Minnesota Press.

Vial, Guy (1978). 'L'Auteur de la deuxième continuation du *Conte du Graal*', in *Mélanges d'études romanes... offerts à Monsieur Jean Rychner* (*Travaux de linguistique et de littérature* 16.1). Strasbourg, 519–30.

—— (1987). *Le Conte du Graal: Sens et Unité; La Première Continuation: Textes et Contenu*. Geneva: Droz.

Vinaver, Eugène (1971). *The Rise of Romance*. Oxford: Oxford University Press.

Vincensini, Jean-Jacques (2005). 'Le *Roman de Mélusine:* Impasses de la discontinuité et sens du chamarré', in Milena Mikhaïlova (ed.), *Mouvances et Jointures: Du manuscrit au texte médiéval. Actes du Colloque international organisé par le CeReS—Université de Limoges, Faculté des Lettres et des Sciences humaines, 21–3 novembre 2002. Medievalia* 55. Orléans: Paradigme.

Walter, Philippe (2004). *Perceval: Le Pêcheur et le Graal*. Paris: Imago.

Walters, Lori (1985). 'Le Rôle du scribe dans l'organisation des romans de Chrétien de Troyes'. *Romania*, 106: 303–25.

—— (1993). 'The Image of Blanchefleur in MS Montpellier, BI, Sect. Méd. H 249', in *Manuscripts* (1993: 2, 437–55).

—— (1994). 'Jeanne and Marguerite de Flandre as Female Patrons'. *Dalhousie French Studies*, 28: 15–27.

—— (1998). 'Parody and Moral Allegory in Chantilly Ms. 472'. *Modern Language Notes*, 113: 937–50.

White, Sarah Melhado (1983). 'Lancelot's Beds: Styles of Courtly Intimacy', in Rupert T. Pickens (ed.), *The Sower and his Seed: Essays on Chrétien de Troyes*. Lexington, KY: French Forum, 116–26.

White, Stephen D. (1998). 'The Politics of Anger', in Barbara H. Rosenwein (ed.), *Anger's Past: The Social Uses of an Emotion in the Middle Ages*. Ithaca: Cornell University Press.

Williams, Andrea M. L. (2006). 'Perceval and the Grail: *Perlesvaus*', in Glyn Burgess and Karen Pratt (eds.), *Arthurian Literature in the Middle Ages, IV The Arthur of the French*. Cardiff: University of Wales Press, 260–4.

Williams, Harry F. (1980–1). '*Le Conte du Graal* de Chrétien de Troyes: Positions critiques et nouvelles perspectives'. *Œuvres et Critiques*, 5: 119–23.

Wilmotte, Maurice (1930). *Le Poème du Gral et ses auteurs*. Paris: Droz.

Wolfgang, Leonora D. (1980–1). 'Prologues to the *Perceval* and Perceval's Father: The First Literary Critics of Chrétien were the Grail Authors Themselves'. *Œuvres et Critiques*, 5: 81–90.

Wood, Michael (2007). 'The Last Night of All'. *PMLA*, 122: 1394–1402.

Wynn, Marianne (1994). 'Wolfram von Eschenbach', in James Hardin and Will Hasty (eds.), *Dictionary of Literary Biography*, vol. 138: *German Writers and Works of the High Middle Ages: 1170–1280*. London: Bruccoli Clark Layman, 185–206.

Zink, Michel (1987–8). 'Chrétien et ses contemporains', in *Legacy* (1987–8: 2, 5–32).

Zornberg, Avivah Gottlieb (2001). *The Particulars of Rapture: Reflections of Exodus*. New York: Image/Doubleday.

Zumthor, Paul (1972). *Essai de poétique médiévale*. Paris: Seuil.

—— (1978). 'Le Texte-fragment'. *Langue française*, 40: 75–82.

—— (1981). 'Intertextualité et mouvance'. *Littérature*, 41: 8–16.

Index

Figures and notes are indexed as **f** and **n**.

Adams, Tracy E. 140**n.39**
advice:
  and Arthurian society 119
  and the Grail 209, 220
  Perceval:
    Gornemant de Gohort 77, 82**n**, 85,
      92, 93, 115, 124, 125, 126, 216;
      mother's 26, 27, 77, 85, 87, 92–3,
      95, 103, 115, 124, 127, 137, 146,
      147, 216–17, 220
  see also education; sexuality
Albéric de Pisançon:
  Alexandre 22–3
Amazawa, Taijiro 75**n.78**
and/both logic 17, 18, 19, 21–2, 23, 24,
  27, 113, 125, 165, 171, 172, 197,
  202, 206, 221, 227
antique romances 20, 87
  Roman d'Eneas (anon) 20, 149
  Roman de Thèbes (anon) 20, 149
  Roman de Troie (Benoît de Sainte-
    Maure) 20, 149
Aristotle 187–8, 189
Arthurian values 27, 94; see also chivalry;
  violence
Atre Périlleux 113
Auerbach, Erich 194, 194**n.17**
authorship 1–2, 32, 33, 34, 35, 38, 40,
  42–4, 46, 57–8, 62, 72, 82–3,
  193–4
  authority 16, 33, 34, 42, 43, 47, 64–5,
    70, 72, 79, 155
  collective 2, 24–31, 41, 59–60
  see also naming

Backman, Clifford R. 169**n.43**
Baldwin, John 175**n.54**
Balsamo, Gian 115**n.58**, 120**n.6**
Barrera, Julio Trebolle 192**n.10**

Baudry, Robert 125**n.13**
Baumgartner, Emmanuèle 8**n.13**, 9,
  30**n.51**, 34**n.2**, 35**n.7**, 36**n.9**, 38,
  39**n.12**, 81**n.92**, 87**n.2**, 120**n.7**,
  130, 139**n.38**, 145**n.48**, 146**n.50**,
  152**n.6**, 163**n.30**, 174**n.51**,
  179**n.64**, 184**n.74**, 201**n.28**,
  219**n.8**, 223, 223**n.14**
Bel Inconnu, Le 35, 108, 120
Bennett, Matthew 151**n.4**, 168**n.41**
Benoît de Sainte-Maure, *see* antique
  romances
Benton, John F. 82**n.96**, 153**n.9**
Berger, Samuel 194**n.16**
Berthelot, Anne 12**n.25**, 23**n.43**, 32, 36,
  83**n.99**
Biau Repaire 51, 58, 60–1, 63, 66, 67,
  199, 203, 209
Bible 26, 29, 79, 80, 166, 168, 192, 193,
  194, 197
biblical references 26, 28, 78, 79, 192–8
Bisson, Thomas N. 124**n.11**, 168**n.41**
Blaess, Madeleine 176**n.56**
Blancheflor 3, 4, 28, 41, 47, 48–9, 51–2,
  56, 60, 63–5, 66–7, 86–7, 89, 92,
  94, 97, 100, 104, 110, 111, 112–
  3, 117, 126, 134, 146, 157, 162,
  183, 196–7, 198, 199, 203, 209
bleeding lance 13, 19, 50, 77, 162, 168,
  176–7, 205, 207, 210, 214, 215,
  220
  see also weapons; Grail quest
Bloch, R. Howard 103, 128**n.20**
Bloom, Harold 94
Blumenfeld-Kosinski, Renate 195**n.20**
Bolduc, Michelle 32**n.1**
Bouchard, Constance B. 18
Braet, Herman 117**n.2**, 135**n.31**
Bran de Lis 105, 107

Brodman, Marian Masiuk 139**n.38**, 143**n.44**
Brown, Catherine 18
Brownlee, Kevin 37**n.10**
Burgwinkle, William E. 150**n.3**, 199**n.27**, 216**n.4**, 221**n.11**
Burns, E. Jane 16**n.33**, 95**n.15**
Busby, Keith 4**n.5**, 5, 5**n.6**, 5**n.8**, 7, 9, 9**n.14**, 9**n.15**, 9**n.16**, 10, 10**n.21**, 53**n.38**, 73**n.74**, 108**n.40**, 138**n.35**, 143**n.44**, 179**n.64**, 189**n.4**, 215**n.2**

canon formation 2, 194
Caradoc 4, 29, 105, 117–18, 136, 137, 138–44, 144**f**, 145, 221–2
Carruthers, Mary 198**n.25**
Castellani, Marie-Madeleine 87**n.2**
Cazelles, Brigitte 150, 175, 176, 185
Cerquiglini, Jacqueline 186**n.77**
Chenu, Marie-Dominique 32, 32**n.1**, 33
chessboard adventures 13, 47, 48, 49, 50, 52
Chessboard Lady 4, 28, 42, 45, 48, 51–2, 65, 100, 104, 117, 146, 222
Cheyette, Frederic L. 169**n.42**
Chickering, Howell 169**n.42**
chivalry 2, 11, 21, 26, 83, 85, 93, 98, 102, 123, 150, 152, 154, 155, 156–8, 165, 172, 174, 176, 184, 199, 206, 216, 217, 223
  Arthurian 76, 83, 124, 178, 181, 223
Chrétien de Troyes:
  Conte du Graal (Perceval) 2, 7, 10–11, 17–19, 21–2, 26–7, 39–40, 42–4, 72–85, 91–5, 95–8, 116–32, 147–8, 167, 170–1, 172, 176, 180, 183, 198, 202, 204, 208, 212, 213–14, 216, 217–19, 220, 222, 226, 227
  Erec et Enide 20, 21, 23, 52, 83, 147, 161, 166
  Cligès 3, 20, 21, 23, 42, 73, 103, 120, 133, 147
  Chevalier au Lion (Yvain) 20, 98, 185
  Le Chevalier de la Charrette (Lancelot) 15, 20, 21, 23, 33, 57

Christian values 29, 83, 90, 165–6, 181, 184
  see also sexuality
Chronicles 152, 192, 193
collective authorship, *see* authorship, collective
continuations 1–3, 9, 213, 216, 220, 226, 227
  First 4, 5, 10, 12, 13, 16, 28, 29, 30, 42, 43, 44, 46, 47, 48, 50, 52, 58, 59, 70, 88, 105–8, 109, 110–14, 117, 118, 135–8, 147, 185, 189, 197, 204, 205, 206, 208, 216, 221, 222
  Second 4, 12, 13, 14, 27–8, 37, 38, 40–1, 43, 44–7, 49**f**, 50–2, 57–8, 61–2, 65, 67–8, 82, 100, 104, 146, 182, 186, 189, 190–1, 200, 204, 205, 211, 222; *see also* Wauchier de Denain
  Third 4, 5, 10, 54, 58, 111–12, 171, 179, 180, 182, 185, 188, 191, 195; *see also* Manessier
  Fourth 3, 4, 5, 22, 28, 30, 37, 40, 41–2, 54, 58, 67, 70, 89**f**, 104, 118, 147, 162, 189, 190–2, 204, 210; *see also* Gerbert de Montreuil
  see also cycles, prose; cycles, romance
Corley, Corin 45, 57**n.46**, 90**n.5**, 179, 180, 181**n.68**
cycles 1–2, 8, 20, 25, 27, 39, 41, 57, 58, 152, 166, 188, 194, 201, 204, 210–11, 220
  Charlemagne 1
  Guillaume d'Orange 1
  Perceval 9–10, 11, 19, 24, 26, 29–30, 33–5, 192, 195, 215, 227
  prose 9, 15, 28, 29, 111, 113, 114, 173, 174–5, 177, 223
  romance 1, 4–5, 15–16
  verse 7, 15, 171
  see also Vulgate Cycle

Davis, Natalie Zemon 140**n.39**
de Combarieu, Micheline 120
de Riquer, Martin 20
Deist, Rosemarie 128, 164**n.40**

Delcourt, Denyse 156**n.6**, 158
Denain, *see* Wauchier de Denain
defamiliarization 166–8, 170
Desclais-Berkvam, Doris 127**n.17**, 144**n.45**
Diamond, Jared 161**n.24**
Doležel, Lubomír 211**n.37**
Dragonetti, Roger 19**n.38**, 23**n.44**, 32**n.1**, 34**n.2**, 35, 35**n.6**, 36**n.8**, 72**n.73**, 77**n.83**, 77**n.86**, 82,128**n.21**, 164**n.32**, 227**n.18**

education 27, 82, 117, 119, 125, 127, 129, 131, 135, 152, 166–7, 170, 193
endings/endlessness 1, 2, 4, 12, 13–14, 16, 17, 22–4, 40, 47, 68, 152, 171, 187–92, 204
  of Chrétien's romance 44, 62, 73, 74, 90, 113, 115, 148, 168–79, 195, 206, 209, 212
  of *Conte du Graal* 52, 194, 216, 222, 227
  and Gerbert 63, 64, 66, 70, 190, 202, 203, 210
  and Manessier 54–9, 62, 63, 112, 186, 206, 225
  of Perceval's Grail quest 28, 35, 49–50, 193, 211, 213, 215
  and Wauchier 51, 52, 191
Escavalon 50, 92, 98, 99–100, 107, 111, 136, 147, 159, 160–3, 177, 210, 211, 220, 226
Ezra 192, 193

family relations 105, 107
  mothers and sons 28, 30, 102, 117, 118, 137, 146, 147
  siblings 114, 117, 135–7, 138, 216, 219
Fisher King 4, 16, 19, 21, 48–9, 50, 53, 57, 58, 77, 91, 114, 215, 216, 124–5, 128, 133–5, 138, 152, 157, 158, 162, 163, 168, 175, 177, 178, 181, 183, 184, 185, 190, 200, 201, 204–5,
205f, 206–8, 208, 211, 220, 225–6
Fleishman, Suzanne 25**n.49**
Flori, Jean 155, 161**n.24**
Fraenkel, Béatrice 34**n.4**
Frappier, Jean 20, 37**n.10**, 108**n.40**, 129**n.23**, 162**n.29**, 175**n.55**, 176, 184**n.74**, 188**n.3**
Friedman, Richard Elliot 153**n.9**
Frye, Northrop 187**n.1**, 194**n.17**

Gallais, Pierre 45**n.20**, 108**n.40**, 132**n.28**, 137**n.35**, 140**n.41**, 145**n.46**, 204**n.31**
Gauvain, *see* Grail Castle; Grail quest; heroes; family relations; heroes; marriage; rape; sexuality; Tent Maiden
Geary, Patrick J. 177**n.58**
gender relations 2, 214, 216, 225, 226
Genette, Gérard 2**n.2**, 188**n.3**
Geoffrey of Monmouth 79
  Historia Regum Britanniae 12, 20, 119, 176
Gerbert (de Montreuil) 4, 5, 15, 22, 28, 29, 30, 38, 40, 41–2, 52, 53, 54, 55, 56, 57, 59, 60, 61–5, 66–71, 73, 76, 79, 85, 88, 89f, 90, 92, 97, 109, 110–11, 112, 113, 114, 186, 188, 190, 192, 194, 195–6, 198–204, 210, 211, 215, 225
  Roman de la Violette 4n, 61, 111n, 145
  see also Continuations, Fourth
Godefroi de Leigni 23, 24, 33, 36, 37, 42, 55, 57
Goodwin, Malcolm 221**n.12**
Gornemant de Gohort, *see* advice, to Perceval
Gouttebroze, Jean Guy 18**n.18**, 80**n.90**, 103**n.29**, 134**n.29**, 135**n.31**, 153**n.9**, 158**n.18**
Gowans, Linda 12**n.23**, 39**n.12**
Grail 1, 3, 6, 9, 11, 15, 17, 19, 22, 24, 26, 27–8, 29, 30, 48, 49, 50, 53, 56, 67, 68, 86–7, 104, 172, 173–9, 186, 190, 196, 197, 207, 211, 213, 215, 217, 219, 220

Grail (*Cont.*)
  and bleeding lance 9, 129, 168, 186,
      197, 199, 200, 210, 214, 216,
      221, 222, 223, 225, 227
  and Christianity 9, 52, 85, 116, 152
  Gauvain 12, 50, 52, 97–8, 99–100,
      102, 109, 113, 174, 189, 197,
      206, 208, 209, 214
  and gender 226
  heroes 4, 14, 15, 28, 56, 67, 111, 178,
      199, 208, 209
  and love 47, 52, 67, 113
  Perceval 11, 12, 28, 47, 48, 51–2,
      66–7, 86–7, 97–8, 113, 125,
      168, 174, 185, 186, 189, 205,
      206, 209, 211, 214, 220–1,
      224f
  rewritings 11–14
  romances 35, 38, 39–40, 41, 43, 47,
      52, 56, 69, 86, 87, 90, 94, 114,
      150, 152, 164–5, 180, 188, 195,
      198–9, 216
  see also bleeding lance, Holy Grail, ivory
      barrels
Grail Castle 5, 43, 53, 57, 100, 114, 196,
      199, 204–5, 209–11, 213, 214,
      225
  Gauvain 4, 16, 47, 50, 58, 69, 109,
      136–7, 189, 197, 205f, 206, 209
  Perceval 3, 4, 12, 28, 46, 47, 48–9, 67,
      69, 97, 111–12, 128, 134, 148,
      158, 166, 184–5, 189, 199, 200,
      218
Grail quest 12, 29, 48, 100, 112, 115,
      150, 163, 173–4, 178, 181, 195,
      199, 222, 223, 226
  Galahad 177, 178
  Gauvain 39, 117, 177
  Lancelot 12, 177, 178
  Perceval 3, 4, 28, 49–52, 67, 86–7,
      177, 178, 181, 185, 199–200,
      203, 209, 224f
Gravdal, Kathryn 94, 95n.15, 121
Guézennec, Sophie 70n.44
Guiromelant 4, 101, 102–3, 114, 132–3,
      136, 165, 168, 196

Hahn, Thomas 88n.3
Haidu, Peter 34n.4, 78n.88, 81n.92,
      83n.99, 92n.8, 94n.12, 97n.20,
      99n.22, 116n.1, 127n.17,
      128n.22, 129n.23, 151n.4,
      160–1n.22, 168n.41, 175n.54,
      190n.5, 212n.41, 216n.4
Harf-Lancner, Laurence 9, 30n.51, 48,
      152n.6, 167n.37
Heng, Geraldine 149n.1
heroes 2, 3, 4, 6, 10, 14, 15, 19, 20–2, 25,
      29, 38, 40, 41, 44, 46, 56, 59, 60,
      69, 75, 76–7, 81, 83–5, 86, 87, 92,
      100, 104, 105, 111, 112, 113–14,
      116, 118, 119, 124, 133, 136–7,
      146, 151, 153, 157, 158, 169,
      172, 175, 178–9, 180, 189, 190,
      196, 220, 197, 198, 199, 204,
      210–11, 223, 226, 227
  doubling of 17, 19, 37, 169, 180
  Gauvain 88–9, 95, 98, 99–100, 105,
      113, 153, 158, 161, 165, 167,
      168, 170, 208
  Perceval 2, 3, 11, 12, 28, 44, 48, 49, 50,
      53, 56, 58, 62, 66, 67, 92, 103–4,
      117, 134, 146, 147, 158, 162, 166,
      198, 203, 206, 209, 214, 216, 222
  see also violence
Heyworth, G. G. 164n.33
Hideous Damsel 48, 75, 126, 154, 177,
      195, 200, 209, 215
Hindman, Sandra 164n.64, 223
Hofer, Stefan 20
Holmes, Urban Tigner 80, 82n.96
Holy Grail 11, 12, 15, 29, 38, 55, 90,
      166, 174, 176, 177, 178, 181, 186
Holzbacher, Ana María 120n.6, 131n.26
Huchet, Jean 93n.11, 101n.25, 120n.6,
      125n.12, 134n.29, 146n.49
Hugh of St Victor:
  Didascalicon 129, 152n.8, 193
Hult, David F. 23n.44, 36n.8
Hunt, Tony 18n.37, 80, 80n.90, 83,
      164n.31
Huot, Sylvia 50n.33, 121, 179n.64,
      191n.6, 223–4

interlace 15, 19, 28, 40, 41, 44, 47, 50, 52, 54, 59–60, 69, 71, 91, 133, 134, 180, 189, 200–1, 216, 220, 222, 227

interpretations 2, 15, 18, 21, 26, 27, 28, 33, 42, 76, 78, 80, 84, 85, 91, 97, 119, 125, 126, 135, 150, 152, 154, 171, 173, 176, 181, 193, 194, 203, 214, 223, 227

intertextuality 15, 14–17
  centrifugal 24, 73, 172
  centripetal 15, 137, 172

Isaiah 29, 152, 159, 160, 163–5, 170, 226
  see also biblical references; utopian vision

ivory barrels 29, 199, 200, 201, 202, 204, 215

Jameson, Frederic 86n.6
Jauss, Hans Erich 116n.1
Jeanne of Flanders/Jeanne de Flandre 28, 46, 54–5, 179n
Jeaste of Sir Gawain 13
Jeffrey, David. L. 212n.42

Kay, Sarah 18, 63n.64, 81n.93, 82–3, 83n.97, 92n.9, 101n.26, 127n.17, 152n.7, 155, 213n.1
Keller, Hans-Erich 62
Kellermann, Wilhelm 45n.21
Kelly, Douglas 23n.43, 34, 128n.21, 133
Kennedy, Elspeth 106n.37, 137
Kjaer, Jonna 62n.50, 69n.66, 70
Klein, Melanie 144n.45, 213, 213n.1, 217n.6
Knightly Tale of Gologros and Gawane 13
Köhler, Erich 134n.29
Koziol, Geoffrey 84n.102
Krause, Kathy 25n.48
Kristeva, Julia 18
Krueger, Roberta L. 95n.15, 121, 127n.17, 146

Lachat, Claude 180n.65
Lacy, Norris 221n.12
Lai du Cor 12, 145

Lai du Mantel 12
Lancelot-Grail 2–3, 9, 15, 16, 56, 58, 178, 179, 180, 181, 195
  see also Vulgate Cycle

Laranjinha, Ana Sofia 92n.8
Larmat, Jean 66n.61
Laurie, Helen C. R. 153n.9
Lefay-Toury, Marie-Noëlle 146
Le Goff, Jacques 154n.11
Le Menn, Gwennolé 143n.43
Le Rider, Paule 124n.11
Leupin, Alexandre 38, 62, 68, 108n.40, 145n.47
Lévi-Strauss, Claude 103n.29, 127n.17, 136
Levy, Raphael 63n.54
Lit de la Merveille 104
Lods, Jeanne 98
Loomis, Roger Sherman 140n.41
Lot, Ferdinand 43, 44, 58, 70n.69, 180

love:
  family ties 2, 14, 22, 85, 99, 146
  erotic 28, 87, 89, 91, 92, 94, 95, 97, 99, 105, 108
  see also Christian values; marriage; sexuality

Luttrell, Claude 78n.87, 80, 81, 83, 164n.31

McCracken, Peggy 90n.6, 95n.16, 117n.3, 132n.27, 137n.34, 143, 179n.62

Maddox, Donald 83n.99, 117n.2, 124, 128, 134n.29, 135n.31, 136, 175, 192n.11, 220

Magic Chessboard 45, 47, 48, 49f, 50

Male Pucele 76, 92, 100–4, 107, 108, 110–11, 167, 183, 220
  see also rape

Malory, Thomas:
  Morte d'Arthur 3, 173

Manessier 4, 5, 7, 10, 11, 15, 22, 28, 29, 38, 40–2, 45, 52, 53, 54–9, 60, 62–4, 66, 72, 85, 89, 90, 111–12, 123, 171, 172, 179–186, 190, 192, 195, 196, 202, 204, 206, 211, 223, 225
  see also Continuations, Third

Marie de Champagne 23, 40, 42, 69
Marie de France 34, 50, 87, 117, 161
Marnette, Sophie 36, 38–9, 39**n.12**, 60
marriage 103, 115, 138, 138–9, 140, 145,
	146, 172, 220
	Gauvain 107, 108, 114, 147, 219
	Perceval 4, 28, 66–7, 104, 111, 114,
		199–200, 217, 219, 223
Marx, Jean 54**n.41**
Matarasso, Pauline M. 177**n.58**
matière de Bretagne 52, 138, 201
Micha, Alexandre 73**n.74**, 123**n.9**, 195**n.21**
Mickel, Emmanuel J. 153**n.9**
Miles, Jack 192**n.10**, 193**n.13**
Minnis, Alastair J. 31**n.1**, 194**n.16**
misogyny 97, 99, *see* Tent Maiden; Male
	Pucele
Mont Dolerous 46, 48, 52, 67
mothers 3, 22, 28–30, 75, 85, 114, 115,
	116–48, 152, 167, 169, 213–14,
	221, 222
	Gauvain 28, 76, 102, 103, 107, 113,
		114, 158, 220
	isolation of 117, 118, 120, 125, 179
	Lady of the Lake 120, 130, 146
	and lovers 14, 104, 220, 227
	and marriage 28
	Perceval 12, 26, 27, 58, 67, 76–7, 81–
		2, 85, 87, 91–3, 95–6, 100, 103–
		4, 114, 154, 156–7, 160, 163–4,
		166, 168–9, 183, 216, 217–19
	and sons 28, 30–1, 116–48, 157, 220,
		227
	see also advice; education; family
		relations; sexuality; Veuve Dame
mysteries 26–7, 31, 75
	Grail romances 11, 22, 86, 90, 150, 204
	of Grail Castle 213

naming:
	anonymity 2–3, 4, 5, 10, 12, 13, 15,
		27, 29, 33–4, 35, 38, 40, 41, 42–4,
		46, 56, 59, 70, 82, 105, 138, 179,
		189, 198, 207, 221
	authors 27, 30, 36, 37, 38–9, 40–2, 44,
		46, 50, 54, 64, 65, 67, 69, 70, 74,
		196, 227

characters 14, 16, 17, 21, 23, 24, 25,
	30, 35, 42, 44, 47, 49, 51, 56, 60,
	61, 67, 76, 78, 91, 92, 95, 99, 110,
	112, 116, 117, 118, 125, 127,
	129, 133, 146, 152, 152, 166,
	167, 171, 176, 179, 180, 181,
	188, 196, 197, 200, 211, 214,
	221, 225
see also authorship
Nicholas, David 179**n.63**
Nixon, Terry 7**n.10**, 70**n.68**
Nykrog, Per 121

Orgueilleux de la Lande 97, 100, 208, 220

Paradis, Françoise 67, 146**n.50**
Partonopeu de Blois 35
Payen, Jean-Charles 187**n.2**, 188**n.3**
Peredur 13
Perceval 8f, 49f, 122f, *see* advice; Chrétien
	de Troyes; cycles; Grail Castle;
	Grail quest; heroes; marriage;
	sexuality; Tent Maiden
Perlesvaus 12, 38, 188
Philip of Flanders 4, 35, 40, 43, 101
Pickens, Rupert 5**n.9**, 6, 11**n.23**, 13**n.29**,
	18, 37**n.11**, 80**n.90**, 103, 128,
	219**n.8**, 220
Pinker, Stephen 160
plowshares, *see* weapons, plowshares
Poirion, Daniel 72, 78**n.87**, 92, 93, 94,
	103**n.89**, 126, 131**n.26**, 156**n.13**,
	190**n.5**, 207**n.34**
Pratt, Karen 195
prequels 13, 15, 32, 188
	Bliocadran 5, 128
	Elucidation 5
Pucele aux Petites Manches 92, 98, 147
Putter, Ad 13, 13**n.31**, 82**n.96**, 84**n.101**,
	111**n.51**, 153**n.9**

Queste del Saint Graal, see Vulgate Cycle

rape 91
	Gauvain 28, 88, 100, 105, 107–8,
		109–12, 113, 165
	Male Pucele 101, 108, 113, 220

Perceval 28, 94, 157
  and Tent Maiden 95–8
Greoreas 101, 108, 165
see also retelling
Raugei, Anna Maria 78**n.87**, 80**n.90**,
  164**n.31**
Red Knight 8f, 76, 77, 121, 122f, 123,
  155–6, 157, 161
Regalado, Nancy Freeman 19**n.38**, 80,
  176**n.57**, 212**n.40**
Régnier-Bohler, Danielle 103**n.29**, 117**n.2**
Reichert, Michelle 132**n.28**
religion 2, 14, 27, 85, 94, 144–5, 172
Renart, Jean:
  Guillaume de Dole ou Roman de la
    Rose 1, 61, 145
retellings 1, 28, 29, 69, 91, 97–8, 105,
  109, 111, 119, 169, 197, 199, 210
  love stories 112–15
rewriting 1, 2–3, 9, 16, 19, 20–1, 24, 28,
  58, 75, 90, 91, 113, 115, 137, 151,
  198, 213, 214, 225, 223
  Grail 11–14, 15, 29, 39, 44, 56, 116,
    118, 128, 147–8, 150, 152, 169,
    172, 175, 186, 188, 199, 202
Rey-Flaud, Henri 92, 92**n.9**, 97**n.20**
Ribard, Jacques 50**n.32**, 95**n.14**, 99**n.21**,
  103
Rider, Jeff 84**n.100**, 93**n.10**, 119**n.5**,
  145**n.48**, 158**n.9**
Rieger, Angelica 191**n.6**
Rieger, Dietmar 95**n.16**
Roach, William 3, 5, 5**n.7**, 5**n.8**,
  7**n.11**, 9, 10, 10**n.21**, 11**n.22**,
  13**n.29**, 37, 40, 40**n.16**, 41,
  42**n.17**, 44, 45, 45**n.20**, 45**n.21**,
  46**n.26**, 46**n.24**, 47**n.26**, 51**n.35**,
  55**n.41**, 57**n.45**, 58, 88**n.4**, 105,
  137, 179**n.63**, 180**n.67**, 189**n.4**,
  195**n.21**, 204**n.31**, 104**n.31**,
  226**n.16**
Robert de Boron 11, 12, 24, 38, 118, 175,
  177, 188, 216
Robertson, D.W. 212**n.41**
Roche de Champguin 28, 75, 102, 114,
  115, 133, 136, 138, 167, 219, 220

Rollo, David 150**n.2**
Roman de la Rose:
  Guillaume de Lorris 35
    and Jean de Meun 23
  Jean Renart 61
    Guillaume de Dole ou Roman de la
      Rose 145
Rossi, Marguerite 141**n.22**
Ryding, William W. 192**n.11**

Saly, Antoinette 83**n.99**, 92**n.8**, 134**n.29**,
  161**n.23**, 167–8**n.38**, 177**n.60**
Sargent-Baur, Barbara N. 75**n.78**,
  81**n.91**, 95**n.15**
Sasaki, Shigemi 58, 100**n.23**
Savage, Grace Armstrong 176**n.57**
Schacter, Daniel L. 197
Schmid, Elisabeth 128**n.20**
Schmolke-Hasselmann, Beate 76**n.79**,
  90**n.7**, 145**n.48**
Schwartz, Debora B. 134**n.30**, 217**n.7**
Segal, Hanna 144**n.45**
Séguy, Mireille 55**n.42**, 204**n.32**
sexuality 26, 28, 91, 97, 102, 104, 107,
  112, 115, 118, 145–6, 147, 216,
  221–3
  adultery 29, 139, 176, 178
  chastity 12, 28, 66, 67, 94, 117, 145–6,
    221
  Gauvain 102, 103, 147
    and mothers 102, 103, 117–18,
      137–43, 145–6, 223
  Perceval 42, 50, 90, 97, 104, 107, 117,
    214, 216, 222
  see also advice; love; marriage; rape
  siblings 114, 138, 216, 219
    and mothers 114, 135–7, 219
Signer, Michael A. 152**n.8**, 193**n.14**
Sinclair, Finn E. 118**n.4**, 135**n.32**,
  221**n.13**
Sir Gawain and the Green Knight 13,
  138**n.35**
Sir Percyvell of Galles 14
Smalley, Beryl 193, 193**n.15**, 194**n.16**
Smith, Gregory A. 154**n.10**
soreplus/sorplus, *see* surplus

Spiegel, Gabrielle M. 128**n.20**, 133, 175**n.54**, 179**n.63**

Stanesco, Michel 72, 73, 119, 129, 129**n.23**, 169**n.42**, 178**n.61**

Stanger, Mary D. 46**n.24**, 179**n.63**

Stanton, Amida 61**n.49**

Steele, Stephen 82**n.95**

Steiner, George 149**n.1**

Stephens, Leslie 51**n.35**, 53**n.37**, 62, 63**n.53**, 191**n.7**

Stiennon, Jacques 179**n.63**

Stones, Alison 9, 223, 223**n.15**

Sturges, Robert 119, 126**n.16**, 129**n.23**, 193**n.15**

Sturm-Maddox, Sara 119

surplus/soreplus/sorplus 51, 65, 92–3, 94, 95, 97, 99, 100, 107, 137, 146, 217, 219

swords 9, 29, 41, 52, 53, 56, 57, 67, 68, 69, 121, 143, 153, 155, 159, 160, 162, 164, 167, 170, 171, 173, 178, 182, 184, 189, 190, 191, 192, 196, 197, 199, 204, 205, 206, 207–8, 210, 211, 223, 226
  see also weapons

Szkilnik, Michelle 46**n.23**, 140**n.39**, 141**n.42**

Tent Maiden 28, 59, 77, 87–8, 91–2, 105, 112, 133, 183, 220
  Gauvain 13–14, 89, 89f, 92, 108, 109, 110, 111, 136–7, 147
  Perceval 90, 91, 92, 95–8, 107, 146, 157, 158, 196, 222

tents 43, 48, 50, 105–6, 139
  biblical comparisons 219, 220

Thompson, Albert W. 204**n.32**

utopian vision 29, 152, 163–5, 169, 226

Van Caenegem, R. C. 84**n.102**

Van Coolput, Colette-Anne 10**n.20**, 108**n.40**, 174**n.51**, 204**n.31**

Van Creveld, Martin 165

Van Liere, Frans 153**n.9**, 193**n.15**

Van Mulken, Margot 25**n.49**, 73**n.74**

Vance, Eugene 18**n.37**

Veuve Dame 28, 124, 126, 129, 136, 157, 158–9, 214, 216–17

Vial, Guy 40**n.16**, 44–5**n.19**, 46, 46**n.24**, 70**n.69**, 160–1**n.22**, 204**n.31**

Vidal-Naquet, Pierre 154**n.11**

Vinaver, Eugène 91

Vincensini, Jean-Jacques 86**n.1**

violence 2, 14, 22, 23, 26, 27, 29, 85, 86, 87–8, 91, 97, 99, 112, 115, 121, 123, 124, 156, 157, 159, 160, 163, 164, 165–6, 167, 168–9, 169–70, 171, 172, 180, 182, 183–4, 186, 215, 216, 220, 221, 226
  ends of 173–9
  and romances 149–53
  see also and/both logic

Virgil:
  Aeneid 172

Vulgate Cycle 12, 15, 29, 85, 90, 147, 172, 175, 179, 186, 194, 199, 223, 226
  Estoire del Saint Graal 12, 15, 38–9
  Estoire de Merlin 12, 16
  Lancelot-Grail 2–3, 138, 174, 180, 195
  Mort le roi Artu 12, 16, 138, 172, 173, 186, 195
  Queste del Saint Graal 4, 12, 15, 16, 25, 27, 38, 67, 83, 85, 104, 114–15, 117, 138, 147, 163, 165, 173, 174–8, 179, 180, 181, 182, 184, 186, 188, 195, 198, 222–3
  see also Chrétien de Troyes, *Conte du Graal*

Wace:
  Roman de Brut 6, 12, 20, 79, 119–20, 132, 138, 176, 195

Walter, Philippe 75**n.78**, 168**n.40**

Walters, Lori 22**n.42**, 46**n.24**, 50**n.33**, 70**n.68**, 179**n.63**, 191**n.6**, 195**n.21**

Wauchier de Denain 4, 5, 28, 38, 40, 43, 44–9, 49f, 50–4, 58 63, 82, 86, 189
  see also Continuations, Second

weapons 154, 155, 157, 160, 161, 164–5, 167, 168, 169, 183

plowshares 29, 153, 159, 162, 164, 170, 171, 182, 226
see also bleeding lance; swords; utopian vision
White, Sarah Melhado 104n.32
White, Stephen D. 151n.4
Williams, Andrea M. L. 12n.24
Williams, Harry F. 150
Wilmotte, Maurice 25, 43–4, 44–5n.19, 46, 54–5n.41
Wolfram von Eschenbach: *Parzifal* 13, 101, 156, 198
Wood, Michael 24n.47, 170–1, 171n.46, 171n.47, 211n.39
words 75, 76, 77, 78, 80, 84, 85, 160, 164, 191, 193, 202, 207, 217
 figurative sense 27, 42, 77, 81, 99, 104
 literal sense 27, 32, 42, 76, 77, 80, 81, 85, 99, 104, 193

questions 1, 2, 3, 14, 19, 21–2, 23, 25, 29–30, 37, 42, 47, 51–2, 53, 63, 65, 68, 70, 77, 79, 82, 85, 86, 87, 94, 100, 109–10, 113, 114, 118, 119, 120, 124, 125, 127, 129, 134, 135, 137, 138, 140, 146, 147–8, 150, 152, 155, 163, 164, 166–7, 168, 169–72, 174–5, 176, 177, 180, 188, 189, 190, 194–5, 197, 200, 201, 206, 208, 210, 211, 212, 213, 214, 215–16, 217, 218, 220–21, 222, 225–6
see also retelling, weapons
Wynn, Marianne 13, 13n.28, 172n.49

Zink, Michel 38, 42n.17, 72n.72
Zornberg, Avivah Gottlieb 17–18n.36
Zumthor, Paul 23, 72, 133, 187–8n.2, 190n.5